CASES AND TEXT
ON
THE LAW OF WILLS

BY

W. BARTON LEACH

PROFESSOR OF LAW, HARVARD LAW SCHOOL

SECOND EDITION
(1949 Revision)

DR. NORMAN A. WIGGINS

BOSTON
LITTLE, BROWN AND COMPANY
1949

DR. NORMAN A. WIGGINS

COPYRIGHT 1947, 1949, BY W. BARTON LEACH

ALL RIGHTS RESERVED, INCLUDING THE RIGHT
TO REPRODUCE THIS BOOK OR PORTIONS
THEREOF IN ANY FORM

PRINTED IN THE UNITED STATES OF AMERICA

PREFACE

When one has spent a large part of his professional career trying to master and teach a branch of the law, any casebook he prepares necessarily reflects his convictions about the subject and the methods of imparting it. This casebook reflects my convictions and I may as well set forth what they are. No claim to originality is made; indeed, what I say here seems to me pretty obvious.

Functions of a course in Wills. These are two: (a) to push the student along the road in acquiring skill in the analysis and synthesis of legal materials, (b) to contribute toward preparing him for a probate and trust practice at the various stages at which lawyers are called upon to participate, viz. planning and drafting, advising, litigating, deciding, legislating. I say "contribute" because traditionally the course on Wills deals with only a small segment of the subject, say 25 per cent, the rest being provided by courses in Trusts (fiduciary administration), Future Interests (the substance of dispositive provisions other than the simplest), and Taxation (the element which increasingly controls the real effectiveness of transfers from one generation to the next).

Length of a course in Wills. With all the affection I have for this subject I cannot justify greater length of treatment than two hours per week for half an academic year — say a total of 32. At Harvard Professor A. James Casner and I give this material 20 hours. This book is designed for any number between these two. It was all very well in Langdell's time for students to wade through the six volumes of Gray's Cases on Property, including one full-sized volume and part of another on wills and related problems. In that day Torts was an upstart subject just elbowing its way into the curriculum, and the Public Law subjects were practically unheard of. Even in my own student days (1921–24) the only large Public Law courses were Constitutional Law and Conflicts; Taxation was considered a subject for specialists, Administrative Law was an oddity designed to provide a stadium for Frankfurter's brilliant open-field running, and Labor Law and Government Regulation of Business were small seminars. Since all of these subjects have assumed major importance I cannot possibly justify more than two semester hours for Wills, and my best judgment is that somewhat less than this is preferable.

Assumptions as to other courses of study. These are the following and may be divided into:

    a. *Prior study:* An elementary course in property, including the historical material through the Statute of Uses. Little, if any,

material in this casebook is dependent upon such prior study, but most students will have had it.
- b. *Concurrent study:* A course in Trusts. A familiarity with the fiduciary concept and fiduciary administration is a necessary adjunct and is probably best studied at the same time, or at least in the same year, as this book.
- c. *Subsequent study:* A course including Federal Estate and Income Taxation. Any student who fails to make a systematic study of this subject is very badly advised. Competent practice of probate law without such study, in or out of law school, is impossible.

This brings us to the course which bears the unfortunate label " Future Interests." It ought to be called something like " The Substance of Gift Transactions, Testamentary and Inter Vivos, for Clients above the Shoe-Salesman Income Level." It ought not to be omitted by anyone who is expecting to engage in a general practice which, he hopes, will ultimately include handling the affairs of clients who range from well-to-do to wealthy. At Harvard and some other schools this course is taken by all students; but I am well aware that in many schools few elect it. For this reason the present book makes no assumption, one way or the other, as to whether the student is taking or will take a course in Future Interests. I personally use the book in the same course with my Cases on Future Interests. However, if it is being used in a school where a large number of students will get no large-scale treatment of Future Interests, certain springboards have been provided as a means of initiating discussion designed to help correct this deficiency:
- a. *Class gifts.* Numerous clauses of the model will (Chapter XI); the cases on Lapse (Chapter VIII, Sec. I).
- b. *Powers of Appointment.* McKallip's Estate, Curley v. Lynch and Matter of Fowles (Chapter IV); clauses in the model will.
- c. *Rule against Perpetuities.* In re Bernard's Settlement (Chapter V); Chapter X.

" Perpetuities in a Nutshell," originally published as a law review article, appears as Chapter X. I require my own students to give it thorough study in preparation for the consideration of Future Interests; this permits the discussion of perpetuities problems to proceed on a much higher level than proved possible previously. For students who are not taking a course in Future Interests a serious study of this Chapter is a matter of common decency to one's clients and elementary protection for one's own professional reputation.

Method of presentation of the subject matter herein. There is no even, consistent pattern of presentation in this book; and that is because the subject matter is not even and consistent in its pedagogical characteristics. It seems to me that the way to teach a subject, and prepare the materials for teaching, is to examine the subject topic by topic, make up your mind as to the probable most fruitful method of attack upon each topic, try out that method for a while, and change it if it doesn't work. This casebook represents the present state of my conclusions after fourteen years of teaching Wills.

A few topics in this field present stimulating and important analytical problems, and these are treated by the full-dress case method:
  a. Restrictions on testation for protection of the widow — a tangle of statutes and cases where counsellor, litigant, judge and legislator all are faced with serious difficulties.
  b. Attempts by testators to make some unattested documents act like wills — the common ground upon which incorporation by reference, non-testamentary act, and power of appointment come together.
  c. Revocation of wills upon misinformation or unfounded expectations.
  d. The handling of those instruments, born of ignorance or ineptness, which would be readily reformed for mistake if they were not wills — a test of how seriously the law can afford to take the Statutes of Wills.
  e. " Ademption " — a situation, dominated by a term drawn from the Civil Law, in which courts have only occasionally remembered that their job is to carry out the testator's intention.

I have not found other topics in this field which justify this type of treatment.

There is a second category of topics which seem to me best treated by illustrative cases or problems for rather summary class discussion. Included in these are advancements, execution of wills, lapse, satisfaction of legacies, certain problems of administration.

A third category is straight text or problems-and-answers. If this material can be taken up in class, so much the better. If time is lacking, the printed page should be sufficient to transmit essentials to the student.

" Perpetuities in a Nutshell " is a category by itself. I do not believe that students can be expected to master this chapter without the assistance of class discussion. The nature and extent of such discussion will naturally depend upon what time is available and whether the students are to take a course in Future Interests.

Estate Planning and the Drafting of Wills. Chapter XI is the latest in a considerable series of ventures in which Professor Casner and I have been trying to find an effective method of introducing students to the art of planning estates and drafting dispositive instruments. The various methods attempted may be described as follows:
  a. Lecturing and writing on specific segments of the problem: for example, Professor Casner's articles on *Class Gifts* (41 Col. L. Rev. 1, 27; 51 Harv. L. Rev. 254, 307; 53 Harv. L. Rev. 207, 249) and my discourse on *Powers to Invade Principal* (9 Am. Law School Rev. 902).
  b. Discussing cases in the classroom with a view to evaluating

the draftsmanship of the instrument being litigated. This is useful but is largely negative. The fact that the case is litigated is in itself evidence of bad draftsmanship, so one tends to get a series of horrible examples.

c. Classroom criticism of instruments drafted by students. This was an unmitigated failure and has been abandoned. The process was extremely dull and prohibitively time-consuming.

d. Presenting documents, some good and some with intentionally planted errors, to the students, directing them to analyze the documents, and in an examination calling for criticisms of specified portions of the documents and analyses of the effects of specified clauses. Professor Casner started using this method in 1946 and prepared a series of documents based upon various client-situations. It has been successful.

e. The method of Chapter XI is really a return to the apprenticeship method of preparing for the legal profession. If this be treason, let the shades of Story and Langdell make the most of it. One presents to the student a client, determines what information from the client is relevant and gets it, prepares the best will one knows how, and then explains to the student why each clause was prepared in that particular way. This Chapter will supplement classroom discussion of types (a) and (b) listed above.

Acknowledgment. The ideas and criticisms of Professors Austin W. Scott and A. James Casner are reflected in many portions of this book and are hereby gratefully acknowledged.

W. B. L.

HARVARD LAW SCHOOL,
MAY, 1947.

NOTE TO 1949 REVISION

The Revenue Act of 1948 is the reason for this Revision. It has required significant changes at pp. 188–189, slight changes elsewhere, and the addition of Appendix II. It should be possible, though inconvenient, for some students to use the regular Second Edition while others in the same class use this volume.

Since 1947 I have bared my professional soul in " Property Law Taught In Two Packages," Vol. 1, No. 1 of the Journal of Legal Education (1948). Some may find it worthwhile to examine "A–B–C of Taxes for Property Lawyers," an appendix to Casner & Leach, Cases on Property.

I have prepared mimeographed " Suggestions for Teachers." A copy can be had, on application to me, by any professor of Wills.

W. B. L.

HARVARD LAW SCHOOL,
JUNE, 1949.

TABLE OF CONTENTS

Preface iii
Table of Cases xiii

CHAPTER I.

Intestacy 1
  A. Essential historical differences between realty and personalty   1
  B. Descent of land in England 3
  C. Distribution of personalty in England 3
  D. Descent and distribution in the United States 5
  E. Should a person leave a will or rely upon the intestate law? . 8
  F. Cases on advancements 9

CHAPTER II.

Protection of Widow and Children against Disinheritance . . 16
  A. History 16
    The writ de rationabili parte bonorum 16
    Dower and curtesy 16
    Descent and distribution to spouses 17
  B. Modern Law 17
    Pretermitted children 18
  C. Cases on protection of the widow 19
  Note: English and Empire Legislation 35

CHAPTER III.

The Execution of Wills 42
  Wills of real property through the Statute of Frauds 42
  Wills of personal property through the Statute of Frauds . . . 42
  The Wills Act (1837) 43
  American statutes 43
  Suggested method of execution of a will 44
  Extraordinary precautions in contemplation of will contest . . 46
  Examples of defectively executed wills 47
  Physically handicapped testator 53
  Competency of witnesses 53
  Holographic wills 56
  Nuncupative wills 58

CHAPTER IV.

Incorporation by Reference and Related Matters 59
  Republication by codicil 59

CHAPTER V.

REVOCATION OF WILLS	101
Revocation by physical act to the testamentary document	101
Revocation by subsequent instrument	101
Protection against spurious revocations	102
Intent to revoke (dependent relative revocation)	102
Revocation by marriage	109
Revocation by divorce	111
"Revocation by conveyance"	111
Revival of revoked wills	111

CHAPTER VI.

CONTEST OF WILLS ON GROUNDS OF MENTAL INCAPACITY, UNDUE INFLUENCE AND FRAUD	115
Mental incapacity	115
Undue influence	116
Fraud	118
Legacies conditional upon legatee not contesting the will	119
Compromise of will contests	120

CHAPTER VII.

MISTAKE, MISNOMER AND MISDESCRIPTION	122

CHAPTER VIII.

LAPSE, ADEMPTION AND SATISFACTION	140
Section 1. Lapse	140
Proper wills can eliminate lapse problems	140
Common disaster clauses	141
Lapsed gifts distinguished from void gifts; realty distinguished from personalty	141
Residuary lapses	142
Lapse statutes	142
Section 2. Ademption and Related Problems	148
Specific legacies and devises and their characteristics	149
General legacies and their characteristics	149
Demonstrative legacies and their characteristics	150
Early history of "ademption" and "revocation by conveyance"	151
Effect of statutes requiring certain formalities for revocation of wills; necessary change in the concept of ademption	151
Note: Is property described as of the time of the will or as of the time of testator's death? Related questions	166
Note: Election required of devisee or legatee whose own property is devised or bequeathed by testator to another	168
Section 3. Satisfaction of Legacies	168

CHAPTER IX.

The Administration of Decedent Estates	176
Section 1. The Grant of Administration	176
The necessity and purpose of administration	176
Types of personal representatives	177
Jurisdiction to appoint a personal representative	178
Enoch Arden & Co.	178
Territorial limits on the powers of the personal representative; ancillary administration	181
Effect of the revocation of letters testamentary or letters of administration	183
The title of the personal representative to personalty and realty	184
Whether rights of action pass to the personal representative	184
Section 2. Outline of the Steps in an Administration	185
The petition for probate or administration and action thereon	185
The issuance of letters; the bond	186
The publication to creditors; short statutes of limitations	186
The inventory	187
The collection and preservation of the assets and the payment of claims	187
The Federal Estate Tax and the personal representative's duties with reference thereto	188
State death taxes	190
Distribution	190
Accounting	190
Routine of administration	191
Section 3. Some Problems in the Conduct of an Administration	193
A. Problems Relating to Creditors	193
Presentment of claims	193
Priorities in insolvent estates	194
Exoneration of mortgaged property	195
B. Investment and Care of Funds	196
C. Contracts of the Personal Representative; Carrying on the Decedent's Business	197
Answers to Problems in Chapter IX	198

CHAPTER X.

Perpetuities in a Nutshell	203
Common Law and Statute	204
I. Statement of the Rule	204
II. Nature of the Rule	204
III. Elements of the Rule	205
A. The Period of Perpetuities	205
B. The required certainty of vesting	207
"Fertile octogenarian" cases	207

"Unborn widow" cases 208
"Administration contingency" cases. 209
   C. "Vesting" in interest 211
IV. Application of the Rule to gifts to classes 213
V. Powers of appointment 215
   A. The validity of the power 216
   B. The validity of appointed interests 217
VI. Severability of invalid conditions and modifying clauses. . 218
VII. Effect of invalidity of an interest under the Rule 219
VIII. Construction and Perpetuities 221
IX. Application of the Rule to various types of interests . . . 223
   A. Contracts, particularly options 223
   B. Revocable trusts; insurance trusts 226
   C. Rights of entry for condition broken; possibilities of reverter 227
   D. Powers of sale in trustees and mortgagees 227
X. Associated Rules 228
   A. Restrictions on accumulations 228
   B. Time restrictions on restraints otherwise valid 229
   C. Time limitations on the duration of trusts 230
XI. Charities 231
XII. Some suggestions as to draftsmanship 232

CHAPTER XI.

PLANNING AND DRAFTING A WILL FOR A PARTICULAR MIDDLE-AGED MAN WITH A FAMILY AND CONSIDERABLE WEALTH 234
Introduction 234
   (1) Investigation 234
   (2) Planning 235
   (3) Drafting 235
Summary of conferences with client 236
   Domicil 236
   Family 236
   Income 237
   Testator's property 237
   Further details on Parsons & Eldridge, Inc. 238
   Other property in the family 239
   Insurance 239
   Former wills 239
   Various facts relevant to the tax situation 239
   Advice given to testator on taxes 239
   Testator's scheme of disposition 242
   Executors and trustees 243
   Immediate pecuniary needs of family during administration 244
   Check with corporate fiduciary 244
   Possibility of wife electing against will 244
   Possibility of contest of will 245

Disposition of this will and previous wills	245
Review of this will	245
Other wills in the family	245
Will of Joseph Albert Thomas	248
Commentary on Will of Joseph Albert Thomas	249
Introductory and revoking clause	249
Residence to the widow, free of mortgage	249
Tangible personalty to widow or issue	249
Summer home to widow for life, remainder to issue; power of sale	251
Heirlooms	255
Pecuniary legacies; annuities; problems as to minors	255
Residuary trust	259
Widow's power to invade principal	259
Power of appointment	261
Ultimate gift to heirs	261
Residuary gift if widow does not survive	265
Various "standard" clauses	267
Spendthrift clause	267
Breadth of power of appointment	267
Release of powers	269
Definition of "issue"	269
"Hotchpot" clause	269
"Reno" clause	269
Adopted children	271
Protection of purchasers	271
Common-disaster clause	271
Provisions as to insanity	273
Taxes payable out of residue	273
Direction to sell certain property within two years	275
Powers of trustee	275
Retention of investments	275
Broad power to deal with trust estate	275
Broad power to invest	275
Making loans	277
Non-income-bearing property	277
Improvement of real estate; demolition of buildings	277
Borrowing	277
Compromise of claims	277
Agents; delegation	277
Reorganizations and mergers	279
Common fund for several trusts	279
Holding assets outside jurisdiction	279
Principal and income	279
Bonds purchased at premium; amortization	279
Other wasting assets	279
Distribution in kind or cash; valuation	279

Powers of executor 281
Exculpatory provisions 281
Provisions for pecuniary aid during administration 283
Income earned by estate during administration 285
Naming executor and trustee; bond 285

APPENDIX I

SELECTED STATUTES ON WILLS, INTESTACY AND ADMINISTRATION . . . 289
    A. England 289
        The Statute of Wills (1540) 289
        The Statute of Frauds (1677) 289
        Stat. 25 Geo II, c. 6 (1752) 289
        The Wills Act (1837) 290
    B. New York 292
        Selected sections of the Decedent Estate Law 292

APPENDIX II

ASPECTS OF THE REVENUE ACT OF 1948 303
    A. Provisions of the Act: Income Splitting and Wealth Splitting 304
    B. Estate Tax Changes Relating to Powers of Appointment . . 306
    C. Estate Plan of J. Albert Thomas: Changes Required by the
       Revenue Act of 1948 309

TABLE OF CASES

Italics indicate that some or all of the opinion of the case is printed. Cases which are not italicized are referred to only in problems or footnotes.

Allen v. Maddock	60
Allott, In re	227, 231
Almosnino, Goods of	64
Ametrano v. Downs	155
Amory v. Meredith	93
Anderson v. Berkley	118
Andrews, Matter of	52
Arneson's Will	53
Atwood, Ex parte	78
Atwood v. *Rhode Island Hospital Trust Co.*	59, *77*, *78*, 86
Baker, In re	94
Balls v. Dampman	215
Bankers' Trust Co. v. Moy	229
Barnes v. Chase	52
Barnum v. Barnum	231
Barrett v. Barrett	220
Barrows' Estate, In re	*155*
Bassett v. Fidelity and Deposit Co.	186
Battell's Will, *In re*	214
Battie-Wrightson, *In re*	139
Beck v. McGillis	169
Beckwith v. Bates	180
Beirne v. *Continental-Equitable Title & Trust Co.*	*31*
Belfield v. Booth	210
Bernard's Settlement, In re	*105*
Bers v. Erie R. R. Co.	169
Beverlin v. First National Bank	214
Bewick, *In re*	209
Bigelow v. Gillott	101
Blackinton, Matter of	196
Boal v. Metropolitan Museum of Art	78
Boehm, Goods of	122, *125*
Bolles v. *Toledo Trust Co.*	*33*, *35*
Bonkowski's Estate, *In re*	109
Boyd's Estate	217
Brackett v. Hoitt	182
Bradley, Matter of	60, 167
Brattle Square Church v. Grant	205, 213, 220, 231
Brett v. Rigden	151
Bridges v. Hitchcock	225
Brown v. Baron	195
Brown v. Boston & Maine R. R.	182
Brown v. Columbia Finance & Trust Co.	218
Bryan's Appeal	64
Bryan v. Bigelow	*69*, 118
Bull's Estate, In re	141
Bundy v. United States Trust Co.	216
Burton v. Newberry	73
Bushell, Goods of	134
Byrnes' Estate, In re	40
Cadell v. Palmer	207
Campbell v. French	107
Carmichael v. *Lathrop*	*170*
Carter, *In re*	222
Cassidy v. Shimmin	182
Cattlin v. Brown	215
Cazassa v. *Cazassa*	*13*
Chardon, *In re*	212
Christ's Hospital v. Grainger	231
Christianson v. King County	184
City Bank Farmers' Trust Co. v. United States	208
Clere's Case, Sir Edward	42
Clifford's Estate	167
Clingan v. Mitcheltree	102
Cochran's Executor v. Kentucky	121
Colman, Goods of	52
Colonial Trust Co. v. Brown	230
Colt v. Industrial Trust Co.	222, 223
Condit v. DeHart	94
Copeland v. Wheelright	120
Corbett v. *Skaggs*	*145*
Cottrell, Matter of	46
Cressy v. Willis	195
Crocheron v. Fleming	167
Crowell v. *Tuttle*	*54*
Cunnius v. Reading School District	181
Curley v. *Lynch*	*92*
Curryer's Will Trusts, *In re*	218
Curtis v. *Curtis*	*160*
Cutler v. Cutler	102
Darnell v. Buzby	46
Davis v. Manson	*77*, *78*
De Paris v. Wilmington Trust Co.	182
Dixon v. Solicitor to the Treasury	109
Dodge v. Detroit Trust Co.	221
Dorr v. Lovering	215
Dumont's Estate v. Commissioner	121
Dye v. Parker	119
Eastman Marble Co. v. Vermont Marble Co.	225
Eaton v. Eaton	*37*, *38*

xiii

xiv   TABLE OF CASES

Eaton's Estate	19	Holland v. Bonner	12
Edgerly v. Barker	214	Hollander v. Central Metal & Supply Co.	225
Elwyn v. DeGarmendia	152, 160		
Equitable Trust Co. v. Pratt	226	Hollis' Hospital, Trustees of, In re	227
Evans v. Walker	211		
Exham v. Beamish	208	Holmes v. John Hancock Mutual Life Ins. Co.	224
Feehan, Matter of	179		
Feeney's Estate	211	Hopper v. Corporation of Liverpool	212
Fernandez v. Wiener	189		
Fifield v. Van Wyck	119	Horn's Estate	165
First National Bank of Boston v. Perkins Institute for the Blind	162	Horsford, Goods of	107
		Hughes v. Hughes	4
First Universalist Society v. Boland	220	Ibey v. Ibey	27
		Inda v. Inda	30
Fisher v. Fisher	120	Institution for Savings v. Roxbury Home for Aged Women	212
Flynn v. Flynn	45		
Forman v. Troup	222	Jackson, In re	134
Fowles, Matter of	94, 141	Jee v. Audley	207, 208
Frazier v. Merchants' Nat. Bank	232	Jodrell, In re	136
Friend, Matter of	208	Johnson, In re	46, 198
Gallagher's Appeal	38	Johnson v. Conover	164
Gardner v. City National Bank	221	Johnson v. McDowell	173
Garrett v. Colvin	12	Johnson v. Preston	209
German Evangelical Church v. Reith	46	Johnston v. Hill	207
		Joynes v. Hamilton	160
Germania Bank v. Michaud	197	Kalina, Matter of	26
Gertman v. Burdick	228	Kavanaugh v. Kavanaugh	19, 20
Ghilain v. Couture	182	Kennell v. Abbott	118
Gifford v. Dyer	125	Kevern v. Williams	222, 223
Gilmore v. Jenkins	12	Kingsbury v. Chapin	151
Glazier v. Glazier	112	Kingston v. Home Life Ins. Co.	225
Goode v. Reynolds	165	Koelhoffer, In re	214
Goodright d. Glazier v. Glazier	112	Koeninger v. Toledo Trust Co.	85
Grafton National Bank v. Wing.	197	Kountz's Estate	220
Gray, Re	139	Ladd, Will of	101
Gray v. Whittemore	218	Leake v. Robinson	213
Greenberg, Matter of	60	Leatherbee v. Leatherbee	46
Guardhouse v. Blackburn	126	Lemayne v. Stanley	52
Guardian, Trust, and Executors Co. of New Zealand v. Smith	167	Lendle, Matter of	166
		Leonard v. Burr	212, 232
Hamilton v. Grange Savings Bank	180	Lewis v. Corbin	119
		Locke v. James	107
Hardyman, In re	60, 167	London & Southwestern Ry. v. Gomm	224, 225
Hare v. O'Brien	182		
Harris v. Harris	35	Longhead v. Phelps	218
Harwood v. Goodright	151	Loring v. Blake	208, 211
Hascall v. King	229	Lougee v. Wilkie	56
Hatcher v. Buford	27	Lovell v. Quitman	101
Hathaway v. Smith	67	Lovering v. Lovering	215
Hattersley v. Bissett	168	Lovering v. Worthington	219
Helvering v. Bullard	208	Lyeth v. Hoey	121
Helvering v. Hallock	189	Lyon v. Osgood	186
Hewson v. Shelley	183	McArthur v. Scott	206
Higinbotham v. Manchester	196	McCauley, Estate of	60
Hiles v. Benton	230	McCoy v. Jordan	115
Hill's Guardian v. Hill	12	McIntyre v. McIntyre	108
Hindmarsh v. Charlton	52	McKallip's Estate	90
Hoff's Appeal	195	McLarney, Matter of	110

TABLE OF CASES

Manhattan Co., President & Directors of v. *Janowitz*	98
Mann v. Registrar	213
Manufacturers Life Ins. Co. v. Von Hamm-Young Co.	226
Maris's Estate	229
Meeker v. Draffen	167, 208
Melvin v. Hoffman	227
Merrill v. Atwood	78
Merrill v. *Boal*	59, 81
Mifflin's Appeal	218
Milam v. *Stanley*	56
Miles's Appeal	101
Miller v. *Richardson*	9, 10
Miller v. Weston	209
Minot v. Paine	218
Mitchell v. Mitchell	27
Moeller v. Kautz	228
Moffatt v. Heon	160
Molineaux v. Raynolds	142
Moore, Appeal of	75, 170
Morehead Banking Co. v. Morehead	197
Morrell v. Morrell	134
Murchison v. Wallace	94
Murray v. *Brooklyn Savings Bank*	27, 30
Mytton v. Mytton	164
National Society for the Prevention of Cruelty to Children v. Scottish National Society for the Prevention of Cruelty to Children	136
National Surety Co. v. Wages	180
Nenaber v. Nenaber	111
Newman v. *Dore*	23, 30
Noell v. Wells	184
Northern Trust Co. v. Perry	139
Norton v. Goodwine	46
Nunn v. *Ehlert*	47, 52
Odell v. Odell	231
O'Hagan, Will of	45
Olney v. Balch	192
Onions v. *Tyrer*	103
Ortman v. Dugan	226
Parfitt v. Lawless	116
Parsons v. Balson	102
Partridge v. Partridge	149
Patch v. *White*	123, 127
Pearks v. Moseley	215, 222
Peirce, *In re*	165
Perkins v. Iglehart	208
Picken v. Matthews	210
Pickens v. *Davis*	112
Piffard, Matter of	94, 96
Pipe Line Cases	222
Powell, *In re*	222
Powell v. Powell	103
Pray v. Hegeman	229
President & Directors of Manhattan Co. v. Janowitz	98
Proctor v. Bishop of Bath	219
Quinlan v. Wickman	220
Rackemann v. Taylor	183
Rausch, Matter of	88
Redman v. *Churchill*	21
Reed v. Harris	101
Reeves, *In re*	60
Rhodes v. Rhodes	134
Richards' Estate, *In re*	221
Richardson, *In re*	58
Ridley, *In re*	230
Ring v. Hardwick	219
Rittenhouse v. Ammerman	197
Rodrigas v. Savings Institution	180
Rudd v. Searles	119
Ruel v. Hardy	107, 114
Scattergood v. Edge	206
Schnakenberg v. Schnakenberg	30
Schott, Goods of	134
Scott v. McNeal	180, 199, 200
Sears v. Putnam	212
Seaver v. Fitzgerald	205, 230
Shepard v. Union & New Haven Trust Co.	215, 222
Siegley v. Simpson	139
Sikes, *In re*	166
Simon v. Grayson	73
Skipworth v. Cabell	107
Slater, In re	163, 166
Smalley, *In re*	118
Smalley v. Smalley	55
Smith's Appeal	218
Smith's Estate v. Commissioner	215, 220
Smith, Goods of	92
Smith, *In re*	195
Smith v. Kibbe	195
Solms' Estate, *In re*	167, 208
Solomon's Estate, *In re*	46
South Norwalk Trust Co. v. St. John	119
Srimati Bibhabati Devi v. Kumar Ramendra Narayan Roy	179
Stanley v. Stanley	134
Stearns v. Stearns	123, 139
Stieglitz v. Migatz	195
Stilwell v. Mellersh	60
Stinson's Estate	52
Storrs v. Benbow	214
Story v. First National Bank & Trust Co.	214
Strong v. Shatto	227
Stubbs v. *Sargon*	74
Swain v. Edmunds	46
Taft v. Stearns	73

TABLE OF CASES

Taltarum's Case	217
Taylor v. State	121
Teed, Matter of	166, 167
Terry, Matter of	212
Thellusson v. Woodford	207, 228
Thomas v. Thomas	195
Thompson v. Pew	143
Tichborne v. Lushington	179
Townshend v. Howard	109
Trautz v. Lemp	210, 222
Truro, Goods of	59, *71*
Tyler, Estate of	46
Tyler, In re	212
Unitarian Society v. Tufts	149
United States v. Delaware & Hudson Co.	222
Van Grutten v. Foxwell	203
Villar, In re	207
Waldo v. Hayes	166
Walker v. Marcellus & Otisco Lake Ry.	213
Ward v. Van der Loeff	107, 207
Warren's Estate	218
White v. Thomas	121
Whitney, Estate of	220
Wilcox, Matter of	205
Wilkinson v. Duncan	218
Willcocks, Re	149
Williams v. Spencer	115
Willis v. *Barrow*	*158*
Wood v. *Hammond*	*136*
Wood, In re	209
Woodard v. Snow	120
Worcester County Trust Co. v. Marble	208
Worcester Trust Co. v. *Turner*	*143*
Worthing Corp. v. Heather	224, 225
Wright's Estate, In re	*123*, 208
Wyatt, Goods of	73

CASES AND TEXT ON WILLS

CHAPTER I.

INTESTACY

A. Essential historical differences between realty and personalty.[1]

In this book we deal with the law governing the passage of property upon death. At the outset it is important to observe that this branch of the law as it relates to real estate grew up under different rules and in a different system of courts than the same branch as it relates to personalty.

Ownership of land, under William the Conqueror and his successors, had more than a proprietary significance. It was the basis of the military, administrative and fiscal organization of the kingdom. Ownership, even in fee simple, was a tenancy in our modern sense; that is, it involved a continuous series of obligations to the lord — fealty, military service of the tenant and his men, money payments upon various occasions. The King was dependent upon the performance of these obligations by his great tenants in capite; and they in turn, as the great estates were divided and sub-divided fan-wise in a hierarchy of lesser tenants, were dependent upon the performance of feudal obligations by these smaller owners. It is not surprising, therefore, that from earliest times the King's courts assumed control of all matters relating to land and impressed upon the land law those doctrines which would tend to make the feudal system work most efficiently from the point of view of the overlords. For example, it was plainly desirable that military obligations of tenants should not be split up in such a way that the lord was forced to rely upon performance of many little obligations by many little tenants instead of one large obligation by a substantial responsible tenant; hence the doctrine of primogeniture and the preference for joint tenancies over tenancies in common, both tending to concentrate ownership. Again, the prosperity of the great lords, and thus indirectly the prosperity of the King, depended upon a continuous flow of those monetary perquisites (reliefs, wardships and marriages) which accrued upon a descent and which were the forerunners of our modern inheritance taxes; hence the common-law prohibition of devises, the doctrine of " worthier title " and the Rule in Shelley's Case, all designed to foster the passage of real estate by descent.

[1] See 1, Holdsworth, Hist. Eng. Law 625–630; 3 id. 534–595. The student would be well advised to read these passages.

Thus it appears that, in origin and development, the law relating to passage of realty upon death is feudal law worked out in the common-law courts.

The ownership and devolution of personalty involved no such public issues. Tangible personalty has never been of great general importance; and in feudal England the agricultural nature of the community and the dogma of the Church that all interest was usury and a mortal sin made the use of gold as capital impossible for Christians. Among a predominantly illiterate population it was natural enough that a dying person should use the last confession as an occasion for giving to the priest his directions as to disposal of his property; and this apparently became the habit. The ecclesiastical courts in mediaeval times came to be the dominant factor in the devolution of personalty upon death, and they administered a set of rules based upon the Roman and Canon systems. It is interesting to note that the title page of Swinburne on Wills (1590) reads as follows: " A Briefe Treatise of Testaments and Last Willes . . . Compiled of such lawes Ecclesiasticall and Civill, as be not repugnant to the lawes, customes or statutes of this Realme, nor derogatorie to the Prerogative Royall." This reliance upon Civil Law sources had a negative and a positive consequence. Negatively, it prevented the law relating to personalty from reflecting the feudal characteristics of the land law; and this was a lasting influence. Positively, it left in the law certain Roman Law rules; but this influence was surprisingly small for two reasons. In the first place, the ecclesiastical courts in the sixteenth and seventeenth centuries lost to Chancery the jurisdiction to supervise the activities of executors and administrators, although they retained other aspects of the probate jurisdiction until the middle of the nineteenth century. In the second place the probate aspects of Roman and Canon law were not very fully developed and yielded readily to the customary habits of thought of the community into which those laws were transplanted.

The modern tendency of courts and legislatures is to assimilate the real-property rules to the rules which govern personalty. But the process of assimilation is by no means complete; and most of the differences can be understood only with reference to the peculiarities of the two systems of law under which the rules arose.

Symbolic of the origin and development of probate law is the nomenclature of testamentary instruments. A " will " (a word of Anglo-Saxon origin) was originally an instrument which disposed of land. A " testament " (a word of Latin origin) was an instrument which disposed of personalty. Hence, if an instrument disposed of both, it was properly a " will and testament." Some rather old-fashioned instruments still contain this double usage; but most modern instruments now use only the word " will."

B. *Descent of land in England.*[2]

The word "descent" is technically applicable only to realty; the word "distribution" serves the same purpose as to personalty.

The principal characteristics of the common law of descent in England were the following:

1. The doctrine of primogeniture — that is, the rule that among several sons and daughters all the real estate descended to the eldest son.
2. The rule that where there were no sons, daughters took together as coparceners. (But note that, in the conception of the law, females taking in coparcenary take as a single heir.)
3. The exclusion of inheritance by ancestors.
4. The doctrine of ancestral property — that is, the rule that in descent to collaterals only those will take who are "of the blood of the first purchaser," i.e. the person who first brought the land into the family. Thus, if John buys Blackacre and allows it to descend to his son James and James dies intestate without issue, brothers or sisters, the land can descend to paternal cousins, but not to maternal cousins.

Side by side with the common law there existed some local customs as to descent. The two best known are the custom of gavelkind by which all sons inherited equally, and the custom of borough English (derived from the fact that in Nottingham it was the custom of the English town but not of the French town) by which the youngest son inherited all.[3]

Intestate land passed (and still passes, in the absence of statute) directly to the heir upon the death of the owner. It does not, as in the case of personalty, pass to an administrator to be by him distributed to the persons entitled.

The Inheritance Act of 1833 (3 & 4 Wm. IV, c. 106) made some changes in the common-law rules without affecting their fundamental basis. The Administration of Estates Act, 1925 (15 Geo. V, c. 23) abolished the doctrine of primogeniture and caused realty to pass upon intestacy in the same manner as personalty.

C. *Distribution of personalty in England.*[4]

At the time of Magna Carta intestate personalty was taken by the ordinary (i.e. the ecclesiastical official having judicial authority, usually the bishop) and administered by him for the good of the soul of the deceased. He was not bound to pay the debts of the intestate or make any distribution to his family. There seem to have been grave abuses. In 1285 the Statute of Westminster II, c. 19, required

[2] See Atkinson, Wills, § 61.
[3] See 3 Holdsw. 259, 271.
[4] See 1 Holdsw. 626–627; 3 id. 556 et seq. Atkinson, Wills, 15, 24 et seq. As to the Civil Law influence imported through the ecclesiastical courts, see Atkinson, "Brief History of English Testamentary Jurisdiction," 8 Mo. L. Rev. 107 (1943).

the ordinary to pay debts; and in 1357 another statute (31 Edw. III, st. 1, c. 11) required the ordinary to appoint as administrator someone " from the next and most lawful friends " of the deceased. Although the administrator had to give bond to the ordinary to guarantee the faithful performance of his duties, there were difficulties in the path of a member of the family who wished to force the administrator to distribute, and these difficulties were accentuated by jurisdictional squabbles between the ecclesiastical courts, the common-law courts and Chancery. The case of Hughes v. Hughes, Carter, 125 (1666), in which a daughter apparently failed to obtain distribution of her father's estate from her brother, caused the Statute of Distribution (22 & 23 Charles II, c. 10) to be passed in 1670.

The scheme of the Statute of Distribution is worth considering because it forms the basis of practically all the American statutes.

1. Rights of the widow. If there are children, she gets ⅓; if no children, ½.
2. Rights of children. If there is a widow, they (and issue of deceased children) get ⅔; if no widow, all.
3. Issue of a deceased child take the share the child would have taken if he had survived. That is, such issue take " by right of representation." This whole scheme of distribution among the descendants of the intestate is known as distribution *per stirpes*.
4. Rights of the next of kin — i.e. nearest relatives other than spouse or issue. They took nothing if there was issue; ½ if there was a spouse but no issue; all if there was neither spouse nor issue. The relatives in the closest degree of kindred took all, provided that issue of deceased relatives of equal degree took by representation (with some restrictions). The degrees of kinship were computed according to the civil law scheme: that is, to compute the degree of kinship of B to A, you count up from A to the common ancestor and then down to B, each step being one degree. This method of computation differs from the common-law method applicable to descent of land and also from the canon-law method which has cropped up to some extent in a few American states.[5]
5. Miscellaneous rules. Collaterals of the half-blood shared equally with those of the whole blood. Relatives by marriage, other than the surviving spouse, had no rights. The doctrine of ancestral property had no application to personalty. An illegitimate could inherit from his spouse or his descendants, but not from any ancestor or collateral.

The Administration of Estates Act, 1925 (15 Geo. V, c. 23) provides that realty as well as personalty shall pass to the administrator, and causes intestate succession of realty to be based upon the same rules as intestate succession of personalty. It provides that if the intestate leaves no spouse, no issue and no relative nearer than great-

[5] See Atkinson, Wills, 30 et seq.

grandparents and their issue, the property shall escheat, — a type of provision which, surprisingly, has appeared in the United States only in Maryland.[6] The most striking feature of this statute, however, is the provision that, where the intestate leaves a widow or minor issue, the bulk of the estate is not distributed outright but is held by the administrator upon statutory trusts prescribed in §§ 46–48. The widow gets personal chattels plus £1000 outright. Then, in the statutory trust of the residue of the estate, she gets the whole income for her life if there are no issue, half if there are issue. The issue take the balance of the income of the trust and also the principal, division being *per stirpes* among those who reach 21 or marry. As of 1946 no American statute has adopted such a system of statutory trusts.

D. Descent and distribution in the United States.

As has been said, the scheme of American statutes of distributions is essentially that of the English Statute of 1670; and this scheme in the main applies alike to realty and personalty. Perhaps the best way to indicate the American practice is to set forth a fairly typical statute — and the Massachusetts act is here selected for this purpose:

MASSACHUSETTS GENERAL LAWS.
(Tercentenary Ed. 1932, as amended by Acts of 1945, Ch. 238)

Chapter 190. *Descent and Distribution of Real and Personal Property.*

§ 1. Share of Surviving Husband or Wife. A surviving husband or wife shall . . . be entitled to the following share in his real and personal property not disposed of by will:

(1) If the deceased leaves kindred and no issue, and it appears on determination by the probate court, as hereinafter provided, that the whole estate does not exceed ten thousand dollars in value, the surviving husband or wife shall take the whole thereof; otherwise such survivor shall take ten thousand dollars and one half of the remaining personal and one half of the remaining real property. . . .

(2) If the deceased leaves issue, the survivor shall take one third of the personal and one third of the real property.

(3) If the deceased leaves no issue and no kindred, the survivor shall take the whole.

§ 2. Distribution of Personal Property. The personal property of a deceased person not lawfully disposed of by will shall . . . be distributed among the persons and in the proportions hereinafter prescribed for the descent of real property.

§ 3. Descent of Real Property. When a person dies seized of land, tenements or hereditaments, or of any right thereto, or en-

---

[6] See Cavers, " Change in the American Family and the ' Laughing Heir,' " 20 Iowa L. Rev. 203, 205 (1935).

titled to any interest therein, in fee simple or for the life of another, not having lawfully devised the same, they shall descend . . . as follows:

(1) In equal shares to his children and to the issue of any deceased child by right of representation: and if there is no surviving child of the intestate then to all his other lineal descendants. If all such descendants are in the same degree of kindred to the intestate, they shall share the estate equally; otherwise, they shall take according to the right of representation.

(2) If he leaves no issue, in equal shares to his father and mother.

(3) If he leaves no issue and no mother, to his father.

(4) If he leaves no issue and no father, to his mother.

(5) If he leaves no issue and no father or mother, to his brothers and sisters and to the issue of any deceased brother or sister by right of representation; and, if there is no surviving brother or sister of the intestate, to all the issue of his deceased brothers and sisters. If all such issue are in the same degree of kindred to the intestate, they shall share the estate equally, otherwise, according to the right of representation.

(6) If he leaves no issue, and no father, mother, brother or sister, and no issue of any deceased brother or sister, then to his next of kin in equal degree; but if there are two or more collateral kindred in equal degree claiming through different ancestors, those claiming through the nearest ancestor shall be preferred to those claiming through an ancestor more remote.

(7) If an intestate leaves no kindred and no widow or husband, his estate shall escheat to the commonwealth.

§ 4. *Degrees of Kindred.* Degrees of kindred shall be computed according to the rules of the civil law; and the kindred of the half blood shall inherit equally with those of the whole blood in the same degree.

§ 5. *Illegitimate Child to Be Heir of His Mother.* An illegitimate child shall be heir of his mother and of any maternal ancestor, and the lawful issue of an illegitimate person shall represent such person and take by descent any estate which such person would have taken if living.

§ 6. *Mother to Be Heir of Illegitimate Child.* If an illegitimate child dies intestate and without issue who may lawfully inherit his estate, such estate shall descend to his mother or, if she is not living, to the persons who would have been entitled thereto by inheritance through his mother if he had been a legitimate child.

§ 8. *Taking by Right of Representation; Posthumous Children.* Inheritance or succession by right of representation is the taking by the descendants of a deceased heir of the same share or right in the estate of another person as their parent would have taken if living. Posthumous children shall be considered as living at the death of their parent.

Chapter 210. *Adoption of Children.*

§ 7. Rights of Adopted Child as to Succession to Property. A person adopted in accordance with this chapter shall take the same share of the property which the adopting parent could dispose of by will as he would have taken if born to such parent in lawful wedlock, and he shall stand in regard to the legal descendants, but to no other of the kindred of such adopting parent, in the same position as if so born to him. If the person adopted dies intestate, his property acquired by himself or by gift or inheritance from his adopting parent or from the kindred of such parent shall be distributed according to chapters one hundred and ninety and one hundred and ninety-six among the persons who would have been his kindred if he had been born to his adopting parent in lawful wedlock; and property received by gift or inheritance from his natural parents or kindred shall be distributed in the same manner as if no act of adoption had taken place. The apportionment and distribution shall be ascertained by the court. A person shall not by adoption lose his right to inherit from his natural parents or kindred.

§ 8. Rights of Adopted Child under Wills, Trusts, etc. The word "child," or its equivalent, in a grant, trust settlement, entail, devise or bequest shall include a child adopted by the settlor, grantor or testator, unless the contrary plainly appears by the terms of the instrument; but if the settlor, grantor or testator is not himself the adopting parent, the child by adoption shall not have, under such instrument, the rights of a child born in lawful wedlock to the adopting parent, unless it plainly appears to have been the intention of the settlor, grantor or testator to include an adopted child.

The Massachusetts statutes also provide that a landowner can set aside, or purchase, during his lifetime an estate of "homestead" which upon his death will pass to his widow and children until the widow dies or remarries and the children all reach 21. See Mass. Gen. Laws (Ter. Ed. 1932) Ch. 188. Upon the death of a husband, the widow may remain in his dwelling house, rent free, for 6 months (G. L. Ch. 196, § 1) ;[7] and the probate court may make her an allowance out of his personal property to support her and her children during that period (G. L. Ch. 196, § 2). Articles of apparel and ornament customarily worn by the widow and children pass to them at the death of the husband-father even though he had title to them during his lifetime (G. L. Ch. 196, § 1). The miscellaneous statutory rules dealt with in this paragraph are equally applicable where there is a will, but they seem part of the general intestacy picture.

[7] This is known as the widow's "quarantine," since it was originally a right to remain only 40 days — in French, a *quarantaine*.

It is to be observed that the Massachusetts statutes do not adopt the doctrine of ancestral property. If A inherits land from his father and then dies intestate, A's heirs on his mother's side can inherit. But there are many American statutes which provide otherwise. These statutes are usually in terms applicable to cases where the land has been received by devise or gift from an ancestor as well as where it is received by descent. Rarely, the statutes are construed to be applicable to personalty.[8]

E. Should a person leave a will or rely upon the intestate law?

Most people who die owning property worth administering leave wills — and with good reason. The scheme of distribution provided by the intestate laws is pretty well designed to make reasonable division among the family of a man who owns a moderate estate, composed of ordinary types of property to be distributed among a usual number of relatives who have much the same needs and are all well-disposed toward each other, — the last specification being the most important of all. But this average man is in practice *avis rarissima*. The intestate laws tend to produce absurdities when the estate is very small or very large.[9] Almost everyone has some types of property which need special attention, perhaps special allocation to certain persons — a small private business, a stamp collection, an involved interest in Florida real estate, great grandmother's portrait. The presumptive distributees of most people are not of equal need; and even if there is equality of need among the present presumptive distributees, an unforeseen sequence of deaths may cause profound dislocation of the distributional scheme the intestate had in mind. For example, a son may die shortly before the intestate, thus causing the son's wife to be deprived of her husband's earning power and her expectancy from her father-in-law at the same time. And there are other difficulties, to wit:

1. The division of personal effects (jewelry, silverware, heirlooms, bric-a-brac, furs, furniture, automobiles, books, linen) among children and grandchildren is the rock upon which many a fine family relationship has been split wide open. The division of the spoils is usually left to the women, and feelings ranging from rankling discontent to passionate hatred are often the result. Daughter Jane says that father always said that her son Harold (who was named after father) should have the grandfather's clock. First question: Shall Harold have it? Second question: If he has it, shall it be taken to be part of Jane's distributive share? However these questions are decided, someone is furious. These difficulties can all be met by a will which allocates these belongings, or orders them sold (every family member being eligible to bid for anything he wants) and the proceeds divided.

[8] See generally Atkinson, Wills, § 29.
[9] See Sayre, op. cit., 42 Harv. L. Rev. at 362 (1929).

2. Servants are not taken care of by the intestate laws. Until such time as the government provides security for domestic help too old or infirm to work it is a matter of obligation for employers to do so.

3. In small estates in which the decedent leaves a widow and minor children, ordinarily the whole should be left to the widow instead of being split up into shares for the children, which will cause expensive and cumbersome guardianships to be set up.

4. In large estates the intestate laws do not provide the protection against payment of unnecessary estate and inheritance taxes in transmission of property to the second generation which can be provided by a simple and flexible trust.

5. In all estates an intestacy brings into potential operation the law of advancements; and in this field the functioning of the general rules upon particular cases is quite as likely to frustrate as to further the probable intention of the decedent. For example, in Miller *v.* Richardson (*infra*) does anyone suppose that General Jackson Oliver wanted Jessie Benn to get the largest share of his estate?

F. Cases on advancements.

The doctrine of advancements is of non-statutory origin.[10] But it was incorporated into the Statute of Distribution of 1670 (§ 5) and is almost universally dealt with by statute in the United States. As will appear, the statutes differ somewhat in terms, but the tendency of courts seems to be to eliminate the effect of such differences.

The law of advancements aims to prevent inter vivos gifts from producing unintended inequalities in the treatment of children by an intestate. (An analogous doctrine, applying where the decedent leaves a will, is dealt with in Chapter VIII, Section 3, " Satisfaction of Legacies.") In the typical clear case one son has come to manhood and has been set up in business by his father. Then, while the other son is still at school, the father dies intestate. It would be manifestly unfair for the elder son to share equally in the remaining property of the father. It is presumed that the father would have equalized the inter vivos gifts to the two sons had he lived, and would now wish the equalization to take place on his death. Thus the elder son can share in the estate only after " bringing into hotchpot " the amount paid out to set him up in business. If the father had paid out $20,000 for this purpose and dies owning $50,000, his total estate is considered to be $70,000; the elder and younger sons share equally in this; but, since the elder has already received $20,000, he gets only $15,000 more, and the younger son gets $35,000 out of the intestate estate.

In England a common case arose where there were two or more daughters and the father died intestate after marrying off one daughter and providing her with the customary marriage settlement. The favored daughter could share in the estate only by bringing her set-

[10] See 2 Holdsw. 579; 3 id. 553.

tlement into hotchpot. The doctrine of advancements is frequently called the " presumption against double portions."

Trouble arises when the nature and motivation of the parent-to-child gifts are less clear than the obvious cases just stated. Miller *v.* Richardson, infra, deals with a family situation where typical gifts have been made to several children. What aspect of the decedent's intention is important in such cases? To be practical, consider how you would argue this case if you represented Alice Love. Of course, for tactical reasons Jessie Benn would have been a fool to appeal. But, if she had appealed, what is the argument against treating her $1000 gift as an advancement?

MILLER *v.* RICHARDSON.

SUPREME COURT OF MISSOURI, 1935.

85 S. W.(2d) 41.

GANTT, Presiding Judge.

On November 26, 1930, General Jackson Oliver, widower, and 90 years of age, died intestate, leaving six children and the children of a deceased son. He left a $97,000 estate of real and personal property. The question of advancements was for determination.[11]

The court found that General Jackson Oliver made gifts as advancements to his children as follows: Arbie Miller, $7,900; Alice Love, $7,865; heirs of John S. Oliver, $7,000; Henry S. Oliver, $3,000; Courtney McCann, $3,000; Anna Richardson, $3,000; Jessie Benn, $1,000. The first three appealed.

The rule is well stated as follows:

" The whole doctrine of advancements rests upon the assumption that ordinarily a parent intends to make an equal distribution of his property among his children, and that a gift of a substantial amount to one child will, in the absence of evidence to the contrary, be presumed to have been intended as an advancement.[12] An advancement is an irrevocable gift, and therefore the use by the parent of the word ' gift ' or ' present ' in connection with the transaction is, standing alone, of little value in determining the parent's intention. * * *

[11] Mo. Rev. Stat. (1929) provide as follows:

§ 311. When any of the children of the intestate who shall have received, in his lifetime, any real or personal estate, by way of advancement, shall choose to come into partition with the other parceners, such advancement shall be brought into hotchpot with the estate descended.

§ 312. Maintaining, educating or giving money to a child under the age of majority, without any view to a portion or settlement in life, shall not be deemed an advancement.

The opinion in the principal case has been substantially shortened.

[12] Compare Mass. Gen. Laws (Ter. ed. 1932) Ch. 196, § 5:

"The presumption is overcome only by clear and convincing evidence." In re Sells' Estate, 197 Iowa, 696, 197 N. W. 922, 923.

In making gifts to the four last-named children, decedent wrote on the checks either " present," " birth present," or " birthday present." The date of the checks was not the birthday of either the donor or donees. We think that he intended said words to identify the checks as gifts. However, there was no evidence tending to show that he intended to make absolute gifts to said children. It will be noted that he gave to Jessie Benn only $1,000. For ought that appears she was in good financial condition.

There was evidence tending to show that in 1915 decedent visited John S., who lived in a small town in Oklahoma and sold patent medicine for a livelihood. He had a wife and nine children. Decedent told him it would be better for the children if they lived on a farm. The son said that he had no money. Decedent gave him $7,000. He purchased a farm with the money for $8,000, and moved his family thereon. He paid the balance due from earnings of the farm. In four years he sold the farm for $16,000. There was no evidence tending to show that decedent intended the $7,000 to be an absolute gift.

There also was evidence tending to show that on November 26, 1927, decedent gave Alice Love a farm of 121 acres. She had ten children and a husband unable to work. At the time decedent stated that Alice needed help and for that reason he gave her the farm. There also was no evidence tending to show that he intended the farm to be an absolute gift.

There also was evidence tending to show that on December 18, 1918, decedent gave Arbie Miller a farm of 80 acres. She kept house for him and worked on his farm. It is contended that the farm was an absolute gift for said services. Arbie did not so consider the gift. On November 10, 1931, she filed a claim against the estate of her father for said services from February 7, 1898, to January 5, 1922, for $21,810, and for said services from January 5, 1922, to April 4, 1929, for $13,225. There also was no evidence tending to show that decedent intended this farm to be an absolute gift.

In the absence of evidence to the contrary, it must be presumed that the gifts were advancements. Lynch *v.* Culver, 260 Mo. 495, 168 S. W. 1138. The judgment should be affirmed.

PROBLEMS.

1. F, a father, had two daughters, Sylvia and Lizzie. In 1903 F bought farm land for $450 and let Lizzie and her husband occupy it under an oral agreement that Lizzie would buy it for $500 when she got enough money to pay it. Lizzie and her husband improved the land until in 1918 it was worth $6,000. F paid the taxes. In 1918 Lizzie paid F $100 and gave him four notes for $100 each, and F gave Lizzie a deed of the land. A few months later Sylvia com-

plained to F that she thought he was discriminating against her. He said, " I won't make any difference between you and Lizzie. I expect you and Lizzie to share equal. Lizzie's place is worth now more than when I bought it; but I'll make that right." In 1919 F died intestate. Is Lizzie chargeable with an advancement upon these facts? Holland v. Bonner, 142 Ark. 214, 218 S. W. 665 (1920).[13] See Atkinson, Wills, pp. 673–674.

2. F, a father, had three sons. Son A finished high-school at the age of 20 and went to work. Son B finished high-school at the age of 18 and went to college, taking an A.B. degree at the age of 22. Son C finished high-school at 17, took an A.B. at 21 and went to law school, receiving his LL.B. at 24. F paid all the expenses of his sons through the schooling above stated and suported them during the summers for this period. F now dies intestate. Have any of the sons received advancements? If so, does the advancement consist of (a) tuition? (b) tuition and expenses during the school year? (c) tuition, expenses during the school year and the fair value of support during vacations? See Hill's Guardian v. Hill, 122 Ky. 681, 92 S. W. 924 (1906); Garrett v. Colvin, 77 Miss. 408, 26 So. 963 (1899).[14]

3. F, a father, in 1930 writes a check for $5,000 in favor of his son, S. There is some ambiguous conversation as to paying the $5,000 back. Later F dies intestate. Is it to S's advantage to have the payment treated as an advancement or as a loan,

    (a) if F dies after the period of the statute of limitations has run?
    (b) if he dies before that time? See Atkinson, Wills, 674.

[13] The Arkansas statutes provide that " If any child of an intestate shall have been advanced by him, in his lifetime, by settlement or portion of real or personal estate, or both of them," such advancement shall be reckoned as part of the property of the intestate and charged against the share of the child advanced. But " The maintaining, educating or giving money to a child or heir, without a view to a portion or settlement in life, shall not be an advancement." Dig. Stat. Ark. (Pope, 1937) §§ 4353–4356.

[14] Ky. Stat. (1936) § 1407 is as follows: " Any real or personal property or money, given or devised by a parent or grandparent, to a descendant, shall be charged to the descendant or to those claiming through him in the division and distribution of the undevised estate of the parent or grandparent." Plainly this statute goes far beyond the others that have been considered in several respects.

Where there is a partial intestacy, a distributee of an intestate share does not have to bring into hotchpot either advancements to him during the decedent's life or gifts to him in the decedent's will unless the contrary is provided by statute. Gilmore v. Jenkins, 129 Ia. 686, 106 N. W. 193 (1906).

CAZASSA v. CAZASSA.

Supreme Court of Tennessee, 1893

92 Tenn. 573, 22 S. W. 560.

WILKES, J. This bill is filed by the widow and younger son of Frank Cazassa against the elder son of Frank Cazassa and his guardian. The objects of the bill are: . . .

Second. To declare certain insurance moneys, amounting to about $14,000, arising from four different life policies, together with the premiums paid thereon, to be an advancement to the elder son, for which he must account upon the settlement of his father's estate.[15] All of these life policies were taken out by the father, one of them being originally payable to his estate, and afterwards transferred to the elder son, and the others taken out originally in the name of and for the benefit of the elder son. . . .

On the trial the Chancellor held . . . a policy for $5,000 in the Mutual Benefit Life Insurance Company was an advancement, but that the other insurance was not an advancement.

This $5,000 policy was in what is styled an "old line company," while the others were certificates in certain benevolent orders. The former was paid up, and had originally been issued in favor of the father's estate, and subsequently transferred to the elder son, while the benefit certificates were taken out in the name of the elder son, and for his benefit. . . .

For complainants, it is insisted that the Court should have charged all the insurance and all the premiums paid thereon as an advancement against the elder son, for which he should account in the further settlement of his father's estate. . . .

As to the insurance money, a new and novel question is presented: Whether insurance taken out by the father in the name of a child, or taken out in his own name and subsequently transferred to a child, shall be treated as an advancement to that child, for which he must account in the settlement of his father's estate; and, if so treated, then for what amount must such child account?

We have been cited by counsel to but one case bearing upon the question, and it is admitted that no other case can be found. The

---

[15] The Tennessee statutes (Code, 1932) provide that "all advancements, whether by settlement or otherwise, in the lifetime of deceased, or by testamentary provision, shall be collated and brought into contribution in the partition and distribution of the real and personal estate of the deceased" (§ 8402a). It is also provided (§ 8404) that if a power is granted to a parent to bestow property in favor of one or more of the children, any property given under such power to a child shall be brought into contribution by such child claiming a share in the distribution of the property of the parent. The statutes do not deal with the valuation of the advancement or the time at which value is to be ascertained.

case cited is Rickenbacker *v.* Zimmerman, 10 South Carolina Reports, 110. In that case it was held that the value of the insurance at the time the policy was taken out and the first premium paid, together with all premiums subsequently paid, must be treated as an advancement.

An advancement is defined to be a gift by a parent to a child by anticipation, in whole or in part, of what it is supposed the child will be entitled to on the death of the parent. . . .

In this case the insurance was purchased by the funds of the father. It was an investment of the money paid as premium by him for the benefit of his son; it was the setting apart and investing of that much of his property, which would otherwise have accumulated in other forms and gone to his distributees just as much as if he had invested the same in some stock or bond for the benefit of his child; and if we add the feature that the father should retain the possession of the bond or stock until his death, the analogy would be complete.

It is true the proceeds of a life policy are by statute protected from seizure for the father's debts, but this in nowise bears upon the matter now under consideration.

The premiums being thus invested in the policy, the proceeds of the same are an advancement to the child in the absence of anything showing that the parent intended it to be a gift and not an advancement.

As a matter of course it is competent for the father to give the policy to his child as a gift, and not as an advancement, as it would be for him to give any other property that he might desire, but in the absence of clear, convincing proof to the contrary, the property will be treated as an advancement, and not as a gift. . . .

The mere fact that the policy is taken in the name of the son is no more evidence that it was intended as a gift instead of an advancement than would be the placing of title to real or personal property in the name of the son. All advancements are gifts, but there may be a gift that is not an advancement if not so intended when made by the parent.

The next question presented is at what sum the insurance should be charged, treating it as an advancement.

In the South Carolina case cited, it was held that the son should be charged with the value of the policy at the time it was taken out and the first premium paid, together with all premiums subsequently paid added to that value, but without interest. This ruling was, however, based upon the statute of South Carolina relating to advancements, which provides that the property advanced shall be estimated at its value at the ancestor's death, but so that neither the improvement of real estate nor increase of personal property shall enter into the computation.

The rule in Tennessee is that advancements shall be charged at their value when made. . . .

Under this rule, we think the property should be charged at its value at the time it comes into the possession and beneficial enjoyment of the child to whom it is given.

We consider this much the better rule, inasmuch as the child gets no possession or beneficial enjoyment until the father's death. In the meantime, if the policy has been allowed to lapse, the child will not be chargeable with anything on account of it. Again, it is said that if anything is charged as an advancement, it should be simply the amount of premium paid, without interest, but the same rule applied to any other property would make the amount paid for the property advanced the criterion of value, instead of what it is actually worth or what may be its real outcome.

We are of opinion, therefore, that the eldest son should be charged, as an advancement, with the net amounts received by him upon all the policies after his father's death. We can see no reason why he should not be charged with the amounts received on the certificates in the beneficial orders as well as that upon the old line policy, nor with the amounts received upon the policies not paid up as well as that paid up in the father's life-time. The final proceeds and outcome of each is earned by, and is the result of, the premiums invested by the father out of his own means, which would otherwise, upon his death, have gone to his distributees.

The decree of the Chancellor as to the . . . insurance money, is modified as herein indicated. . . .

CHAPTER II.

PROTECTION OF WIDOW AND CHILDREN AGAINST DISINHERITANCE.[1]

A. History.

From early times the widow (and to some extent, the children) of a decedent were protected from disinheritance.

The writ de rationabili parte bonorum. As to personalty, it was settled in the twelfth and thirteenth centuries that if a man left a widow and no issue, the widow was entitled to one-half of his property and could not be deprived of it by will; if he left a widow and children, the widow was entitled to one-third and the children one-third. The man's power of testation extended only to one-half and one-third respectively of his estate. The rights of widow and children in this situation were enforced by the writ *de rationabili parte bonorum.*[2] But this writ, and the rule it enforced, fell into decadence; and it later became settled that a man could make a will of his personal property which would deprive his widow and children of any interest in it.[3] This has always been the common law of the United States. The statutes on the subject are later discussed.

Dower and curtesy. As to realty, the institution of dower and curtesy protected the surviving spouse. Dower: The widow had a life estate in one-third of all freeholds of which her husband was at any time seised during coverture. Curtesy: The widower, if issue of the marriage were born alive but not otherwise, had a life estate in all freeholds of which his wife was at any time owner during coverture. While both spouses were alive dower and curtesy were obviously contingent interests — contingent upon which spouse survived the other; during the joint lives they were known respectively as inchoate dower and curtesy initiate. When one spouse died the dower (or curtesy) became consummate. Both dower and curtesy were exempt from the claims of the decedent's creditors —

---

[1] See generally Sayre, "Husband and Wife as Statutory Heirs," 42 Harv. L. Rev. 330 (1929).

[2] 3 Holdsw. 550.

[3] The tripartite division of a decedent's property survives in Scottish law almost exactly as above described. Where there are issue and a widow, testator can dispose of only one third (the dead's part) but cannot take away the *jus relictae* (the widow's part) or the *legitim* (called, believe it or not, the bairn's part). But, as in modern American law, as hereafter appears, inter vivos transfers can render these rights of widow and children valueless. Gloag and Henderson, Introduction to the Law of Scotland (2 ed. 1933) 480 et seq.

an important attribute, which has considerable modern significance. Dower and curtesy became important parts of the American land law and they continue to exist except so far as they have been abolished or modified by statute.

Descent and distribution to spouses. In passing it should be recalled that in England the spouse was a distributee of personalty under the Statute of Distribution but was not an heir of realty. The decedent could cut off the surviving spouse's right as distributee by making a will; therein this right differed from dower, curtesy and (under the older law) the rights secured by the writ *de rationabili parte bonorum.*

B. *Modern Law.*

Common-law dower and curtesy were well designed to give appropriate rights to a surviving spouse in a social order where the chief form of wealth was land and the chief form of income was rents and profits from land. The widow's dower (life estate in one-third of her husband's lands) provided for her after his death the support he was obligated to furnish in his lifetime. The husband's curtesy gave him after his wife's death the same rights in her lands that he exercised when she was alive. But in the United States since the industrial revolution the nature of wealth and income has changed. Stocks and bonds and the income from them have replaced land and its rents. Dower and curtesy no longer give the needed protection.

To meet this situation practically all states have enacted statutes which provide that a surviving spouse can, by renouncing any benefits which may be conferred by the decedent's will, receive a designated part of the decedent's estate. Sometimes this designated part is the share which the survivor would have taken if the decedent had died intestate; sometimes it is one-third of the decedent's property; sometimes more complicated provisions are made to compute the survivor's share. Observe the differences between this forced share and common-law dower: (1) Common-law dower applies only to land, the statutory forced share to both personalty and land; (2) Common-law dower exists with regard to property of which the husband was seised at any time during coverture; the statutory forced share exists only with regard to property which the husband owns at the time of his death; (3) Common-law dower was free from the claims of the husband's creditors, whereas the statutory forced share is free of such claims only in a few states.[4] The cases which appear in this Chapter concern common types of problems which arise with reference to the statutory forced share.

In some states common-law dower and curtesy have not been abolished even though a statutory forced share is provided. In such states it is rarely wise for a surviving spouse to claim dower or

[4] However, the homestead rights and family allowance made to the widow (see p. 7, supra) are almost universally held to be free of the husband's debts.

curtesy;[5] but the possibility of such a claim being made is a constant nuisance in conveyancing transactions and a constant source of bothersome clouds on title. The complexity of the problem where common-law dower continues to exist is indicated by the situation which arises in Massachusetts when a husband dies leaving a will.[6] The widow's choices are three:

(1) She can elect to take the interest, if any, given her by the will. She exercises this election by allowing six months to pass from the date of probate of the will without electing to take her dower or statutory forced share. If the will so provides, she can have dower in addition to the testamentary provisions; but such a clause is rarely found.

(2) She can elect to "waive the will" (i.e. renounce its provisions) and take her statutory forced share. She exercises this election by filing a renunciation with the probate court not more than six months after probate of the will.

(3) She can elect to waive the will and her statutory forced share and take dower. She exercises this election by filing a claim of dower within six months of the approval of the administrator's or executor's bond and filing a renunciation of the will within six months of the probate of the will. The widow should be advised to elect her dower only if her husband's estate is insolvent or practically so; for dower is exempt from the claims of creditors whereas the statutory forced share and testamentary provisions for the widow are not.[7]

Pretermitted children. The modern law gives no protection to the child whom his parent wishes to disinherit. However, statutes usually protect the "pretermitted" child — i.e. the child whom the parent has neglected through oversight. Thus, in Massachusetts, it is provided that

"If a testator omits to provide in his will for any of his children or for the issue of a deceased child, they shall take the same share of his estate which they would have taken if he had died intestate, unless they have been provided for by the testator in his lifetime or unless it appears that the omission was intentional and not occasioned by accident or mistake." (Gen. Laws Mass., Ter. Ed., 1932, Ch. 191, § 20.)

Note that (1) the statute protects issue of deceased children as well as children; (2) the statute applies to children and issue born after the execution of the will as well as to those who are living at that time; (3) the evidence of intentional omission need not appear on

---

[5] See Newhall, Settlement of Estates and Fiduciary Law in Massachusetts (3d ed. 1937) p. 449.

[6] If he dies intestate the widow must choose whether she is to take her intestate share, described in the preceding chapter, or dower.

[7] On this triple election see generally Newhall, Settlement of Estates and Fiduciary Law in Massachusetts (3d ed. 1937) Chapters 19–21.

the face of the will but may be furnished by oral testimony or unattested writings. Several similar statutes differ from the Massachusetts act in one or more of these particulars; but the after-born child is protected almost everywhere.

C. *Cases on protection of the widow.*

The New York statute as to the widow's right to renounce the will and claim a statutory share in her husband's estate is Decedent Estate Law, § 18, appearing at p. 292, infra. It covers three and a half printed pages and has been amended six times. You would expect that such a statute would now be lucid in meaning and airtight to evasion. As a matter of fact the statute does not solve, indeed does not even face, the problem of the husband who is determined to disinherit his wife; for it gives to the wife a right to " her share of the estate as in intestacy " and thus leaves it open to the husband to reduce or eliminate that share at will by inter vivos gifts which withdraw assets from " the estate." Whatever real protection the widow has is derived from decisions of the courts which distort the words of the statute beyond recognition and put serious strain upon accepted trust doctrine.

Other legislatures have been equally remiss. They have passed statutes which make graceful and friendly gestures to the surviving spouse but, despite a flood of litigation, have uniformly failed to protect the statutes against evasion.

It well may be that legislatures have no intention of giving substantial rights to a widow whose relationship to her husband was such that a desire to disinherit her lay uppermost in his mind. It cannot be ignored that legislatures are predominantly male; and there are no statistics to establish that marital infelicity is less prevalent among the elected. Again the emancipation of womanhood may have progressed to the point where statutory protection of the widow is out of step with the times. But these are reasons for repealing the statutes, not for leaving them porous.

In this situation it is not surprising that courts have had a bad time. The following cases represent (a) a sampling of various shadings of judicial opinion (b) the writhings of the New York courts in trying to develop a sensible body of law within the confines of their statutory system. Kavanaugh v. Kavanaugh (p. 20) contrasts the claims of fiancée and wife on judicial chivalry. The Eaton Estate (Problem, p. 37) warns of pitfalls in drafting ante-nuptial agreements and divorce settlements.

The Note on British Empire legislation (p. 35) suggests that, at least where confidence in the judiciary runs high, there may be better ways of protecting the family than the ones we have adopted in the United States.

KAVANAUGH v. KAVANAUGH.

SUPREME JUDICIAL COURT OF MASSACHUSETTS, 1932.

279 Mass. 238, 181 N. E. 181.

CROSBY, J. This suit in equity was heard by a judge of the Superior Court who made the following findings: The plaintiff and the defendant Joseph B. Kavanaugh were married to each other on November 9, 1921. At the time they became engaged to marry, he was the owner of certain real estate situated in Boston and described in paragraph 2 of the bill of complaint. On occasions before and during said engagement, and thereafter from the date of their marriage until their separation in 1928, he represented to her that he was the owner of the premises and that they were not encumbered. On September 20, 1921, he conveyed the property by quitclaim deed to his brother, Albert L. Kavanaugh, the other defendant, without consideration, but not intending it to be an absolute conveyance, and for the purpose of preventing any rights therein accruing to the plaintiff through her approaching marriage to him; of this purpose the grantee had knowledge. The deed was deposited in the safe of the defendant Albert L. Kavanaugh in his law office in Lewiston, Maine, until July 11, 1923, when he caused it to be recorded in the Suffolk registry of deeds, and returned to him; it has since remained in his possession. The trial judge further found that Joseph B. Kavanaugh concealed from the plaintiff the fact of this antenuptial conveyance, and continued to manage, control and retain for himself the income from the premises until the fall of 1928, when the plaintiff was granted a decree, by the Probate Court for the county of Suffolk, to the effect that she was living apart from her husband for justifiable cause; since that time Albert L. Kavanaugh has retained said income for himself.[8] A final decree was entered in which it was ordered, adjudged and decreed that the defendant Joseph B. Kavanaugh was " seised in fee simple in his own right " of the real estate in question; that by the deed dated September 20, 1921, he transferred the property to his brother Albert L. Kavanaugh, without consideration, and with the fraudulent intention and purpose of depriving the plaintiff of her marital rights in the property, and that Albert L. Kavanaugh took said transfer with knowledge of said fraudulent purpose. The decree further recited that the defendant Albert L. Kavanaugh " is hereby forever enjoined from asserting or claiming ownership or being seised in fee simple in his own right in said described property by, through or under said . . . deed dated September 20, 1921;

---

[8] Observe that there was no finding that (1) the ownership of this real estate was an inducement to the plaintiff to marry or that (2) the ownership of this real estate was necessary to permit the husband to comply with the decree for separate support.

and the codefendant Joseph B. Kavanaugh be and he is hereby decreed to be sole owner in fee simple of said described estate "; that costs be taxed in the sum named to be paid by the defendants to the plaintiff, and that execution issue therefor. From this decree both defendants appealed. No question is raised as to the form of the decree.

The evidence not being reported the findings must stand, as it does not appear that they are mutually inconsistent or plainly wrong. L. E. Fosgate Co. *v.* Boston Market Terminal Co., 275 Mass. 99, and cases cited. The judge found that the conveyance was made, without consideration, for the purpose of preventing the plaintiff from acquiring any rights in the property upon her marriage with Joseph B. Kavanaugh, with the full knowledge of the grantee. This constituted a fraud practised upon the plaintiff. She had a right to rely upon the good faith and honesty of her husband. She could assume that he would not enter into a fraudulent transaction with his brother to deprive her of her marital rights after they had become engaged, and before they were married. Allen *v.* Allen, 213 Mass. 29, 34. Tucker *v.* Andrews, 13 Maine, 124, 128. Smith *v.* Smith, 2 Hals. Eq. 515, 522. In the case last cited it was said: " I am of opinion that a voluntary conveyance by a man, on the eve of marriage, unknown to the intended wife and made for the purpose of defeating the interest which she would acquire in his estate by the marriage, is fraudulent, as against her." See also Wheeler *v.* Kirtland, 12 C. E. Green, 534, 535; Pinkinson *v.* Pinkinson, 93 N. J. Eq. 583; Wildeman *v.* Wildeman, 98 N. J. Eq. 109; Daniher *v.* Daniher, 201 Ill. 489; Petty *v.* Petty, 4 B. Mon. 215. It follows that the decree must be affirmed with costs.

REDMAN *v.* CHURCHILL.

Supreme Judicial Court of Massachusetts, 1918.

230 Mass. 415, 119 N. E. 953.

CARROLL, J. The appellant is the widow of Chauncey S. Churchill who died October 5, 1914. By his will he gave her one third of his real and personal property " belonging to me and standing in my name, but no part of the real or personal property held by me as executor or trustee of the estate of my mother, Parmelia S. Churchill, or of the property in which I have a life interest and power of disposition by will." The residue of his estate " or over which I have, under the will of my mother or otherwise, the power of distribution," he gave in trust for the benefit of his children. In 1913 he transferred and assigned to himself as executor of his mother's will certificates of stock and mortgages which were in fact his own, to the amount of at least $50,000. The executors filed their account showing a payment to Mrs. Churchill of $825.69, which was one third of the property standing in the name of the husband at the time of his death. This account was allowed in the Probate Court and Mrs. Churchill appealed to the Supreme Judicial Court.

She contends she is entitled to receive from the executors in addition to the amount of $825.69, — which was one third of all the property standing in her husband's name at the time of his death, — one third of the certificates and mortgages which he assigned and transferred to himself as the executor of his mother's will. It was agreed that these assignments and transfers were made for the purpose of preventing his wife from receiving any part of this property. The single justice before whom the case was heard was of opinion that the property conveyed was not within the description " belonging to me and standing in my name," and reserved the case for the consideration of this court.

The language of the will and the evidence of his intention introduced at the hearing, showed that the testator intended to give his wife one third only of the property which he owned and which stood in his name when he died, and did not intend to include in this bequest any portion of the property which he had transferred to his mother's estate and which he held as the executor of her will. The certificates of stock and mortgages, of which Mrs. Churchill now claims a share as legatee under her husband's will, were not his property. They had been transferred and were a part of his mother's estate.

Even if the question of fraud were open in these proceedings, there is nothing to show that the husband practised any legal fraud on the appellant. He had the right to dispose of his personal property during his lifetime without her consent, and she cannot impeach a gift made by him as a fraud upon her because made to prevent her from acquiring any portion of it. He could make a gift to himself as executor of his mother's will, and when this was done the property was no longer his. . . . The wife had no right to insist that the husband should hold all the property he owned during his marriage until his death, and such a conveyance or gift is not a fraud on the marital rights of his wife. . . . The testator had a right to convey to a third person who was the executor of another's will, property which belonged to himself, and he could transfer his own property to himself as executor of his mother's will, by way of gift. . . .

As the securities transferred to his mother's estate did not belong to the testator and did not stand in his name when he died, and as the executors have paid to Mrs. Churchill one third of all the property which did belong to him and which stood in his name when he died, the decree of the Probate Court allowing the account should be affirmed.

NEWMAN v. DORE.

Court of Appeals of New York, 1937.

275 N. Y. 371, 9 N. E.(2d) 966.

[Appeal from a judgment holding that the trust described in the opinion was invalid as to the settlor's wife.]

Lehman, J. . . . Ferdinand Straus died on July 1, 1934, leaving a last will and testament dated May 5, 1934, which contained a provision for a trust for his wife for her life of one-third of the decedent's property both real and personal. In such case the statute did not give the wife a right of election to take her share of the estate as in intestacy.[9] She receives the income for life from a trust fund of the amount of the intestate share, but does not take the share. That share is one-third of the *decedent's estate.* It includes no property which does not form part of the estate at the decedent's death. The testator on June 28, 1934, three days before his death, executed trust agreements by which, in form at least, he transferred to trustees all his real and personal property. If the agreements effectively divested the settlor of title to his property, then the decedent left no estate and the widow takes nothing. The widow has challenged the validity of the transfer to the trustees. The beneficiary named in the trust agreement has brought this action to compel the trustees to carry out its terms. The trial court has found that the "trust agreements were made, executed and delivered by said Ferdinand Straus for the purpose of evading and circumventing the laws of the State of New York, and particularly sections 18 and 83 of the Decedent Estate Law." Undoubtedly the settlor's purpose was to provide that at his death his property should pass to beneficiaries named in the trust agreement to the exclusion of his wife. Under the provisions of the Decedent Estate Law the decedent could not effect the desired purpose by testamentary disposition of his property. The problem in this case is whether he has accomplished that result by creating a trust during his lifetime.

The validity of the attempted transfer depends upon whether "the laws of the State of New York and particularly sections 18 and 83 of the Decedent Estate Law" prohibit or permit such transfer. If the statute, in express language or by clear implication, prohibits the transfer, it is illegal; if the laws of the State do not prohibit it,

---

[9] Decedent Estate Law, § 83 specifies the interest which the surviving spouse takes by intestacy; this share is one-third of all property outright. Decedent Estate Law, § 18 provides that, where a testator dies leaving a will executed after Aug. 31, 1930, the surviving spouse may elect to take his or her share by intestacy unless (inter alia) the decedent creates a trust of one-third of all his property and gives the income thereof to the surviving spouse for life. For the text of Section 18, see Appendix, p. 292.

the transfer is legal. In strict accuracy, it cannot be said that a " purpose of evading and circumventing " the law can carry any legal consequences. " We do not speak of evasion, because when the law draws a line, a case is on one side of it or the other, and if on the safe side is none the worse legally that a party has availed himself to the full of what the law permits. When an act is condemned as an evasion what is meant is that it is on the wrong side of the line indicated by the policy if not by the mere letter of the law." (Bullen v. Wisconsin, 240 U. S. 625, 630.) In a subsequent case it was said of a defendant: " The fact that it desired to evade the law, as it is called, is immaterial, because the very meaning of a line in the law is that you intentionally may go as close to it as you can if you do not pass it." (Superior Oil Co. v. Mississippi, 280 U. S. 390, 395, both opinions by Mr. Justice HOLMES.) . . .

The statute gives to a spouse a property right. The question is, how far the statute protects that right even while it remains only expectant and contingent. . . . Here, we should point out that the courts below have not based their decision primarily upon the finding that the trust agreements were executed for the purpose of evading and circumventing the law of the State of New York. The courts have also found, and the evidence conclusively establishes, that the trust agreements were made for the purpose of depriving the decedent's widow of any rights in and to his property upon his death. Under the trust agreements executed a few days before the death of the settlor, he reserved the enjoyment of the entire income as long as he should live, and a right to revoke the trust at his will, and in general the powers granted to the trustees were in terms made " subject to the settlor's control during his life," and could be exercised " in such manner only as the settlor shall from time to time direct in writing." Thus by the trust agreement which transferred to the trustees the settlor's entire property, the settlor reserved substantially the same rights to enjoy and control the disposition of the property as he previously had possessed, and the inference is inescapable that the trust agreements were executed by the settlor, as the court has found, " with the intention and for the purpose of diminishing his estate and thereby to reduce in amount the share " of his wife in his estate upon his death and as a " contrivance to deprive * * * his widow of any rights in and to his property upon his death." They had no other purpose and substantially they had no other effect. Does the statute intend that such a transfer shall be available as a means of defeating the contingent expectant estate of a spouse?

In a few States where a wife has a similar contingent expectant interest or estate in the property of her husband, it has been held that her rights may not be defeated by any transfer made during life with *intent* to deprive the wife of property, which under the law would otherwise pass to her. (Thayer v. Thayer, 14 Vt. 107; Evans v. Evans, 78 N. H. 352; Dyer v. Smith, 62 Mo. App. 606; Payne v.

Tatem, 236 Ky. 306.) In those States it is the intent to defeat the wife's contingent rights which creates the invalidity and it seems that an absolute transfer of all his property by a married man during his life, if made with *other* purpose and intent than to cut off an unloved wife, is valid even though its effect is to deprive the wife of any share in the property of her husband at his death. (Dunnett *v.* Shields & Conant, 97 Vt. 419; Patch *v.* Squires, 105 Vt. 405.) The rule has been stated that " while the wife cannot complain of reasonable gifts or advancements by a husband to his children by a former marriage, yet, if the gifts constitute the principal part of the husband's estate and be made without the wife's knowledge, a presumption of fraud arises, and it rests upon the beneficiaries to explain away that presumption." (Payne *v.* Tatem, *supra*, p. 308.)

Motive or intent is an unsatisfactory test of the validity of a transfer of property. In most jurisdictions it has been rejected, sometimes for the reason that it would cast doubt upon the validity of all transfers made by a married man, outside of the regular course of business; sometimes because it is difficult to find a satisfactory logical foundation for it. Intent may, at times, be relevant in determining whether an act is fraudulent, but there can be no fraud where no right of any person is invaded. " The great weight of authority is that the intent to defeat a claim which otherwise a wife might have is not enough to defeat the deed." (Leonard *v.* Leonard, 181 Mass. 458, 462, and cases there cited.) Since the law gives the wife only an expectant interest in the property of her husband which becomes part of his estate, and since the law does not restrict transfers of property by the husband during his life, it would seem that the only sound test of the validity of a challenged transfer is whether it is real or illusory. That is the test applied in Leonard *v.* Leonard (supra). The test has been formulated in different ways, but in most jurisdictions the test applied is essentially the test of whether the husband has in good faith divested himself of ownership of his property or has made an illusory transfer. " The good faith required of the donor or settlor in making a valid disposition of his property during life does not refer to the purpose to affect his wife but to the intent to divest himself of the ownership of the property. It is, therefore, apparent, that the fraudulent interest which will defeat the gift *inter vivos* cannot be predicated of the husband's intent to deprive the wife of her distributive share as widow." (Benkart *v.* Commonwealth Trust Co., 269 Penn. St. 257, 259.) In Pennsylvania the courts have sustained the validity of the trusts even where a husband reserved to himself the income for life, power of revocation and a considerable measure of control. (Cf. Lines *v.* Lines, 142 Penn. St. 149; Potter Title & Trust Co. *v.* Braum, 294 Penn. St. 482; Beirne *v.* Continental-Equitable Title & Trust Co., 307 Penn. St. 570.) . . .

In this case the decedent, as we have said, retained not only the income for life and power to revoke the trust, but also the right to control the trustees. We need not now determine whether such a trust is, for any purpose, a valid present trust. It has been said that " where the settlor transfers property in trust and reserves not only * * * a power to revoke and modify the trust but also such power to control the trustee as to the details of the administration of the trust that the trustee is the agent of the settlor, the disposition so far as it is intended to take effect after his death is testamentary * * * " [10] (American Law Institute, Restatement of the Law of Trusts, § 57, subd. 2.) We do not now consider whether the rule so stated is in accord with the law of this State or whether in this case the reserved power of control is so great that the trustee is in fact " the agent of the settlor." We assume, without deciding, that except for the provisions of section 18 of the Decedent Estate Law the trust would be valid. . . .

Judged by the substance, not by form, the testator's conveyance is illusory, intended only as a mask for the effective retention by the settlor of the property which in form he had conveyed. We do not attempt now to formulate any general test of how far a settlor must divest himself of his interest in the trust property to render the conveyance more than illusory. Question of whether reservation of the income or of a power of revocation, or both, might even without reservation of the power of control be sufficient to show that the transfer was not intended in good faith to divest the settlor of his property must await decision until such question arises. In this case it is clear that the settlor never intended to divest himself of his property. He was unwilling to do so even when death was near.

The judgment should be affirmed, with costs.[11]

PROBLEMS.

1. T was on bad terms with his second wife. His daughter by a first marriage sided with her father in the family disputes.

    (a) T bought $5000 of Series " G " United States Savings Bonds and registered them in the name of himself, payable on death to the daughter. (Under Treasury Regulations he could surrender the bonds for redemption and receive cash; but he could not eliminate the name of the beneficiary during the latter's lifetime.)

    (b) T had two life insurance policies, one payable to his estate and one payable to his wife. He exercised his right to change beneficiaries, naming his daughter in each policy.

After T's death the widow waived the will under Decedent Estate Law § 18. Are the bonds and the insurance proceeds to be included in T's estate in determining the widow's rights? Matter of Kalina,

[10] See Scott on Trusts (1939 and Supp.) §§ 57.1, 57.2. Particularly note National Shawmut Bank *v.* Joy, 315 Mass. 457, 53 N. E. (2d) 113 (1944) overruling McEvoy *v.* Boston Five Cents Savings Bank, 201 Mass. 50, 87 N. E. 465 (1909).

[11] See Scott on Trusts (1939 and Supp.) §§ 57.5 and 58.5.

184 Misc. 367, 53 N. Y. S.(2d) 775 (1945); Ibey v. Ibey, 43 A.(2d) 157 (N. H. 1945). Mitchell v. Mitchell, 290 N. Y. 779, 50 N. E.(2d) 106 (1943), affirming 265 App. Div. 27, 37 N. Y. S.(2d) 612 (1942).

2. T died at the age of 58 during an operation for an abdominal cancer. The day before going to the hospital he drew out the entire balance of his bank account and handed the currency (some $4000) to his brother, saying that he was giving it to him because he thought there was precious little chance of pulling through the coming operation and he " wanted to keep the money in the family." T's widow waived the will under a usual type of statute. Can she obtain a statutory share of the $4000? Hatcher v. Buford, 60 Ark. 169, 29 S. W. 641 (1895).

MURRAY v. BROOKLYN SAVINGS BANK.

SUPREME COURT, APPELLATE DIVISION, FIRST DEPARTMENT, 1939.

9 N. Y. S.(2d) 227

SUPREME COURT, SPECIAL TERM, NEW YORK COUNTY, 1939.

258 App. Div. 132, 15 N.Y.S. (2d) 915.

ROSENMAN, J. [Supreme Court, Special Term] The deceased, Lawrence J. O'Neill, at the age of 55, married Mary Margaret O'Neill, 29, on November 11, 1934. Their marriage was not entirely a happy one, but they lived together until April 11, 1938. On that day the deceased died, intestate. The deceased had threatened to leave his wife on several occasions; and had also declared that he would leave her nothing when he died.

The decedent left him surviving no mother, father or children. His widow, two sisters and a number of nephews and nieces alone are entitled to share in his intestate estate of which the widow is the administratrix.

Upon his death it was discovered that the greater portion of his property consisted of various savings accounts in the defendant banks totaling $13,411.76.

The pass books to the accounts in the defendant banks were found in the decedent's trunk after his death. They were not in the individual name of the decedent, but in the name of " Lawrence J. O'Neill in trust for " the various persons who are now the plaintiffs in this action.

Each of the plaintiffs claims the moneys on deposit in the account standing in his or her name as beneficiary thereof, under the rule promulgated in Matter of Totten, 179 N. Y. 112, 71 N. E. 748, 70 L. R. A. 711, 1 Ann. Cas. 900. Since the decision in that case this form of deposit has become popularly known as a " Totten Trust." The administratrix, on the other hand, claims all the moneys in these accounts as part of the decedent's estate under the recent ruling in Newman *v.* Dore, 275 N. Y. 371, 9 N. E.(2d) 966, 112 A. L. R. 643. The defendant banks have no interest in this action, except that they seek to be protected by a decree of this court in paying the sums on deposit to the persons entitled thereto. . . .

All of the above beneficiaries were relatives either by blood or by the deceased's former marriage. Although they showed that they were legitimate objects of the deceased's bounty, they gave no consideration for the accounts; no delivery of the pass books was made to them during the deceased's lifetime; nor were they given any control of the accounts by the deceased at any time. The plaintiffs apparently did not even know of the existence of these accounts.

The deceased maintained absolute and complete control over all the accounts right up to his death. He withdrew whatever he wished to give to others or to use himself. He treated the money as his own, surrendering neither ownership nor indicia of ownership so long as he lived.

The court in Matter of Totten, 179 N. Y. 112, at pages 125 and 126, 71 N. E. 748, at page 752, laid down the rules applicable to this form of deposit: " A deposit by one person of his own money in his own name as trustee for another standing alone, does not establish an irrevocable trust during the lifetime of the depositor. It is a tentative trust merely, revocable at will, until the depositor dies or completes the gift in his lifetime by some unequivocal act or declaration, such as delivery of the pass book or notice to the beneficiary. *In case the depositor dies before the beneficiary without revocation, or some decisive act or declaration of disaffirmance, the presumption arises that an absolute trust was created as to the balance on hand at the death of the depositor.*"

It is undisputed that the deceased here died before the beneficiaries and that there was no decisive declaration or act of disaffirmance. Consequently, in the absence of anything further to give the widow additional rights, the plaintiffs would come within the rule enunciated, and would be entitled to the bank balances due.

Here, however, complications arise by virtue of § 18 of the Decedent Estate Law. By that section " a personal right of election is given to the surviving spouse to take his or her share of the estate as in intestacy, subject to the limitations, conditions and exceptions " contained in said section.

This section prohibits a testamentary disposition of property in excess of what the widow would have been entitled to in case of intestacy. It does not prohibit anyone from transferring in good faith any or all of his property during his lifetime. The question here presented is whether these Totten Trusts were transfers during the lifetime of the deceased which take precedence over § 18 of the Decedent Estate Law or whether they were, in legal contemplation, testamentary dispositions of property at the death of the decedent which must yield to the mandatory provisions of the section. . . .

In commenting on [Matter of Totten], Austin Wakeman Scott, in 43 Harvard Law Review, 521, at page 542, says: " The New York courts in dealing with savings bank trusts sometimes speak as though no trust arises until the death of the depositor. If this is so, the trust would seem clearly testamentary, since the depositor's death is a condition precedent to the creation of the trust. Apparently what is meant, however, is that a trust is created at the time of the deposit but that the trust is revocable, in whole or in part by the depositor; the trust is subject to a condition subsequent of revocation rather than a condition precedent of the death of the depositor. Even so, in view of the extent of the control of the depositor over the deposit, the trust in substance appears to be testamentary. It is clear that a similar trust of property other than savings bank deposits would be invalid. In view, however, of the convenience of this method of disposing of comparatively small sums of money without the necessity of resorting to probate proceedings, there seems to be no sufficiently strong policy to invalidate these trusts. Not only is the amount involved usually comparatively small, but it is easy to identify, and there is no great danger of fraudulent claims resulting from the absence of an attested instrument." . . .

A parallel to the provisions of the trust agreement in Newman v. Dore may be found in the usual Totten Trust, such as the one in the case at bar. The settlor, of course, is the depositor; the depositor is also the trustee; the beneficiary named in the bank account occupies the same position as the beneficiary of the express trust agreement. Under a Totten Trust, (1) the depositor retains the enjoyment of the entire income so long as he lives; (2) he may revoke the deposit either by notifying the depository or withdrawing all the funds; and (3) he can control his own actions as trustee in exercising his rights as depositor. . . .

All the elements rendering the conveyance illusory in Newman v. Dore, i.e. reservation of income, power of revocation and reservation of control, are present in a Totten Trust. . . .

Judgment must be directed for the defendant administratrix. . . .

UNTERMYER, J. [Supreme Court, Appellate Division, First Department] . . . We would agree with the conclusion of the Special Term that these " Totten trusts " which reserved to the deceased during his lifetime all the attributes of ownership, constituted transfers which would be " illusory " under the decision of Newman v. Dore, supra, and accordingly subordinate to the rights of the widow under Section 18 of the Decedent Estate Law if Lawrence J. O'Neill had left a last will and testament. . . . There, as here, the settlor had reserved all the benefits of ownership until his death and there, as here, the trust only became absolute and irrevocable upon his death. But in Newman *v.* Dore the decedent had left a last will and testament which gave to the widow a standing under Section 18 of the Decedent Estate Law. . . . In the present case the decedent left no will. The inquiry thus arises whether the widow of a decedent who has died intestate is in a position to complain of the creation of a " Totten trust " which has necessarily resulted in depleting the estate.

We fully appreciate the difficulties which surround the answer to that problem. If it be held that the widow is not in a position to assail such transfers as " illusory," then the husband may effectively disinherit her by creating " Totten trusts " and then failing to execute a will. However, it must be remembered that the same result might in any event be accomplished by an absolute transfer made during the husband's life. If, on the contrary, a transfer by means of the creation of a " Totten trust " may be assailed as " illusory " by the widow of a decedent who has died intestate, then it may be assailed by any other distributee, though not entitled to the protection of Section 18, since under the statute (Section 83) there is no distinction in the quality of their expectancies, if such they may be called. . . .

We think, under the statute (Decedent Estate Law, Section 18) that the widow has no standing to complain of a transfer by the creation of a " Totten trust " where the decedent has not left a will against which the widow can elect to take. . . . We do not believe it to have been the purpose of the statute in such cases to invalidate a form of trust which for generations has been recognized as a lawful and convenient method for the transmission of property. Yet, that is the effect of refusing to enforce these trusts at the instance of the classes of persons enumerated in Section 83. . . .

Since Lawrence J. O'Neill died without leaving any will, his widows' rights, like those of all other distributees enumerated in Section 83, are such, and only such, as existed before the enactment of Section 18. It follows that the general rule sustaining against distributees the validity of " Totten trusts " is applicable here. . . .

Judgment reversed.[12]

[12] In Schnakenberg *v.* Schnakenberg, 262 App. Div. 234, 28 N. Y. S.(2d) 841 (1941) decedent left a will executed before August 31, 1930. (Decedent Estate Law, § 18 applies " where a testator dies after August 31, 1930, and leaves a will thereafter executed.") In 1931 decedent had created a large inter vivos trust, reserving the right to revoke, to amend, and to withdraw capital. The Appellate Division, Second Department ruled that the widow could set aside this trust under Newman *v.* Dore. The Court felt " constrained to disagree with the holding in Murray *v.* Brooklyn Savings Bank " and went on to say, " A widow may have no right to elect pursuant to the Decedent Estate Law, § 18, and yet may rely upon it in support of her action to set aside a revocable trust as illusory where the very purpose of the decedent in so conveying was to avoid its application . . . The grievance of the widow in the Newman case, supra, as here, relates not to a direct violation of that law, but to evasion thereof in reducing the quantum of the estate."

In Inda *v.* Inda, 288 N. Y. 315, 43 N. E.(2d) 59 (1942), an intestate left two

BEIRNE v. CONTINENTAL-EQUITABLE TITLE & TRUST CO.

SUPREME COURT OF PENNSYLVANIA, 1932.

307 Pa. 570, 161 A. 721.

[In 1929 Thomas L. Beirne created a trust of the bulk of his property for the benefit of himself for life and, after his death, for the benefit of named individuals and charities. His wife was not beneficiary. He reserved the right to amend or revoke and exercised the former power.

The lawyer who drew the will testified that Beirne had asked him whether he could keep his wife from getting any of the trust property. The lawyer advised him that he could and recommended the trust instrument as above described. At the same time he prepared a will for Beirne in which Mrs. Beirne was given $40 per month, contingent upon her not contesting the will or electing to take against it.

At Beirne's death the widow elected to take against the will and brought a bill in equity to have the 1929 trust declared void as to her.

The trial court ruled that the trust was a dry trust, testamentary in character and vested no title in the trustee; also that the transaction was fraudulent and void as to the widow.]

SIMPSON, J. . . . It is clear beyond question that the deeds are not testamentary in character and that the trusts created are active, and not dry or passive . . . The trustee has active duties to perform . . . The trustee had a discretionary power to continue the assets in their then present form, if it saw fit to do so, or to sell them and reinvest the proceeds in other securities. . . .

The other point involved is far more interesting and important. There are many early decisions which hold that, so far as concerns his personal estate, a husband may do what he pleases with it, and the wife cannot be heard to complain. The reason for this conclusion is well stated in 6 S. & R. 535-6: " A man can never be said to commit a fraud on the contingent rights of others, where it depends on his

---

savings bank accounts in the names of himself (by a fictitious name) and another, " Joint accounts, either or the survivor may draw." Under Banking Law § 239 there is a conclusive presumption that such a form of deposit evidences an intention to vest the deposit in the survivor. The Court of Appeal ruled that the widow had no interest in these deposits, and said, " There being no will in the case at bar, section 18 of the Decedent Estate Law has no application, as that section only applies when there is a will in existence. . . . We need not decide the question whether section 83 of the Decedent Estate Law gives a spouse rights comparable to those conferred by Section 18 thereof. Even if we assume this to be so, the case is none the less governed by Section 239 of the Banking Law."

own act whether they shall ever exist. The rights of [the wife], other than to her common law dower, he could defeat in the same manner as he could the succession of his heirs." So, also, it was said in Lines *v.* Lines, 142 Pa. 149, 165: " It is the settled law of this State that a man may do what he pleases with his personal estate during his life. He may even beggar himself and his family, if he chooses to commit such an act of folly. When he dies, and then only, do the rights of his wife attach to his personal estate." Those decisions are all based on the general rule that if one has the legal right to do a particular thing, the law will not inquire into his motive for doing it. . . .

In the cases first above cited, and the others in their train, the question of the husband's or wife's intent to commit an actual fraud on the other spouse was not considered, perhaps was not attempted to be shown. In the later authorities, . . . however, it is treated as the vital factor, and if actual fraud upon the other spouse is shown to have been the real cause of the transfer of the assets, the general rule is applied, as in other cases of actual fraud, and the conveyance is held void. Thus in Hummel's Est., 161 Pa. 215, 217, it is said the husband " may give away or squander his property and thus reduce himself and wife to poverty, according to the authorities; but no case has gone so far as to sustain a voluntary obligation given and received with intent to defraud the wife's rights." . . . " But the fraudulent intent is the indispensable foundation for any such limitation of his control " (Young's Est., 202 Pa. 432, 441; Windolph *v.* Girard Trust Co., 245 Pa. 349, 363), and this is not shown merely by proving that " the husband's intent [was] to deprive the wife of her distributive share in his estate as widow " (Windolph *v.* Girard Trust Co., supra, page 364; Potter Title and Trust Co. *v.* Braum, 294 Pa. 482, 485); nor, as we have already shown, does the fact that he retained a life estate in the income of the assets conveyed, or that he reserved a right to revoke the trust whenever he chose to do so, in any way affect the matter. . . .

KEPHART, J., dissenting. I disagree with the decision of the majority by which it is held that by the simple expedient of a deed of trust a husband may accomplish that which he cannot do by his will, and may deprive his wife of any right or claim to his personal property after his death. During the early years of married life, she may have helped him to acquire this very property. Indeed, it is the joint efforts of husband and wife which are usually responsible for the prosperous condition of the husband. The ultimate goal of the two is to accumulate sufficient property, real and personal, not only that their children may, in a measure, be properly cared for; but, more especially, that in old age each may be provided for, notwithstanding the death of the other. The common practice has invariably been to place property thus acquired in the name of the husband. Indeed, placing it otherwise is looked upon, at times, with suspicion. . . .

While deeds and other instruments disposing of property in anticipation of marriage are declared void as against the other party to the marriage contract, it is now possible, under the decision in the instant case, to entirely set aside such rights without fear after the fact of marriage. . . .

I cannot go along with the court to this extent. I believe that to permit such an invasion of the wife's marital rights by making it possible for her husband to deprive her of them at his pleasure is against the best interests of society, and that such decision may be fruitful of consequences that will become exceedingly harmful. . . . I frankly concede that there must be a certain liberality with respect to the alienation of personal property; it cannot be burdened with postmortem or contingent claims that would cause titles to be in turmoil whenever property is thus transferred. In transferring such interests they should be freed from such claims. But that is far different from upholding the deliberate attempt that is here made by the husband to deprive his wife of her postmortem rights and still retain for himself all the benefits of the property until his death.

What the husband did in this case was to transfer to a third party, as trustee, personal property. He was to receive the entire income and all the benefits from this trust for his life. He had the right to control and manage it in the hands of the trustee. He could change the beneficiaries even to the day of his death. He had the right to revoke the trust and retake physical possession of the property at any time. In other words, his hand never left the property nor its benefits until his death severed the connection. He placed the property in the name of this third party as trustee solely to prevent his wife from having any share whatever in it after his death. It would seem to me that the mere statement of such facts ought to be sufficient in themselves to require a court of law to defeat the husband's purpose. . . . [Here follows a lengthy analysis of the earlier Pennsylvania cases.]

BOLLES v. TOLEDO TRUST CO.

SUPREME COURT OF OHIO, 1944.

144 Ohio State 195, 58 N. E.(2d) 381

[George A. Bolles executed a series of inter vivos trusts, reserving the right to amend and revoke. Upon his death his widow obtained an extension of her right to elect whether to take under or against his will and brought this proceeding for a determination by the court whether the assets subject to the inter vivos trusts would be included in his estate if she should elect to take against the will.]

TURNER, J. Our question: Whether, by the device of a revocable living trust, a husband relinquishes such dominion over the personal property in such trust as will bar his widow's right to a distributive share of such personal property upon her election to take under the statute of descent and distribution. . . .

Section 8617, General Code, provides: " All deeds of gifts and conveyance of real or personal property made in trust for the exclusive use of the person or persons making the same shall be void and of no effect, but the creator of a trust may reserve himself any use or power, beneficial or in trust, which he might lawfully grant to another, including the power to alter, amend or revoke such trust, and such trust shall be valid as to all persons," [except that creditors can reach any beneficial interest or any such power].

There is, therefore, in this state authority for amendable and revocable living trusts, valid as to all persons except creditors. But the question remains as to what interest or dominion, if any, the husband held at the time of his death. . . .

We recognize the right of the husband to dispose of his personal property during his lifetime without the consent of his wife (Section 7998, General Code), but we do not recognize the right of the husband to bar his wife of her right to a distributive share in the property which the husband possessed at the time of his death (Section 10504-55, General Code, 114 Ohio Laws, 356). It is not necessary to hold that the terms and administration of either trust No. 331 or trust No. 520 created a mere agency to come to the conclusion that Mr. Bolles during his lifetime had substantial enjoyment and dominion over the small amount of property in trust No. 331 and of the substantial amount of property in trust No. 520. . . .

To the extent that such an arrangement, if allowed to stand, would deprive the widow of her distributive share of property, it is voidable at the instance of the widow. . . .

We reiterate that where there is an absolute, *bona fide* transfer by a husband of his personal property during lifetime the wife at his death may not assert her right to a distributive share of such personal property. However, where there is not an absolute transfer of his property during the husband's lifetime, the widow may assert her right to a distributive share. . . . [Here the Court comments upon Newman *v.* Dore, p. 23 ante.]

We may go a step further and say that irrespective of the husband's intention, if the effect of the device resorted to is such as to cut down or deprive the widow of the right given her under Section 10504-55, General Code, such device is voidable when challenged by the widow. . . .

As Mr. Bolles did not in his lifetime relinquish absolute dominion over the personal property remaining in this trust at the time of his death, we hold that in the event the widow elects to take under the statute of descent and distribution, she will be entitled to her distributive share of the property in those trusts at the time of her husband's death, otherwise trusts Nos. 331 and 520 are valid trusts.[13]

NOTE: ENGLISH AND EMPIRE LEGISLATION

The Inheritance (Family Provision) Act, 1938, 1 & 2 Geo. VI Ch. 45, provides in part as follows (some words omitted):
" Where a person dies domiciled in England leaving
   (a) a wife or husband;
   (b) a daughter who has not been married, or who is, by reason of some mental or physical disability, incapable of maintaining herself;
   (c) an infant son; or
   (d) a son who is, by reason of some mental or physical disability, incapable of maintaining himself;
and leaving a will, then, if the court on application by or on behalf of any such wife, husband, daughter or son is of opinion that the will does not make reasonable provision for the maintenance of that dependant, the court may order that such reasonable provision as the court thinks fit shall be made out of the testator's net estate for the maintenance of that dependant:

" Provided that no application shall be made to the court by or on behalf of any person in any case where the testator has bequeathed not less than two-thirds of the income of the net estate to a surviving spouse and the only other dependant or dependants, if any, is or are a child or children of the surviving spouse.

"'Net estate' means all the property of which a testator had power to dispose by his will (otherwise than by virtue of a special power of appointment),"

[13] In a subsequent case (Harris v. Harris, 147 Ohio St. 437, 72 N. E. 2d 378, 1947) the Ohio Fiduciaries Research Association filed a brief as amicus curiae urging that the Bolles Case be overruled or limited to its facts. The brief pointed out among other things that
(a) Since the Michigan courts did not allow the widow to reach property placed in a revocable and amendable trust an Ohio settlor need only go to Detroit to do what he wished, and this would produce a flight of revocable trust capital from Ohio;
(b) If it is the policy of Ohio to subject revocable trusts to the claims of the widow this should be done by legislation which can operate prospectively only and which can simultaneously create a comprehensive and workable body of law with adequate safeguards;
(c) The Bolles Case raises many incidental practical questions of difficulty. Suppose, for example, that, after creating a revocable trust, the settlor incurs large debts and dies insolvent. The widow waives the will and claims a share in the revocable trust. Is this share now subject to the claims of the creditors? If it is, the widow will get practically nothing and the creditors will get a windfall. If it is not, the widow will be preferred to the creditors, whereas Section 10504-55 of the Code prescribes that she shall take her share subject to the claims of creditors.

less debts, taxes and administration expense.[14] As in the case of much other legislation, this statute is derived from a New Zealand prototype: Testator's Family Maintenance Act of 1900, N.Z. Stat. (1900), No. 20. (If it be thought that the British were glad to see such an experiment tried out on the colonials before it was installed among people who really counted, it might also be mentioned that the New Zealanders tried it out on the natives for six years before they adopted it for themselves. Native Land Court Act, § 46, N.Z. Stat. (1894), No. 43.) All six states of Australia and two Canadian provinces have enacted similar legislation.[15]

Two articles from English legal periodicals [16] yield the following quotations: " In New Zealand, actions under the Act have not resulted in any large increase of litigation, nor do they represent an undue proportion of the cases that come before the Courts for decision. Taken over a period of 5 years —

    Average number of wills proved annually 4396
    Average wills contested under the Act   77

In the absence of the Act it may be assumed that some at least of the applicants in the 77 cases would have contested the wills on the ground of undue influence, lack of testamentary capacity, etc. . . . The courts [in Australia and New Zealand] have taken a very generous view of the extent of their powers under these Acts . . . The language of these Acts is somewhat different to the English Act . . . So far [1941], the authorities on the [English] Act show that the judges tend to lean against interfering with testamentary dispositions, except where a strong case is made out."

In the English cases the courts have been severe in awarding costs against unsuccessful petitioners where the court feels that the application should not have been made. This is an obvious deterrent to applications based on spite or the what-can-we-lose theory.

Observe that the Act defines " net estate " in such a way as to exclude inter vivos transfers by the testator — provided he does not reserve to himself a general power of appointment. The widow and children are still at the mercy of living trusts designed to exclude them, even where the settlor reserves the usual power to revoke and amend.

[14] For the legislative history of the English act, see Dainow, " Limitations on Testamentary Freedom in England," 25 Cornell L. Q. 337 (1940).

[15] Dainow, " Restricted Testation in New Zealand, Australia and Canada," 36 Mich. L. Rev. 1107 (1938). This article deals at length with judicial interpretations and applications of the statutes.

[16] Gold et al., " Freedom of Testation: The Inheritance (Family Provision) Act," 1 Modern L. Rev. 296 (1938); " Applications under the Inheritance (Family Provision) Act, 1938," 191 Law Times 168 (1941).

SIMES & BASYE, MODEL PROBATE CODE (1946)
(Michigan Legal Studies)

§ 33. *Gifts in fraud of marital rights.*

(a) *Election to treat as devise.* Any gift made by a person, whether dying testate or intestate, in fraud of the marital rights of his surviving spouse to share in his estate, shall, at the election of the surviving spouse, be treated as a testamentary disposition and may be recovered from the donee and persons taking from him without adequate consideration and applied to the payment of the spouse's share, as in case of his election to take against the will.

(b) *When gift deemed fraudulent.* Any gift made by a married person within two years of the time of his death is deemed to be in fraud of the marital rights of his surviving spouse, unless shown to the contrary.

Comment. This section makes no attempt to define the expression " in fraud of marital rights." It is believed that only by judicial decision can that be done. Among the situations which courts would have to classify in this connection is that where a married person sets up an inter vivos trust reserving to himself a life estate and a power to revoke the trust. . . .

Subsection (b) lays down an aid in determining whether a gift is fraudulent where the proof is slight. Under this section it is possible to show that a gift made within two years of the death of a married person is not fraudulent, but the burden of proof is upon the person asserting the absence of fraud.

Problem.

1. Charles S. Eaton was the proprietor of " Thompson's Spa," a Boston restaurant netting a profit of about $100,000 annually. In 1909, at the age of 53 he married one Ella F. Bartlett, aged 38, of Pasadena. By an antenuptial contract it was provided that Charles should in his will (1) bequeath not more than 10 per cent of his estate to persons other than his wife and issue, (2) devise and bequeath the residue of his estate in equal shares, one share to Ella and one share to each son; Ella agreed to accept this provision in lieu of all her rights in Charles's property.[17] In 1914 Charles and Ella be-

---

[17] Although the Reporter and the Court in Eaton *v.* Eaton occupy seventeen pages of the report with statements of fact, the exact terms of the contract do not anywhere appear. Examination of the original record reveals that the agreement was as follows so far as here material (many words omitted):

" Charles does hereby covenant that he will by a will duly executed provide that, after making legacies not exceeding in value one-tenth part of the estate, both real and personal, of which Charles shall die seized or possessed according to the value thereof as the same shall be stated in the inventory of his estate filed in the probate court, of the residue of his estate a share shall

came estranged. For the purpose of increasing the property which his sons would take and reducing the property Ella would take, Charles formed a partnership with two of his sons and admitted them as equal owners with him of Thompson's Spa, valued at $800,000. He also gave to his sons property worth $320,000. At his death the terms of his will complied with the terms of the antenuptial agreement. What are Ella's rights? Eaton v. Eaton, 233 Mass. 351, 124 N. E. 37 (1919).[18]

D. Who bears the loss when the widow elects against the will?

When the widow exercises her statutory right to waive the will she does so for the purpose of getting more money. This means that someone else will get less money. But who? A usual rule and a recognized fact bear on this problem. The rule is: Normally the residue bears administration expense, debts, taxes, and any other charges or losses. The fact is: Normally the residuary legatees are the persons closest to the testator and the primary objects of his bounty. Where the testator has made large pecuniary legacies the widow's renunciation may seriously distort the scheme of distribution unless the rule is modified to fit the fact. This is the problem with which the two following cases deal.

A related question is whether the interest renounced by the widow will be devoted to reducing the loss of legatees whose shares are reduced to provide the interest claimed by the widow. This is considered in Chapter X of Leach, Cases on Future Interests.

GALLAGHER'S APPEAL.

Supreme Court of Pennsylvania, 1878.

87 Pa. St. 200.

Robert C. Gallagher died in 1872, leaving a will, wherein he made certain provisions for his widow, Jane Gallagher, devised certain real estate to his sister, Sophia Oswald, and bequeathed all the residue of his estate, excepting certain specific legacies, to his nephews and nieces, in proportions named therein. There was no

---

be set aside equal in value to the amount that would go to his wife if she survived him if said residue were divided in equal parts among his wife and his surviving children, that is to say, one part to his wife and one part each to each surviving child. And Ella covenants that in case Charles shall provide for her by will as hereinbefore set forth and said will shall be duly admitted to probate, she will accept the provisions thereof in full satisfaction of all her rights in the property of said Charles, statutory or otherwise, and all claims which she might have against the estate of said Charles if she should survive him."

[18] In this case Sherman L. Whipple represented the Eaton estate; Charles F. Choate, Jr., Mrs. Eaton.

issue of Robert C. and Jane Gallagher, and the widow refused to accept the provisions of the will and claimed the one-half of the real estate for life, under the intestate law. The value of the widow's interest in the land devised to Sophia Oswald was $1000, or $60 per annum, and in the distribution of the estate she [Sophia] claimed that a fund sufficient to raise $60 should be set apart and retained, so that she might enjoy the property devised to her free from any encumbrance, as she contended the testator intended she should.

The court, Junkin, P. J., made a decree that the assets should be marshalled, and that an amount sufficient to make her whole should be taken from the residuary legatees and devisees, and in an opinion said:

"It is certain that testator intended that his sister should enjoy in fee the real estate devised to her, and it is equally certain that she was among the first objects of the testator's bounty; and that she is restricted in the enjoyment of her devise is apparent.

"The case is novel, in this, that the encumbrance did not exist in the testator's lifetime, nor was it created by him. It springs out of a right which he could not control, is a mere encumbrance, leaving the fee simple in the devisee. It is not a debt created by the testator, nor a lien which his personal estate is bound to discharge. It is an estate in the land itself, and can such a charge be removed? In principle, how does a dower charge differ from a mortgage, or any other charge which defeats the enjoyment of the lands devised, or subjects the devisee to the expense of removing it? Such a charge (mortgage or judgment), where it is the debt of the testator, would be paid out of the residuary estate at the expense of the residuary legatees, unless the testator has directed otherwise. . . . But should this principle fail in its application to this estate, there remains the general rule, as laid down in Sandoe's Appeal, 15 P. F. Smith 314, to wit: 1. Where a widow elects not to take under a will, her substituted devises and bequests are a trust in her, for the benefit of the disappointed claimants, to the amount of their interest therein; 2. A court of equity will sequester the benefit intended for the wife to secure compensation to those whom her election disappoints. Then add the general rule, that specific legatees and devisees shall be first satisfied, and any deficiency or loss must fall upon the residuary legatees, and we think this question is decided. Sophia Oswald, as a devisee of the half lot and house, is deprived of one-half the benefits of the devise while the widow lives, and the rule requires that she be made whole, at the expense of the residuary legatees, and we must marshal the assets to effect that result."

From the foregoing decree this appeal was taken. . . .

PER CURIAM. We discover no substantial error in this case. The decree is, therefore, affirmed and appeal dismissed, and the costs ordered to be paid by the appellants.

IN RE BYRNES' ESTATE.

Surrogate's Court, New York County, New York, 1933.

149 Misc. 449, 267 N. Y. Supp. 627.

Foley, Surrogate.

In this accounting proceeding, questions have arisen as to the effect upon the terms of the will, of the withdrawal by the widow of the testator of her elective share, under section 18 of the Decedent Estate Law. In a previous special proceeding, I held that the terms of the will did not sufficiently comply with the statute so as to prevent the election by the widow. It was decided that she was entitled to take her statutory share.[19] That determination was affirmed by the Appellate Division and by the Court of Appeals (141 Misc. 346, 252 N. Y. S. 587, affirmed 235 App. Div. 782, 257 N. Y. S. 884, affirmed 260 N. Y. 465, 184 N. E. 56).

The net estate remaining after the payment of administration expenses and debts is approximately $180,000. The widow is entitled, as her statutory elective share, to one-half of the net estate, approximately $90,000. The will provided for preliminary legacies or trusts aggregating $40,000 to three educational, religious, and charitable corporations. The residue was bequeathed in trust to the widow for her life or until her remarriage. . . . Upon the death or remarriage of the widow, the remainder was bequeathed to such of the children of the testator's brother, Ronald M. Byrnes, who were living at the time of the death or remarriage of the widow and to the issue of a deceased child of said brother living at either of those events. Secondary trusts were created for the life of each child of the brother, living at the death of the testator. There are certain contingent gifts over in the event of the absence of issue which are not material here.

The first question for determination is, Shall the amount withdrawn, by reason of the election of the widow, be charged wholly out of the residuary trust fund? Or, shall the amount withdrawn by the widow be equitably apportioned out of the pecuniary legacies, the charitable trust funds and the residuary fund?

I hold that the latter method should be adopted and that each of the pecuniary legatees, the charitable trusts, and the remaindermen must ratably contribute to the withdrawn share of the widow.

---

[19] The statute (as amended in 1930) provides that the widow may elect to take her intestate share unless the testator has devised or bequeathed in trust an amount equal to or greater than the intestate share, with income thereof payable to the surviving spouse for life. The will of Byrnes bequeathed the residue of his estate in trust to pay the income to his wife for life *or until remarriage*. This was held not to bring the will within the exception to the statute and thus was held to allow the wife to elect her intestate share.

Since one-half of the net estate has been withdrawn by the widow, each legacy, whether outright or in trust, and the residuary trust fund, as it would have been originally constituted, must be reduced by one-half. The charitable gifts amounting to $40,000 will thereby be reduced to the sum of $20,000. The residuary trust fund, which would have amounted to the sum of $140,000, if the widow had not elected, will be reduced to approximately $70,000.

In the drafting of section 18 of the Decedent Estate Law, which conferred this new right of election upon a surviving spouse, the decedent estate commission gave serious consideration to the effect of the withdrawal of the intestate share upon the terms of the will.

We are dealing here with a right of election which is absolute. No question is involved, therefore, as to the source of payment of the limited benefits given by paragraphs (b) and (e) of subdivision 1 of the section. The situation here is covered by subdivision 2, which reads as follows: "Where any such election shall have been made, the will shall be valid as to the residue remaining after the elective share provided in this section has been deducted and the terms of the will shall as far as possible remain effective."

This subdivision was purposely drawn in general terms with a deliberate design to vest in the courts an equitable authority over the apportionment of the charge, caused by the withdrawal by the surviving spouse. The alternative of attempting to draft and impose meticulous rules applicable to every estate was rejected by the commission.

CHAPTER III.

THE EXECUTION OF WILLS.

Wills of real property through the Statute of Frauds. Under the feudal law land was not devisable except by local custom, e.g. the Custom of Kent. But as early as the fourteenth century a feoffment to uses, with what we should now call a power of appointment reserved in the feoffor, in substance gave the ability to devise to any landowner who wished to acquire it. It worked this way: A, owning Blackacre, would enfeoff B and his heirs to the use of A for life and then to the uses of A's will; A by will would declare a use in favor of C and his heirs; and, upon A's death, C would acquire an equitable title to Blackacre which a court of equity would enforce by directing B to convey the legal title to C.[1] The passage of the Statute of Uses in 1536 cast doubts, at least, upon the continued effectiveness of this familiar method of evading the feudal prohibition of devises.[2] Consequently, in 1540 the Statute of Wills (32 Hen. VIII, c. 1) was passed making lands devisable at law with certain exceptions which have long since been removed. The Statute of Wills gave to a landowner the power to devise " by his last will and testament in writing " — a modest enough formal requirement. A century and a quarter later the Statute of Frauds (1677) required that a devise or bequest of any land or tenement.

> " shall be in writing, and signed by the party so devising the same, or by some other person in his presence and by his express direction, and shall be attested and subscribed in the presence of the said devisor by three or four credible witnesses."

Wills of personal property through the Statute of Frauds. There was never any legal objection to wills of personal property. Indeed, among the righteous, unless death was sudden, intestacy was considered a disgrace. At an early period it seems to have been customary for the priest to receive the will orally as part of the last confession; but as time went on written wills of personalty became more usual. Not, however, until the Statute of Frauds (1677) were formal requirements imposed as to such wills. It was there provided that no nuncupative (i.e. oral) will of property in excess of £30 should be valid unless (a) it was proved by the oath of three witnesses present

---

[1] For an example see Sir Edward Clere's Case, 6 Co. Rep. 17b (1599).
[2] See Bacon, Reading upon the Statute of Uses (Rowe's Ed., 1804) p. 140, note 80.

when it was made, and (b) the testator bade the persons present to bear witness to his will, and (c) the will was made in the last sickness of the testator, and (d) the testimony was given within six months or committed to writing within six days after the will was made. But there was still no requirement that a written will of personalty be attested. So the law remained in England until 1837.

The Wills Act (1837), 7 W. IV. & 1 Vic. c. 26. This statute imposed identical formal requirements upon wills of realty and wills of personalty. It required that a will

> "shall be in writing, shall be signed at the foot or end thereof by the testator, or by some other person in his presence and by his direction; and such signature shall be made or acknowledged by the testator in the presence of two or more witnesses present at the same time, and such witnesses shall attest and shall subscribe the will in the presence of the testator."

In view of the fact that some American states have statutes modelled upon the requirements of the Statute of Frauds concerning land while others have statutes modelled upon the Wills Act, a comparison of the principal formalities prescribed by these two English statutes has more than academic interest:

(1) As to signature. The Wills Act requires signature "at the foot or end thereof," a requirement not in the Statute of Frauds.

(2) As to number of witnesses. The Wills Act requires two; the Statute of Frauds, three.

(3) As to attestation. The Wills Act requires that the witnesses be present at the same time, whereas the Statute of Frauds could be satisfied by several witnesses attesting separately. Both statutes require that the witnesses attest in the presence of the testator.

American Statutes.[3] In the main American statutes tend to follow the Wills Act, but the variations are often considerable. For example, the New York Statute (Decedent Estate Law, § 21) reads as follows:

> "Every last will and testament of real or personal property, or both, shall be executed and attested in the following manner:
>
> 1. It shall be subscribed by the testator at the end of the will.
>
> 2. Such subscription shall be made by the testator in the presence of each of the attesting witnesses, or shall be acknowledged by him, to have been so made, to each of the attesting witnesses.
>
> 3. The testator, at the time of making such subscription, or at the time of acknowledging the same, shall declare the instrument so subscribed, to be his last will and testament.
>
> 4. There shall be at least two attesting witnesses, each of whom

---

[3] See generally, Bordwell, "The Statute Law of Wills," 14 Ia. L. Rev. 1, 172, 283, 428 (1928–29).

shall sign his name as a witness, at the end of the will, at the request of the testator.[4]"

Observe that the requirement that the testator declare the instrument to be his will is a new one, but that the requirements of the Wills Act that the witnesses be present at the same time and subscribe in the presence of the testator are not imposed. Most states require only two witnesses; but the New England states (except Rhode Island) and Georgia and South Carolina still insist upon the three witnesses originally prescribed in the Statute of Frauds.

But it is not useful to examine the requirements of the individual states as to formalities; for no lawyer does a competent job unless he has a will executed in such manner that it will be valid according to the law of any state in which it may be offered for probate. The maximum formalities should *always* be observed. Why is this so? For the reason that the law of the place in which the will is executed may govern the validity of the will at the testator's death with reference to little or none of his property. By the rules of Conflict of Laws the validity of a will as a disposition of personalty is determined by the law of the domicil of the testator *at the time of his death;* the validity of a will as a disposition of real estate is determined by the law of the state in which the realty is located. Restatement of Conflict of Laws, §§ 249, 306. Thus if A, while domiciled in Massachusetts, makes his will, then moves to New Jersey and dies owning Pennsylvania real estate and a fund of stocks, bonds and cash, the validity of his will is determined by the law of New Jersey as to the personalty and by the law of Pennsylvania as to the realty. The law of Massachusetts is not determinative as to any property.[5]

Suggested method of execution of a will. A will meets all existing American formal requirements if it is executed as follows:

1. The testator, not less than three witnesses and the attorney supervising the execution of the will are brought into a room. The door is closed, not to be again opened until the ceremony is finished.

2. The testator examines the will, states to the witnesses that it is his will and that he wishes them to act as witnesses to the will and to his signature thereon. It is, of course, not necessary

---

[4] Decedent Estate Law § 22 also requires that witnesses to wills write their places of residence opposite their names. However, the penalty for violation of this provision is a fine of $50 upon the witness; the omission of the address does not invalidate the will or prevent the witness from being a competent witness.

[5] The Uniform Wills Act, Foreign Executed, provides that a will is valid if executed according to the law either of the testator's domicil or of the place where the will was executed. This statute or an equivalent has been adopted in a considerable number of states. See Bordwell, "Statute Law of Wills," 14 Ia. L. Rev. at 443–444 (1929).

or customary for the witnesses to read the will or otherwise to be familiar with its contents.

3. The testator puts his signature on the margin of each page of the will for purposes of identification.

4. The testator signs the will at the end thereof, all witnesses looking at the signature as it is written.[6]

5. One witness reads the attestation clause aloud. The witnesses then sign their names and write their addresses. As each witness signs the testator and all other witnesses observe the signature being made.

The testimonium and attestation clauses of a will are sufficient if they read as follows:

"IN WITNESS WHEREOF, I, the said John Doe, herewith set my hand to this my last will, typewritten on nine sheets of paper (including the attestation clause and signatures of witnesses) upon the margin of each one of which I have also written my name, this first day of September, nineteen hundred and forty-seven.

(Signature)   John Doe

"On the first day of September, nineteen hundred and forty-seven, John Doe declared to us, the undersigned, that the foregoing instrument was his last will, and he requested us to act as witnesses to the same and to his signature thereon. He thereupon signed said will in our presence, we being present at the same time. And we now, at his request, in his presence, and in the presence of each other do hereunto subscribe our names as witnesses. And we and each of us declare that we believe this testator to be of sound mind and memory.

(Signature)   Henry Jones
12 Elm St., Cambridge, Mass.
(Signature)   John Smith
25 Oak St., Arlington, Mass.
(Signature)   Arthur Brown
35 Ash St., Cambridge, Mass."

Whether it is advisable to insert an attestation clause in a will may be judged with reference to the following cases which are assumed to arise in a jurisdiction which requires the maximum formalities:

PROBLEMS.

1. (*The witness who forgets.*) W is the only witness surviving T, the testator. He identifies his signature but testifies that he has absolutely no memory of the transaction. Is the will entitled to probate,

    a. if it contains a full attestation clause of the type appearing above? Flynn v. Flynn, 283 Ill. 206, 213, 119 N. E. 304 (1918); Will of O'Hagan, 73 Wis. 78, 40 N. W. 649 (1888).

    [6] A seal is not required in any American state.

b. if it contains only the word " Witnesses " ahead of the signatures of the witnesses? Estate of Tyler, 121 Cal. 405, 53 P. 928 (1898).

2. (*The witness who dies.*) No witness survives T. Various persons take the stand and identify the signatures of the testator and of the witnesses. Is the will entitled to probate,
    a. if it contains a full attestation clause of the type appearing above? Darnell *v.* Buzby, 50 N. J. Eq. 725, 727 (1893); 5 Wigmore, Evidence §§ 1505, 1511 (3d ed. 1940).
    b. if it contains only the word " Witnesses " ahead of the signatures of the witnesses? Leatherbee *v.* Leatherbee, 247 Mass. 138, 141 N. E. 669 (1923); Swain *v.* Edmunds, 53 N. J. Eq. 142, 143 (1894); 22 Mich. L. Rev. 623 (1924).
    c. if it contains an attestation clause which states that the witnesses signed in the presence of the testator but does not state that they signed in the presence of each other? Norton *v.* Goodwine, 310 Ill. 490, 142 N. E. 171 (1924); In re Johnson, 115 N. J. Eq. 249, 171 A. 307 (1934).

3. (*The witness who attacks the will.*) W is the only witness surviving T. He identifies his signature but testifies that T did not declare the instrument to be his will and that the other witnesses were out of the room when W signed. Is the will entitled to probate,
    a. if it contains a full attestation clause of the type appearing above? In re Solomon's Estate, 145 N. Y. Supp. 528 (Surrogate's Court, 1914); Matter of Cottrell, 95 N. Y. 329 (1884).
    b. if it contains only the word " Witnesses " ahead of the signatures of the witnesses? German Evangelical Church *v* Reith, 327 Mo. 1098, 1109–10, 39 S. W. (2d) 1057 (1931).

Extraordinary precautions in contemplation of will contest. Any will can lead to a contest, but some positively ask for it. This is so where the next-of-kin are ignored in favor of a charity or an unpopular spouse or where one relative is preferred over another. To take a couple of examples out of the writer's experience:
    (a) An elderly recluse has a record of keeping eighteen or twenty cats in her house, biting the postman when he tries to deliver registered mail, and living in unsanitary conditions in an ancient house despite having means adequate to provide a much better standard of living. Her next-of-kin are cousins. Her will leaves her entire estate to a university to establish a scholarship fund in memory of her father.
    (b) A widow in her seventies has two sons. One lives near her and sees her frequently; she approves of his habits of life. The other lives in another state and sees her infrequently; she disapproves of his habits of life and dislikes his wife. Her will leaves the whole estate to the first son and his family.

Something more than routine execution is appropriate for this type of will.

It should be pointed out to the testator that his natural desire to keep his will confidential must yield to the necessity of protecting it from contest. The testator should state to the witnesses who his relatives are, what his will provides, and why he is making these dispositions. In the case of relatives whom he is not benefiting he should give his reasons for neglecting them. It is also frequently desirable for the testator to state the nature and extent of his property. Within a day or two a detailed memorandum as to what the testator said should be written up, read over carefully by each witness and signed. The memorandum should be kept with the will.

This process performs several useful functions with a view to assuring ultimate probate. It enables the probate court, and jury if any, to be informed by the most direct possible evidence as to what the testator did and said at the instant of execution of the will. It gives to the witnesses an opportunity of observing the speech, action and thought of the testator as a basis for their testimony as to his mental capacity. It records the evidence in such form that it can be made available with accuracy at any time in the future.

The choice of witnesses is important. Included among them should be some who are mature, experienced persons having no prior knowledge of the testator, his family or the beneficiaries of the will. Such persons will be in the same neutral position that a judge or jury will later assume; and their testimony will properly be given great weight. It may also be desirable to include among the witnesses persons who have known the testator for a considerable period and who, therefore, can place the conversation of the testator against a general background; but such persons are rarely in a position of complete neutrality as to the result of the will contest and should not alone be relied upon. There is, of course, no reason to restrict the witnesses to the minimum required by the statute.

Examples of defectively executed wills. A habit of meticulous compliance with formal requisites is an extremely important part of a lawyer's equipment, for courts consistently require strict adherence to the statutes. Nunn *v.* Ehlert, infra, is fairly representative of the microscopic treatment which courts habitiually give to the statutes of wills; and the Problems which follow this case indicate some of the mistakes that can be made.

NUNN *v.* EHLERT.

SUPREME JUDICIAL COURT OF MASSACHUSETTS, 1914.

218 Mass. 471, 106 N. E. 163.

LORING, J. This appeal from a decree of the Probate Court comes before us upon a report by a single justice of this court which sets forth all the evidence introduced before him. The single justice found that the testimony of each subscribing witness was " entirely credible and not open to doubt," and made a finding that the instrument was properly executed and that it ought to be admitted to probate as the will of Thomas Nunn. By the terms of the report, if the finding was wrong the decree of the Probate Court (disallowing the will) is to be affirmed. But, if the finding is sustained, that decree is to be reversed and a decree entered admitting the instrument to probate.

A facsimile of the will is made part of the report. The will was written on ordinary foolscap paper, that is to say, on paper folded at the top and with lines ruled upon it. The whole paper is in the handwriting of the deceased. A copy of the ending of it is set forth in the footnote.[7] . . .

According to Mrs. Marshall's testimony it appeared that a few days before she and her husband signed the instrument here in question the deceased had asked her if she and her husband would sign his will; that later on, he came into their kitchen and took the will out of his pocket; that " it was folded up "; that as he turned it over she saw handwriting on it and recognized the writing as the writing of the deceased, but could not " recognize any word "; that they were sitting on opposite sides of a table, and the deceased " reached " the folded paper across to her and she signed; that he held on to the paper while she signed; that it was folded " just so I could sign comfortably," and so that she saw nothing above where she put her name. She saw no signature below the edge made by the folding of the paper. She further testified that she then got up out of the chair in which she sat while signing her name; that her husband sat down and signed his name, and that the deceased held on to the paper folded as above described until both had signed. He then blotted the signatures, put the paper in his pocket and went away. She further testified that when she caught sight of the writing while the paper was being turned over she did not distinguish any words or see any signature. This testimony was corroborated by that of her husband. He was explicit in his testimony that no change was made in the arrangement of the paper while his wife and he signed, and that the deceased did not point to any signature in the will. In his

---

[7] " In testimony whereof I hereunto set my hand and in the presence of three witnesses declare this to be my last will and testament, this first day of March A. D. 1908 Thomas Nunn of Malden in the said Commonwealth.

" On this first day of March 1908. Thomas Nunn of Malden in said Commonwealth, signed the foregoing instrument in our presence, declaring it to be his last will, and as witnesses thereof we three at his request and in his presence hereto subscribe our names:

Signed. Thomas Nunn

Mrs. Mary E. Marshall.
John Marshall.
Thomas G. Andrews.

Thomas Nunn."

testimony he said, " I don't remember of seeing any signature." It should be added that after his death the instrument now presented as the will of the deceased was found in his box in a safety deposit vault.

This case, therefore, presents the question whether a will is duly attested when the signature of the deceased is hidden from the witnesses when they attest and subscribe the will.

Our statute of wills (in substance a re-enactment of the statute of frauds, St. 29 Car. II, c. 3, § 5) is in these words: " Every person of full age and sound mind may by his last will in writing, signed by him or by a person in his presence and by his express direction, and attested and subscribed in his presence by three or more competent witnesses, dispose of his property, real and personal," with some additions not necessary to be stated. R. L. c. 135, § 1.

In Chase v. Kittredge, 11 Allen, 49, 63, a statement was made of the meaning of the word " attested " in what is now R. L. c. 135, § 1. The decision in Chase v. Kittredge was that a subscribing witness cannot sign before the testator has signed. In making that decision Mr. Justice Gray delivered an exhaustive opinion upon the acts required by statute to make a valid will. In the course of that opinion he said: " The statute not only requires them (the witnesses) to attest, but to subscribe. It is not sufficient for the witnesses to be called upon to witness the testator's signature, or to stand by while he makes or acknowledges it, and be prepared to testify afterwards to his sanity and due execution of the instrument, but they must subscribe. This subscription is the evidence of their previous attestation, and to preserve the proof of that attestation in case of their death or absence when after the testator's death the will shall be presented for probate. It is as difficult to see how they can subscribe in proof of their attestation before they have attested, as it is to see how they can attest before the signature of the testator has made it his written will." Chief Justice Robertson gave a similar definition of the word " attest " in Swift v. Wiley, 1 B. Mon. 114, 117. He said: " To attest the publication of a paper as a last will, and to subscribe to that paper the names of the witnesses, are very different things, and are required for obviously distinct and different ends. Attestation is the act of the senses, subscription is the act of the hand; the one is mental, the other mechanical, and to attest a will is to know that it was published as such, and to certify the facts required to constitute an actual and legal publication: but to subscribe a paper published as a will, is only to write on the same paper the names of the witnesses, for the sole purpose of identification." . . .

Taken literally, R. L. c. 135, § 1, requires that the instrument in writing shall be " signed " by the deceased (or by a person in his presence and by his express direction), in the presence of the witnesses. But as matter of construction it was early established that an acknowledgment by the deceased in the presence of the witnesses of a previous signature was equivalent to signing the instrument in their presence. . . .

It may be taken to be settled, therefore, first, that the attestation required by R. L. c. 135, § 1, consists in the witnesses seeing that those things exist and are done which the statute requires must exist or be done to make the written instrument in law the will of the deceased; second, that although the act required by R. L. c. 135, § 1, is that the will shall be " signed " by the deceased, yet as matter of construction an acknowledgment by the deceased of a previous signature, made in the presence of the attesting witnesses, is equivalent to signing in their presence.

With these two propositions established we come to the question presented in the case at bar, namely: Is there an acknowledgment by the deceased of a previous signature where the signature at the time is hidden from the witnesses? Chief Justice Shaw put that (the case of a hidden signature) as an example of an instance where without question there was not an acknowledgment by the deceased of his signature. In his charge to the jury, set forth in Hall v. Hall, 17 Pick. 373, 375, already referred to, he said: " That to maintain the issue on the part of the executor, and to establish the will, it was necessary to prove that the testatrix signed the will in presence of the witnesses; or that she acknowledged the signature as hers in their presence; and that they severally signed it as witnesses in her presence; and that such acknowledgment was a sufficient compliance with the statute. But in the latter case such acknowledgment may be shown, either by proof of an express acknowledgment and declaration that the signature to the will is hers, or by such facts as will satisfy the jury, that she intended to make such declaration or recognition of her signature. If a mere reference is made to a paper, especially if produced by another person, and not held in her own custody, or if it is folded up, and there is no pointing to or referring to the signature, if she publishes, declares and acknowledges such document to be her will, this is not such an acknowledgment of the signature as will supersede the necessity of an actual signature in the presence of the witnesses, and will not warrant the jury in finding that it was duly signed in the presence of the witnesses." And the law is settled in accordance with this view in England (Hudson v. Parker, 1 Rob. (Eccl.) 14; Blake v. Blake, 7 P. D. 102); in New York (In re Will of Mackay, 110 N. Y. 611; In re Laudy, 148 N. Y. 403); in Minnesota (Tobin v. Haack, 79 Minn. 101); and in Oregon (Richardson v. Orth, 40 Ore. 252). An opposite conclusion was reached in In re Dougherty's estate, 168 Mich. 281.

Apart from authority it is manifest that a person does not acknowledge a signature to be his where no signature can be seen. All that he does in such a case is to acknowledge the fact that he has signed. While an acknowledgment of a signature then exhibited to the witnesses is equivalent to signing in their presence, an acknowledgment to the witnesses of the fact that a signature has been made is not the equivalent of signing in their presence. It follows that where the signature is hidden there is not the equivalent of the statutory requirement that the writing shall be "signed" in the presence of the attesting witnesses.

It is true that Hudson v. Parker, 1 Rob. (Eccl.) 14, and Blake v. Blake, 7 P. D. 102, were decided under St. 1 Vict. c. 26, § 9, which in terms requires that the signature shall be "made or acknowledged by the testator in the presence of two or more witnesses." But it is of no consequence whether the conclusion (that the signature must be made by the testator in the presence of the witnesses or acknowledged by him in their presence) is reached as matter of construction (as in R. L. c. 135, § 1) or as matter of express enactment (as it is under 1 Vict. c. 26, § 9). The conclusion, however reached, being the same, cases in both jurisdictions are equally in point. . . .

Cases like Ella v. Edwards, 16 Gray, 91, where it is held that a will can be allowed on proof of the authenticity of the signatures of the deceased and of the attesting witnesses when these witnesses are all dead or for any other reason cannot be produced, do not conflict with the conclusion reached by us in the case at bar. These are not cases holding that the ultimate fact to be proved is not a signing by the deceased or the acknowledgment by him of a previous signature then exhibited to the witnesses. They are cases deciding how that fact may be proved when the attesting witnesses are dead, or for other reasons cannot testify; and they decide that in such cases the ultimate fact to be proved may be proved by circumstantial evidence aided by the doctrine "omnia rite esse acta praesumuntur." . . .

The proponent also has relied upon Gould v. Chicago Theological Seminary, 189 Ill. 282. That was a case where the attestation was held valid although the previous signature of the deceased was hidden from the subscribing witnesses when the deceased asked them to sign, saying that the paper was his will. But the Illinois Act (Ill. Rev. Sts. c. 148, § 2) does not provide that the testator shall acknowledge a previous signature. The Illinois act provides that the attesting witnesses must declare on oath "that they were present and saw the testator or testatrix sign said will, testament or codicil, in their presence, or acknowledge the same to be his or her act and deed." It was held as matter of construction of that statute that what is to be acknowledged by the deceased is that the paper signed by the subscribing witnesses is his will. . . .

It is undoubtedly the fact that Thomas Nunn thought that he had made his will, and it is a matter of regret, under these circumstances, to have to come to the conclusion that the paper which he signed, thinking that it was his will, is not in law his will. But that regret arises in every case in which a deceased person has failed to comply with those requirements, which, as a matter of public policy, the Legislature has thought proper to exact in case a person wishes to dispose of his property by will. The Legislature might have provided (as it has been held that the Legislature of Illinois did provide) that if the paper was signed by the deceased it would be enough if he acknowledged it to be his will in the presence of the persons who signed the paper as witnesses. But that is not the provision which was adopted in R. L. c. 135, § 1, and the earlier acts of which this is the re-enactment.

It follows that by the terms of the report the decree of the Probate Court must be affirmed.

PROBLEMS.

In all of the cases hereafter briefly stated expensive litigation as to the validity of the will was produced by sloppy execution; and in most of the cases the will was held void. Examine these cases for the purpose of discovering wherein the defect lay and how the difficulty could have been avoided. It is assumed, unless the contrary is stated, that the relevant statute requires the maximum formalities.

1. T wrote his will upon his wife's social correspondence paper, consisting of a single sheet folded so that it made four natural pages. He wrote on the first right-hand page (which he numbered "1"), then on the second right-hand page (which he number "2"), then on the first left-hand page (which he numbered "3"). His signature and the signatures of the witnesses appeared on page "3." Matter of Andrews, 162 N. Y. 1, 56 N. E. 529 (1900); Stinson's Estate, 228 Pa. 475, 77 A. 807 (1910).

2. T asked three people to witness his will and then wrote his will in his own handwriting as follows: " I, T, hereby make my last will. I leave all my property to my wife." This was written in the presence of the witnesses who thereupon signed the instrument in the presence of T and of each other. Then T said, " Oh, I forgot to sign it myself." He thereupon signed his name above the signatures of the witnesses. The Mass. statute stated in Nunn. v. Ehlert (p. 47 supra) is applicable. Barnes v. Chase, 208 Mass. 490, 94 N. E. 694 (1911). Compare Lemayne v. Stanley, 3 Lev. 1 (1691).

3. T, with all witnesses in his bedroom, signed the will. He then was very exhausted and the doctor suggested that the witnesses should move into the next room. They did so, leaving the door open and signed the will as witnesses at a table which was not visible from T's bed. Goods of Colman, 3 Curt. Eccl. 118 (1842).

4. T called in two witnesses. He signed the will in their presence and they signed as witnesses. Then it occurred to T that he should have three witnesses. One of the witnesses stepped out and got another witness. When all four persons had assembled, T and each of the original two witnesses pointed to their respective signatures on the will and acknowledged that they had made them. Thereupon the third witness signed. The statute requires three witnesses. Hindmarsh v. Charlton, 8 H. L. Cas. 160 (1861).

Physically handicapped testator. Paralysis is no obstacle to the making of an effective will since the statutes permit signature by someone other than the testator if made " in his presence and by his express direction." Blindness is a greater difficulty because the attestation has to take place in the " presence " of the testator, and " presence " usually means " within sight." But the statutes of wills are not designed to deny testation to the blind, so in their situation the superintending control must be transferred to the other senses. Through the senses of hearing and touch the blind testator should participate in the ceremony to the greatest possible extent.

PROBLEM.

Ole Arneson, age 80, was bed-ridden and blind. One Quale told a lawyer that Ole wanted to leave all his property to him, so the lawyer drew up a will for Ole to that effect. A neighbor, Forseth, took the will in to Ole and translated it to him orally in Norwegian, which was Ole's native tongue. Ole said that was what he wanted. He asked Forseth to sign it for him, which Forseth did, a Mrs. Hagestead being also in the room. Forseth then signed as a witness and said to Mrs. Hagestead that she should sign as a witness, which she did. When she signed she was at the foot of Ole's bed with her back to him. Is the will validly executed? Arneson's Will, 128 Wis. 112, 107 N. W. 21 (1906). (The applicable statute requires only two witnesses.)

Competency of witnesses. The Statute of Frauds (1677) required attestation by " credible " witnesses. This meant that if one of the witnesses was a beneficiary of the will or the spouse of a beneficiary or otherwise received a benefit, the will was void. The Statute 25 Geo. II C. 6 (1752) changed this situation by providing that " if any person shall attest the execution of any will or codicil . . . to whom any beneficial devise, legacy, estate, interest, gift or appointment of or affecting any real or personal estate . . . shall be given or made, such devise, legacy, interest, gift or appointment, shall, so far only as concerns such person attesting the execution of such will or codicil, or any person claiming under him, be utterly null and void; and such person shall be admitted as a witness." Existing legislation in the United States in the main follows this pattern.[8]

It is fairly easy to eliminate as witnesses legatees and their husbands and wives, but there are certain types of indirect interests which even the most cautious attorney may not be able to discover. This leads to the conclusion that reliance upon the minimum number of witnesses provided by the statute may be improvident.

[8] See Bordwell, " Statute Law of Wills," 14 Ia. L. Rev. at 17-25 (1928).

CROWELL v. TUTTLE.

Supreme Judicial Court of Massachusetts, 1914.

218 Mass. 445, 105 N. E. 980.

Appeal from a decree of the Probate Court for the County of Essex allowing a certain instrument as the last will of Charles Rodrick, late of Swampscott.

The appeal was heard by De Courcy, J. The justice found that the instrument presented for proof was executed by Rodrick as his last will on August 7, 1912, in the presence of three attesting witnesses, Albert H. Barrows, Loring Grimes, and Frank O. Ellis, that they signed in his presence, that he was of sound and disposing mind and memory and that the execution of the will was not procured by undue influence. The justice found also the facts which are stated in the opinion. He ruled that by guaranteeing the mortgage note of the Chapel Congregation of the Church of Christ of Swampscott there described Ellis was not rendered incompetent to act as a witness to the will. Accordingly he ordered that a decree be entered allowing the instrument in question as the last will of Charles Rodrick, and remanding the case to the Probate Court for further proceedings. At the request of the parties, the justice reported the case for determination by the full court. . . .

Hammond, J. At the time Ellis signed his name as an attesting witness he was a guarantor on the outstanding note named in the bequest to the church; and one of the questions is whether by reason of this fact he was rendered incompetent to be such a witness.

By the fifth item of the will the sum of $300 was bequeathed to the church corporation " on the express condition " that it be " applied to the reduction of the present mortgage on the property of said church." This mortgage was given by the corporation to secure the payment of a promissory note dated January 30, 1889, wherein the corporation promised to pay to the order of the Lynn Institution for Savings the sum of $4,500 in one year from date, " with interest payable semi-annually . . . at the rate of five per centum per annum during said term and for such further term as said principal sum or any part thereof remains unpaid." Upon the back of this note appears a writing under seal of even date with the note, whereby six persons, of whom Ellis is one, jointly and severally " guarantee the payment of the within note and interest thereon to the [payee] and its assigns, hereby expressly waiving all demand and notice." The interest on this note has been regularly paid, and from time to time partial payments have been made upon the principal, so that at the time the will was executed it had been reduced to $500. The note was a promise to pay a certain sum " in one year from date," and interest so long as any part of the principal should remain unpaid.

As to interest at least, it was a continuing promise. The guaranty was as broad as the note.

It is urged, however, by the petitioner that since the mortgaged estate was worth much more than the amount due on the note Ellis was not interested in its payment. But the holder could look solely to the note, nevertheless, and collect of the guarantors without reference to the value of the estate. The liability of the guarantors remained the same. It is also urged by the petitioner that the guarantors had a perfect defense in the statute of limitations. But this position is untenable. The guarantors are liable to pay the interest which may arise in the future.

It is plain, therefore, that at the time of the execution of the will Ellis had a direct pecuniary interest in the subject matter of this bequest. This interest was small, but as was said by Wilde, J., in Hawes v. Humphrey, 9 Pick. 350, 356, " such an interest, however minute, will disqualify a witness." See also the authorities cited in 3 Dane Abr. c. 90, art. 4.

Although many changes have been made by our statutes in the rules of the common law as to the competency of witnesses, no statute has been passed which allows a person having a direct, private, pecuniary interest in a legacy such as Ellis here had, to be a competent witness to the execution of a will.

It follows that the ruling that Ellis was a competent witness was erroneous. It becomes unnecessary to consider the other questions raised by the report. The decree admitting the will to probate should be reversed, and the case remanded to the Probate Court.[9]

Problems.

1. T's will is witnessed by H, one of T's three heirs and next of kin. The will gives $5000 to H and the residue to X. If there had been no will, H would have received $8000. Is the will valid? How much does H get? Smalley v. Smalley, 70 Me. 545 (1880).

2. Same facts as Problem 1 except that H would have received $3000 if there had been no will. Is the will valid? How much

[9] At the time this case was decided Rev. Laws c. 135, §§ 1 and 2, were in force, reading as follows:

"Every person . . . may by his last will in writing signed by him or by a person in his presence and by his express direction, and attested and subscribed in his presence by three or more competent witnesses, dispose of his property. . . . A beneficial devise or legacy which is made in a will to a subscribing witness thereto, or to the husband or wife of such witness, shall be void unless there are three other competent subscribing witnesses to such will."

The statute was amended in 1918 to provide as follows (G. L. c. 191, § 2):

" Any person of sufficient understanding shall be deemed to be a competent witness to a will, notwithstanding any common law disqualification for interest or otherwise; but a beneficial devise or legacy to a subscribing witness or to the husband or wife of such witness shall be void unless there are three other subscribing witnesses to the will who are not similarly benefited thereunder."

does H get? Bordwell, "Statute Law of Wills," 14 Ia. L. Rev. 24 (1928).

3. T executes a valid will devising Blackacre to Annie. Then T executes a codicil providing as follows: "I revoke the gift of Blackacre to Annie contained in my will and I give Blackacre to Annie for life, remainder to Catherine. Annie and Catherine were two of the three witnesses to the will. Who gets Blackacre? See Lougee v. Wilkie, 209 Mass. 184, 95 N. E. 221 (1911).

Holographic wills. In some nineteen states [10] unattested wills are valid if they are written *throughout* in the handwriting of the testator. Most statutes also require that the will be dated and that the date be entirely in the testator's hand. If any part of the will consists of a printed form or typewriting (even the testator's typing) it does not come within the terms of the statutes.

The most serious difficulty with holographic wills arises when letters are offered for probate, as in the following case.

MILAM v. STANLEY.

Supreme Court of Kentucky, 1908.

33 Ky. 783, 111 S. W. 296.

Appeal from Logan Circuit Court.

Opinion of the court by Judge Hobson, affirming.

W. R. Fletcher was convicted in the Logan Circuit Court of rape and sentenced to be hung. He appealed to this court, where the judgment was affirmed. He applied to the Governor for clemency and his application was denied. The date of his execution was fixed for February 15, 1907. On February 12, 1907, he wrote the following letter:

"My Dear Loving Daughters:

"I guess my last hope is gone. I don't want you all to grieve after me for I think I will be better off than to be in jail, for I think I am prepared to go and want to ask one thing of you all is to meet me in heaven. Jennie, Lula and Bettie and Mary, I want you to understand that I am as innocent of the charge which I have to die for as an angel in heaven, and it does me good to know that God knows that I am not guilty. Jennie, tell John to see that my body is taken home and buried in our own graveyard, and get Stinson to preach my funeral. Tell him I am at rest. I want to make you and Lula a deed to that house and lot, and I don't want you and her to ever have any trouble over it. Jennie, I don't do this because I think more of you and Lula than I do of Mary and Bettie, but I do it because you both

[10] Atkinson, Wills, § 133.

attended to your dear old mother so good. I hope to soon meet her in heaven. Jennie, Mary has got enough of my money to bury me, I guess. So this is from your loving father,

"W. R. Fletcher.

"To Jennie and Lula, may God bless you all, is my prayer.

"Yours,

"W. R. F."

He was executed on February 15, and afterwards the letter was offered for probate as his will. The appeal before us is prosecuted from the judgment of the circuit court admitting the paper to probate. It is insisted that the paper is not testamentary in character; that it only indicates an intention to make Jennie and Lula a deed to the house and lot, and that the deceased having died without executing this intention by making a deed, the paper can not be probated as a will.

In determining whether the paper is testamentary or not the court will look, not only at the language of the instrument, but at the situation of the maker and at his intention. W. R. Fletcher knew when he wrote this paper that he was to die on February 15. His last hope of life was gone, and knowing that he was to die on the fifteenth, he wrote this letter to his daughters. The letter shows on its face that it is inartificially written; but his meaning is sufficiently apparent. He did not have in mind that he was thereafter to make his daughters a deed to the house and lot. What he had in mind was that he wished them to have the house and lot, and not to have any trouble over it; for he added, " I don't do this because I think more of you and Lula than I do of Mary and Bettie but I do it because you both attended to your dear old mother so good." These words show that he had in mind not something that he was going to do, but something he was then doing. In other words, they show that he intended them to have the house and lot by virtue of the letter he was then writing, and not by virtue of some instrument he was thereafter to write. A will may be in any form. The words in which the intention of the testator is expressed are immaterial if it sufficiently appears from the instrument that he was making a disposition of his property testamentary in character. In Clark v. Ransome, 50 Cal. 595, the following note written in expectation of death was probated as a will: "Dear Old Nance: I wish to give you my watch, two shawls, and also $5,000. Your old friend, E. A. Gordon." In Beyers v. Hope, 48 Am. Rep. 89, the decedent wrote on the back of a business letter, addressed to a man and his wife, the following, addressed to the wife: "After my death you are to have $40,000. This you are to have, will or no will. Take care of this until my death." In Hunt v. Hunt, 17 Am. Dec. 438, the decedent endorsed on the back of a note, these words: "If I am not living at the time this note is paid, I order the contents to be paid to A. H." H died before the note was paid. In Fickle v. Snepp, 49 Am. Rep. 449, the instrument was in form a promissory note; in all these cases the papers were probated as a will. Indeed the general rule is that an instrument is a will if properly executed whatever its form may be, if the intention of the maker to dispose of his estate after his death is sufficiently manifested. (Babb v. Harrison, 70 Am. Dec. 23).

Under these principles the circuit court properly admitted the paper to probate as the will of W. R. Fletcher.[11]

Nuncupative Wills. In many states nuncupative (i.e. oral) wills are recognized as to small amounts of personal property, if the will is made in the last sickness of the testator. There are usually requirements as to the place of death, the prompt reduction of the will to writing and prompt probate. Nuncupative wills of soldiers and sailors on active service are usually recognized without the restrictions applicable to other nuncupative wills.[12]

[11] In re Richardson, 94 Cal. 63 (1892), is another case in which a letter was offered as a holographic will. Whatever may be the views of Southerners, loyal Harvard men will mourn that this letter of a man of such sterling judgment was held nontestamentary in character. It was addressed to his sister in Savannah and read as follows:

" Nina, — I want to know everything about mother, and all about you. your children. I have reached the point of perfect independence, pecuniarily. My health is probably ruined and I want to anticipate possibilities. You and your children get everything. Your boy I want given the best of educations. I would like him to go to Harvard. I would like to have him a lawyer; don't bring him up a prejudiced Southerner; but teach honor; make it dearer than life, and he must, with the blood in his veins, be a man.
BROTHER."

[12] See generally, Bordwell, "' Statute Law of Wills," 14 Ia. L. Rev. at 26 l 34 (1928).

CHAPTER IV.

INCORPORATION BY REFERENCE AND RELATED MATTERS.[1]

The statutes of wills require that a " will " be executed with certain formalities designed to minimize the risk of fraud, forgery and coercion. Yet, despite these statutes, there are many documents, not physically a part of the testator's will and not executed with the statutory formalities, which may determine the takers of the testator's property. In this chapter we deal with these extrinsic documents. We find them given effect on the grounds, variously, that they are " incorporated by reference," or that they constitute the exercise of a " power of appointment," or that they are " non-testamentary acts." The difficulty common to all these devices lies in reconciling them with the letter and the spirit of the statutes of wills.

These three doctrines present analytical problems of no slight complexity. They also offer an unusual field of play for the ingenuity of advocates. After you have mastered Goods of Truro (p. 71) consider how pleased you would have been to conceive the theory upon which the Dowager's silverware was saved for the Baron. Contrariwise, suffer through Atwood v. Rhode Island Hospital Trust (p. 77) with the counsel whose ineptitude had allowed this situation to arise; then share their sigh of relief as they stumble out into the sunshine again by grace of a fortuitous precaution tardily recognized as a forlorn hope of salvation (Merrill v. Boal, p. 81). The last three cases in the chapter show the New York courts making very heavy work of being individualistic and functional.

Republication by codicil. It will be recalled that at common law land in England was not devisable, except by local custom. In 1540 the Statute of Wills permitted devises, but the courts interpreted it as applying only to lands owned by the testator at the time of executing the will. Thus, if T executed a will in 1600, devising to A " all lands I shall own at the time of my death," then acquired Blackacre in 1605 and died in 1610, Blackacre did not pass to A. This was the rule forbidding devise of after-acquired property.

However, in the case supposed, if T in 1607 executed a codicil to his will, this codicil " republished " the will, or " made it speak again " as the courts said; and Blackacre, having been acquired before the date of the codicil, passed to A on the death of T.

---

[1] See generally 3 Restatement of Property (1940) § 348, Comments c to f; Scott on Trusts (1939 and supp.) §§ 54.1 to 54.4; Evans, " Incorporation by Reference, Integration and Non-Testamentary Act," 25 Col. L. Rev. 879 (1925).

Observe that republication is a doctrine of the *re-execution of valid instruments*. There is a properly attested will and a properly attested codicil, and the only question is: As of what date is the will considered to be executed. In this the doctrine of republication differs from the three above enumerated (incorporation by reference, non-testamentary act, power of appointment), for in all of these three there is, or may be, an unattested document into which some attested document must breathe testamentary life if it is to have effect. These three concern themselves with *validation of invalid instruments*.

PROBLEMS.

1. In 1940 T, owning a house lot in Plainville, executed a will devising to A "the real estate I now own in Plainville," giving the residue to R, and nominating E as executor of the will. In 1942 T bought a large tract of land in Plainville. In 1943 he gave the house lot to his son, S. In 1945 E died and T executed a codicil nominating F as executor of the will. When T dies in 1947 does the tract bought in 1942 pass to A? In re Reeves, (1928) 1 Ch. 351; Stilwell *v.* Mellersh, 20 L. J. Ch. (N.S.) 356, 361 (1851). Compare In re Hardyman and Matter of Bradley, referred to at p. 167, infra.

2. N. Y. Decedent Estate Law § 18 gives a right of election to the widow "where a testator dies after August 31, 1930 and leaves a will thereafter executed." T died in 1931, leaving a will executed in 1927 and a codicil thereto executed in 1931. Does his widow have a right of election? Matter of Greenberg, 261 N. Y. 474, 185 N. E. 704 (1933).

3. Several states invalidate charitable devises and bequests made within short periods before the testator's death. The California Civil Code provides that no bequest or devise to a charity shall be valid "except the same be done by will duly executed at least thirty days before the decease of the testator." T executed a will in 1927 leaving $10,000 to a church. He executed a codicil on February 1, 1931, adding two residuary legatees. He died on February 3, 1931. Does the church take? Estate of McCauley, 138 Cal. 432, 71 P. 512 (1903).

ALLEN *v.* MADDOCK.

JUDICIAL COMMITTEE OF THE PRIVY COUNCIL, 1858.

11 Moore P. C. 427.

APPEAL from the Prerogative Court of Canterbury.

The RIGHT HON. T. PEMBERTON LEIGH.

On the 1st of December, 1851, Anne, the wife of Joseph Emanuel Allen, but who was separated from her husband, and who had assumed, and was known by, the name of "Foote," drew up in her own handwriting, and signed and sealed, a paper of that date, described in its commencement as the "last will and testament of me, Anne Foote, of Bath, which I make and publish for all my worldly substance." By this instrument she gave several legacies, and appointed executors, but made no disposition of the remainder of her property.

She had a power, under the settlement made on her marriage, to make a will, but the paper in question was attested by only one witness, and was, therefore, not valid.

On the 13th of September, 1856, being then on her death-bed, she duly executed a codicil, thus headed: "This is a codicil to my last will and testament." By this codicil, she gives to her servant, Eliza Baker, the sum of £100, "with as much of my furniture as, in the opinion of my executor, will be sufficient to furnish a sitting-room and a bed-room." The codicil appoints no executor, and contains no other reference to the will.

On the following day, the 14th of September, the testatrix died. On her death, search was made for her testamentary papers by Sir Thomas Herbert Maddock, who was one of the executors appointed by the paper described as her will, and to whom, in pursuance of the testatrix's direction, a letter announcing the event had been sent immediately upon her death. The codicil was found in a chest in her bed-room, and the disputed paper was found in another chest which had been, shortly before her death, removed from her bed-room into an adjoining room. This paper was enclosed in a sealed envelope, on which are written the words, "Mrs. Anne Foote's will."

No other testamentary paper of any description was found.

Under these circumstances, these two papers have been admitted to probate by the judge of the Prerogative Court; and against this decree the present appeal is brought as regards the will.

The objection relied on is, that there is no such distinct reference to this paper in the codicil, as to enable the court to receive parol evidence in order to identify it; that it is not identified by the description of a "will," for that, in truth, it is not a will; that it is not identified either by date or by any reference to its contents, or by annexation to the codicil, so as to distinguish it from other papers of a like description, if more than one were found; and that to admit this paper to probate on the ground that no other is produced to satisfy the description, would be to incorporate the will in the codicil, merely by parol evidence, and not by the effect of the reference contained in the codicil itself.

It becomes necessary to examine, with some minuteness, the rules of law and the decided cases applicable to this subject.

Before the "Act for the Amendment of the Laws with respect to Wills," 7 Will. IV and 1 Vict., *c.* 26, was passed in the year 1837, no formalities of any kind being necessary in the execution of a will or codicil as to personal estate, the effect of a well-executed testamentary instrument upon one not well executed could hardly come before a Court of Probate. But such questions arose very frequently in the temporal courts, with respect to the disposition of real estate; and the Statute alluded to having placed wills, as to real and personal property, on the same footing, it should seem that the authorities upon this point with respect to real estate, whether before or since the Statute, in the courts of law, are now equally applicable to the Court of Probate, with regard to personalty. In considering them, however, it is necessary to bear in mind this distinction between cases before the Statute, and subsequent cases, namely, that, before the Statute, a testamentary paper not executed so as to affect real estate, was valid as to personalty; was really a will or codicil, and might, therefore, strictly answer that description in a subsequent reference to it by that name; whereas since the Statute came into operation, no paper not properly executed and attested can, in strictness, be for any purpose a will or codicil.

It is necessary also to remember the distinction between the admissibility of evidence to prove a testamentary paper, and of evidence to explain its meaning, that direct evidence of intention, declarations of the testator by word, or in writing, and other testimony of a similar character, are admissible, when the will is disputed, but that no such evidence can be received in order to explain the expressions which he has used. Still, in construing his will, the court is entitled, and is bound, to place itself in the situation of the testator with respect to his property, the objects of his bounty, and every other circumstance material to the construction of the will, and for this purpose to receive, if occasion require it, parol evidence of those circumstances, and to expound his meaning with reference to them.

In the celebrated treatise of Sir James Wigram, cited at the bar, these rules are stated, discussed, and explained in a manner which has excited the admiration of every judge who has had to consult it. After collecting and stating the effect of the several authorities, Sir James Wigram sums up (as it appears to us with perfect accuracy) the result in these terms: "Every claimant under a will has a right to require that a court of construction, in the execution of its office, shall — by means of extrinsic evidence — place itself in the situation of the testator, the meaning of whose language it is called upon to declare. It follows that — with the light which that situation alone affords — the testator's meaning can be determined by a court; the court which so determines does, in effect, declare that the testator has expressed his intention with certainty, or, in other words, that his will is free from ambiguity." (Prop. v. par. 96.)

It may be said that, on the present occasion, the Court of Probate is, to a certain extent, a court of construction; for it has to determine what is the meaning of the reference made by the testatrix in her codicil, to her last will and testament (the executor under which is to determine upon one of the gifts in the codicil), and whether any, and, if any, what, instrument found at her death is thereby referred to.

This question is one of fact which obviously must be explained, and can only be explained by parol evidence. At first sight there is no difficulty; there is no ambiguity whatever in the expression by which the reference is made. Parol evidence must necessarily be received to prove whether there is or is not in existence at the testatrix's death any such instrument as is referred to by the codicil. For this purpose, inquiry must be made and evidence must be offered to show what papers there were at the date of the codicil, which could answer the description contained in the codicil; and the court having by these means placed itself in the situation of the testatrix, and acquired, as far as possible, all the knowledge which the testatrix possessed, must say, upon a consideration of those extrinsic circumstances, whether the paper is identified or not. If the will in question had been properly executed, there can be no doubt that it would have been treated as the instrument referred to by the codicil; yet it must, in that case, have been proved, or assumed, that there was no later will revoking it. This last fact is one which is in truth a necessary foundation of the establishment of every testamentary paper.

That a description in a will may be applied to a subject inaccurately described in it, if it should be shown by parol evidence that there is no subject to which it applies with accuracy, can admit of no doubt. " If the description in the will is incorrect, evidence, that a subject — having such and such marks upon it — exists, must be admissible, that the court may determine whether such subject, though incorrectly described in the will, be that which the testator intended." (Wigram's " Extrinsic Evidence in Aid of the Interpretation of Wills," Prop. v. par. 64.)

Is, then, the evidence in this case sufficient to identify the paper propounded as the will? No other paper has been found to which the description can apply; here is a paper kept by the testatrix up to the time of her death in her own possession, to which, according to her view of that paper, it does apply with the strictest accuracy.

If we are to read the codicil with the knowledge of what the testatrix knew, namely, that she had this testamentary paper, and that she had no other, can it be doubted that this is the paper referred to? . . .

The facts on which we rely are that the paper in question was written by the testatrix, was found locked up in her possession at her death, in a sealed envelope, on which there was an indorsement describing it as her will; and that after diligent search no other paper has been found answering the description, and that the only trace of any other testamentary paper in the evidence is the proof of an earlier will, which the testatrix destroyed.

Their Lordships, therefore, are of opinion, that the decree complained of must be affirmed, and they think that the costs of all parties must come out of the estate.

Problem.

1. Testatrix wrote a letter as follows: " My dear Nephew, — You will be doing me a charity if you will comply with my last wishes; I always found you very kind, and I hope you will not refuse my last request. . . ." The letter proceeded to give directions as to disposal of her property. She sealed this in an envelope and put it in her desk. Several months later she was told that a paper giving directions as to disposal of property on death should be witnessed. So, in the presence of two witnesses, she wrote on the outside of the envelope, " I confirm the contents of the enclosed document." She signed, and the two witnesses signed. The sealed envelope was found among her papers at her death. Is the letter entitled to probate? Goods of Almosnino, 1 Sw. & Tr. 508 (1859).

BRYAN'S APPEAL.

Supreme Court of Errors of Connecticut, 1904.

77 Conn. 240, 58 A. 748.

APPEAL from a judgment of the Superior Court in New Haven County, GAGER, J., refusing to admit to probate a certain written instrument as part of the will of Philo S. Bennett of New Haven, deceased. *No error.*

TORRANCE, C. J. The Court of Probate for the district of New Haven approved and admitted to probate a certain writing as the last will of Philo S. Bennett, deceased. That will contained, as its 12th clause, the following: "I give and bequeath unto my wife, Grace Imogene Bennett, the sum of fifty thousand dollars ($50,000), in trust, however, for the purposes set forth in a sealed letter which will be found with this will." At the time this will was offered for probate there were also offered for probate as a part of it, under the 12th clause of the will, two writings hereinafter referred to as exhibits *B* and *C*.

The Court of Probate refused to approve or admit to probate as parts of said will each and both of these exhibits; and from that part of its decree an appeal was taken to the Superior Court, by William J. Bryan individually, and as trustee under the will as he claims it to be. The will admitted to probate is in the record called Exhibit *A*; while exhibits *B* and *C* are letters which, as the appellant claims, constitute a part of the will. The will was executed in New York, and is dated the 22d day of May, 1900.

Exhibit *B* is a letter from the testator to his wife, of which the following is a copy: —

"New York, 5/22/1900.

"My Dear Wife, — In my will just executed I have bequeathed to you seventy-five thousand dollars (75,000) and the Bridgeport houses, and have in addition to this made you the residuary legatee of a sum which will amount to twenty-five thousand more. This will give you a larger income than you can spend while you live, and will enable you to make bountiful provision for those you desire to remember in your will. In my will you will find the following provisions:

"'I give and bequeath unto my wife, Grace Imogene Bennett, the sum of fifty thousand dollars (50,000), in trust, however, for the purposes set forth in a sealed letter which will be found with this will.'

"It is my desire that fifty thousand dollars conveyed to you in trust by this provision shall be by you paid to William Jennings Bryan, of Lincoln, Nebr., or to his heirs if I survive him. I am earnestly devoted to the political principles which Mr. Bryan advocates, and believe the welfare of the nation depends upon the triumph of those principles. As I am not as able as he to defend those principles with tongue and pen, and as his political work prevents the application of his time and talents to money making, I consider it a duty, as I find it a pleasure, to make this provision for his financial aid, so that he may be more free to devote himself to his chosen field of labor. If for any reason he is unwilling to receive this sum for himself, it is my will that he shall distribute the said sum of fifty thousand dollars according to his judgment among educational and charitable institutions. I have sent a duplicate of this letter to Mr. Bryan, and it is my desire that no one excepting you and Mr. Bryan himself shall know of this letter and bequest. For this reason I place this letter in a sealed envelope, and direct that it shall be opened only by you, and read by you alone. With love and kisses, P. S. Bennett."

Exhibit C was a typewritten duplicate of Exhibit B, except that the words "with love and kisses, P. S. Bennett," at the end of Exhibit B, were not contained in Exhibit C, nor was Exhibit C signed by the testator.

Respecting these exhibits the appellant in the Superior Court offered evidence tending to prove the following facts: that about a week or ten days before the date of the will, at the city of Lincoln, Nebraska, the testator, and Mr. Bryan and his wife, prepared a blank draft form of the will, which was subsequently filled out and executed,[2] and that Exhibit C was then also prepared as a blank

[2] The fact that Bryan supervised, and probably drafted, the instruments in this case raises two interesting questions: (a) his motive in having the gift come in this secret and tortuous method, (b) his skill as a lawyer. The question of motive is fairly clear: There were obvious reasons why The Great Commoner would not welcome advertisement of a $50,000 gift from an eastern capitalist. On the question of skill Bryan's biographer, Mr. Wayne C. Williams (1936), gives some helpful data and some views which should be soothing to any law

draft form from which Exhibit *B* was to be, and was subsequently, drawn; that Exhibit *B* was in the handwriting of the testator, and was by him placed in a sealed envelope bearing the following indorsement in his handwriting: " Mrs. P. S. Bennett. To be read only by Mrs. Bennett, and by her alone, after my death. P. S. Bennett. (Seal) "; that the testator, on the day after the date of the will, placed said will and said envelope containing Exhibit *B* in his box in a vault in the Wool Exchange Building in New York City, where they remained as he put them until after his death, the will being " separate from said letter and said sealed envelope "; and that Exhibit *C*, from the time it was drawn up, remained in Bennett's custody till his death, and was found soon after that event among his private papers, in an envelope subscribed in Bennett's handwriting as follows: " Copy of letter in Safe Deposit Company vault, Wool Exchange."

The appellant then offered Exhibit *C* in evidence as part of the will, claiming that it was the original and equivalent of the paper Exhibit *B*, " and that it was substantially the sealed letter referred to in paragraph 12 of the will." The court excluded the evidence. The appellant thereupon offered in evidence, as part of the will, the letter Exhibit *B*, and the court excluded it. The appellant also offered parol evidence tending to prove that Exhibit *B* was the instrument to which reference was made in clause 12 of the will, but the court excluded such evidence. Subsequently the jury, under the direction of the court, rendered a verdict to the effect that exhibits *B* and *C* " are not either separately or together a part of the last will of said Philo S. Bennett, deceased "; and judgment followed in accordance with the verdict.

From the opinion of the trial court, which is made part of the record, the rulings of the court seem to have been based upon several distinct grounds, which may be briefly indicated: (1) Apparently

---

student nursing an inferiority complex. He points out that Bryan attended Illinois College (where, incidentally, he got his future wife fired from the Female Academy by taking her on an unauthorized buggy ride) and then the Union College of Law at Chicago. There Bryan showed " his keen interest in constitutional law and his grasp of the fundamental principles of jurisprudence. The law school had a debating society and Bryan shone here as he had in Illinois College." These activities were mixed with " excursions to places of interest about the big city " and " jokes and good clean fun." " Bryan stood high in his classes, not the top but above the average, and at graduation his graduating theme was a justification of the jury system. To those critics who in later years described Bryan as ignorant and unlearned and without intellectual ability, a reply is really not needed. It is enough to say that a law course of two years in any established law school in and of itself makes for an intellectual discipline and a mental grasp that lifts any student from the class of the unlearned. This study of the great structure of English common law and of American constitutional law affords a mental discipline unsurpassed by any other mental training afforded in our institutions of higher learning. Bryan was an educated man and every lawyer in America can resent the slur upon him " (pp. 45–46).

While we are on the subject, could the matter have been arranged so that secrecy would have been attained and Bryan's rights safeguarded? If so, how?

upon the ground that the doctrine of incorporation by reference does not prevail as to wills, under our statute relating to their making and execution; (2) that even if that doctrine prevails here, no paper in the present will is by reference made a part of it, according to the rules universally applied in jurisdictions where the above doctrine prevails; and (3) that the letter, Exhibit *B,* shows on its face an intent on the part of the testator that it should not constitute a part of his will.

As we think the rulings of the court below can be vindicated upon the second of the grounds above mentioned, it will be unnecessary to consider the other two grounds; but in thus resting our decision upon the second ground we do not mean to intimate that it could or could not be made to rest upon the first or third.

Before considering the second ground a word or two regarding the first ground may not be out of place. Under the rule prevailing in England, an unattested document may, by reference in a will, under certain conditions and limitations, become by such reference incorporated in the will as a part of it; and that too whether the document referred to is or is not a dispositive one; and one of the leading cases upon this subject is that of Allen *v.* Maddock, 11 Moore's P. C. C. 427, decided in 1858. This is known as the doctrine of incorporation by reference; and the principle upon which it rests does not differ essentially from that which is applied in incorporating unsigned writings in a signed instrument so as to constitute a memorandum in writing under the statute of frauds. The English rule appears to prevail in many of our sister States; but the question whether it prevails in this State, and if so, with what limitations and under what conditions, was left undetermined in Phelps *v.* Robbins, 40 Conn. 250, and has never been passed upon since. In the present case we find it unnecessary to decide those questions; but for the purposes of the argument we shall assume, without deciding, that the doctrine of incorporation by reference in a will prevails here.[3]

Two of the conditions, without the existence of which the English rule will not be applied, are concisely, but we think correctly, stated in Phelps *v.* Robbins, supra (272), as follows: "First, the paper must be in existence at the time of the execution of the will; and, secondly, the description must not be so vague as to be incapable of being applied to any instrument in particular, but must describe the instrument intended in clear and definite terms." In a California case upon this subject this language is used: "But before such an extrinsic document may be so incorporated, the description of it in the will itself must be so clear, explicit and unambiguous as to leave its identity free from doubt." Estate of Young, 123 Cal. 337, 342. In an important and well considered English case, decided in 1902, the court uses this language upon this subject: "But it is clear that, in order

---

[3] It was later established that the doctrine of incorporation by reference does not exist in Connecticut. Hathaway *v.* Smith, 79 Conn. 506, 65 A. 1058 (1907).

that the informal document should be incorporated in the validly executed document, the latter must refer to the former as a writing existing — that is, at the time of the execution — in such terms that it may be ascertained. . . . The document which it is sought to incorporate must be existing at the time of the execution of the document into which it is to be incorporated, and there must be a reference in the properly executed document to the informal document as an existing one, and not as a future document." In the Goods of Smart, L. R. (1902) P. D. 238, 240.

Tested by the rules as thus laid down in the cases above cited, and in numerous others that might be cited, the will in the present case fails to comply with the required conditions under which incorporation by reference can take place in the case of wills. In clause 12 of the will in question here a large sum of money is given to Mrs. Bennett " in trust, however, for the purposes set forth in a sealed letter which will be found with this will." There is not in the language quoted, nor anywhere else in the will, any clear, explicit, unambiguous reference to any specific document as one existing and known to the testator at the time his will was executed. Any sealed letter, or any number of them, setting forth the purposes of the trust, made by anybody, at any time after the will was executed, and " found with the will," would each fully and accurately answer the reference; and if we assume that the reference calls for a letter from the testator, it is answered by such a letter or letters made at any time after the will was drawn. The reference is " so vague as to be incapable of being applied to any instrument in particular " as a document existing at the time of the execution of the will; " the vice is that no particular paper is referred to." Phelps *v.* Robbins, 40 Conn. 250, 273. Such a reference as is made in the present will is, in fact as well as in law, no reference at all; certainly it is not such a reference as the rules under the doctrine of incorporation by reference require in the case of wills.

A reference so defective as the one here in question cannot be helped out by what is called parol evidence; for to allow such evidence to be used for such purpose would be practically to nullify the wise provisions of the law relating to the making and execution of wills. We know of no case, and in the able and helpful briefs filed in this case have been referred to none, where a reference like the one here in question has been held to incorporate into the will some extrinsic document.

Assuming then, without deciding, that the doctrine of incorporation prevails in this State, as claimed by the appellant, we are still of the opinion that the rulings of which he complains were correct.

There is no error.

In this opinion the other judges concurred.[4]

[4] " Reading the opinion in the light of history and in the light of the authorities, and especially in the light of common sense, it would seem that the

BRYAN v. BIGELOW.

SUPREME COURT OF ERRORS OF CONNECTICUT, 1905.

77 Conn. 604, 60 A. 266.

[This case arose out of the facts stated in Bryan's Appeal, supra. In this proceeding Bryan as executor brought a bill for instructions to determine the disposition of the $50,000. Bryan argued the case pro se.]

HALL, J. The real question to be considered is whether the trust upon which the $50,000 was given to Mrs. Bennett has been lawfully created; if it has not, the money should not be paid to her, either as an individual or as a trustee. Mrs. Bennett herself makes no claim, either as an individual or as a trustee, to any interest in the money, as a legatee under the twelfth clause of the will. . . . The controversy is therefore one between Mr. Bryan as an individual and as an alleged trustee under the sealed letter, Exhibit 1, upon the one hand, and the residuary legatees, of whom Mrs. Bennett is one, upon the other; the issue between them being whether a valid bequest of the $50,000 named in the sealed letter and in section 12 of the will, has been made to Mrs. Bennett in trust, either by force of the sealed letter itself, or by the twelfth paragraph of the will, or by the sealed letter and said paragraph together. . . .

The letter cannot operate as a declaration of the trust upon which the money was bequeathed to Mrs. Bennett. Our statute of wills is not only directory but prohibitory. Irwin's Appeal, 33 Conn. 128. To treat this letter as an operative declaration of trust would be, in effect, to hold that a testamentary disposition of property could be made by an instrument not executed in conformity with the statute regulating such transfers of property. . . .

That the twelfth clause of the will, unaided by the sealed letter, makes no disposal of the equitable interest in the $50,000 named therein, admits of no question. To what purposes the sum given to Mrs. Bennett in trust is to be devoted, and in whom the beneficial interest in that sum is to vest, is neither stated nor attempted to be stated in paragraph 12, independently of Exhibit 1.

But it is urged that the twelfth clause of the will and the sealed letter, read together, clearly show the purposes to which the testator

---

Connecticut Court was not at all disposed towards a western political leader of the radical or progressive type, not from anything said in the opinion, but from the strained and utterly inconsistent position which the court took in holding that the will and the letter did not particularly refer each to the other! As a plain matter of fact and common sense the reference was so direct and unmistakable that there was no possible room for doubt or ambiguity. . . . Probably his [Bryan's] greatest victory was in the finding of the Superior Court of Connecticut that Mr. Bryan had exercised no undue influence upon Mr. Bennett." Williams, William Jennings Bryan (1936) 249–250.

intended the $50,000 given to Mrs. Bennett in trust should be devoted by her, and show a valid bequest to her as trustee; and that the sealed letter and other exhibits offered in evidence should have been received for the purpose of showing such intention of the testator, and of thus enabling the court to properly construe the will.

It may be conceded that such an intention of Mr. Bennett is clearly shown by these exhibits, but it does not follow that they are for that reason admissible as evidence, or that they can be considered in construing the will. While extrinsic evidence may be admitted to identify the devisee or legatee named, or the property described in a will, also to make clear the doubtful meaning of language used in a will, it is never admissible, however clearly it may indicate the testator's intention, for the purpose of showing an intention not expressed in the will itself, nor for the purpose of proving a devise or bequest not contained in the will. . . .

The sealed letter and other exhibits were not admissible in the case at bar for the purpose of identifying the beneficiary of the trust described in paragraph 12, for not only is there no beneficiary or trust described in that section, but it clearly appears from the language of the will that it was the intention of the testator that neither the name of the beneficiary nor the purpose of the trust upon which the bequest was made to Mrs. Bennett should be disclosed by the will, but that they should be stated in another instrument. . . .

The excluded evidence was not admissible to rebut a resulting trust to the residuary legatees. "The resulting trusts which can be rebutted by extrinsic evidence are those claimed upon a mere implication of law, not those arising on the failure of an express trust for imperfection or illegality." Woodruff *v.* Marsh, 63 Conn. 125, 141.

The cases of Dowd *v.* Tucker, 41 Conn. 197, Buckingham *v.* Clark, 61 id. 204, and other cases in which trusts *ex maleficio* have been declared against persons who have obtained property by promising to apply it to certain purposes, have been cited as applicable to this proceeding. Assuming that while the $50,000 was still in the hands of the executor the Superior Court, as a court of equity, might, in this proceeding, in directing to whom the money should be paid, have considered whether if paid to Mrs. Bennett, or the residuary legatees, they or either of them could be held to be trustees *ex maleficio* by reason of an express or implied promise to apply the money to the purposes named in the sealed letter, we cannot find error in the judgment of the Superior Court, since neither the evidence excluded nor the facts proved show any agreement, express or implied, by Mrs. Bennett or the other residuary legatees, to accept the money upon the trust described in Exhibit 1, or that during the lifetime of the testator they even knew of any of the provisions of the twelfth clause of the will. Proof that Mrs. Bennett possessed such knowledge was not prevented by the rulings of the court sustaining the demurrer to Mr. Bryan's answer and denying his motion for leave to file a cross-complaint. These rulings were not upon the ground that evidence of that fact was inadmissible, and an opportunity was apparently given to the claimant Mr. Bryan, during the trial of the case, to offer the evidence of Mrs. Bennett, without objection, as to the facts upon which a disclosure was asked for.[5] Further discussion of these rulings is unnecessary, since they did not prevent the claimant Mr. Bryan from proving upon the trial all the facts alleged in his answer and cross-complaint.

There is no error.[6]

GOODS OF TRURO.

PROBATE AND DIVORCE DIVISION, ENGLAND, 1866.

L. R. 1 P. & D. 201.

THE Dowager Lady Truro died on the twenty-first of May, 1866, leaving a will dated the fifteenth of September, 1865, and a codicil dated the tenth of October, 1865. The will contained the following clause: "I likewise bequeath to the present Baron Truro, in affectionate recollection of his kindness to me, all my library and books and maps, except such parts thereof as I shall herein or after or by codicil otherwise dispose of; and also all my engravings, paintings, pictures, and drawings, save and except such parts thereof as I shall herein or after or by codicil otherwise dispose of; also all my household bed and table linen, and also all such articles of silver plate and plated articles *as are contained in the inventory signed by me and deposited herewith.*"

The will was deposited by the deceased at Messrs. Coutts', the bankers, in an envelope with an indorsement in her writing, and in the same envelope with the will was found an inner envelope containing a list of plate. The list, which was in several sheets, was

---

[5] "During the trial, counsel for Mrs. Bennett and the other residuary legatees stated that if counsel for Mr. Bryan desired to call Mrs. Bennett as a witness as to whether she had been informed during her husband's lifetime of the contents of the twelfth section of the will, they would not object to the introduction of the evidence. She was not called and no evidence was offered upon that subject." 77 Conn. at 610.

[6] In the absence of proof that Mrs. Bennett knew of the letter during her husband's lifetime there is no authority for giving the $50,000 to Bryan. Scott on Trusts, § 55.5. If Mrs. Bennett knew of the letter and of the provision in the will to which the letter referred it is probable that an agreement to comply with the letter could be implied; and, if there had been no reference to the letter in the will but only an outright gift to Mrs. Bennett, Bryan would have succeeded. Scott on Trusts, § 55.1. But the mention of the letter in the will, and the consequent indication that *some* secret trust exists, would prevent Bryan from succeeding in some jurisdictions, even though Mrs. Bennett had impliedly agreed to the arrangement. Scott on Trusts, § 55.8.

In a word Bryan could hardly have done worse in setting up this transaction.

headed, " List of plate and plated articles left by my will dated the fifteenth of September, 1865, to the present Baron Truro. AUGUSTA E. TRURO." The list was signed by the deceased in several places, and on the last sheet was her signature and the date, twenty-first of September, 1865. Affidavits were filed showing that the will and the list were deposited with Messrs. Coutts on the twenty-first of September, 1865, and that the codicil was deposited at a subsequent date. One of the affidavits also proved that when the will was executed the attention of the testatrix was called to the importance of signing the inventory and depositing it with her will, and that she intimated her intention of acting upon that suggestion. . . .

Sir J. P. Wilde. I have very serious doubts whether I could allow this list to form part of the probate if the question depended upon the words of the will, because, although to some extent they point to an existing document, I should, construing them by the existing facts, read them as meaning, not that the document had been signed at the time when the will was executed, and would be deposited with it, but as meaning that it would be signed and deposited when the will should be deposited. There is no distinct reference to an existing document. For, though the testatrix, in using the words, " signed by me, and deposited herewith," would *prima facie* seem to mean " now already signed and deposited," yet those words, like all others in a written document, must be construed in connection with the existing and surrounding state of things. Now, the will could not have been deposited at the time at which the testatrix was speaking, and the list when produced was plainly not signed till the twenty-first of September. The true meaning, therefore, of the words, as spoken at that date, would seem to be, " a list which I intend to sign and deposit," &c. It is, however, unnecessary to decide whether the list is incorporated with the will, because I am of opinion that it is entitled to probate by force of the codicil. . . .

Where the will, if treated as executed on the date of the codicil, and read as speaking at that date, contains language which, within the principle of Allen *v.* Maddock, would operate as an incorporation of the document to which it refers, testamentary effect may be given to such document. But when this is not the case, the mere fact of unexecuted papers having been written or signed between the date of the will and that of the codicil will not suffice to add such papers to the will by force of republication, or to make that testamentary which would not have been so if the will had been originally executed at the later date.

Applying that doctrine to the present cases, and treating this will as having been re-executed on the date of the codicil, its language runs thus: " And also all such articles of silver plate and plated articles as are contained in the inventory signed by me and deposited herewith." Now, construing these words by the light of the events which had then happened, they appear with sufficient distinctness to refer to a document then existing. For the inventory referred to had then been signed by the testatrix and deposited at the bankers. The operation of the codicil as a re-execution of the will, therefore, gets rid of all difficulty, and I admit the will and the codicil to probate, together with the inventory signed by the testatrix.

PROBLEMS.

1. On March 25, 1932 S. M. Seligsohn executed his will. Paragraph 4 gave $6000 to his executors to be paid out by them " as shall be directed by me in a letter that will be found in my effects and will be dated March 25, 1932. No person having an interest in this will shall inquire into the application of said moneys." No letter dated March 25, 1932 was found in the testator's effects; but there was found a letter to the executors, dated July 3, 1933, which recited the provisions of Paragraph 4 and directed them to pay $4000 out of the $6000 to Mrs. Esther Cohn. On November 25, 1933 the testator executed a codicil to his will, confirming it but making no reference to Paragraph 4 or to the letter. Testator died in 1935. Is the letter entitled to probate? Simon *v.* Grayson, 15 Cal.(2d) 531, 102 P. 1081 (1940), commented on in 39 Mich. L. Rev. 1055 (1941).

2. T duly executed his will in 1847. Sometime in the next two years he wrote interlineations into the will. Then in 1854 he duly executed a codicil which began, "This is a codicil to my will dated 1847." Are the interlineations entitled to probate? Goods of Wyatt, 2 Sw. & Tr. 495 (1862).

3. T executed his will on December 7, 1837, and it was properly attested. On October 12, 1838, he executed a codicil in which he made gifts to his grandchildren; and this codicil was attested by two of his grandchildren, William and Ann. On April 8, 1839, T executed a second codicil which was properly attested and which provided, "This is a codicil to my last will dated December 7, 1837. I hereby bequeath to my daughter Elizabeth £600." Are William and Ann entitled to receive the gift made to them in the first codicil? Burton *v.* Newberry, 1 Ch. D. 234 (1875).

4. Eustace duly executed a will in 1906 leaving all his property to Mary Wells. Mary Wells procured the execution of this will by exerting undue influence upon Eustace. In 1912 Eustace duly executed an instrument as follows: "This is a codicil to my will of 1906. I devise my real estate in Des Moines, Iowa, to Mary Simpson; and I appoint Mary Simpson executrix of this codicil." This 1912 instrument was not procured by undue influence? What instrument or instruments are entitled to probate? Taft *v.* Stearns, 234 Mass. 273, 125 N. E. 570 (1920).

STUBBS v. SARGON.

COURT OF CHANCERY, ENGLAND, 1838.

3 Myl. & Cr. 507.

THE LORD CHANCELLOR. [LORD COTTENHAM.] The second question is, Whether the ultimate devise of the premises in Little Queen Street be void under the Statute of Frauds. The devise is to trustees to keep in repair the premises, and, subject thereto, to pay the rents to the testatrix's sister, Mary Innell, during her life, and after her decease, in trust to dispose of and divide the same unto and amongst her partners who should be in copartnership with her at the time of her decease, or to whom she might have disposed of her business, in such shares and proportions as her trustees should think fit and deem advisable.

Upon the first head of objection, namely, the Statute of Frauds, it was argued that the will contained no disposition of itself, but that it was a reservation to the testatrix of the power of completing the devise by investing the intended devisee with the character described in the will, and that Habergham v. Vincent, 2 Ves. Jr. 204; 4 Bro. C. C. 353, was in point in support of that proposition. The difference between the two cases is, that the will in Habergham v. Vincent contained no devise of the remainder; it only declared that the remainder should be for such persons and for such estates as the testator should, by any deed or instrument attested by two witnesses, appoint. This was no disposition of the property; but a reservation by will, inoperative till the testator's death, of a power to dispose, in his lifetime, of freehold property, by an instrument not attested according to the Statute of Frauds.

In the present case, the disposition is complete. The devisee, indeed, is to be ascertained by a description contained in the will; but such is the case with many unquestionable devises. A devise to a second or third son, perhaps unborn at the time — many contingent devises — all shifting clauses — are instances of devises to devisees who are to be ascertained by future events and contingencies; but such persons may be ascertained, not only by future natural events and contingencies, but by acts of third persons. Suppose a father, having two sons, and having a relation who has a power of appointing an estate to some one of them, makes his will, and gives his own estate to such one of his sons as shall not be the appointee of the other estate — or with a shifting clause. Here the act of the donee of the power is to decide who shall take the father's estate; but there is nothing in the Statute of Frauds to prevent this, because the devise by the will is complete, that is, the disposition is complete — the intention is fully declared, though the object to take remains uncertain. If the subsequent act removing that uncertainty, and fixing the identity of the devisee, were to be considered as testamentary, in the case above supposed, the donee of the power would be making or completing the will of the father, that is, one man would be making another man's will. The act, therefore, is not testamentary; and, if not, then why should not the act be the act of the testator himself? It is objected to upon the ground of its being testamentary; but if it be not testamentary when done by a stranger, it cannot be so when done by the testator. If it were otherwise, a testator could not devise lands, or give legacies charged upon land, to such person as might be his wife at his death — to such children as he might have — or to such servant as he might have in his service at his death. . . . I think, therefore, the objection upon the ground of the Statute of Frauds cannot be supported. . . .

APPEAL OF MOORE.

PREROGATIVE COURT, NEW JERSEY, 1900.

61 N. J. Eq. 616, 47 A. 731.

REED, VICE-ORDINARY. James Moore died August fourteenth, 1897, leaving a will [executed prior to 1893]. . . .

The will contained the following clause:

" In making division of my property aforesaid as above directed I hereby further direct that certain amounts of money that I have already advanced or may hereafter advance to certain of my children, shall in each case be charged against the portion of each of said children, and be inventoried as part of the estate of which I may die seized, at the full amount of the charge in each instance, but without interest thereon. All such charges are contained in sealed envelopes to be found with this my last will. All other evidence of indebtedness against any of my said children, which I may have at my death, I hereby give and bequeath to such debtors, respectively, to each child the evidence of his or her indebtedness, and discharge each of said debtors from all his or her obligations in respect to such and all indebtedness for any such advances or debts, except such as I have heretofore specified as being left with this my will.

" These amounts I cannot at present certainly indicate, as they are liable to be changed before my death by payments to be made or by further advances by me."

After the testator's death the executors found the will in a sealed envelope, and with it three other papers, signed by the testator, one of which was in the following form:

" Elizabeth, N. J., February 22d, 1893.

" The sum of $14,000 is to be charged to account of my son Thomas (without interest) for money heretofore advanced by me to him in accordance with the provisions of my will contained in the third section thereof.

" James Moore."

The point taken by Thomas Moore, the exceptant, is that " this paper is an attempt to add to, change or complete the provisions of a will by a subsequent paper not executed with the formalities required by the statute of wills."

There is no doubt that a testator can provide that the amount to be received by a legatee shall be dependent upon a condition of fact to be ascertained *aliunde.* Some of these conditions are noted by Chief-Justice Denio, in his opinion in the leading case of Langdon *v.* Astor's Executors, 16 N. Y. 1, 26.

This is so, even though the condition may be brought about by the testator himself. Stubbs *v.* Sargon, 3 Myl. & C. 507.

The testator could have provided that all advances made to, or debts owing by, a legatee, whether made or incurred before or after the execution of the will, should be deducted from his portion. Such amount may be ascertained by parol evidence, and may be varied by advancements made subsequent to the execution of the will. 1 Underh. Wills, 447.

A frequent testamentary provision is that such debts or advancements as are charged on testator's books against legatees shall be deducted, and these provisions are valid. Robert *v.* Corning, 89 N. Y. 227.

When a testator provides that such advancements as are indicated by entries, to be subsequently made by him, shall be deducted from the share or legacy, a mere entry, it seems, unless there have been advancements in fact, will not suffice. Hoak *v.* Hoak, 5 Watts, 80.

Parol evidence is admissible to support the book entries. Estate of Mussleman, 5 Watts, 9; Gilman *v.* Gilman, 63 N. Y. 41.

In the present case I think it appears that, before the execution of the will, testator had paid to, and for the benefit of, the exceptant moneys, which were never repaid, to an amount in excess of $14,000. It is to this sum that the testator alludes when he speaks of the amounts of money "that I have already advanced." The checks produced, taken in connection with the explanation of the exceptant himself, seem to establish this fact. . . .

Now, the testator having the right to provide that such advances should be charged to the portion of exceptant, the question remains, did he defeat his intention to charge some of the advances by providing that the amount which he intended to charge should be evidenced by a paper made subsequently to the execution of his will?

In my judgment the paper which contained the charge is not to be regarded as testamentary in its character. The effect of the contents of the paper was restrictive. Suppose the testator had said, I charge all the debts owing to me, which I have not discharged or forgiven at the time of my death, and the receipt, release or paper evidencing such discharge will be found with my will. This would seem analogous to a provision containing a gift of certain property, unless it should be conveyed before the testator's death. The fact that he mentioned where such deed or conveyance could be found, if made, would be in no degree material. It being proved that more than $14,-000 had been advanced to this legatee, the paper which expressly charged him with only $14,000 was impliedly a gift of the remainder of the advances. . . .

ATWOOD v. RHODE ISLAND HOSPITAL TRUST CO.

CIRCUIT COURT OF APPEALS, FIRST CIRCUIT, 1921

275 Fed. 513.

BEFORE BINGHAM, JOHNSON, and ANDERSON, Circuit Judges.

This is a proceeding in equity, in which it is sought to have the residuary clause of the will of Theodore M. Davis declared inoperative and void. Kate Atwood, a resident of Massachusetts and a half sister of the testator, brings the suit in her individual capacity and as executrix of the estate of Gertrude Galloway, a sister of the testator. Theodore Davis Boal, a resident of Pennsylvania and executor of the will of Annie B. Davis, widow of the testator, is also a party plaintiff. . . .

Mr. Davis resided at Newport, Rhode Island.[7] August 14, 1911, he

[7] This sterile sentence — "Mr. Davis resided at Newport, Rhode Island" — hardly does justice to the human factors involved in this litigation. More informative is the Supreme Court of Rhode Island in Davis v. Manson, 180 A. 714 (1918) from which the following data are taken:

Theodore M. Davis was born in 1837 and was a New York lawyer, strong of will, successful in his practice, and fortunate in his investments. He is also "said to have been able." In 1890, at the age of 53, he retired from practice and took up permanent residence at The Reef, a mansion he had built at Newport. He developed a strong interest in Egyptology which led him, beginning with 1897, to spend about half the year in Egypt. When he was in Newport, however, he and his wife — "a gentle and patient woman" — were not alone. Prominent in their lives were Theodore Davis Boal, Mrs. Boal (née Mathilde de Lagarde), Cecile de Lagarde (Mrs. Boal's sister), Mrs. Emma B. Andrews, and Miss Annie Ghio.

Theodore Boal was a nephew of Mrs. Davis whom Davis took from his parents at the age of eight to educate, Davis being childless. In 1886 Boal was sent to Boston to take the entrance examinations for Harvard, "became involved in some difficulty with the driver of a herdic," and, to get out of the difficulty, pawned a watch which Davis had given him. Davis heard of the episode and sent him back to his parents in Iowa. Some years later Davis relented, sent Boal to the Beaux Arts in Paris and put up $4,000 at the time of his marriage to Mlle. Mathilde de Lagarde. Boal's wife was a frequent visitor at The Reef, where she seems to have been highly regarded.

Cecile de Lagarde acted as an intermediary by whom Mr. Davis sent to Mrs. Boal payments for the education of her son and other monies.

Mrs. Andrews, a woman of masterful mind with an interest in Egyptology, signed a trust agreement in which he made the Rhode Island Hospital Trust Company, trustee. August 16, 1911, he delivered the trust deed and securities of more than $2,000,000 in value to the Trust Company, and August 17, 1911, the Trust Company signified in writing its acceptance of the property and agreed to carry out the trust.

Under the terms of the trust the trustee was to manage the property, and pay the net income to Mr. Davis during his life, and upon his decease convert a sufficient amount of it into cash and pay forthwith certain sums to designated beneficiaries. The remainder of the trust estate, not required for the payment of certain benefits and annuities, was to be held in trust to pay the net income to Mrs. Davis and Mrs. Andrews. Upon the decease of the survivor the trustee was directed to divide the principal of the remaining trust estate into equal parts, and to pay over said parts, free of all trusts, to certain persons designated in the deed of trust, comprising about 30 in all. In the deed Mr. Davis reserved the right at any time dur-

---

was first a frequent visitor at the Davis home, then a permanent resident. She accompanied Davis and others of his party to Egypt each year. She was disliked and feared by the other women at The Reef.

Miss Annie Ghio had been the private secretary of Mr. Justice Gray for 15 years, then came with Davis as secretary, first on a temporary basis, then permanently.

The Supreme Court emphasizes that, with all of these ladies who made up Davis's household and shared his generosity, " it is obvious that his relations were devoid of censurable familiarity."

Be that as it may, in 1911 Mrs. Davis found the place too crowded and moved to Atlantic City with an allowance of $14,000 annually provided by Davis. There Boal became her principal adviser and the intermediary for business communications between Davis and his wife.

In 1915 Davis died. Thereupon Mrs. Davis produced a purported letter of 1912 from Davis, promising, in consideration of Mrs. Davis waiving dower rights to land in Michigan (where dower did not have to be released by a non-resident anyway, but " Mr. Davis may not have known about this "), to leave one million dollars to Mrs. Davis by will. Shortly thereafter Mrs. Davis died, leaving a will in which Boal was named executor and principal beneficiary.

The million-dollar agreement was contested. Boal and Cecile de Lagarde were the principal witnesses as to its validity. The court found that no such agreement was made, and this was affirmed in Davis v. Manson, supra.

Other litigation — beyond the two principal cases and Davis v. Manson — as to the estate of that lawyer who was " said to have been able," is as follows:

Boal v. Metropolitan Museum of Art, 292 Fed. 299 (S. D. N. Y. 1922); s.c. 292 Fed. 303 (S. D. N. Y. 1923), rev'd 298 Fed. 894 (C. C. A. 2d, 1924); s.c. 19 F.(2d) 454 (C. C. A. 2d, 1927); Merrill v. Atwood, 48 R. I. 72, 135 A. 402 (1926); Atwood v. R. I. H. T. Co., 30 F.(2d) 707 (D. R. I. 1929), aff'd 34 F.(2d) 18 (C. C. A. 1st, 1929); Ex Parte Atwood, 280 U. S. 523 (1929).

For a still longer probate dispute involving 32 reported cases between 1839 and 1893, see the litigation over the will of Daniel Clark of Louisiana as set forth in Frankfurter and Shulman, Cases on Federal Jurisdiction and Procedure (1937) 484n. For popular books dealing with the Clark Estate litigation, see Kane, New Orleans Woman (1946); Harmon, The Famous Case of Myra Clark Gaines (1946).

ing his life to revoke "any or all of the trusts herein declared," and "add to, annul, change, or modify in any respect whatsoever any of the trusts or powers hereby created or conferred."

On the same day that he signed the trust deed, August 14, 1911, but subsequent to its execution, Mr. Davis executed his will, the ninth or residuary clause of which is in question. October 4, 1911, he executed a codicil to his will in which, after making certain modifications, he confirmed his will except as therein modified. October 5, 1911, which was the day after the execution of the codicil, he added four beneficiaries to the trust, giving them sums varying from $5,000 to $15,000 and amounting in the aggregate to $35,000. October 17, 1913, he made a further modification of the trust instrument by adding a new beneficiary, with a gift of $5,000, and cancelling the provision made in the original trust deed of $3,000 to Amelia Burgnon. Neither of these modifications was executed as required by the statute of wills.

In the residuary clause of his will the testator provided as follows:

"Ninth: I give, devise and bequeath all the remainder of the property, real and personal, . . . to my said executors, or any duly appointed administrator of my estate, in trust nevertheless, to convert the whole of said property into cash as soon as reasonably possible, with power to sell the same or any part or parts thereof at either private or public sale, and the net proceeds of such sale or sales to pay over to the said Rhode Island Hospital Trust Company to be held, managed and disposed of as a part of the principal of the estate and property held by it in trust for my life and the lives of others in the same manner as though the proceeds of such sales had been deposited by me as a part of said trust estate and property. . . ."

ANDERSON, C. J. We are clear that the plan disclosed in the will and the inter vivos trust together is obnoxious to the statute of wills, falling plainly within the condemnation of the rule pungently stated by Sir George Parker in Johnson *v.* Ball, 5 De G. & Sm. 85, 91, where he said:

"A testator cannot by his will prospectively create for himself a power to dispose of his property by an instrument not duly executed as a will or codicil."

This is exactly what Davis undertook to do as to the residue of his testamentary estate.

The case is on all fours with Olliffe *v.* Wells, 130 Mass. 221, and the other numerous cases to the same effect.

Reading the ninth clause of the will in connection with the trust instrument, which contains full power of revocation and modification, Davis said:

"I give the residue of my estate to said Trust Company to be disposed of to such persons and in such proportions as I may have instructed or shall hereinafter instruct said Trust Company."

Such instructions might be given in writing or orally. A cablegram from him sent from Egypt would have been legally sufficient to change the destination of the entire trust fund, including the increment from his testamentary estate under the residuary clause. Indeed, the defendants concede that oral instruction would, as matter of law, have been equally effective; that writings are of no importance, except as persuasive evidence. Nor is the fact that in this case the trust fund was upwards of $2,000,000 and the residue of the testamentary estate by comparison small, of any import; the plan devised would have been equally effective if the inter vivos trust had been $5,000, divisible under the trust instrument into fractions to various named persons (and subject to change or modification at any time, orally or in writing), and the augmentation under the will had been $5,000,000.

Manifestly, then, the real disposition of this residuary estate is made, not by the will, but by the shifting provisions in the trust instrument. No amount of discussion or elaboration could make plainer the absolute destruction by such plan of the safeguarding provisions in the statute of wills. . . .

But it is contended that this case can be distinguished from Olliffe v. Wells, because, in the language of Denio, C. J., in Langdon v. Astor's Ex'rs, 16 N. Y. 9, the trust in this case is not " indifferent in itself and having no pertinency, except its effect upon his testamentary dispositions."

Applying this somewhat abstruse and confusing language to this case, we understand it to mean that, because the trustee named in Mr. Davis' will had, with reference to some of Mr. Davis' property, functions to perform other than those created by the will alone, the gift to such trustee is thereby made valid; in other words, that because the respondent Trust Company had, apart from the provisions in the will, a trust relationship to Davis, the bequest to it became valid, although it would have been invalid if this Trust Company had stood towards the testator as Wells stood in Olliffe v. Wells, with no trust relationship except that arising under the will itself.

In our view, this is a distinction without any legal difference. The real question is whether the residue of this estate was disposed of by Mr. Davis' will. Plainly it was not. No additional sanctity attaches to this trust because as to the property vested in the same trustee by Mr. Davis during his lifetime it had duties enforceable either in a court of equity or to the performance of which it was bound by contract. No multiplication of words or refinement can alter the result above stated — that Davis had by this plan sought " prospectively to create for himself the power to dispose " of property vested in him at the time of his death by instruments not executed in accordance with the statute of wills.

It seems equally clear to us that this case does not fall within the rule which permits a testator to determine to some degree the objects of his testamentary bounty by his own subsequent conduct, as, for instance, in cases of gifts to servants in the employ of the testator at his decease, or to surviving partners, or to the persons or institutions caring for the testator in his last sickness. It is, of course, true that the volition of the testator as to who shall be his servants or partners, or final attendants, is a factor in selecting the objects of his testamentary bounty. But it is not the only factor. The volition and acts of such legatees are also factors in determining whether the designated relationship shall or shall not exist at the time of the testator's death. There is a great practical as well as legal difference between such relationship — arising " in the ordinary course of his affairs or in the management of his property " — and a relationship which arises solely out of the bounty-giving volition of the testator.

. . . The result is that, on principle and authority, we find ourselves constrained to conclude that the residue of the personal property of Theodore M. Davis, held by the respondent Trust Company, is . . . held under a resulting trust for the plaintiffs. . . .

BINGHAM, C. J. (dissenting). As I understand the law, it is that an extraneous fact referred to in a will by which the intended object or objects of a testator's bounty may be identified can be shown in evidence to make certain those objects, and that this is so, even though the extraneous fact referred to may be the result of a future act of the testator, provided that future act is one of a business nature and has reason for its existence apart from any disposition of the property under the will. It cannot be said in this case that the deposit of securities of the value of $2,000,000 by Mr. Davis with the Trust Company was not a business transaction and did not have pertinency in itself, apart from any disposition of property made by him in his will.

MERRILL v. BOAL.

SUPREME COURT OF RHODE ISLAND, 1926.

47 R. I. 274, 132 A. 721.

[The will and trust which are the subject matter of the preceding case are here again in litigation.]

RATHBUN, J. The above entitled cases were tried together by a justice of the Superior Court sitting without a jury. The cases were before said court on appeal from a decree of the Probate Court of the city of Newport denying the petitions filed by said Merrill and Bugnon respectively to have a certain written instrument in the form of a trust deed from Theodore M. Davis, late of said Newport, deceased, to the Rhode Island Hospital Trust Company, admitted to probate as a part of his will in so far as said instrument affected the disposition of his property after his death. Each case is before us on the appellant's exception to the decision of said justice dismissing the appeal and also on the exception of appellees — although said decision was in their favor — to certain rulings and a finding of said justice.

It appears that in the summer of 1911 said Davis arranged with the Rhode Island Hospital Trust Company for the latter to manage a portion of his property under a trust agreement which was afterwards reduced to writing by the attorney for the Trust Company. The written agreement, which is the instrument in question, conferred upon the Trust Company as trustee broad powers for the management and control of such securities and property as he should deliver to the trustee, and, pursuant to the agreement, he delivered to the Trust Company property of considerable value to be held, managed and finally disposed of in accordance with the terms of the trust agreement. The trust instrument provided that the trustee should pay the income from the trust property to Mr. Davis during his lifetime and, upon his decease, after making certain specified payments and providing for certain annuities for persons named, pay the net income in equal shares to Mr. Davis' wife and another person during their joint lives. The instrument further provides that after the decease of the survivor the trustee shall divide the remainder of the trust estate into as many equal parts as may be necessary, and transfer, pay over, and convey varying specified numbers of said parts to persons named, if respectively living, at Mr. Davis' decease. Mr. Davis' signature to said instrument was witnessed by two witnesses and the appellants contend that the instrument was executed not only with all the formality required by law for executing a will but also with the intention that said instrument should operate in connection with an instrument, hereinafter referred to as the will, to dispose of property which he should leave at his death. The attorney who prepared the trust instrument also drew for Mr. Davis, at the same time, another instrument, bearing the same date, in the form of a will. Said will and trust instrument together purported to dispose of the property, which Mr. Davis should leave at his death, substantially in accordance with a will which was in existence at the time the will and trust instrument in question were being prepared. If resort cannot be had to the trust instrument to ascertain the persons and the shares which they are to take, the whole of the residuary property must pass as intestate estate.

The appellants contend that these two instruments together constitute Mr. Davis' will. It was his intention that both instruments should be executed at the same time but the trust instrument, although in existence bearing his signature when the will was executed, was not witnessed until August 16, 1911, two days after the execution of the will. However, Mr. Davis later added a codicil to the will and the execution of the codicil, of course, amounted to a republication of the will. See In the Goods of Truro, 14 Wkly. Rep. 976, 14 L. T. Rep. N. S. 893. By the ninth clause of the will Mr. Davis referred to the trust instrument by referring to the trust, the terms of which were contained in said instrument. By said clause he gave the residue of his property to the executors or administrators of his estate in trust to reduce to cash as soon as reasonably possible and to pay the net proceeds " to the said Rhode Island Hospital Trust Company to be held, managed and disposed of as a part of the principal of the estate and property held by it in trust for my life and the lives of others in the same manner as though the proceeds of such sales had been deposited by me as a part of said trust estate and property." . . .

Was the instrument executed with the formalities required by the Statute of Wills in force in Rhode Island? . . .

Mr. Davis acknowledged his signature to the instrument in question in the presence of two witnesses, who were present at the same time, and who thereafter at his request, in his presence and in the presence of each other witnessed his said signature. The testimony of the witnesses who testified that said signature was acknowledged and witnessed as above stated was clear and uncontradicted, and it was a question of law whether said signature was witnessed as required by the statute regulating the execution of wills.

Mr. Davis' signature was witnessed by one person who wrote his name to the left of that of Mr. Davis and under the words " In presence of:." The second witness instead of signing as did the first wrote the ordinary acknowledgment clause, signed his name, affixed his official seal and wrote beneath his signature the words " Notary Public." It appears that the acknowledgment of Mr. Davis was taken with his consent but not at his request. His request of the second witness was the same as that of the first. The appellees contend that the second witness, because of his taking the acknowledgment and signing as notary public did not attest and subscribe the will as required by § 4303, G. L. 1923.

Said § 4303 provides that, " no form of attestation shall be necessary." Was the second person signing any less a witness because he did more than was required by statute? What he did was to sign his name with his official title and certify that Mr. Davis personally appeared before him; that Mr. Davis was known to him and known by him " to be the person executing the foregoing instrument and acknowledged the same to be his free act and deed." The authorities hold that if a person who is called upon to witness a will attaches to the instrument his official certificate of the maker's acknowledgment of the due execution thereof such unnecessary acts are mere surplusage and do not affect the validity of his signature as a witness to the will. . . .

It is contended by the appellees that the instrument was not executed *animo testandi*.

It must be admitted that said instrument was intended to, and did, create a valid *inter vivos* trust operating in *praesenti* and that the instrument does not refer to the residuary estate mentioned in the will. The will, however, does refer to the trust instrument, indirectly we admit, but with sufficient clearness so that there is, and can be, no question as to the identity of the instrument which the testator had in mind, and the will directs that the residue of the property mentioned in the will be reduced to cash and paid to the Trust Company to be finally distributed in accordance with the terms of the residuary clause of the trust instrument. As we have said, the will and the trust instrument were prepared at the same time by the same person and there can be no doubt whatever that Mr. Davis intended that the two instruments should, after his death, operate together to dispose of property left by him at his decease. The two instruments having to all intents and purposes been executed at the same time and each with the required formalities and with the intention that the two should operate together to dispose of property left by the testator at his death, what more is required?

Said § 4303 provides that the testator shall sign the will in the presence of two or more witnesses present at the same time or acknowledge his signature thereto in a like manner " and such witnesses shall attest and shall subscribe the will in the presence of the testator . . . and no other publication shall be necessary." Perhaps it did not occur to Mr. Davis that a part of the trust instrument was a part of his will but he must have known that said instrument was to serve in a dual capacity: First, to provide for the management and distribution of the property which he placed in trust, and second, in pointing out the persons who were to take the residuary estate set out in the will and in determining the shares which they would respectively take. When a person executes at the same time two instruments with the required formalities, and with the intention that the two shall operate together after his decease to dispose of property which he left at death, and the instruments together purport so to do, he has acted *animo testandi*. A person may act *animo testandi* without knowing that he is making a will and it is inmaterial what kind of an instrument he thinks he is making if only he manifests a clear intent to dispose of his property after his decease and observes the statutory formalities. . . .

After examining the two instruments and the facts surrounding their execution the conclusion is unavoidable that the trust instrument, although executed to operate *in praesenti* as to property transferred to the trustee, was executed *animo testandi* as to the residue mentioned in the will. . . .

By the terms of the trust instrument Mr. Davis reserved to himself the right to revoke or modify the trust at any time during his life, or to annul, change or modify " any of the dispositions of income or of principal of my said trust estate." The appellees contend that by reserving the right to change the disposition of income and principal of the trust estate Mr. Davis reserved the right to change without compliance with the Statute of Wills the persons who are to take and the shares which they are to take of the residuary property referred to in the will. We seriously doubt that he had any such intention. It is more probable that he, in making the reservation, was thinking only of the trust estate and the disposition thereof. But having the intention that the two instruments, unless modified, should regulate after his death the disposition of the property left by him at his decease, is it of any importance what his ideas were as to an effective method of modifying either of these instruments so as to change the disposition of the residuary property? Wills are ambulatory, that is subject to revocation or change at the pleasure of the testator and many persons have made wills apparently with the belief that a provision could be stricken out or a new one inserted without complying with the statutory formalities; at least many such attempts to modify wills have been made, but such attempts do not revoke or invalidate the will, and according to the better rule, are entirely ineffectual, provided the original language remains legible. 40 Cyc. 1097, 1196. If a person in making his will attempts by specific terms to reserve the right to change the will without complying with the statutory requirements, such attempted reservation is, of course, ineffectual as a reservation but the will would not, by reason thereof, be invalid. . . .

All of the appellees' exceptions applying to matters involved in our consideration of the causes are overruled. The appellants' exception to the decision of said justice is sustained. . . .[8]

KOENINGER v. TOLEDO TRUST CO.

Court of Appeals of Ohio, Lucas County, 1934.

49 O. App. 490, 197 N. E. 419.

OVERMYER, J. This is an action to construe a will, and comes befor this court on appeal from the common pleas court of Lucas county, where a decree was entered for the defendants, the Toledo Trust Company and others.

On June 1, 1926, the decedent, Gustav Waldner, entered into a contract with the defendant, the Toledo Trust Company, by the terms of which he established a trust fund of which he was to be beneficiary during his lifetime, his widow to be the beneficiary after his death, and his daughter, Lillian W. Koeninger, the plaintiff herein, to be the sole beneficiary after the death of her mother. The

[8] Two of the five justices dissented on the ground that Davis did not execute the trust instrument *animo testandi*.

Toledo Trust Company was named trustee, and the petition alleges that the trust company later acquired title, as trustee, to all the estate of decedent, both real and personal, not specifically disposed of by certain legacies in decedent's will. Contemporaneous with the execution of the trust agreement, the donor transferred to the trustee two notes valued at $15,000. This was the only property transferred to the trustee during the donor's lifetime.

Two days after the execution of the trust agreement the donor executed his will, containing item 3, a residuary devise to the Toledo Trust Company of all the property not previously disposed of, " to be managed and disposed of in accordance with the terms and provisions of a certain trust agreement by and between said Toledo Trust Company and myself, dated June 1, 1926, and known as Trust No. 170." The Toledo Trust Company was named executor of the will.

Nine days after the execution of the will the donor executed a supplementary trust agreement in which he named two new beneficiaries, but in all other respects he specifically ratified and reaffirmed all the provisions of the original agreement of June 1. The controversy arises over the question as to what effect, if any, the execution of the supplemental agreement of June 12 had upon the original agreement of June 1, which had been specifically incorporated into his will on June 3.

It is conceded by plaintiff that the original trust agreement of June 1 was properly incorporated in the will by reference, but plaintiff claims that said original agreement of June 1 was discharged and wholly superseded by the execution of the supplemental agreement of June 12, and that since the latter agreement postdated the will, it could not be incorporated therein by reference, and the residuary devise in item 3 of the will failed, and therefore as to all the property which would otherwise pass by the will, Gustav Waldner died intestate, thereby causing the property therein mentioned to vest at once in the plaintiff as the sole heir at law, subject only to her mother's dower rights.

The defendants contend that since the original trust agreement of June 1 became a part of the will by incorporation therein, the testamentary trust was not affected by the execution of the supplementary agreement of June 12, since the latter agreement was not executed in conformity with the statute of wills. . . .

The plaintiff . . . relies largely on the case of Atwood *v*. Rhode Island Hospital Trust Co. (C. C. A. 275 F. 513, 521, 24 A. L. R. 156, the clause in testator's will in that case containing this language:

" I give the residue of my estate to said Trust Company to be disposed of to such persons and in such proportions *as I may have instructed or shall hereafter instruct said Trust Company.*" [9]

[9] This is slippery work with quotation marks. The quoted sentence is not what the testator provided in his will (which is Paragraph Ninth appearing at the end of the statement of facts in the Atwood Case, supra) but is the argu-

It does not attempt to incorporate in the will any definite existing document, as does the will in the case at bar. In the Atwood Case that clause was properly held void because it did not contain a definitely ascertainable disposition of the property sought to be devised. The court there specifically found that the will " does not incorporate by reference any existing trust instrument." In fact, an examination of the will in the Atwood Case fails to show any reference to any existing document, and leads to the conclusion that if there had been an incorporation by reference a different conclusion would have been reached.

. . . Having in mind the primary purpose of seeking the true intention of the testator, and of carrying into effect that intention so far as the law permits, we are of opinion that the finding and judgment of the court of common pleas were correct. The provision in the supplementary trust agreement directing the transfer of ten acres of land to the donor's nephew, Gustav H. Eppler, which land passed to the trustee by devise in the will, is therefore ineffective and void. The provision in said supplementary trust agreement directing the payment of $500 to the donor's nephew, John G. Eppler, after the death of donor and his wife, is valid, but that sum can be paid only out of the property transferred by Gustav Waldner during his lifetime to the trustee under the trust agreement.

It is true the original trust agreement reserved the right to alter, change, or extend that agreement, but when the donor carried that trust agreement into his will he waived this right if not done by an instrument complying with the statute of wills. It was the manifest intention of Gustav Waldner to provide for his widow a safe and comfortable income during her life, and, at her death, the daughter, plaintiff herein, was to be the sole beneficiary. This was entirely natural and regular. His first trust agreement and his will make full, clear, and unmistakable provisions for the natural objects of his bounty. After the trust agreement and the will were executed he evidently felt that his two nephews should have been rememberd, and he thereupon undertook to modify his will, which included the trust agreement, by modifying the trust agreement, which, if the will had not intervened, he would have had a legal right to do. The testator, however, could not alter the will by a supplemental agreement which did not comply with the statute of wills. . . .

Having been executed subsequent to the making of the will, and attempting to modify the former trust agreement which had already been incorporated in his will, the supplemental trust agreement, not complying with the statute of wills, must fail. . . .

A decree is accordingly entered for the defendants in accordance with the above opinion.[10]

---

mentative paraphrase by Circuit Judge Anderson in the third paragraph of the opinion.

[10] Commented on in 49 Harv. L. Rev. 498 (1936); 21 Corn. L. Q. 492 (1936). See 1 Scott on Trusts (1939 & Supp.) § 54.3.

MATTER OF RAUSCH.

Court of Appeals of New York, 1932.

258 N. Y. 327, 179 N. E. 755.

Cardozo, Ch. J. Herman Rausch left a will dated November 25, 1927, whereby he gave one-fifth of his residuary estate " to the New York Trust Company of New York City, to be held by said Trust Company in trust for the benefit of my daughter Florence Skillings, under the same terms and conditions embodied in the Trust Agreement made between myself and the said New York Trust Company, dated April 15, 1922, the principal to be disposed of as contained in the said agreement, and which agreement is hereby made part of my will, as if fully set forth herein."

The testator's daughter had been judicially declared to be a person of unsound mind and had been committed to an asylum. The trust agreement assigns to the trustee specified shares of stock to be applied to her support. It also states that by a will previously made the grantor has set apart for her use a sixth of his residuary estate, " to be held by the Trustee as an addition to and part of the trust estate hereby created, and the Trustee upon receiving such share of the grantor's residuary estate, shall administer it as a part hereof and as directed in this indenture." Provision is also made for the disposition of the interests in remainder when the trust is at an end. The only change effected by the will of 1927 is to make the share of the residue a fifth instead of a sixth.

The Surrogate held upon objections by the next of kin that the will was valid in all its parts. The Appellate Division reversed, and held that as to a fifth of the residuary estate there had been a violation of the rule forbidding the incorporation of unattested documents, and that the testator to that extent had died intestate. The case is now here upon appeal by the legatees affected.

At the execution of this will there was in existence a valid deed of trust whereby a trustee was under a duty to apply the subject-matter of the grant to uses there declared. All that the later will does is to give additional property to the same trustee to be held in the same way. We are told by the decision below that this may not be done unless the terms of the deed of trust are repeated in the will.

The rule against incorporation, well established though it is, is one that will not be carried to " a drily logical extreme " (Matter of Fowles, 222 N. Y. 222, 233). It is one thing to hold that a testator may not import into his will an unattested memorandum of his mere desires and expectations, his unexecuted plans (Booth v. Baptist Church of Christ, 126 N. Y. 215, 247). It is another thing to hold that he may not effectively enlarge the subject-matter of an existing trust by identifying the trust deed and the extent and nature of the increment. In the view of the law, a corporation as an individual and a corporation as trustee are separate personalities (Collins v. Hydorn, 135 N. Y. 320, 324, 325). What is taken as trustee is taken subject to the trust, for it can be held no other way. A gift to a trust company as trustee of a trust created by a particular deed identifies the trust in describing the trustee, like a gift to a corporation for the uses stated in its charter. Only a quibble will find a difference between a gift to a trust company as trustee under a deed and a gift to the same company with instructions to hold what is given in accordance with the deed. The quibble becomes the more transparent when we recall that by the terms of the deed the trustee had bound itself in advance to accept a sixth of the estate if so directed by the will. The legacy when given was not the declaration of a trust, but the enlargement of the subject-matter of a trust declared already. A philanthropist during his life establishes a foundation as trustee for a specific trust. The mind rebels against the formalism that would invalidate a bequest for no better reason than the omission to state the purpose of the trust again. We do not mean that a gift, though merely one of enlargement, would be held to be effective if the declaration of the trust had been by word of mouth alone. The possibility of fraud or error would be too strong in such circumstances to permit the gift to stand (Reynolds v. Reynolds, 224 N. Y. 429, 431). Even in courts where incorporation is permitted more liberally than it is with us, the reference must be to a document or something equivalent thereto (Wilcox v. Attorney-General, 207 Mass. 198), the document must be in existence at the time of the making of the will, and the tests of identification must be precise and definite (Matter of Shillaber, 74 Cal. 144; Watson v. Hinson, 162 N. C. 72). Here the extrinsic fact, identifying and explaining the gift already made, is as impersonal and enduring as the inscription on a monument.

The books abound in nice distinctions. They are tests to guide the judgment rather than invariable rules or standards. The one most frequently drawn is between documents expressing the terms of the bequest and documents identifying the thing intended to be bequeathed (Hatheway v. Smith, 79 Conn., 506, 519, 521; Booth v. Baptist Church of Christ, supra). We pointed out, however, in the Fowles Case (supra, p. 233) that " the two classes of cases run into each other by almost imperceptible gradations " (citing Langdon v. Astor's Executors, 16 N. Y. 9, 26, 31). To insist upon a will so self-contained and self-sufficient as to make resort to things extrinsic needless in every possible contingency is to lose sight of the significance of language, its function and capacities. " Words," we have said, are " symbols, and we must compare them with things and persons and events " (Matter of Fowles, supra, p. 232). A father bequeaths a legacy to his son by canceling whatever indebtedness appears upon his books. No one doubts the validity of such a gift (Langdon *v.* Astor's Executors, 16 N. Y. 9, 24, 26, 28; Robert *v.* Corning, 89 N. Y. 225, 242), yet to understand the extent of the legacy we must go beyond the will itself. " Signs and symbols " must be turned " into their equivalent realities " (Marks *v.* Cowdin, 226 N. Y. 138, 143). How far the process will be extended is a question of degree (Marks *v.* Cowdin, supra; Matter of Fowles, supra; Doherty *v.* Hill, 144 Mass. 465, 468, 469). We exclude the will that remits us to other words of promise, the expression of a plan or purpose inchoate and imperfect. Another result may follow where by comparison of the description with some " manifest, external, and continuing fact " (Doherty *v.* Hill, supra; Marks *v.* Cowdin, supra) we learn the terms of a regulation that is consummate and subsisting. Much will depend upon the extent to which the door is likely to be opened to chicanery or mistake if there is relaxation of the requirement of a self-sufficient integration. The rule against incorporation is not a doctrinaire demand for an unattainable perfection." It has its limits in the considerations of practical expediency that brought it into being. Here the identification of the donee is itself an expression of the gift, the discovery of the one being equivalent to the ascertainment of the other. . . .

The order of the Appellate Division should be reversed and that of the Surrogate's Court affirmed with costs in the Appellate Division and in this court payable out of the estate.

McKALLIP'S ESTATE.

SUPREME COURT OF PENNSYLVANIA, 1936.

324 Pa. 438, 188 A. 343.

[Margaret J. McKallip executed a will in 1919, giving life interests in income to certain nieces and the principal to certain charities. When about to sail for South America in 1922, the testatrix duly executed a codicil providing as follows: " I leave Ida Crum Campbell authority to change my will according to personal dictation — Boat sailing." The testatrix died in 1925. Thereafter, Ida Crum Campbell executed an instrument in which, after reciting that the testatrix's property was seriously depleted before her death by the embezzlement of a broker and that the testatrix's chief object was to provide an education for her nieces, she purported to exercise the power given her by the will by increasing the value of the interest of the nieces and decreasing the value of the interest of the charities. The orphan's court held that Ida Crum Campbell had a valid power and that she had validly exercised it. The charities appealed.]

DREW, J. . . . Questions upon the validity . . . of "the authority to change my will" are presented by appellants. We think the court below has answered them correctly.

The codicil clearly represents in lay fashion an intention to give a collateral power of appointment — 'an authority to deal with an estate, no interest in which is vested in the donee of the power.' Dickinson v. Teasdale, 1 DeGex, J. & S. 52, 60. When the intention to create a power is plain, it should be given effect; no technical form of words is necessary. Fraeff v. DeTurk, 44 Pa. 527.

Such a collateral power, broad as it is, does not violate our Wills Act (20 P. S. § 181 et seq.) which prescribes exclusive methods for the revocation of wills. This has been held in other jurisdictions with similar statutory limitations. Dudley v. Weinhart, 93 Ky. 401, 20 S. W. 308; Cf. Goods of John Smith, L. R. 1 P. & D. 717. Apparently Illinois stands alone in an opposite view. Zierau v. Zierau, 347 Ill. 82, 179 N. E. 432,[11] with critical comment in 27 Ill. Rev. 297. Nor is the gift of such an authority a delegation of the privilege, personal to each testator, to dispose of property on death. See Meade King v. Warren, 32 Beavan, 111, 116.

Both conclusions just reached follow from the traditional and technical analysis of powers. Originally enforced in equity only, the appointed interests operated as shifting uses and executory devises. The exercise was viewed merely as the event upon which the use went over. See Sugden, Powers (3d. Am. Ed.) xii. Before that event the estates that might be vested by appointment were classed as future or contingent uses created by testator or settlor. See Sugden, supra, 82. After the Statute of Uses, the use thus shifted was at once invested with legal title where the statute applied. The same learning applies to collateral powers allowing the broadest discretion to the donee. See Sugden, supra 108, passim. Thus it is impossible to take the view that the Wills Act (20 P. S. § 181 et seq.) is

---

[11] In this case Testator provided that "My beloved wife shall have the right and power to make any changes and alterations of this my last will and testament after my death (before hers — she sees fit)." The wife exercised the power by filing an instrument declaring the operative paragraphs of the will " revoked and made null and void " and substituting herself as sole legatee. In holding this action ineffectual the court said:

"Such an attempt is in contravention of our statute on wills. (Smith's Stat. 1931, chap. 148, sec. 1.) The right to make a testamentary disposition of one's property is purely statutory, and no authority is conferred by which a testator can legally delegate this right to another. The power to change or alter any or all the provisions of a will is the power to revoke. A testator cannot delegate the power of revoking his will to someone else to execute at his option after the testator's death. (Schouler on Wills, 6th ed., § 589, p. 670.) While living, the testator could not have revoked or changed his will in the manner followed by his widow in her three different attempts, as our statute (Smith's Stat. 1931, chap. 148, § 19) provides that no will, testament or codicil shall be revoked otherwise than by burning, canceling, tearing, or obliterating the same by the testator himself, or in his presence by his direction and consent, or by some other will, etc."

planned to defeat the intention to create a power of appointment. Neither can we say so merely because the result intended is ineptly expressed as an authority to change the will. . . .

Decree affirmed at appellants' cost.

Problem.

T duly executed a will. Then he duly executed a codicil making substantial changes in the gifts of the will. The codicil provided, " I give my wife the option of adding this codicil to my will or not, as she may think proper or necessary." The wife filed an instrument with the probate court declaring that she wished the codicil added. Is this effective? Goods of John Smith, L. R. 1 P. & D. 717 (1869).

CURLEY v. LYNCH.

Supreme Judicial Court of Massachusetts, 1910.

206 Mass. 289, 92 N. E. 429.

[Eugene Lynch died in 1909 leaving a will, executed January 19, 1909, which provided that a considerable portion of his estate should pass to trustees in trust to pay the income to his wife Mary for life. Then at his wife's death said property " shall be, as soon as practicable, paid and delivered free and discharged from any and all trusts under this my will, as my wife shall in and by her last will and testament devise and bequeath the same." Mary predeceased her husband by three days. She left a will, executed January 15, 1909, containing a residuary clause as follows: " All the rest of my property . . . I give, devise and bequeath to my nieces and nephews, there being seven in number." The question of the effect of these wills was presented by a bill in equity before the single justice of the Supreme Judicial Court and was by him reserved for determination by the full bench.]

Sheldon, J. The provisions made by Eugene Lynch in his will for the benefit of his wife lapsed and became of no effect by reason of her decease in his lifetime. . . . And the power of appointment given to her fell with the life estate which preceded it. That power did not and could not come into existence until the death of Lynch himself. And as his wife, the only person who could have exercised the power, was dead before that time, the power itself never came into existence. It is as if no such power had been created by the will of Lynch. . . .

If we assume that the language of Mrs. Lynch's will could be regarded as an exercise of the power which she would have had under her husband's will if she had survived him,[12] then we may also assume that the mere fact of her appointment having preceded the creation of the power under which it was made would not have prevented it from taking effect. . . . But the difficulty here is not a mere question of time; it goes deeper than that. Mrs. Lynch never enjoyed a power of appointment at all. In all the cases above referred to the power was vested in its donee when his appointment took effect. But here there could be no power in existence until the husband's death, and there never was a time when Mrs. Lynch had any such power vested in her. It follows that any attempted appointment by her was a mere nullity.

But it has been contended that Eugene Lynch adopted the provisions of his wife's will and by reference incorporated them into his own will. Dexter v. Harvard College, 176 Mass. 192. Allen v. Boomer, 82 Wis. 364. Goods of Limerick, 2 Rob. Eccl. 313. Undoubtedly he might have done so, as it appears that his will was made after hers and with knowledge of its contents. Nor do we doubt that it was competent to prove these facts. But his language, even considered in the light of these facts, falls far short of the effect contended for. The words that he used were that the fund should " be, as soon as practicable, paid and delivered free and discharged from any and all trusts under this my will, as my wife shall in and by her last will and testament devise and bequeath the same." These words refer unmistakably to whatever last will his wife should leave at her decease, whenever she might execute it, and not solely to the will which, as he knew, she had then executed, but which until her death was still ambulatory, and could be altered or revoked as she might choose. He made no reference in terms to that particular will. This was not a reference in clear and precise terms to an existing document plainly and specifically identified; it was the creation of a general power which his wife might exercise by any future will. He did not restrict his bounty to the particular beneficiaries whom she had already named; he intended that this part of his estate should go to those to whom she might in future appoint it by any new and final will that she might make. He did not seek to incorporate into his own will the specific provisions which he had read in hers. The industry of counsel has referred us to a multitude of decisions upon this subject; but we know of none which could be wrested into a support of the contention that has been made. . . .

In accordance with the terms of the report, a decree is to be entered instructing the petitioners that Mrs. Lynch took no valid power of appointment under the will of her husband, and did not by her will make a valid appointment of any part of his estate, and that her nephews and nieces do not under his and her wills take any interest

[12] See Amory v. Meredith, 7 Allen 397 (Mass. 1863), Leach, Cases on Future Interests (1935) 714.

in his estate, but that the part of his estate which would have been at his wife's disposal if she had survived him must go to his next of kin as intestate estate.[13]

MATTER OF FOWLES.

COURT OF APPEALS OF NEW YORK, 1918.

222 N. Y. 222, 118 N. E. 611.

CARDOZO, J. The will of Charles Frederick Fowles, made on April 29, 1915, is before us for construction. By the second article of the will he gave to his wife, Frances May Fowles, $5,000. By the fourth article he gave her the contents of his estate "Fairmile Court." By the eighth article he gave his residuary estate to trustees . . . 22½ per cent of the entire residue was to be paid by the trustees "pursuant to the provisions of such last will and testament as my said wife may leave (hereby conferring upon my said wife the power to dispose of the said one-half by last will and testament duly executed by her)." If she failed to execute the power, the corpus was to be held in trust for his daughters by a former wife, with remainder to their children. To them also were given upon like trusts, and with like remainders, the other shares of the residue. [The Surrogate ruled that 22½ per cent of the residue passed to the executor of Frances May Fowles to be distributed in accordance with her will. The Appellate Division reversed this order.]

The controversy grows out of the ninth article which reads as follows: "In the event that my said wife and myself should die simultaneously or under such circumstances as to render it impossible or difficult to determine who predeceased the other, I hereby declare it to be my Will that it shall be deemed that I shall have predeceased my said wife, and that this my Will and any and all its provisions shall be construed on the assumption and basis that I shall have predeceased my said wife."

Husband and wife were lost at sea on May 7, 1915, with the steamship Lusitania. There is nothing to show which was the survivor. The wife left a will made at the same time as the husband's. She recites the power of appointment, and undertakes to execute it. She gives her residuary estate (including the property affected by the power) to trustees for the use of a sister during life with remainder over. Whether this gift in its application to the husband's estate is made valid and effective by the ninth article of his will is the chief question to be determined.

[13] *Contra,* Murchison *v.* Wallace, 156 Va. 728, 159 S. E. 106 (1931); 3 Restatement of Property, § 348, Comment f. On the same subject but not exactly in point are Condit *v.* De Hart, 62 N. J. L. 78, 40 A. 776 (1898); Matter of Piffard, 111 N. Y. 410, 18 N. E. 718 (1888); In re Baker [1934] W. N. 94.

Of his intention, there can be no doubt. In that, we all agree. He was about to set sail with his wife upon a perilous journey. He knew that disaster was possible. He knew that if death came, there would be no presumption to whom it had come first (Newell *v.* Nichols, 75 N. Y. 78; St. John *v.* Andrews Institute, 117 App. Div. 698; 191 N. Y. 254). He told the courts what he wished them to do if all other tests of truth should fail. They were to distribute his estate as they would if his wife were the survivor. We cannot know whether she was in truth the survivor or not: there is no break in the silence and obscurity of those last hours. The very situation which was foreseen has thus arisen. If intention is the key to the problem, the solution is not doubtful. We are now asked to hold that under the law of the state of New York, a testator may not lawfully declare that a power executed by one who dies under such conditions shall be valid to the same extent as if there were evidence of survivorship.

Two rules of law are supposed to stand in the way. One is the rule that a power created by will lapses if the donee dies before the will takes effect. The other is the rule that wills must be executed in compliance with statutory formalities, and are not to be enlarged or diminished by reference to extrinsic documents which may not be authentic. A testator is not permitted at his pleasure to violate these rules. He does violate them, it is said, by indirection, if he may dispense with evidence of survivorship and still sustain the gift which purports to execute the power. If the wife had survived a single second, the gift would certainly be valid. That would be so though she had signed her will while her husband was yet alive and before the power took effect (Stone *v.* Forbes, 189 Mass. 163, 168; Airey *v.* Bower, 12 A. C. 263; Hirsch *v.* Bucki, 162 App. Div. 659, 665). It is possible that she did survive, but it is also possible that she did not. The latter possibility, it is said, renders the gift void. We do not think it does.

It is true that a power created by will lapses if the donee of the power dies before the maker of the will (Curley *v.* Lynch, 206 Mass. 289; Sugden on Powers [8th ed.], 460; Farwell on Powers [2d ed.], p. 226). That is because a will has no effect till the death of the testator. Whatever power it creates, comes into being at that time. But to say this, does not answer the question before us. The question is not whether this power of appointment lapsed. The question is whether the testator has avoided the consequences of a lapse. More concretely, it is whether the law permits him to provide that if the donee's survivorship is incapable of proof, he will give his estate none the less to whomever she has named. That is what this testator said, not in words, but in effect. . . . One obstacle, and one only, can be thought of. That is the rule against the incorporation of extrinsic documents, testamentary in character but not themselves authenticated in accordance with the statute. It is said that this rule is violated when a testator, to keep a power alive, ratifies its execution, adopts the will which executes it as his own, and thus in effect averts a lapse. We do not share that view.

Everything that this testator did is justified by our decision in Matter of Piffard (111 N. Y. 410, 414, 415).[14] The distinction between that case and this is purely verbal. There is none in substance. In that case the testator authorized his daughter to dispose of a share of his estate by will. If she died before him, leaving a will in execution of the power, he directed his executors to transfer the share to her executors or trustees. We upheld the validity of that provision. We said that it might not be "possible to sustain the power of appointment as such." We held, however, that the daughter's will might be referred to "not as transferring the property by an appointment, but to define and make certain the persons to whom and the proportions in which the one-fifth should pass by the father's will in case of the death of the daughter in his lifetime." There was a like decision upon like facts in Condit v. De Hart (62 N. J. L. 78). . . .

The rule against incorporation has not been set aside. It has been kept within bounds which were believed to be wise and just. The rule is sometimes spoken of as if its content had been defined by statute, as if the prohibition were direct and express, and not inferential and implied. But the truth is that it is the product of judicial construction. Its form and limits are malleable and uncertain. We must shape them in the light of its origin and purpose. All that the statute says is that a will must be signed, published and attested in a certain way (Decedent Estate Law, § 21; Consol. Laws, ch. 13). From this the consequence is deduced that the testator's purpose must be gathered from the will, and not from other documents which lack the prescribed marks of authenticity (Booth v. Baptist Church of Christ, 126 N. Y. 215, 247). It is a rule designed as a safeguard against fraud and mistake. In the nature of things, there must be exceptions to its apparent generality. Some reference to matters extrinsic is inevitable. Words are symbols, and we must compare them with things and persons and events (4 Wigmore on Ev. § 2470). It is a question of degree (Langdon v. Astor's Executors, 16 N. Y. 9, 26, 31; Robert v. Corning, 89 N. Y. 225, 242). Sometimes the distinction is said to be between documents which express the gift and documents which identify it (Hathaway v. Smith, 79 Conn. 519, 521; Booth v. Baptist Church of Christ, supra). But

[14] In Matter of Piffard T's will bequeathed a share of his estate to his daughters. A codicil provided as follows (omitting unnecessary words): "I direct that my daughters, Sarah and Ann, shall have power by their wills heretofore or hereafter executed, to dispose of the share of my estate bequeathed to them in my will; and to that end I direct that such share shall be paid to the executors or trustees named in and by the several wills of my said daughters in case of the death of them, or either of them, in my lifetime, instead of to my said daughter or daughters."

the two classes of cases run into each other by almost imperceptible gradation (Langdon *v.* Astor's Executors, supra). One may ratify assumptions of power, extinguish debts, wipe out wrongs, confirm rights, by the directions of one's will (Bizzey *v.* Flight, L. R. 3 Ch. Div. 269; 1 Jarman on Wills, 99). In these and other cases, the expressions of the gift and the description of its subject-matter must often coalesce. No general formula can tell us in advance where the line of division is to be drawn.

It is plain, therefore, that we are not to press the rule against incorporation to " a drily logical extreme " (Noble State Bank *v.* Haskell, 219 U. S. 104, 110). We must look in each case to the substance. We must consider the reason of the rule, and the evils which it aims to remedy. But as soon as we apply that test, the problem solves itself. There is here no opportunity for fraud or mistake. There is no chance of foisting upon this testator a document which fails to declare his purpose. He has not limited his wife to any particular will. Once identify the document as *her* will; it then becomes his own. He authorizes her to act, and confirms her action (Condit *v.* De Hart, supra, 62 N. J. L. 78). For the purpose of the rule against incorporation, the substance of the situation is thus the same as it always is when a will creates a power. The substance is that a power which would otherwise have lapsed, has been kept alive by the declaration that its execution, however premature, is ratified and approved. But the execution of a power does not violate the rule against incorporation. It can make no difference for that purpose whether the execution is authorized in advance or made valid by relation. There is no greater impairment in the one case than in the other of the principle of the integrity and completeness of testamentary expression. The source of title may be in one case the appointment, and in the other the confirmatory will. But if we go beneath the form and reach realities, the truth is that under the sanction of the will, a power has been executed. That is the principle which underlies the ruling in Matter of Piffard and Condit *v.* De Hart. We reaffirm it now. To hold that the purpose of this testator has been adequately or inadequately declared according to the accident of time at which death came to him or his wife in the depths of the ocean, is to follow the rule against incorporation with blind and literal adherence, forgetful of its origin, its purpose, and its true and deep significance. . . .

The order of the Appellate Division should be reversed and the decree of the Surrogate's Court affirmed with costs in the Appellate Division and in this court to be paid out of the estate.

CRANE, J. (dissenting). . . . The eighth clause of the will does not refer to any specific or existing will of his wife, according to which this part of the residuary estate is to pass, but has reference to the last will which she might make. Thus if she had survived him she could have changed her will as often as she pleased. Even in those states which do not follow our law, but have adopted the English doctrine of incorporation by reference, these facts would not justify reading Mrs. Fowles' will into that of her husband. (Curley *v.* Lynch, 206 Mass. 289). [Two others of the seven judges also dissented.] [15]

PROBLEM.

1. T dies in 1939 leaving a will executed in 1937 which provides, "I devise Blackacre to such person as A shall by will appoint, whether or not A survives me." A's will provides, "I appoint to B the property over which T's will has given or shall give to me the right of appointment." Is B entitled to get Blackacre,
   a. if A's will was executed in 1938 and A dies in 1940?
   b. if A's will was executed in 1938 and A dies in 1938?
   c. if A's will was executed in 1936 and A dies in 1940?
   d. if A's will was executed in 1936 and A dies in 1938?

See 3 Restatement of Property § 348, Comment f.

PRESIDENT & DIRECTORS OF MANHATTAN CO. *v.* JANOWITZ

SUPREME COURT, SPECIAL TERM, NEW YORK, 1939.

APPELLATE DIVISION, SECOND DEPARTMENT, NEW YORK, 1940.

[Janowitz, the testator, executed a revocable and amendable trust in 1933. The property was worth $392,000 in 1933 and $306,000 at Janowitz's death in 1937. In his will, executed in 1935, he left the bulk of his $131,000 estate to the trustee of the 1933 instrument to be administered as part of the trust. He amended the trust four times: twice before the date of his will, a third time on the date of his will

---

[15] Another married couple who perished in the Lusitania disaster were Victor and Rheta Shields of Cincinnati. It became important to determine which survived the other because (a) Victor's life insurance passed to Rheta only if she survived him and (b) each was the sole beneficiary of the other's will. Victor's survivorship was established with considerable ingenuity. Rheta's body was never found and there was no evidence that she was seen again after the torpedo struck. Victor's body was recovered in a life belt at sea 71 days after the disaster. It was identified by dental work, tailor's marks and engravings on his watch. Evidence was obtained that Victor finished his lunch at 2:10 p.m., 10 minutes before the torpedo struck. An autopsy showed (a) that his stomach contained a meal which had undergone 3 to 4 hours of the digestive process and (b) that the lungs still contained air. From this it was deduced that death came from exposure, not drowning, and occurred between 5 and 6 p.m. 57 Am. L. Rev. 911 (1923).

See Tracy & Adams, "Evidence of Survivorship in Common-Disaster Cases," 38 Mich. L. Rev. 801 (1940).

but delivering the amendment to the trustee some hours after the execution of the will, and a fourth time two months after the will. The amendments are not stated in detail, but they appear not to have altered the basic scheme of distribution of the original trust.

The widow and children of the testator now contend that the will is invalid so far as the above provisions are concerned.]

ALDRICH, J. [Supreme Court, Special Term] . . . The Rausch case is controlling here on the general validity of the provision of the will. . . . As to the first two amendatory instruments, both of which were executed and duly delivered to the trustee prior to the date of the will, it seems clear that these are to be regarded as a lawful part of the disposition to be made under the will by virtue of the trust indenture. The fourth amendatory instrument which was executed and delivered subsequent to the date of the execution of the will cannot be included without an extension of the doctrine of incorporation beyond any limit presently indicated by the decisions of the Court of Appeals. As to that particular instrument it will be adjudged that for the purposes of a distribution under the will it is of no effect. The third amendatory instrument presents a more troublesome problem. . . . Its execution by the donor and its subsequent delivery on the same day to the trustee are conclusively established. To deny effect to such instrument under the circumstances would be to carry the rule against incorporation to " a drily logical extreme." To summarize, it will be adjudged that the will is valid and that thereunder the [property bequeathed to the trustee] passes under the indenture of trust as modified by the three first amendatory instruments. . . .

JOHNSTON, J. [Appellate Division, Second Department] Matter of Rausch is an exception to the well-settled rule in this State against incorporation by reference. That case, however, must be limited to its own peculiar facts. There the trust agreement was in existence at the time the will was executed. Here . . . the third supplemental indenture did not become effectual until after the will was executed, and the fourth supplemental indenture did not come into existence until approximately two months after the will was executed. There the trust agreement was unamendable and irrevocable. Here the trust indenture is amendable and revocable. . . . To permit the incorporation of the trust indenture, as amended, would allow the testator to alter his will by an instrument not published and attested as required by the Statute of Wills. The statute may not be so circumvented. Moreover, if the property is to pass under the original and three supplemental indentures, as the court below has decreed, then the purpose and intention of the testator is frustrated because he intended that his property should be disposed of as provided in the original and four supplemental indentures. . . .

Nor may [the will] be upheld on the ground that the trust indenture and its amendments were facts of such independent significance, apart from their effect upon the disposition of the property devised and bequeathed by the will, that they might be referred to for the purpose of determining the terms of the intended testamentary trust. The reservation of power to amend the trust indenture and its repeated exercise eliminated all independent significance that might be attached to the trust indenture. . . .[16]

[16] Commented on in 39 Col. L. Rev. 1256 (1939); 26 Cornell L. Q. 172 (1940); 3 U. of Detroit L. J. 103 (1940); 10 Fordham L. Rev. 82 (1941); 29 Georgetown L. J. 797 (1941); 25 Minn. L. Rev. 254 (1941); 18 N. Y. U. L. Q. 284 (1941); 50 Yale L. J. 342 (1940).

CHAPTER V.

REVOCATION OF WILLS.

Revocation by physical act to the testamentary document. The usual problems concerning the revocation of wills arise out of amateur attempts to revoke. An old man on his death bed tells his housekeeper to throw his will in the fire; she does, but someone else snatches it off before there is any substantial burning.[1] Or the testator crosses out a word here and a clause there and tears a paragraph off the bottom of one page.[2] Or he writes on the back of the will, " I hereby cancel this will." [3] Whether or not there is a revocation in whole or in part under such circumstances depends upon a meticulous interpretation of the local statute. The statutes are usually based on the English Statute of Frauds (which declared that a will could be revoked by " burning, canceling, tearing, or obliterating ") or the English Wills Act (which prescribed " burning, tearing, or otherwise destroying "). Nice questions of statutory construction arise (e.g. Does the phrase " *otherwise* destroying " in the Wills Act require the " burning " to amount to destruction?), but a study of them is not profitable. They can be studied when, as and if they arise in practice. For no lawyer, if consulted, would think of advising a testator to rely upon a revocation by physical act to the testamentary document.

Revocation by subsequent instrument. All statutes allow a will to be revoked by a subsequent will or codicil and nearly all permit such revocation by an instrument which performs no other function than to revoke, provided that the formalities required of a will are complied with.[4] The mere fact that an instrument is entitled " Last Will and Testament " does not necessarily constitute a revocation of a previous will though, of course, the prior will is superseded to whatever extent the subsequent will makes inconsistent dispositions. There should be an express clause revoking all previous wills and codicils if that is the intention of the testator. Or, if the intention is otherwise, there should be an express clause providing exactly what instruments exist and how far they are to be considered as still effective.

[1] See Doe dem. Reed *v.* Harris, 6 Ad. & El. 209 (1837).
[2] See Bigelow *v.* Gillott, 123 Mass. 102 (1877); Miles's Appeal, 68 Conn. 237 (1896); Lovell *v.* Quitman, 88 N. Y. 377 (1882).
[3] Will of Ladd, 60 Wis. 187 (1884).
[4] Bordwell, "Statute Law of Wills," 14 Iowa L. Rev. at 286 (1920).

Protection against spurious revocations. The fact that a will *can* be revoked by destruction or mutilation of the document raises a difficulty. Suppose the testator dies and either his will is not found at all or it is found torn in pieces. If the will is merely lost, it can be probated if its contents can be established; if someone other than the testator destroyed or mutilated it, the same is true. But how is it to be determined whether the will is lost or destroyed and, if the latter, who destroyed it? In the absence of direct evidence, there is a presumption of revocation if the will is found mutilated among the testator's effects or if the will is not found at all but was last seen in the testator's custody.[5] The possibilities of knavery in this situation are obvious. Any lawyer who draws a will for his client should advise him (a) to make any change or revocation of his will only by subsequent instrument under legal advice, (b) to put his will in such a place that no unauthorized person can lay hands on it during his life or after his death. In most states there is a provision for the deposit of wills with the probate court during the life of the testator.[6] Such deposit is an excellent protection against accident and fraud and should be advised.

Intent to revoke. An effective revocation requires (a) a specified act, i.e. either a physical mutilation of the document or the execution of a revoking instrument, plus (b) an intent to revoke. All statutes declare in terms that mutilation is effective to revoke only if done " with the intention of revoking." The act without the intent is of no avail.

PROBLEM.

1. T's house was destroyed by fire. His will was in a desk drawer in the house and was also destroyed. After the fire someone mentioned to him that his will was gone. He replied, " I'm glad it's gone. I was going to tear it up anyway." Is the will revoked? Parsons *v.* Balson, 129 Wis. 311, 109 N. W. 136 (1906); Cutler *v.* Cutler, 130 N. C. 1, 86 S. E. 301 (1915); Clingan *v.* Mitcheltree, 31 Pa. 25 (1856).

A still more difficult set of problems involving the intent to revoke constitutes the subject matter of the doctrine of " Dependent Relative Revocation " with which the following cases are concerned.[7]

[5] Atkinson, Wills (1937) 375.
[6] E.g. Mass. Gen. Laws (Ter. ed. 1932) c. 191, § 10.
[7] See generally articles on " Dependent Relative Revocation," by Joseph Warren, 33 Harv. L. Rev. 337 (1920); Cornish, 5 So. Calif. L. Rev. 273 (1932); Evans, 16 Ky. L. J. 251 (1928); Bernstein, 7 U. S. C. Selden Soc. Y. B. 48 (1943).

ONIONS v. TYRER.

Court of Chancery, 1717.
2 Vern. 742.

Mr. Tyrer, in 1707, made a will, duly attested by three subscribing witnesses, and thereby had disposed of his real estate, and being afterwards minded to make some alteration in his will, in the year 1711 he made a second will touching his real estate, and with a clause in it revoking all former wills; but there being no table in the room where the testator lay sick and subscribed his will, the three subscribing witnesses did not attest it in his presence, but went into a lower room out of the testator's sight, and there wrote their names as witnesses to the publishing this latter will; and it was also in proof in the cause that he called for [the 1707 will] and directed his wife to cancel it, and the witness swore she heard her tear it; and the question now was, whether the former will was well revoked, or not.

Lord Chancellor [Lord Cowper] was of opinion, that the former will stood good; for the latter will being void, and not operating as a will, would not amount to a revocation; and as to the actual cancelling of the former will, it is plain he did it only upon a supposition that he had made a latter will at the same time, and both wills as to the main, were much to the same effect, and with little variation as to the disposition of the real estate; and in case it had been a good cancelling of the will at law, it ought to be relieved against, and the will set up again in equity, under the head of accident, and decreed it accordingly.

POWELL v. POWELL.

Probate and Divorce Division, 1866.
L. R. 1 P. & D. 209.

Walter Powell died on the 18th of June, 1865. He executed a will on the 3rd of March, 1862, by which he left all his property to his grandson, Edward Burfoot Powell, the plaintiff, whom he appointed his executor, and another will on the 29th of March, 1864, by which he revoked all former wills, and bequeathed all his property to his nephew Walter Powell, whom he appointed his executor. This latter will he destroyed in the early part of the year 1865, and under the circumstances connected with its destruction there arose a question on the doctrine of dependent relative revocations. . . .

Mrs. Elizabeth Willis deposed, that early in 1865, the testator, whose housekeeper she was, seemed disturbed in his mind, and on her inquiring the cause, he said he was not easy in his mind about the last will he had made, leaving his property to his nephew, Mr. Walter Powell; that one day he got out two or three wills, and asked her to read them to him, and as she could not read very well, he called in the charwoman, who read the wills of 1862 and 1864 to him; that he then placed the will of 1862 under his arm, and said that was the will he intended to stand, and he tore the will of 1864, which was, by his request, put into the fire and burnt in his presence. [The belief of the testator, that by destroying the 1864 will he thereby revived the 1862 will, was erroneous. Section 22 of the Wills Act provides that "no will . . . which shall be in any manner revoked, shall be revived otherwise than by the re-execution thereof, or by a codicil executed in manner hereinbefore required."]

SIR J. P. WILDE. . . . I conceive that the doctrine of dependent relative revocation properly applies to facts such as this case involves. This doctrine is based on the principle that all acts by which a testator may physically destroy or mutilate a testamentary instrument are in the nature equivocal. They may be the result of accident, or, if intentional, of various intentions. It is, therefore, necessary in each case to study the act done by the light of the circumstances under which it occurred, and the declarations of the testator with which it may have been accompanied. For unless it be done *animo revocandi*, it is no revocation. What, then, if the act of destruction be done with the sole intention of setting up and establishing some other testamentary paper, for which the destruction of the paper in question was only designed to make way? It is clear that in such case the *animus revocandi* had only a conditional existence, the condition being the validity of the paper intended to be substituted, and such has been the course of decision in the various cases quoted in argument. But then it is said, that this method of reasoning has only hitherto been applied to cases in which the destruction of the script has accompanied the execution of the instrument intended in substitution; and that no decided case can be found in which the instrument intended to be established has been a long previously executed paper. But I fail to perceive a distinction in principle between the two cases. For what does it matter whether a testator were to say, "I tear this will of 1860 because I have this day (1st of January, 1861) executed another designed to replace it"; or, "I tear this will of 1860 because I desire and expect that the effect of my so doing will be to set up my old will of 1840?" In either case, the revocatory act is based on a condition, which the testator imagines is fulfilled. In both cases the act is referable, not to any abstract intention to revoke, but to an intention to validate another paper; and as in neither case is the sole condition upon which revocation was intended fulfilled, in neither is the *animus revocandi* present. It is only necessary to add that, in the above observations, it has been assumed that the act of destruction was referable, wholly and solely, to the intention of setting up some other testamentary paper. And such was, I think, upon the evidence given in this case, the reasonable conclusion of fact. Cases may, and probably will, arise in which the intention is either mixed or ambiguous, and such are for future consideration. The only case cited that requires special mention is that of Dickinson v. Swatman. [30 L. J. (P. M. & A.) 84.] But Sir C. Cresswell, in that case, does not appear to have been satisfied that the sole intention in destroying was to set up the previous will. He is reported to have said, " At all events, to make it a case of dependent relative revocation, you would have to shew that he did not intend to revoke the second will unless by doing so the first would have been revived."

The Court pronounces, therefore, for the will of the 29th of March, 1864, as contained in the draft thereof produced and sworn to by Mr. Newman, the attorney who made it.

The costs of all parties out of estate.

IN RE BERNARD'S SETTLEMENT.

CHANCERY DIVISION, 1916.

[1916] 1 Ch. 552.

[Under a marriage settlement Mary Bernard had a special testamentary power of appointment among her children. The settlement contained a gift in default of appointment to the children equally. There were born to Mary three sons and six daughters. By her will, dated February 3, 1877, she appointed the fund to her six daughters equally and bequeathed to each daughter a pecuniary legacy and a share of the residue of her estate. By a third codicil, dated April 28, 1898, she purported to change the appointment and gifts to her daughter Margaret. By way of preamble the codicil read, " Whereas I am desirous that the share of my said daughter Margaret Bernard of and in the said settled funds and the said legacies and share of my residuary property or the income thereof shall not be paid or transferred to her but be held upon the trusts for her benefit hereinafter declared. . . ." She thereupon declared that she revoked the appointments and the gifts to Margaret and appointed and gave the same amounts to trustees in trust to apply the income, or such part thereof as the trustees should determine, to the support of Margaret for her life and upon Margaret's death to pay the principal and accumulations to such of Margaret's sisters as should survive her. The appointment in remainder and the discretionary trust as to income during the life of Margaret are obviously void under the Rule against Perpetuities.[8]]

[8] To understand the Perpetuities points you should read, infra, from the middle of page 215 to the middle of page 218. Be sure you understand Case 30 (p. 216) and Case 32 (p. 217).

NEVILLE, J. . . . The important question arises whether under those circumstances the invalidity of the appointment in the codicil destroys the appointment that had been made in favour of the plaintiff by the will, or whether under the circumstances, having regard to the intention of the testatrix and her attempted exercise of the power in the codicil failing, the valid earlier exercise of the power by the will is operative. . . . I think the question which the Court has to determine is, Did the testator intend by the second appointment to revoke in any case the prior appointment, or did he really only intend to revoke it for the purpose of carrying out the alteration made in his second appointment and without having any intention of revoking the previous gift except for the purpose of the altered appointment? Turning to the case before me, I think the intention of the appointor is reasonably clear. The testatrix is dealing with a provision she has made for her daughter. In the first instance she has given her an equal share with her other daughters in the funds to be appointed. But then she desires to control the provision she has made for her daughter, and I think the recital in the codicil itself indicates the purpose for which the revocation of the previous absolute gift to the daughter was made. She says, " Whereas I am desirous that the share of my said daughter Margaret Bernard of and in the said settled funds and the said legacies and share of my residuary property or the income thereof shall not be paid or transferred to her but be held upon the trusts for her benefit hereinafter declared concerning the same respectively." Now, is not that a clear expression of her intention? She says, in effect, " I am not intending to deprive my daughter altogether of what I have given her, but what I am seeking to do is to ensure that it shall be properly applied for her maintenance." It seems to me that obviously the intention of the testatrix is only to revoke the previous appointment for the purpose of giving effect to the increased security which she thought her daughter would have by the protecting clauses that she has added in the codicil. There is only one thing which does no doubt militate against that view, and that is the gift over upon the death of the daughter. But I do not think that is strong enough to enable me to come to the conclusion that the testatrix intended to revoke her bounty under her previous appointment in all respects and not only for the purpose of giving effect to the substituted provisions in the codicil. I hold, therefore, applying the rule which Lord Romillys lays down, that in this case, the appointment by the third codicil having failed, the original appointment made by the will remains operative.

PROBLEMS.

1. T duly executed a will which in part provided as follows: " I bequeath my bank stock to Rosina. I bequeath $500 to Ralph."

Later T pasted a strip of paper over the word "Rosina" and wrote the word "Mary" on it. He also pasted a strip of paper over the figures "$500" and wrote "$100" on it. Who gets the bank stock? What, if anything, does Ralph get? Ruel *v.* Hardy, 90 N. H. 240, 6 A. (2d) 753 (1939); Locke *v.* James, 11 M. & W. 901 (1843); Goods of Horsford, L. R. 3 P. & D. 211 (1840).

2. T's will provided legacies for the grandchildren of M. T executed a codicil as follows: "I revoke the legacies to the grandchildren of M, they being all dead." One of the grandchildren was still living and survived T. Does the grandchild get his legacy? Campbell *v.* French, 3 Ves. Jr. 321 (1797).

3. T's will provided legacies for the grandchildren of M. T executed a codicil as follows: "I revoke the legacies to the grandchildren of M." M testifies that on the day the codicil was executed she told T that all her grandchildren were dead and that he then said, "Well, then, I had better cancel the legacies to them." One of the grandchildren was still living and survived T. Does the grandchild get his legacy? See Skipworth *v.* Cabell, 19 Grat. 758 (Va. 1870).

4. Burnyeat executed a will bequeathing his residuary estate in trust for his wife for life and then for such of his nephews and nieces as his wife should by will appoint and in default of appointment to his nephews and nieces equally. He then executed a codicil which (1) made his wife's life estate terminable upon her remarriage to any person not a British subject, (2) revoked the power of appointment, (3) directed that after termination of his wife's life estate the trustees should transfer the principal to such of his nephews and nieces as should reach the age of 21. Due to the fact that Burnyeat's mother and father were still living at his death the gift to nephews and nieces in the codicil was held to violate the Rule against Perpetuities. Upon the marriage of Burnyeat's widow to a citizen of Holland, where does the property go? Ward *v.* Van der Loeff, [1924] A. C. 653.

McINTYRE *v.* McINTYRE.

SUPREME COURT OF GEORGIA, 1904.

120 Ga. 67, 47 S. E. 501.

[The testator made numerous obliterations and interlineations in his will and crossed off the signature, acts which would have constituted a revocation if accompanied by the proper intent. There was evidence that at the time he did these things he intended to make a new will; but he died before any such will was made. In the trial court the jury found for the old will. The Supreme Court of Georgia reversed on the ground that instructions on the burden of proof had been erroneous. A portion of the opinion dealing with the issue of dependent relative revocation is here given.]

SIMMONS, C. J. . . . Reference is made in the brief of counsel for the defendant in error to what is known as the doctrine of " dependent relative revocation." Under the operation of this doctrine it has been held that if a testator cancel or destroy a will, with a present intention to make a new will as a substitute for the old, and the new will is not made, or if made fails of effect for some reason, it will be presumed that the testator preferred the old will to an intestacy, and this testament will be given effect. We believe this doctrine to be sound, when properly understood and properly qualified. It is a doctrine of presumed intention, and has grown up as a result of an effort which courts always make to arrive at the real intention of the testator. Some of the cases appear to go to extreme lengths in the application of this doctrine, and seem to defeat the very intention at which they were seeking to arrive. The doctrine, as we understand it and are willing to apply it, is this: The mere fact that the testator intended to make a new will, or made one which failed of effect, will not alone, in every case, prevent a cancellation or obliteration of a will from operating as a revocation. If it is clear that the cancellation and the making of the new will were parts of one scheme, and the revocation of the old will was so related to the making of the new as to be dependent upon it, then if the new will be not made, or if made is invalid, the old will, though canceled, should be given effect, if its contents can be ascertained in any legal way. But if the old will is once revoked, — if the act of revocation is completed, — as if the will be totally destroyed by burning and the like, or if any other act is done which evidences an unmistakable intention to revoke, though the will be not totally destroyed, the fact that the testator intended to make a new will, or made one which cannot take effect, counts for nothing. In other words, evidence that the testator intended to make or did actually make a new will, which was inoperative, may throw light on the question of intention to revoke the old one, but it can never revive a will once completely revoked. . . . Applying what has been said to the facts of the present case, the following result is reached: There was evidence from which the jury could have found that when the testator canceled the old will he intended to make a new one. The canceled paper itself bore evidence of such an intention. If this was his intention, and he did not intend for the cancellation to operate as a revocation unless the new will was made, then the finding ought to be in favor of the propounder. On the other hand, there was evidence from which a jury could find that the cancellation was intended to operate as a revocation; and if this is the truth, the finding ought to be against the will, notwithstanding it may appear that the testator contemplated the making of another will. These are questions for the jury to decide. . . .[9]

PROBLEM.

1. George started on a journey from California to his home in Portland, Maine; but when he arrived in Denver he was too sick to proceed further. One Howard was very kind to him. Three weeks later George made his will, giving a legacy of $2000 to Howard. Then Lewis, George's brother, arrived from Maine and took charge of George. George sent a note to the lawyer who drew the will that he wanted the will because he was going to destroy it and make another one. He crossed the signature off the will, crossed out the legacy to Howard, and, using the old will as a draft for the new one, inserted interlineations which would leave all his property to Lewis except a $300 legacy and certain books which were intended for one Cushing. George never did anything more about making another will and died two weeks later. George's estate amounts to $7000. Lewis is his only heir. Is the will revoked? Townshend v. Howard, 86 Me. 285 (1894).

Revocation by marriage. By the English common law a woman's will was revoked by her marriage, — an obvious corollary to the rule that a married woman could not make a will. A man's will was not revoked by marriage (for his wife was not an heir anyway and hence revocation would do her no good) but was revoked by marriage plus birth of issue. The fact that the bases for these English rules no longer exist in the United States throws the American common law into considerable doubt. Some courts follow the English rules, disregarding the disappearance of their reasons; others have developed independent rules to square with the greater rights given to married women in this country.[10] But in most states the common law is relatively unimportant, since the question of revocation by marriage is governed by express statutes.[11]

These statutes vary considerably from the common law and from each other.[12] The New York statute (Decedent Estate Law, § 35) is worth examining because it has been very carefully worked out

---

[9] Accord, Dixon v. Solicitor to the Treasury, [1905] P. 42. But see In re Bonkowski's Estate, 266 Mich. 112, 253 N. W. 235 (1934).

[10] See generally Atkinson, Wills (1937) 396–404.

[11] Statutes which, like the English Statute of Frauds, provide that wills shall not be revoked except by certain acts to the document and certain subsequent instruments, do not prevent revocation by marriage; for revocation by marriage is considered to be a revocation by operation of law and hence not within the purview of a statute which deals with intended revocation by act of the testator. Atkinson, Wills (1937) 396–397.

[12] See Bordwell, "Statute Law of Wills," 14 Ia. L. Rev. 298–301 (1929).

and frequently amended and because it incorporates most of the variations from the common law that will be found in other states. It reads as follows:

"If after making any will, such testator marries, and the husband or wife survives such testator, such will shall be deemed revoked as to such survivor, unless provision shall have been made for such survivor by an ante-nuptial agreement in writing; and such surviving husband or wife shall be entitled to the same rights in, and to the same share or portion of the estate of said testator as he or she would have been, if such will had not been made. . . ."[13]

Observe the differences between this and the common-law rules:

1. The same rules apply to men and women; birth of issue is immaterial. This is a common feature of American statutes.
2. The will is revoked only as to the spouse; the rest of the will stands and the spouse takes the share he or she would have taken by intestacy. This is not so common. Compare statutes which entitle a surviving spouse to "waive the will," even if made after marriage, and take an intestate share (Chapter II, supra).
3. The will is not affected if the spouse does not survive the testator, whereas under the common law the marriage (plus birth of issue, in the case of a man) revoked the will and the failure of the spouse to survive the testator made no difference. Statutes differ as to the significance of survival of the spouse; in some states survival of the wife is required for revocation whereas survival of the husband is not. Under some statutes birth and survival of issue revokes a will made before marriage.
4. The will is not revoked if there has been a written ante-nuptial agreement. This exception is much less extensive than that which is usually found. Ordinarily it is provided that a will is not revoked by a marriage in contemplation of which it was made. Sometimes it is required that the spouse and issue be provided for in the will. But under the quoted New York statute the fact that a will was executed in contemplation of marriage and that it makes provision for the intended spouse and the issue of the marriage does not save it from revocation in the absence of a written ante-nuptial agreement.

It is obvious that the variations of state law as to the effect of marriage and/or birth of issue upon wills are such as to make it advis-

[13] This statute applies to wills executed before September 1, 1930. As to wills executed after that date the rights of the surviving spouse are governed by the complex provisions of D. E. L. § 18, p. 292, infra. An earlier form of the New York statute was, "A will executed by an unmarried woman shall be deemed revoked by her subsequent marriage." W executed a will while married to H1; H1 then died and W married H2. It was held that her will was not revoked by the marriage because she was not "an unmarried woman" when she executed it! Matter of McLarney, 153 N. Y. 416, 47 N. E. 817 (1897).

able for each student to make a study and analysis of the law on this subject in the state in which he expects to practice.

Under the common-law rule and under most statutes a will is not affected by marriage so far as it exercises powers of appointment where the gift in default of appointment is not to the heirs or next-of-kin of the donee of the power.

Revocation by divorce. The generally accepted view is that provisions for a spouse are revoked by divorce if, but only if, a property settlement attends the divorce. Some statutes expressly provide for revocation by divorce; the form of others is such as to exclude by implication this type of revocation.[14]

"*Revocation by conveyance.*" When T executes a will devising Blackacre to A and then conveys Blackacre to B and dies, it is plain that A gets nothing. We now say that A's devise is adeemed. But in the older books it was commonly said that A's devise was "revoked by conveyance." This phrase was to a considerable extent descriptive of the effect of T's transfer to B prior to the Wills Act of 1838, for before that date a devise of land was for many purposes treated as operating at the time of execution of the will and land acquired after execution of the will could not be devised by it. But since the abolition of the rule forbidding devise of after-acquired property, there has been no reason for differentiating either the rules or the terminology relating to real estate from those relating to similar problems concerning personality; hence at the present time the term "ademption" is applied to this situation. This matter is treated in Chapter VIII, Section 2, infra.

Revival of revoked wills. The question whether a will is reinstated, or "revived," by the revocation of a revoking will raises fundamental questions as to the nature of wills and the process of revocation. The matter may be discussed with reference to the following case:

PROBLEM.

T executes a will in 1930 by which he devises Blackacre to Mary and gives the residue of his property to John.
- a. In 1935 T executes an instrument entitled "Codicil to my will of 1930" in which he devises Blackacre to Elizabeth. In 1940 he destroys the codicil.
- b. In 1935 T executes an instrument entitled "Last Will and Testament" which contains no clause of revocation but which devises Blackacre to Elizabeth and gives the residue of T's property to Arthur. In 1940 he destroys this will.
- c. In 1935 T executes an instrument entitled "Last Will and Testament" which contains a clause revoking all prior testa-

---

[14] See, for example, Nenaber *v.* Nenaber, 55 S. D. 257, 225 N. W. 719 (1929); 5 Wis. L. Rev. 377 (1930).

mentary dispositions, devises Blackacre to Elizabeth and gives the residue of T's property to Arthur. In 1940 T destroys this will.

Under each of these circumstances what effect should be given to the 1930 instrument, assuming that there is no evidence whether or not T intended to revive the 1930 instrument? Should there be a different result if there is evidence that T intended revival? [15]

Lord Mansfield had a simple solution to these difficulties. Said he, in Goodright d. Glazier *v.* Glazier, 4 Burr. 2512 (1770), " A will is ambulatory till the death of the testator. If the testator lets it stand till he dies, it is his will; if he does not suffer it to do so, it is not his will. Here, he had two. He has cancelled the second; it has no effect, no operation; it is as no will at all, being cancelled before his death. But the former, which was never cancelled, still stands as his will." A contrasting view, which originated in the English ecclesiastical courts is commonly adopted in the United States, as indicated by the following case:

PICKENS *v.* DAVIS.

Supreme Judicial Court of Massachusetts, 1883.

134 Mass. 252.

Appeal from a decree of the Probate Court, allowing the will of Mary Davis. . . .

C. Allen, J. The two questions in this case are, first, whether the cancellation of a will, which was duly executed, and which contained a clause expressly revoking former wills, has the effect, as matter of law, to revive a former will which has not been destroyed, or whether in each instance it is to be regarded as a question of intention, to be collected from all the circumstances of the case; and secondly, if it is to be regarded as a question of intention, whether subsequent oral declarations of the testator are admissible in evidence for the purpose of showing what his intention was. These are open questions in this commonwealth. . . .

A majority of the court has come to the conclusion that the destruction of the second will in the present case would not have the effect to revive the first, in the absence of evidence to show that such was the intention of the testator. The clause of revocation is not necessarily testamentary in its character. It might as well be executed as a separate instrument. The fact that it is inserted in a

---

[15] For the tangled state of the authorities, see Atkinson, Wills (1937) 421-424. In about half of the states the doctrine of revival is abolished by statute to a greater or less extent. It was abolished in England by Section 22 of the Wills Act (1838).

will does not necessarily show that the testator intended that it should be dependent on the continuance in force of all the other provisions by which his property is disposed of. It is more reasonable and natural to assume that such revocatory clause shows emphatically and conclusively that he has abandoned his former intentions, and substituted therefor a new disposition of his property, which for the present, and unless again modified, shall stand as representing his wishes upon the subject. But when the new plan is in its turn abandoned, and such abandonment is shown by a cancellation of the later will, it by no means follows that his mind reverts to the original scheme. In point of fact, we believe that this would comparatively seldom be found to be true. It is only by an artificial presumption, created originally for the purpose of preventing intestacy, that such a rule of law has ever been held. It does not correctly represent the actual operation of the minds of testators, in the majority of instances. The wisdom which has come from experience, in England and in this country, seems to point the other way. In the absence of any statutory provision to the contrary, we are inclined to the opinion that such intention, if proved to have existed at the time of cancelling the second will, would give to the act of such cancellation the effect of reviving the former will; and that it would be open to prove such intention by parol evidence. . . .

In the present case, there was no evidence tending to show that the testatrix intended to revive the first will; unless the bare fact that the first will had not been destroyed amounted to such evidence. Under the circumstances stated in the report, little weight should be given to that fact. The will was not in the custody of the testatrix, and the evidence tended strongly to show that she supposed it to have been destroyed.

The question, therefore, is not very important, in this case, whether the subsequent declarations of the testatrix were admissible in evidence for the purpose of showing that she did not intend, by her cancellation of the second will, to revive the first; because, in the absence of any affirmative evidence to prove the existence of such intention, the first will could not be admitted to probate. Nevertheless we have considered the question, and are of opinion that such declarations were admissible for the purpose of showing the intent with which the act was done. The act itself was consistent with an intention to revive, or not to revive, the earlier will. Whether it had the one effect, or the other, depended upon what was in the mind of the testatrix. It would in many instances be more satisfactory to have some decisive declaration made at the very time, and showing clearly the character of the act. Evidence of declarations made at other times is to be received with caution. They may have been made for the very purpose of misleading the hearer as to the disposition which the speaker meant to make of his property. On the other hand, they may have been made under such circumstances as to furnish an entirely satisfactory proof of his real purpose. It is true, that it may not be proper to prove the direct act of cancellation, destruction or revocation in this manner. But when there is other evidence of an act of revocation, and when the question of the revival of an earlier will depends upon the intention of the testator, which is to be gathered from facts and circumstances, his declarations, showing such intention, whether prior, contemporaneous, or subsequent, may be proved in evidence. . . .

The result is, that, in the opinion of a majority of the court, the will should be disallowed, and the decree of the Probate Court *reversed*.[16]

---

[16] The close relationships between the doctrines of Revival and Dependent Relative Revocation is obvious. In each case the intention of the testator is the vital factor. In Ruel *v.* Hardy, 90 N. H. 240, 6 A. (2d) 753 (1939) Woodbury, J. emphasizes the necessity of receiving evidence of the declarations and circumstances of the testator in the Dependent Relative Revocation cases.

CHAPTER VI.

CONTEST OF WILLS ON GROUNDS OF MENTAL INCAPACITY, UNDUE INFLUENCE AND FRAUD.

The common grounds alleged for contests of wills are (1) that the will was not executed in the manner prescribed by the applicable statute of wills, (2) that the testator did not have sufficient mental capacity to make a will, (3) that the will, or some part thereof, was executed under the undue influence of some person, (4) that the will, or some part thereof, was induced by the fraud of some person. We have already considered problems of execution of the will in Chapter III; in this chapter we deal with the last three of these grounds of contest.

Mental incapacity.[1] Problems of sanity are almost entirely fact problems, involving on the part of the advocate considerable ingenuity in the discovery, marshalling and presentation of evidence, particularly in view of the rather bizarre rules of evidence on this matter which exist in a considerable number of states.[2] The rule of law is simple: A man has sufficient mental capacity to make a will if, at the time of execution of the will, he is capable of understanding the nature and extent of his property, appreciating the nature of the claims upon him of the natural objects of his bounty and formulating an orderly scheme of disposition. The test is very definitely ad hoc, and it is not severe. A man may be insane for other purposes, may even have been adjudged insane, and yet have sufficient capacity to make a will. On the other hand, juries have frequently upset unsympathetic wills upon relatively meager evidence. In many states a jury trial of the issue of sanity is allowed only where a prima facie case of unsoundness of mind is made out to the satisfaction of the probate judge.

As a matter of professional ethics, it is clear that a lawyer should refuse to prepare a will for a person whose mental capacity he believes to be inadequate.

[1] See generally Atkinson, Wills (1937) 186–206.
[2] For example, in Massachusetts, an ordinary witness cannot be asked whether in his opinion the testator was sane; but the following question is proper: "Did you notice any facts which indicated that the testator was not of sound mind?" McCoy v. Jordan, 184 Mass. 575, 69 N. E. 358 (1904). Again, an attesting witness can testify that at the time he signed as a witness he believed the testator to be sane; but he cannot testify that he now believes that at that time the testator was sane. Williams v. Spencer, 150 Mass. 346, 23 N. E. 105 (1890).

Undue influence.[3] All wills are the product of a number of influences upon the testator; yet so long as the will represents the volitional choice of the testator between competing claims, the influence is not "undue." Advice and persuasion are proper. But when the external influence is such as to substitute the volition of another for that of the testator, then the will, or that part of it which is affected by the influence, is invalid. Obviously this is a vague line to draw; and obviously the problems involved are again essentially fact problems.

There is frequently a close relationship between allegations of insanity and of undue influence. Testimony which may be insufficient to establish unsoundness of mind may nevertheless indicate a subnormal power of resistance to suggestion and may, therefore, be one link in the chain of evidence supporting a claim of undue influence.

If the lawyer preparing a will learns that the testator intends to make a gift to him or to any member of his family, he should immediately dissociate himself from its preparation. By this it is meant that he should not prepare the will himself and should advise the testator to seek independent counsel not professionally associated with himself. This ethical obligation is enforced by the rule, applicable in nearly all courts, that there is a rebuttable presumption of undue influence with reference to gifts made to the person who drafted the will and who stands in the attorney-client or other confidential relationship to the testator.[4]

A very difficult ethical question arises with reference to the nomination of executors and trustees in a will and the preparation of clauses relating to their powers and immunities. When a client asks advice concerning a will, he is entitled to receive, and the attorney is professionally obligated to give, advice designed solely to produce the greatest benefit for the testator and the legatees named in the will. Is this possible where the lawyer himself is named executor or trustee or both or where the will names as fiduciary a trust company which is a steady client of the lawyer and which sent the particular testator to him? The possible conflicts of interest and loyalty are many. For example,

---

[3] See generally Atkinson, Wills (1937) 207–218.

[4] This presumption is an aspect of the general attitude of suspicion with which gifts to persons in confidential relationships are regarded. An inter vivos gift to a person in a confidential relationship (e.g. an attorney, a religious adviser) is presumed to have been obtained by undue influence. In some states this rule is also applied to testamentary gifts; but there are strong reasons contra. Parfitt *v.* Lawless, L. R. 2 P. & D. 462 (1872). In most states a testamentary gift to a person in a confidential relationship is merely regarded with suspicion, unless such person was also the draftsman of the will. See Costigan, Cas. Wills (3d ed. 1941) 307–308.

(a) It is certainly to the advantage of the trustee to have a trust created and to have it last as long as possible; but it may be to the interest of the beneficiaries to have an outright gift or a short trust.
(b) It is almost always to the advantage of the trustee to be a sole trustee, for then compensation does not have to be divided; but it may be to the advantage of the beneficiaries to have joint trustees.
(c) It is usually to the advantage of an individual trustee to have a stipulation in the will that no bond of the trustee is required, for this eliminates bothersome supervision (and sometimes joint control of funds) by a surety company; but it is usually to the advantage of the beneficiaries to have surety-company protection.
(d) It is inevitably to the advantage of the trustee to have a clause in the will which relieves him from various liabilities to which the law might otherwise subject him; but such clauses are of at least doubtful value to a beneficiary.
(e) It is inevitably displeasing to the trustee to have a clause in the will providing that the trustee can be superseded by a new trustee at the option of the life tenant; but such a clause is almost always advantageous to the beneficiaries.

The Executive Committee of the Association of the Bar of the City of New York (Year Book, 1931, pp. 167–8) has declared that " a lawyer should not advise a prospective testator or donor as to the making of a will or trust if the lawyer already occupies a relationship to a proposed or potential fiduciary which might embarrass him in advising fully and freely as to all matters involved in the formation and terms of such will or trust. Such embarrassment exists where the prospective testator or creator of the trust has come to the attorney at the instance of any person or institution seeking to be named as fiduciary." The Committee on Professional Ethics of the same association has declared that it is not " necessarily improper " for an attorney to draft a will in which he is named as executor and trustee and in which he is exempted from giving bond.[5] There are obvious difficulties in reconciling a rule that one may draft a will in which he himself is named as trustee with a rule that he may not draft a will in which a trust company with which he is associated is named as trustee.[6] The American Bar Association Canons of Professional Ethics do not deal with the matter specifically. Canon No. 6 states that " it is unprofessional to represent conflicting

[5] Committee on Professional Ethics, Association of the Bar of the City of New York, Questions Answered by the Committee, 1925–1930, p. 59.

[6] On this see Griswold, " The Trust Division and the Bar," A. B. A. J. 236–238 (1932).

interests, except by express consent of all concerned given after a full disclosure of the facts." Certainly the current practice is not to refuse to draft wills for those who wish to name the draftsman executor or trustee. It should be observed, however, that this situation is fraught with the gravest danger of overreaching and professional impropriety and that, at the very least, the client should be made aware of the nature and implications of clauses which are of benefit to the draftsman in his capacity as fiduciary.

Fraud. Fraud differs from undue influence in that it is deception rather than coercion. Frequently the two are mixed. Once again the lawyer's problems are chiefly factual; but in cases of fraud there is often a very difficult legalistic problem as to the remedy to be applied. Where A by fraud induces T to give a legacy to A that T would otherwise have given to his friend, B, a refusal of probate as to this legacy is punitive but not compensatory. It punishes A, but it does not help B, since the disallowance of probate will cause the property to pass by intestacy or into the residue. Can B be helped? The obvious objection to helping him is that the evidence establishing (a) the fraud and (b) that the legacy would otherwise have gone to B, is oral; there is no writing giving the property to B; and the policy of the statutes of wills militates against allowing B to have the property in the absence of a writing. Nevertheless there is a growing tendency to impose a constructive trust upon A in favor of B in all cases where B has been deprived of interests in a decedent estate through fraud. This is true even though the fraud was that of a third person. It applies where T has been prevented from making a will or revoking one as well as where he has made a different one than he otherwise would have.[7] The main problems relating to fraud may be considered with reference to the following cases.

PROBLEMS.

1. Edward went through a marriage ceremony with Catherine in 1783. Unknown to Catherine, Edward had been married in 1775 and his wife was still living, although he had deserted her in 1781 and never saw her again during Catherine's life. Catherine died believing that she was legally married to Edward. By will she bequeathed " to my husband Edward, £150." Is Edward entitled to the legacy? Kennell *v.* Abbott, 4 Ves. Jr. 802 (1799). Cf. Anderson *v.* Berkley, [1902] 1 Ch. 936; In re Smalley, [1929] 2 Ch. 112.

2. T told his son-in-law, Charles, to draw a will which devised Blackacre to A and Whiteacre to B. Charles drew a will which

---

[7] See generally 3 Scott on Trusts (1939 & Supp.) §§ 489 to 489.6; Restatement of Restitution, § 184 (1937); J. Warren, " Fraud, Undue Influence and Mistake," 41 Harv. L. Rev. 309 (1927); Atkinson, Wills (1937) 218–227. As to the effect of a promise by A that, if a legacy is given to him, he will give it to B, see Bryan *v.* Bigelow, supra p. 69; Restatement of Restitution, § 186.

omitted any reference to Whiteacre and thus allowed Whiteacre to pass by descent to Charles's wife, Lera. Charles fraudulently told T that the will gave Whiteacre to B, and in reliance upon this statement T executed it. What are B's rights? Dye v. Parker, 108 Kan. 304, 194 P. 640, 195 P. 599 (1921); Lewis v. Corbin, 195 Mass. 520, 81 N. E. 248 (1907); 3 Scott on Trusts § 489.5.

Legacies conditional upon legatee not contesting the will.[8] It is fairly common for a testator to provide in some form of words that a legatee shall lose his legacy if he contests the will. Such clauses give rise to several questions. (1) First, there is the question whether such clauses are invalid as being conditions *in terrorem*. Some courts rule that the condition is void unless there is a gift over of the legacy to some other person in the event that the legatee contests; a mere provision for forfeiture of the legacy will not be given effect.[9] This view is not widely held, but the fact that it was the English rule and that some American courts appear to have adopted it indicates the advisability of including a gift over. (2) A more serious question is whether the forfeiture will be imposed when the legatee contests unsuccessfully [10] but with probable cause. A number of states hold that it will not, for the reason that a contrary rule would cause decedent estates to pass under wills not executed in accordance with the statutes and written by persons of insufficient mental capacity.[11] But the majority view is that probable cause does not protect the contesting legatee. The reasoning of these cases has been cogently put by Chief Justice Rugg in Rudd v. Searles, 262 Mass. 490, 500, 160 N. E. 882 (1928): " Contests over the allowance of wills frequently, if not invariably, result in minute examination into the habits, manners, beliefs, conduct, idiosyncracies, and all the essentially private and personal affairs of the testator, when he is not alive and cannot explain what may without explanation be given a sinister appearance. To most persons such exposure to publicity of their own personality is distasteful, if not abhorrent. The ease with which plausible contentions as to mental unsoundness may be supported by some evidence is also a factor which well may be in the mind of a testator in determining to insert such a clause in his will. Nothing in the law or in public policy, as we understand it, requires the denial of solace of that nature to one making a will. A will contest not infrequently engenders animosities and arouses hostilities among the kinsfolk of the testator, which may never be

[8] See generally Atkinson, Wills (1937) 357.
[9] Fifield v. Van Wyck, 94 Va. 557, 563, 27 S. E. 446 (1897).
[10] Obviously, if the contest of probate is successful the condition falls with the rest of the will.
[11] For example, South Norwalk Trust Co. v. St. John, 92 Conn. 168, 176–177, 101 Atl. 961 (1917).

put to rest and which contribute to general unhappiness. Moreover, suspicions or beliefs in personal insanity, mental weakness, eccentricities, pernicious habits, or other odd characteristics centering in or radiating from the testator, may bring his family into evil repute and adversely affect the standing in the community of its members. Thus a will contest may bring sorrow and suffering to many concerned. A clause of this nature may contribute to the fair reputation of the dead and to the peace and harmony of the living." (3) Third, there is often a question of construction: What constitutes a " contest "? These forfeiture clauses can be drafted with such precision as to eliminate this question, but they seldom are. The question may arise when the legatee files a *caveat* to the will but then abandons it, or where the legatee does not appear in the proceeding himself but gives assistance to another person who contests, or where the legatee does not seek to prevent probate of the will but later attacks a gift as a violation of the Rule Against Perpetuities. Much will depend upon the wording of the particular clause; and the decisions are not uniform even with reference to clauses which are substantially identical.[12]

Compromise of will contests. Most will contests end in compromise. One would expect to find that such agreements between the parties would involve payments by the legatees under the will to the contestants; and this is usual. But frequently enough one finds that the compromise provides for substantial alterations in the terms of the will; and circumstances sometimes suggest that the desire for such alterations was the chief aim of the contestants. Thus in one case [13] the compromise resulted in the elimination of spendthrift restrictions upon a gift to a contestant; and in several cases the " compromise " has been effected by nullifying future interests to unborn persons,[14] a practice which has been severely criticized.[15]

When an agreement has been reached between the parties to a will contest, the technique of putting it into execution may have considerable effect upon the amount of income, succession, estate and gift taxes that will be payable. Often an agreement of compromise can be accomplished by any of the following three methods: (1) allowance of the will and a payment by the legatees to the contestants, (2) disallowance of the will and a payment by the contestants to the legatees, (3) revision of the will by compromise agreement and court decree. Tax advantages may well flow from selecting one or another of these possible methods. The possible situations are so

---

[12] See Atkinson, Wills (1937) 358.

[13] Woodard *v.* Snow, 223 Mass. 267, 124 N. E. 35 (1919).

[14] Fisher *v.* Fisher, 253 N. Y. 260, 170 N. Y. 912 (1930); Copeland *v.* Wheelright, 230 Mass. 131, 119 N. E. 667 (1918).

[15] Schnebly, " Extinguishment of Contingent Future Interests by Decree and Without Compensation," 44 Harv. L. Rev. 378 (1930).

CHAP. VI.] CONTEST OF WILLS 121

diverse and the solution is so far dependent upon the local probate procedure and the wording of the applicable tax statutes that no more can here be done than to indicate that the problem exists.[16]

[16] See Lyeth v. Hoey, 305 U. S. 188 (1938); Dumont's Estate v. Commissioner, 150 F. (2d) 691 (3rd CCA, 1945); White v. Thomas, 116 F. (2d) 147 (5th CCA, 1940); 54 Harv. L. Rev. 1072 (1941). Compare Cochran's Exr. v. Kentucky, 241 Ky. 656, 44 S. W. (2d) 603 (1931) with Taylor v. State, 149 S. E. 321 (Ga. App. 1929). For general treatments, see Note, " Succession tax as affected by compromise of will contests," 78 A. L. R. 716 (1932); Tye, " Tax Status of Will Compromise Agreements." 19 Taxes 350 (1941); Magill & Maguire, Cas. Taxation (4th ed. 1947) 739–746; Griswold, Cas. Federal Taxation (2d ed. 1946) 379–385.

CHAPTER VII.

MISTAKE, MISNOMER AND MISDESCRIPTION.[1]

Introduction.

THE first case in this Chapter deals with a type of mistake — "mistake in the inducement" — which is obviously closely related to the problems of fraud[2] and of dependent relative revocation.[3] The rest of the cases are of two types: (1) those in which a verbal error has crept into the will, an error which the testator would have recognized as such if it had been called to his attention, and (2) those in which the words of the will are the words intended by the testator but are ambiguous or misleading when read in the light of the circumstances of the formulation of the will. In this latter classification the words may describe no person or no property, or two persons or two pieces of property, or a person or piece of property which extrinsic evidence indicates the testator did not intend.

In all of these cases two questions arise. The first is, How far can a court go in examining evidence extrinsic to the document for the purpose of discovering that there is a mistake or ambiguity and deciding what the testator really intended? Plainly this is a problem in determining how far one is willing to ignore the safeguards imposed by the statutes of wills. The second question is, Assuming that a mistake has been located, what remedy will be provided? Reformation would be a natural remedy in an inter vivos transaction; but the fact that testamentary transfers are almost invariably voluntary and the dangers of allowing reformation on parol evidence when the person whose words are being reformed is invariably dead, have caused the courts to deny that they have a jurisdiction to reform. Can the equivalent of reformation be obtained by refusing probate to words inserted by mistake or by "construing" words in the light of circumstances which substantially alter their usual meanings? These are the questions upon which the following cases offer illumination.

Some of these cases (particularly Goods of Boehm, p. 125) cannot be appreciated except in the framework of the older English pro-

---

[1] See generally J. Warren, "Fraud, Undue Influence and Mistake," 41 Harv. L. Rev. 309, 329 (1928); J. Warren, "Interpretation of Wills — Recent Developments," 49 Harv. L. Rev. 689 (1936); Atkinson, Wills (1937) 237–244.

[2] See Chapter VI.

[3] See Chapter V.

cedure relating to the probate and construction of wills. (1) So far as a will dealt with personal property, it was subject to the jurisdiction of two courts. The ecclesiastical court (later superseded by the Probate Division of the High Court of Justice) was the court of probate and determined what words constituted the will of the testator and who should be appointed as executor; then its function ceased. The problem of construing the words admitted to probate was a function of the Chancellor (later superseded by the Chancery Division of the High Court of Justice). The artificial results produced by this division of function between courts of probate and courts of construction is pointed out by the dissenting Justices in Patch v. White (p. 127). (2) So far as a will dealt with real estate, it was subject solely to the jurisdiction of the common law courts, which acted both on the issue of probate and the issue of construction, — except that the construction of equitable interests was a matter for the Chancellor. It was possible, therefore, that a will would be admitted to probate by the ecclesiastical court or its successor with reference to personalty and denied probate by a jury before whom the issue was tried in the King's Bench with reference to land. It was even possible that the jury trying an issue of ejectment as to Blackacre under the will of T might find one way and a different jury trying the same issue as to Whiteacre under the same will might find the other.

At the present time, in most of the United States, a single court deals with personalty and realty in decedent estates and decides all issues, including both probate and construction. But it is frequently important for a modern probate court to realize that its paternity is mixed and that it inherits the combined powers of three ancient judicial bodies. A fuller realization of this might have been important in Stearns v. Stearns (Problem 2, p. 139).

IN RE WRIGHT'S ESTATE.

King's Bench, Province of Saskatchewan, 1937.

[1937] 3 W. W. R. 452.

Embury, J. The deceased originally lived in England with his family, consisting of a wife, a daughter and a son. In 1910 he came to Canada and for about two years corresponded with his wife in terms of confidence and affection. After this time all communications between them ceased. Meantime his son died but in 1913 the testator had conversations with a friend in which he referred to his wife and daughter but not to the son. Later in making an income tax return he stated he had a wife living in England to whom he intended to return in a short time.

Some few days before he died he had a conversation with his landlady to the effect that he had a wife living who was not a wife to him as she had left him for another man. There is no other evidence to the effect that he had ever had any thought of such a state of affairs being true. In fact on the evidence it was quite untrue.

Shortly before he died the deceased made a holograph will in the following words:

"To C. Burrows: Although of sound mind today I am a sick man, and in case The Grim Reaper catches up with me I wish to leave everything I own, personal effects and bank balance after everything is paid for — which will be Dr. F. Munroe & my funeral expenses. Bal. of everything to go to Marion Honeysette at 2143 Rose St. She is to have everything as I have no living relations.
Signed FRANK WRIGHT.

"Late of Regina Daily Star."

. . . As a fact at the time, as I have said, he had a wife and daughter living, with whom or of whom there is no evidence that he had had communication or information for many years.

The words of the will should be analyzed carefully to see what the deceased had in mind, "A sick man," "before The Grim Reaper catches up with me," meaning thereby, as I take it, "being on the verge of death." Written at such a time these are solemn words. No matter what may have happened previously they must be taken to represent his state of mind when he wrote this holograph will and so at that time he must be taken to have had in mind that he had "no living relations." To go further into the wording of the document it is as if he had said "she is to have everything because I have no living relatives," or to go a step further "since I have no immediate relatives to succeed I give all my property to so and so," and to interpret further still "I would allow all my property to go to my relatives — but having none I will it to so and so."

I believe the principle of interpretation involved has been considered and approved in the following cases:

Campbell *v.* French (1797) 3 Ves. Jun. 321, 30 E. R. 1033, Lord Chancellor (Loughborough):

"Testator by his will gave legacies to A. and B. describing them as grandchildren of C. and their residence in America: by a codicil he revoked these legacies; giving as a reason, that the legatees were dead: that fact not being true, they were held entitled upon proof of identity."

Thomas *v.* Howell (1874) L. R. 18 Eq. 198, at 211, 30 L. T. 244:

"The rule is to find out what the testator means, and give effect to his intention. Now what does the testator mean here? When he says that, presuming and believing a certain state of things, he gives an additional sum of £4,000, on what principle can I say that his belief did not influence him in making this gift, and how can I double the legacies, when in fact the supposed state of things was an entire mistake?" . . .

It seems to me that the principle advanced above is entirely applicable to the present circumstances and so there will be judgment that the estate should pass to the mother [wife] and daughter, as though the will had never been executed.

PROBLEMS.

1. Suppose that the will in In re Wright's Estate had omitted the words "as I have no living relations" and that the testator's landlady had testified that he told her on the day he wrote the will that he was leaving all his property to Marion Honeysette because he had no living relations. Would the result have been different? Gifford *v.* Dyer, 2 R. I. 99 (1852).

2. Suppose that the will in In re Wright's Estate had omitted the words "as I have no living relations" and that the testator's landlady had testified that she heard Marion Honeysette tell him that she had just come back from England and had ascertained as a fact that his wife and daughter were dead. Would the result have been different? See Restatement of Restitution, § 184 (1937); 3 Scott on Trusts (1939 & Supp.) § 489.1.

GOODS OF BOEHM.

PROBATE DIVISION, 1891.

[1891] P. 247.

MOTION for a grant of probate of a will with certain alterations.

The testator, Sir J. E. Boehm, R.A., died December 24, 1890, leaving a will duly executed bearing date December 12, 1889.

The instructions for the preparation of the will were given to Mr. Mills, an old friend, who conveyed them to the testator's solicitor, by whom they were laid before counsel to prepare a draft will.

From the affidavits of these gentlemen it appeared that by his instructions the testator directed that two sums of 10,000*l.* each, part of a specific sum of 24,000*l.* dealt with in the will, should be set apart to be settled to the use and benefit of his two unmarried daughters, Miss Georgiana Boehm and Miss Florence Boehm, and their children, after the death of his wife, who was to have the life interest if she survived him. By inadvertence the conveyancing counsel in settling the draft inserted the word "Georgiana" in both the clauses of the will relating to the gifts to the unmarried daughters, and omitted the word "Florence" altogether; so that there were two gifts of 10,000*l.* to Miss Georgiana Boehm, while Miss

Florence Boehm was left totally unprovided for.[4] This error was repeated in the engrossed copy of the draft which was ultimately executed by the testator. The draft of the will, together with an epitome of its provisions, was taken to the testator by Mr. Mills. The draft was never read over to him, but the epitome was. In the epitome the names " Georgiana " and " Florence " were accurately given, and the testator read it over and made corrections in it. The testator did not read the will over at the time of execution, and it was perfectly certain that his attention was not drawn to the mistake, which was only discovered after his death.

JEUNE, J. I am asked to grant probate of the will of Sir Joseph Edgar Boehm with the word Georgiana omitted in two places, in what, on the face of the will, professes to be a gift in her favour. I had some doubt about deciding this matter on motion; but as representatives of all existing interests agreed to its being so decided, and future interests will be protected rather than prejudiced by this mode of dealing with this question, I see no objection to adopting it. It is clear from the evidence that the testator intended to give 20,000*l.* in equal moieties to trustees for each of his daughters, Florence and Georgiana, and the instructions for the will correctly expressed this; but the draftsman, instead of inserting in the draft of the will a clause of gift in favour of Georgiana, and then a similar clause in favour of Florence, inserted the name of Georgiana in the second clause as well as in the first. It is proved that the testator did not read or have read over to him the will, but did read what professed to be an epitome of it, such epitome being in accordance with the instructions, and correctly representing the testators' intentions. In a sense, therefore, the word Georgiana was clearly inserted in the two places in question in error, though the real and complete mistake was in not inserting Florence in place of Georgiana. . . . In the present case no such difficulty occurs as arose in Fulton *v.* Andrew, Law Rep. 7 H. L. 448, . . . from a presumption of knowledge and approval arising from the reading of, or hearing read, a will by a competent testator, because here the evidence is that the testator, relying on the epitome, never read or heard the will read.[5]

[4] The testator had three daughters, Effie Josephine Herapath, Georgiana Boehm, and Florence Boehm. The will gave a £4,000 trust fund to Effie. It gave a £10,000 trust fund "for the benefit of my said daughter Georgiana Boehm her children and any husband of hers"; and it gave another £10,000 trust fund "for the benefit of my said daughter Georgiana Boehm her children and any husband of hers." J. Warren, " Interpretation of Wills — Recent Developments," 49 Harv. L. Rev. 689, 712 (1936). In this article Professor Warren poses the question: How would this case have been decided if the testator had had three unmarried daughters instead of two?

[5] In Guardhouse *v.* Blackburn, L. R. 1 P. & D. 109 (1866), Sir J. P. Wilde said, " The fact that the will has been duly read over to a capable testator on the occasion of its execution, or that its contents have been brought to his notice in any other way, should, when coupled with his execution thereof, be

My difficulty at the argument was that, in the above cases, to strike out the word or words inserted in error left the will what the testator intended it should be. Here, to strike out the word Georgiana and to leave a blank in its place does not leave the will what the testator intended it should be, and I am not aware that there is any exact authority for striking a word out of a will under these circumstances. . . . But I think that the application of the principle of striking out a word clearly inserted in mistake may be safely extended, if it be an extension, to a case where the effect of its rejection may be to render ambiguous, or even insensible, a clause of which it formed part. If a person by fraud obtained the substitution of his name for that of another in a will it would be strange if his name could not be struck out, although the rest of the clause in which it occurred became thereby meaningless. It may be that in the present case the effect of striking out the name in question will be, on the construction of the will, as it will then read, to carry out the testator's intentions completely. It is not for me to decide that. But even if to strike out a name inserted in error and leave a blank have not the effect of giving full effect to the testator's wishes, I do not see why we should not, so far as we can, though we may not completely, carry out his intentions. I am, therefore, willing to grant probate of this will as prayed with the omissions specified.

PATCH *v.* WHITE.

Supreme Court of the United States, 1886.

117 U. S. 210, 6 Sup. Ct. 617.

Error to the Supreme Court of the District of Columbia.

Bradley, J. Ejectment for two undivided thirds of a lot of land in Washington City, known on the plats and ground plan of the city as lot No. 3, square 406, fronting 50 feet on E Street north: plea, not guilty.

The plaintiff, John Patch, now plaintiff in error, claims the lot under Henry Walker, devisee of James Walker. The latter died seized of the lot in 1832, and by his last will, dated in September of that year, devised to Henry Walker as follows, to wit: "I bequeath and give to my dearly-beloved brother, Henry Walker, forever,

---

held conclusive evidence that he approved as well as knew the contents thereof." In that case a codicil, referring to the will, declared that all legacies "therein and herein given" should be paid out of personal property. The contention was that the words "therein and" were inserted by mistake. Evidence on this point was excluded when it was conceded that the will had been read over to the testator. See Roland Gray, "Striking Words Out of a Will," 26 Harv. L. Rev. 212 (1912).

lot numbered six, in square four hundred and three, together with the improvements thereon erected, and appurtenances thereto belonging." The testator did not own lot number 6, in square 403, but did own lot number 3, in square 406, the lot in controversy; and the question in the cause is, whether the parol evidence offered and by the court provisionally received, was sufficient to control the description of the lot so as to make the will apply to lot number 3, in square 406. The judge at the trial held that it was not, and instructed the jury to find a verdict for the defendant. The court in General Term sustained this ruling and rendered judgment for the defendant; and that judgment is brought here by writ of error for review upon the bill of exceptions taken at the trial.

The testator, at the time of making his will, and at his death, had living a wife, Ann Sophia, an infant son, James, a mother, Dorcas Walker, three brothers, John, Lewis, and Henry (the latter being only eleven years old), and three sisters, Margaret Peck, Louisa Ballard, and Sarah McCallion, and no other near relations, and all of these are provided for in his will, if the change of description of the lot given to Henry is admissible; otherwise Henry is unprovided for, except in a residuary bequest of personal property in connection with others. The following are the material clauses of the will. After expressing the ordinary wishes and hopes with regard to the disposal of his body and a future life, the testator adds: "And touching worldly estate, wherewith it has pleased Almighty God to bless me in this life, I give, devise, and dispose of the same in the following manner and form." He then gives and bequeaths to his wife one-third of all his personal estate, forever, and the use of one-third of his real estate for life, remainder to his infant son, James. He then proceeds: "I bequeath and give to my dear and affectionate mother, Dorcas Walker, forever, all of lot numbered seven, in square one hundred and six, as laid down on the plan of the City of Washington, together with all the improvements thereon erected and appurtenances thereto belonging.

"I bequeath and give to my dearly-beloved brother, John Walker, forever, all of lot numbered six, in square one hundred and six, with the two-story brick house, back building, and all appurtenances thereto belonging.

"I bequeath and give to my dearly-beloved brother, Lewis Walker, forever, lots twenty-three, twenty-four, and twenty-five, in square numbered one hundred and six, together with a two-story brick building, with a basement story back building, and all appurtenances thereto belonging and erected on one or more of said lots.

"I bequeath and give to my dearly-beloved brother, Henry Walker, forever, lot numbered six, in square four hundred and three, together with the improvements thereon erected and appurtenances thereto belonging."

Then, after giving to his three sisters, and his infant son, respectively, other specific lots with houses thereon, he proceeds as follows:

"I also bequeath and give to my infant son, James Walker, forever, the balance of my real estate *believed to be and to consist in* lots numbered six, eight, and nine, with a house, part brick and part frame, erected on one of said lots, in square one hundred and sixteen; lots thirty-one, thirty-two, and thirty-three, in square numbered one hundred and forty, and a slaughter-house erected on one of said lots; lots numbered eight and eleven, in square numbered two hundred and fifty; and lot numbered twenty-eight, in square numbered one hundred and seven; and further, I bequeath and give to my infant son, James Walker, one thousand dollars, to be paid out of my personal estate, and applied at the discretion of his guardian hereinafter appointed, for the education of my son, James Walker." He then adds:

"The balance of my personal estate, whatever it may be, I desire shall be equally divided between my mother, Dorcas Walker, my sister, Sarah McCallion, and my brothers, John, Lewis and Henry Walker."

It is clear from the will itself—

1. That the testator intended to dispose of all his estate.

2. That he believed he had disposed of it all in the clauses prior to the residuary clause, except the specific lots thereby given to his son.

3. That when he gave to his brother, Henry, lot number 6, in square 403, he believed he was giving him one of his own lots. On general principles, he would not have given him a lot which he did not own; and he expressly says, "touching worldly estate, wherewith it has pleased Almighty God to bless *me* in this life, I give, devise, and dispose of *the same* in the *following* manner."

4. That he intended to give a lot with improvements thereon erected.

Now, the parol evidence discloses the fact, that there was an evident misdescription of the lot intended to be devised. It shows, first, as before stated, that the testator, at the time of making his will, and at the time of his death, did not, and never did, own lot 6, in square 403, but did own lot 3, in square 406; secondly, that the former lot had no improvements on it at all, and was located on Ninth Street, between I and K Streets, whilst the latter, which he did own was located on E Street, between Eighth and Ninth Streets, and had a dwelling house on it, and was occupied by the testator's tenants — a circumstance which precludes the idea that he could have overlooked it.

It seems to us that this evidence, taken in connection with the whole tenor of the will, amounts to demonstration as to which lot was in the testator's mind. It raises a latent ambiguity. The question is one of identification between two lots, to determine which was in the testator's mind, whether lot 3, square 406, which he owned, and which had improvements erected thereon, and thus corresponded with the implications of the will, and with part of the description of the lot, and rendered the devise effective; or lot 6, square 403, which he did not own, which had no improvements thereon, and which rendered the devise ineffective.

It is to be borne in mind that all the other property of the testator, except this one house and lot, was disposed of to his other devisees, at least that was his belief as expressed in his will, and there is no evidence to the contrary; whilst this lot (though he believed he had disposed of it), was not disposed of at all, unless it was devised to his brother, Henry, by the clause in question. In view of all this, and placing ourselves in the situation of the testator at the time of making his will, can we entertain the slightest doubt that he made an error of description, so far as the numbers in question are concerned, when he wrote, or dictated, the clause under consideration? What he meant to devise was a lot that he owned; a lot with improvements on it; a lot that he did not specifically devise to any other of his devisees. Did such a lot exist? If so, what lot was it? We know that such a lot did exist, and only one such lot in the world, and that this lot was the lot in question in this cause, namely, lot number 3, in square 406. Then is it not most clear that the words of the will, " lot numbered six, in square four hundred and three," contained a false description. The testator, evidently by mistake, put " three " for " six," and " six " for " three," a sort of mis-speech to which the human mind is perversely addicted. It is done every day even by painstaking people. Dr. Johnson, in the preface to his Dictionary, well says: " Sudden fits of inadvertence will surprise vigilance, slight avocations will seduce attention, and casual eclipses of the mind will darken learning." Not to allow the correction of such evident slips of attention, when there is evidence by which to correct it, would be to abrogate the old maxim of the law: " *Falsa demonstratio non nocet.*"

It is undoubtedly the general rule, that the maxim just quoted is confined in its application to cases where there is sufficient in the will to identify the subject intended to be devised, independently of the false description, so that the devise would be effectual without it. But why should it not apply in every case where the extrinsic facts disclosed make it a matter of demonstrative certainty that an error has crept into the description, and what that error is? Of course, the contents of the will, read in the light of the surrounding circumstances, must lead up to and demand such correction to be made.

It is settled doctrine that, as a latent ambiguity is only disclosed by extrinsic evidence, it may be removed by extrinsic evidence.[6]

[6] " There be two sorts of ambiguities of words; the one is *ambiguitas patens* and the other is *ambiguitas latens*. *Patens* is that which appears to be

CHAP. VII.]　　　　　　　MISTAKE　　　　　　　　　131

Such an ambiguity may arise upon a will, either when it names a person as the object of a gift, or a thing as the subject of it, and there are two persons or things that answer such name or description; or, secondly, it may arise when the will contains a misdescription of the object or subject: as where there is no such person or thing in existence, or, if in existence, the person is not the one intended, or the thing does not belong to the testator. . . .

In view of the principles announced in these authorities, the case under consideration does not require any enlargement of the rule ordinarily laid down, namely, the rule which requires in the will itself sufficient to identify the subject of the gift, after striking out the false description. The will, on its face, taking it altogether, with the clear implications of the context, and without the misleading words, "six" and "three," devises to the testator's brother, Henry, in substance as follows: "I bequeath and give to my dearly beloved brother, Henry Walker, forever, lot number —, in square four hundred and —, together with the improvements thereon erected and appurtenances thereto belonging — being a lot which belongs to me, and not specifically devised to any other person in this my will." In view of what has already been said there cannot be a doubt of the identity of the lot thus devised. It is identified by its ownership, by its having improvements on it, by its being in a square the number of which commenced with four hundred, and by its being the only lot belonging to the testator which he did not otherwise dispose of. By merely striking out the words "six" and "three" from the description of the will, as not applicable (unless interchanged) to any lot which the testator owned; or instead of striking them out, supposing them to have been blurred by accident so as to be illegible, the residue of the description, in view of the context, so exactly applies to the lot in question, that we have no hesitation in saying that it was lawfully devised to Henry Walker.

The judgment is reversed, and the cause remanded, with directions to award a new trial.

Woods, J. dissenting (with whom concurred MATTHEWS, GRAY and

---

ambiguous upon the deed or instrument: *latens* is that which seemeth certain and without ambiguity for any thing that appeareth upon the deed or instrument, but there is some collateral matter out of the deed that breedeth the ambiguity.

"*Ambiguitas patens* is never holpen by averment. . . .

"Therefore if a man give land to I. D. et I. S. et haeredibus, and do not limit to whether of their heirs; it shall not be supplied by averment to whether of them the intention was the inheritance should be limited. . . .

"But if it be *ambiguitas latens*, then otherwise it is. As if I grant my manor of S. to I. F. and his heirs, here appeareth no ambiguity at all upon the deed; but if the truth be that I have the manors both of South S. and North S. this ambiguity is matter of fact; and therefore it shall be holpen by averment." Bacon, Maxims of the Law (1597), Regula XXV (sometimes XXIII) in 7 Works of Francis Bacon (Spedding, Ellis & Heath ed., 1879) 385.

BLATCHFORD, JJ.) Latent ambiguities are of two kinds: first, where the description of the devisee or the property devised is clear upon the face of the will, but it turns out that there are more than one estate or more than one person to which the description applies; and, second, where the devisee or the property devised is imperfectly, or in some respects erroneously, described, so as to leave it doubtful what person or property is meant.

It is clear that if there is any ambiguity in the devise under consideration it belongs to the latter class. But there is no ambiguity. The devise describes the premises as lot six, in square four hundred and three. It is conceded that there is such a lot and square in the city of Washington, and but one; and it is not open to question what precise parcel of land this language of the devise points out. It clearly, and without uncertainty, designates a lot on 9th Street, between I and K Streets, well known on the map of the city of Washington, whose metes and bounds and area are definitely fixed and platted and recorded. The map referred to was approved by President Washington in 1792, and recorded in 1794. Thousands of copies of it have been engraved and printed. All conveyances of real estate in the city made since it was put on record refer to it; it is one of the muniments of title to all the public and private real estate in the city of Washington, and it is probably better known than any document on record in the District of Columbia. The accuracy of the description of the lot devised is, therefore, matter of common knowledge, of which the court might even take judicial notice.

Nor is any ambiguity introduced into the description by the words "with the improvements thereon erected and the appurtenances thereto belonging," or by the testimony which was offered to prove that at the date of the will and of the death of the testator the lot described in the devise was unimproved. It is plain that the words "improvements thereon erected" were a conveyancer's phrase of the same nature as the words which immediately followed them, namely, "and the appurtenances thereto belonging," and the whole phrase is simply equivalent to the words "with the improvements and appurtenances." The words "with the improvements thereon erected" were not intended as a part of the description of the premises, which had already been fully and accurately described, but were used, perhaps, as a matter of habit, or perhaps out of abundant but unnecessary caution, to include in the grant improvements that might be put upon the premises between the date of the testator's will and the date when it took effect, namely, at his death. The phrase is one not commonly used to identify the premises, and was not so used in this devise. There is persuasive evidence of this in the will. For in eight other devises of realty the testator particularly describes the character of the improvements. Thus, in the devise to his brother, John Walker, the improvements are described as a "two-story brick house, back building;" in the devise to Lewis Walker as "a two-story brick building, with a basement story back building;" in the devise to Margaret Peck of four lots, as "a two-story frame house erected on lot 27;" in the devise to Louisa Ballard, as a "three-story brick house;" in the devise to Sarah McCallion, as a "frame house;" in the devise to James Walker of two lots, as "two two-story brick houses;" and in the residuary devise to James Walker of the testator's real estate as "a house part brick and part frame," and "a slaughter-house." There is no proof that any of the other real estate mentioned in the will was improved. . . .

It is, therefore, beyond controversy that if the testator had been the owner of lot numbered six, in square four hundred and three, it would have passed by the devise, and the sufficiency of the description could not have been challenged. The only ground, therefore, upon which the plaintiff can base his contention that there is a latent ambiguity in the devise, is his offer to prove that the testator did not own the lot described in the devise, but did own another which he did not dispose of by his will. This does not tend to show a latent ambiguity. It does not tend to impugn the accuracy of the description contained in the devise. It only tends to show a mistake on the part of the testator in drafting his will. This cannot be cured by extrinsic evidence. For, as Mr. Jarman says, "As the law requires wills, both of real and personal estate (with an inconsiderable exception), to be in writing, it cannot, consistently with this doctrine, permit parol evidence to be adduced either to contradict, add to, or explain the contents of such will; and the principle of this rule evidently demands an inflexible adherence to it, even where the consequence is a partial or total failure of the testator's intended disposition; for it would have been of little avail to require that a will *ab origine* should be in writing, or to fence a testator around with a guard of attesting witnesses, if, when the written instrument failed to make a full and explicit disclosure of his scheme of disposition, its deficiencies might be supplied, or its inaccuracies corrected, from extrinsic sources." 1 Jarman on Wills, 4th and 5th eds., 409.

If there is any proposition settled in the law of wills, it is, that extrinsic evidence is inadmissible to show the intention of the testator, unless it be necessary to explain a latent ambiguity; and a mere mistake is not a latent ambiguity. Where there is no latent ambiguity there no extrinsic evidence can be received.

. . . The opinion of the court in this case allows, what seems to us to be an unambiguous devise, to be amended by striking out a sufficient description of the premises devised, and the blank thus made to be filled by ingenious conjectures based on extrinsic evidence. This in the face of the statute of frauds in force in the District of Columbia, where the premises in controversy are situated. Fifty years after the unequivocal devise in question, as written and executed by the testator, had, as required by law, been placed upon the records of the District for the information of subsequent purchasers and incumbrancers, it is allowed to be erased, and, by argument and inference, a new one substituted in its place. This is not construing the will of the testator; it is making a will for him.

The decision of the court subjects the title of real estate to all the chances, the uncertainty, and the fraud attending the admission of parol testimony, in order to give effect to what the court thinks was the intention of the testator, but which he failed to express in the manner required by law.

Problems.

1. T's will devised to his widow " all my lands in the county of Hants." T had lands in the county of Hants and also in the county of Wilts. He had instructed his solicitor to draw a will leaving all his lands to his widow. The solicitor had thought that all T's lands were in Hants and so had added the words " in the county of Hants." T read over the will before signing it. Then he said to his wife in the presence of her brother, " You are getting all my real estate. I'm sure you will be happy at Tedworth." Tedworth was an estate owned by T in the county of Wilts. Can the words " in the county of Hants " be stricken out? See Stanley v. Stanley, 2 J. & H. 491 (1862); [7] Morrell v. Morrell, 7 P. D. 68 (1882); Rhodes v. Rhodes, 7 App. Cas. 192, 198 (1882).

2. T directed his solicitor to include in his will a bequest to the Bristol Royal Infirmary. By mistake the solicitor made the bequest to the " British Royal Infirmary." Can " Bristol " be substituted in the will for " British "? Goods of Bushell, 13 P. D. 7 (1887); but see Goods of Schott [1901] P. 190.

IN RE JACKSON.

Chancery Division, 1933.

[1933] Ch. 237.

[The executor of the will of Mary Jackson issued this summons for the purpose of obtaining a construction of the words " my nephew Arthur Murphy " in the gift of one-fifth of the residue of her estate. Three claimants appeared: (1) A nephew named Arthur Murphy, resident in Australia, (2) a nephew named Arthur Murphy, resident in Southwaite, and (3) a person named Arthur Murphy who

[7] It will be observed that some variations of the facts in Stanley v. Stanley have been made in stating this problem.

was the illegitimate son of testatrix's sister, Margaret, and who had married one of testatrix's nieces. This third Arthur Murphy had handled testatrix's financial affairs during the latter part of her life. In a prior will testatrix had given her residuary estate to six persons, one of whom was described as "my nephew, Arthur Murphy, son of my sister Margaret."]

FARWELL, J. The will is a short one, and on the face of it presents no difficulty. The testatrix gave her residuary estate to her two brothers and two sisters and " my nephew Arthur Murphy " in equal shares. Evidence is undoubtedly admissible as to the existence of her brothers and sisters, and whether she had a nephew whose name was Arthur Murphy, and the evidence shows that she had in fact two legitimate nephews, both named Arthur Murphy, each being the son of a brother, and both answer the description exactly. That state of affairs gave rise at once to an ambiguity as to which nephew the testatrix intended to benefit, and in order to solve that problem, evidence as to the state of the family generally is admissible, and I have read this evidence, from which it appears as follows. One of these two nephews lives in Australia and had some communications with his aunt in her lifetime. There is also some evidence of a quarrel between his father and the testatrix, but no weight can be attached to this. Had he been the only legitimate nephew he would undoubtedly have taken. The other legitimate Arthur Murphy lives in this country, and there is evidence as to his having been in communication with the testatrix. But he is the son of the testatrix's brother Arthur Murphy, to whom she gave another share of her residuary estate, and it does not seem very likely that she would give a further share to his son.

Now on that evidence alone I should have come to the conclusion that it is impossible to tell which of these two nephews was intended by the testatrix, and had the matter ended there I must have found that there was an intestacy on the ground of uncertainty. But the matter does not end there, because the evidence shows that one of the testatrix's sisters had a son born out of wedlock, who was also named Arthur Murphy, and that he was in close relationship with the testatrix, and had married one of her nieces, and therefore in some sense may be called a nephew. Now in the circumstances what course ought I to adopt? If there had been one legitimate nephew only named Arthur Murphy that nephew would undoubtedly have been entitled to the legacy, and no evidence at all as to the existence of the illegitimate nephew would have been admissible: see Wigram on Extrinsic Evidence, Prop. II.[8] But as soon as it appears

---

[8] "Where there is nothing in the context of a will, from which it is apparent, that a testator has used the words in which he has expressed himself in any other than their strict and primary sense, and where his words so interpreted are sensible with reference to extrinsic circumstances, it is an inflexible

from the evidence that there is more than one nephew who exactly answers the description in the will, the Court is entitled to have evidence of the state of the family generally, and to be put to some extent in the position of the testatrix in order to ascertain not what the testatrix intended but what the words which she has used were intended to mean. Now if from that evidence it appears that neither of the legitimate nephews was intended by the words which the testatrix has used, but that the words were used to describe the illegitimate nephew, I am, I think, bound to give effect to that evidence as a whole. I cannot disregard it, and if it convinces me that the testatrix intended by the words " my nephew Arthur Murphy " her illegitimate nephew, in my judgment I must give effect to it. . . .

Looking at the whole of the evidence in this case I can have no doubt that the illegitimate nephew was the person intended to be designated by the words " my nephew Arthur Murphy," and in those circumstances in my judgment I am bound to hold that he is the person entitled to the share of residue, and I will so declare.

WOOD *v.* HAMMOND.

Supreme Court of Rhode Island, 1889.

16 R. I. 98.

Durfee, C. J. We are asked to decide certain questions arising under the will and codicil of the late Daniel W. Lyman. . . .

Second. The will contains the following bequest, to wit: " To The

---

rule of construction, that the words of the will shall be interpreted in their strict and primary sense, and in no other, although they may be capable of some popular or secondary interpretation, and although the most conclusive evidence of intention to use them in such popular or secondary sense be tendered."

But see In re Jodrell, 44 Ch. D. 590, 614 (1890), per Bowen, L. J.: " [The rule against disturbing a plain meaning is] not so much a canon of construction as a counsel of caution "; National Society for the Prevention of Cruelty to Children *v.* Scottish National Society for the Prevention of Cruelty to Children, [1915] A. C. 207.

Compare 3 Restatement of Property, § 242, Comment c: " The meaning expressed by the language employed in a conveyance [which, by Restatement definition, includes a will or a trust] is to be derived from reading such conveyance as an entirety. . . . The necessity for the reading of a deed or will as a whole does not, however, justify a construction which relies solely on its language and excludes evidence as to the circumstances of its formulation. Such an exclusion is often the result of the so-called 'single plain meaning rule,' which unduly stresses the controlling force of the ordinary meaning of the words employed. This rule, in so far as it causes such exclusion, is disapproved, since language is so colored by the circumstances of its formulation that the exclusion of otherwise admissible evidence as to such circumstances is never justified."

Nursery I give five thousand (5,000) dollars." There was no corporation having the corporate name of "The Nursery" when the will was written, but four charitable corporations claim the bequest. The case was sent to a master for him to investigate their claims and report thereon, and it now comes before us on exceptions to his finding. It appears that A.D. 1872 an act was passed by the General Assembly creating a corporation under the name of the "Providence Nursery," and that an amendment thereto was passed A.D. 1879, changing the name to "The Rhode Island Children's Hospital and Nursery of Providence." The principal work of this corporation was to care for poor children under three years old, day and night. It was a well known charity, and was popularly called "The Nursery." It had appealed to the public for pecuniary aid by entertainments and otherwise as "The Nursery." The testator was accustomed to contribute to it as "The Nursery," and to speak of it by that name. But in April, 1881, more than four years before the testator made his will, it had abandoned its work for lack of funds, and had transferred its property and the children whom it was caring for to St. Mary's Orphanage, a charitable corporation in East Providence, and the testator had since then discontinued his contributions to it. St. Mary's Orphanage has maintained the Nursery since the transfer, in connection with its other work, having on an average half its inmates in the Nursery. In 1884 the testator was asked to contribute to the Orphanage. He said, "You mean the Nursery." The solicitor said, "No, the Orphanage." To which he replied, "It is the same thing," and contributed. The early friends of The Nursery often called the Orphanage The Nursery after its transfer. It seems to us that the Orphanage makes a better case for the bequest than the Rhode Island Children's Hospital and Nursery, for evidently the bequest was intended for the benefit of The Nursery as a favorite charity, and should go to the corporation as the medium through which the benefit would reach its destination.

We think it also makes a better case than the Grace Memorial Home, which, prior to its incorporation, carried on its work under the name of the "Day Nursery." Its work began only a few months before the execution of the will, and without either assistance, or, so far as appears, favor from the testator.

The fourth claimant is The Providence Shelter for Colored Children, which was for children between three and twelve years old, and in some instances under three years old. Its charter provides: "No children are to be received into the Shelter under three years of age, unless attended by peculiar circumstances." It is a children's home rather than a nursery. It was never popularly known as The Nursery, and it does not appear that the testator ever took an interest in it or contributed to it. His cousin, Mrs. Frances J. Chapin, who is interested in it, testifies that he was in the habit of calling it "the Nigger Nursery;" that he wrote his will at her house, and consulted her about the legacies; that he read it to her before signing it; that she asked him to leave something to the Shelter, and he replied that he had left $5,000 to it; that she told him he had made a mistake and called it The Nursery; that he replied, "You know what I mean, I mean the Nigger Nursery," pointing toward the Shelter; that she asked him to change the word, but he said, "You know what I mean," and declined because he did not wish to scratch anything out. The testimony is not within the rule under which extrinsic testimony is ordinarily received to elucidate the testamentary intent, namely, that when a devise or bequest is expressed in terms which apply indifferently to two or more persons or institutions claiming the benefit thereof, then extrinsic testimony may be resorted to to show which of them was intended. For, as we have seen, the Shelter was never called or known as The Nursery, and, properly speaking, it is not a nursery. The effort is to impose upon the will by extrinsic testimony a meaning which, taking it as it naturally applies to existing facts and circumstances, it does not express. It is an effort which contravenes the fundamental requirement of the law that a will shall be in writing; that is, that it shall be a written expression of the testator's intention.

But granting that the testimony is admissible, it does not carry conviction. The testator knew that there was a charity called "The Nursery," and if he had intended to give to The Shelter instead of The Nursery, it is incredible that he would have refused to alter the bequest, or, indeed, that he would have put it originally in a form to need alteration. His excuse that he did not wish to scratch anything out was evidently a pretence; for it is in evidence that the will has both an interlineation and an erasure. His entire talk about "The Nigger Nursery," and "You know what I mean," and the pointing, seem to us much more like a playful method of putting his cousin's request aside than like a serious purpose to accede to it. His calling The Shelter "the Nigger Nursery" does not, to say the least, indicate a benevolent feeling toward it.

The master found in favor of St. Mary's Orphanage. We confirm his finding. We think the legacy should be paid to the Orphanage, not for its general purposes, however, but for the benefit of "The Nursery" which it maintains. . . .

Problems.

1. T gave a legacy of $6000 "to my friend Richard H. Simpson." Two claimants appeared. The first was named Richard H. Simpson; he was acquainted with T, had met him once. The second was Hamilton Ross Simpson. Evidence was offered (1) that H. R. Simpson was called "Rotary Bill" by T because of his skill in handling a rotary snowplow; (2) that T addressed letters to him as "R. H.

Simpson" or "H. R. Simpson"; (3) that T had known him for years, worked with him and been his employer; (4) that T had told X that he had made a gift to Rotary Bill in his will; (5) that T had told Y that he intended to reward those who had stood by him and helped him to do the work out of which he realized his fortune. How much of this evidence is admissible? Who is entitled to the legacy? Siegley v. Simpson, 73 Wash. 69, 131 P. 479 (1913); Northern Trust Co. v. Perry, 105 Vt. 524, 168 A. 710 (1933).

2. Fannie Stearns died leaving a will in which legacies were given to her children and in which the residuary clause read as follows: "I give, devise and bequeath all the rest of my personal estate to my husband Thomas." Evidence was offered (1) that Fannie had no more personal estate, but had $15,000 of real estate; (2) that Fannie and Thomas agreed that they would each make a will leaving all property to the other except for legacies for the children; (3) that in pursuance of this agreement they went together to a scrivener and told him to make wills for them which should leave to the other all property except prescribed legacies for the children; (4) that the residuary clause in the will which was drawn by the scrivener for Thomas omitted the word "personal." How much of this evidence is admissible? Who is entitled to the real estate? Stearns v. Stearns, 103 Conn. 213, 130 A. 112 (1925).[9]

3. T's will read in part as follows, "I give to Annie Stevens £1000 [to be paid out of my account in the National Provincial Bank]. I give to Maria Middleton the balance of my account in the said bank after paying thereout the legacy to Annie Stevens." The words in brackets were stricken out by T before the execution of the will. Are the stricken words admissible in evidence to determine the meaning of the gift to Maria Middleton? In re Battie-Wrightson, [1920] 2 Ch. 330.

4. T's will gave property to "my brother, John Norman Gray." T had a brother John Gray and another brother Norman F. Gray. Evidence is offered that T stated to John, after the execution of the will, that he had given him $5000. Is this admissible? Re Gray, [1934] Ont. W. N. 17.

[9] In this case it was held that Thomas took none of the real estate. Moreover, the litigation took a longer period than that allowed for a surviving spouse to waive the will; and it was held that he had lost his right to waive the will while waiting for the courts to determine what the will meant. 103 Conn. at 225.

CHAPTER VIII.

LAPSE, ADEMPTION AND SATISFACTION.

The three problems which compose the subject matter of this chapter have this in common: They all arise out of changes which occur between the execution of the will and the death of the testator. They are aspects of the ambulatory nature of a will. Where T makes a bequest to A, A may predecease T (which raises the issue of lapse) or the property bequeathed may be disposed of by T before his death (which raises the issue of ademption) or T may make a similar inter vivos gift to A (which raises the issue of satisfaction).

Section 1.

Lapse.

Proper wills can eliminate lapse problems. If a problem of lapse arises with reference to a given will, that fact in itself is a reproach to the draftsman. A will provides for distribution upon a future event, the death of the testator, and the most elementary foresight and common sense plainly require provision for the possibility that one or more legatees may die before that event occurs. Depending on the result desired, gifts should be made in some such forms as the following:

1. " To A, if he survives me."
2. " To A, if he survives me; or, if A shall not survive me, to his issue who shall survive me; but if neither A nor any of his issue shall survive me, then nothing shall pass under this Article of my will."
3. The residue " to such of A, B, and C as shall survive me."
4. The residue " to be divided in equal shares, one share for each child of mine who shall survive me and one share for the issue[1] who shall survive me of each child of mine who shall

---

[1] Of course, the substitutional gift to issue should be defined in such a way that questions cannot arise as to who is included in the term " issue " and how distribution is to be made among such persons. One way of solving this problem is to provide that " wherever a gift to 'issue' of a person is made in this will, the gift shall pass to those children or more remote descendants of such person as would receive the personal property of such person if he died intestate, domiciled in Massachusetts, owning only personal property, and having only said children and more remote descendants as his next of kin, on the date when the said gift becomes distributable." To eliminate one other possible problem, most testators provide that " adopted children shall be treated in all respects under this will as if they had been born to their adopting parents."

predecease me; but if no child or issue of a child of mine shall survive me, then the residue of my estate shall pass to The X Hospital."

Common disaster clauses. The clauses recommended in the last paragraph assume that it is known whether the legatee survived the testator. But this is not always so. Sudden death to groups of people is an increasingly notable characteristic of our automotive, air-minded, atom-blessed civilization. The testamentary draftsman can do something toward saving the estates of the victims from dissipation in useless litigation. With this objective in view consider the relative desirability of the following clauses:

a. "I leave one-half of my estate to the persons specified in such will as my wife shall leave, if she survives me or if we shall die simultaneously or under such circumstances that it is impossible to determine which survived the other."

b. "I leave all my estate to my husband. But if he shall die so nearly together with me that there shall not have been a reasonable time and opportunity to probate my will and thereby formally to establish rights thereunder, then I give my estate to the American Museum of Natural History."

c. "I leave $10,000 to A if he survives me. . . . If any legatee and I die in a common disaster under such circumstances that it cannot be determined which of us died first, the said legatee shall be deemed to have predeceased me."

d. "I leave $10,000 to A if he survives me. . . . If a legatee dies within 30 days after my death he shall be deemed not to have survived me, for purposes of this will." [2]

Lapsed gifts distinguished from void gifts; realty distinguished from personalty. Where the named taker is living at the execution of the will, but dies before the testator, the gift is said to lapse. Where the named taker is already dead at the time of execution of the will, the gift is said to be void. As far as personal property is concerned lapsed and void gifts are, and always have been, treated alike; they pass into the residue. But where real property is concerned the situation is somewhat complicated.

At common law (i.e. before the Wills Act of 1838 in England and similar statutes in the United States) real estate acquired after the execution of a will could not pass by that will. For rather doubtful historical and constructional reasons a will of land was thought of as operating at the date of *execution* of the will, subject to postpone-

---

[2] Clause (a) is, of course, Matter of Fowles, p. 94, supra. Clause (b) is found in In re Bull's Estate, 175 Misc. 197, 23 N. Y. S. (2d) 5 (1940). Clause (c) is a common provision found in many wills. Clause (d) is found in a substantial number of modern wills. For general discussion, see Note: "Wills; Common Disaster; Survivorship; Problems of Drafting," 25 Cornell L. Q. 316 (1940); 2 Page on Wills (3d ed. 1941) §§ 908–912.

ment of operation of the devise until the testator's death and also subject to revocation. Let us assume that T owned Blackacre, Whiteacre, and Greenacre in 1790; in that year, T executed a will which devised Blackacre to A and all the residue of T's realty to B. The effect of this will was the same as if T had specifically devised Whiteacre and Greenacre to B; that is, a residuary devise was treated as a compendious specific devise (due to the notion that wills of real estate operated at once and could not include any land later acquired). Now when A died in the life of T, did Blackacre become part of the residue? No, argued the courts; this was analogous to after-acquired property. So the lapsed devise went to the heir, not into the residue. Carrying out the same thought, the English courts ruled that if A had been dead at the time of execution of the will (i.e. if the devise had been void rather than subject to lapse) then Blackacre would pass into the residue, because at the time of the will there was no effective devise which prevented Blackacre from being included in the compendious specific devise (i.e. the residuary devise) to B. This latter refinement was not generally adopted in the United States; here, at common law, both lapsed and void devises passed to the heir.

The passage of statutes making after-acquired land devisable removed any vestige of justification for treating lapsed and void devises differently from lapsed and void legacies. Therefore, the weight of authority now holds that lapsed and void devises pass to the residue, not to the heir.[3] There are some statutes which specifically so provide.[4]

Residuary lapses. Lapsed and void legacies and devises now fall into the residue; they do not pass by intestacy. But what if there is a lapse in the residue? This is the problem with which the two cases printed in this Section deal.

Lapse statutes. Almost all states have a statute designed to minimize the effects of lapse.[5] Typically the statute provides that if a gift is made to a relative of the testator, and the legatee predeceases the testator leaving issue surviving the testator, the issue will be given the legacy.[6] The principal variations in the statutes are the following:

1. Some states allow the statute to operate with regard only to legacies to children; some allow it to operate with regard to all legacies, whether to relatives or strangers.
2. Some states do not require that the legatee leave issue sur-

---

[3] Molineaux *v.* Raynolds, 55 N. J. Eq. 187 (1896).
[4] Lee, "Devolution of Void and Lapsed Devises," 25 Col. L. Rev. 447 (1925).
[5] For the statutes, see Bordwell, "Statute Law of Wills," 14 Iowa L. Rev. 428 (1929). As to the problems arising under such statutes, see Mechem, "Problems under Anti-Lapse Statutes," 19 Iowa L. Rev. 1 (1933).
[6] The Massachusetts statute quoted at p. 144, infra, is fairly typical.

viving the testator, but allow the legacy to pass to the heirs of the named legatee, whether issue or collaterals.

It is important to observe that the usual lapse statute does not prevent the gift to the legatee from failing; it creates a substitutional gift in his issue (rarely, his heirs). Therefore the legacy cannot usually be reached by the creditors of the named legatee.

Many difficult problems arise in the construction of these statutes. Is the wife of the testator a " relative "? The answer is, No. Does the statute apply to void legacies as well as lapsed legacies, i.e. where the legatee was dead at the making of the will as well as at the death of the testator? There is some conflict on this and something depends upon the wording of the particular act. But the most important (and in some respects the most difficult) problem is whether the lapse statutes apply to gifts to classes. Where there is a gift " to my children " and one child living at the time of the will predeceases the testator leaving issue who survive him, do the issue take the share the child would have taken had he survived? A consideration of this problem requires some considerable understanding of class gifts and is more appropriately dealt with in connection with a general treatment of future interests.[7] Another problem, also closely connected with the law of future interests, is whether the lapse statutes apply to attempts to exercise powers of appointment in favor of persons who have died.[8]

WORCESTER TRUST CO. *v.* TURNER.

SUPREME JUDICIAL COURT OF MASSACHUSETTS, 1911.

210 Mass. 115, 96 N. E. 132.

[The will of Horace A. Young contained the following provisions so far as they are relevant to this case:
1. Article Ninth provided, " To my sister-in-law, Lydia Young, I bequeath the sum of two thousand dollars."
2. Other articles made like pecuniary gifts to numerous other persons, including the testator's nephew, Warren E. Sibley, and his niece, Victoria M. Worcester.
3. The residuary clause provided, " I bequeath [the residue of my estate] to be divided among the first sixteen legatees named in this will, in proportion to the several amounts given to each."

Lydia Young, Warren E. Sibley, and Victoria M. Worcester were

[7] The effect of lapse statutes with reference to class gifts is dealt with in Leach, Cas. Future Interests (2d ed. 1940) Ch. IX, Sec. 2; Restatement of Property (1940) § 298.

[8] On this see Thompson *v.* Pew, 214 Mass. 520, 102 N. E. 122 (1913); Leach, Cas. Future Interests (2d ed. 1940) 597; 3 Restatement of Property (1940) § 350.

three of said first sixteen legatees. They all predeceased the testator. Lydia Young left issue surviving the testator; the other two did not.]

SHELDON, J. (1) It is rightly agreed by all parties that the legacies given by the eighth, ninth and seventeenth clauses of the will to Warren E. Sibley, Lydia Young and Victoria M. Worcester have lapsed; that to Mrs. Young because she was not a relation of the testator within the meaning of R. L. c. 135, § 21 [9] . . . and the others because neither of these two legatees left issue. . . .

The amounts of these legacies fall into the residue and become a part of the amount to be distributed under the fifth clause of the thirtieth article of the will.

(2) This fifth clause of the thirtieth article of the will is strictly residuary. It disposes of whatever residue may be left by ordering that " to be divided among the first sixteen legatees named " in the will, " in proportion to the several amounts given to each." This is a bequest as directly to those sixteen individuals and no others as if they were specified by name, instead of being identified by the order in which they are named in the will. It is not such a disposition as was made in cases relied on by some of the defendants in which beneficiaries were identified by description only and not by name, and, because a will speaks as of the time of the testator's death, it was held that those must take who answered to it only at the time when the will was made. Or, more exactly, it is the first sixteen legatees who are named in the will, whether they actually take under it or not, who are described here and who really answer to the testator's description both at the time of his making his will and at that of his death.

It is also plain that these sixteen legatees take their shares of the residue severally, and not as a class. . . . As in Sohier *v.* Inches, 12 Gray, 385, the gift is to each one absolutely, and in legal effect is made to each by name (Jones *v.* Crane, 16 Gray, 308), and there are no words importing survivorship. A division is to be made in stated proportions among them, which of itself indicates that they are to take neither as joint tenants nor as members of a class, and that there is to be no increase by survivorship among them. . . .

(3) It follows from these considerations that each one of the residuary bequests to Mrs. Young, Sibley and Mrs. Worcester, lapsed like their general legacies. Best *v.* Berry, 189 Mass. 510, 512, and cases cited. The question arises how the amount of these bequests is now to be distributed. The general rule to be applied in such

---

[9] This statute (now Mass. Gen. Laws, c. 191 § 22) provides as follows: " If a devise or legacy is made to a child or other relation of the testator, who dies before the testator, but leaves issue surviving the testator, such issue shall, unless a different disposition is made or required by the will, take the same estate which the person whose issue they are would have taken if he had survived the testator."

cases is well settled and is scarcely disputed. It was succinctly stated by Lathrop, J., in Lyman *v.* Coolidge, 176 Mass. 7, 9: " Where a legacy lapses which is part of the residue, it cannot, according to our decisions, fall into the residue because it is itself a part of the residue, and it must pass as intestate estate." . . .

It may be granted, as was said in Lombard *v.* Boyden, 5 Allen, 249, and Best *v.* Berry, 189 Mass. 510, that this rule would not prevail against a manifest intention of the testator that such a lapsed residuary bequest, instead of being treated as intestate property, should go to increase the shares of other residuary legatees. But upon examination of this will in all its parts and consideration of the able arguments which have been addressed to us we have not been able to find the expression of such an intent in the language used. It is not enough that he had, as undoubtedly he did have, a general intent to dispose of all his property by his will. . . .

The pecuniary legacies given in the earlier part of the will to Lydia Young, Warren E. Sibley and Victoria M. Worcester fall into the residue; and the residue thus increased is to be divided among the first sixteen legatees named in the will as written, except that the shares of the residue which thus would come to these three deceased legatees are to be distributed as intestate estate to the next of kin of the testator. . . .

CORBETT *v.* SKAGGS.

SUPREME COURT OF KANSAS, 1922.

111 Kan. 380, 207 P. 819.

[The will of Samuel S. Kincaid made pecuniary bequests to 10 nephews and nieces and then bequeathed the residue of his estate to seven of the nephews and nieces, naming them, " the same to be divided among them in the same proportion as their former bequests bear to the whole sum bequeathed to them." The pecuniary gifts to the nephews and nieces who were not also made residuary legatees contained an added clause as follows: " But he (she) is to have no share in the residue and remainder of my estate."

Two of the residuary legatees predeceased the testator leaving no issue. The trial court ruled that the residue was to be divided among the other five nephews and nieces and that no part thereof passed by intestacy. The three nephews and nieces who were pecuniary legatees but not residuary legatees appealed, since they would share in any distribution of the residue by intestacy.]

MASON, J. . . . (2) A lapsed legacy ordinarily falls into the residue and inures to the benefit of the residuary legatees. It is a rule of the English common law, however, which has met with considerable acceptance in this country, that on the death before the testator of one of several residuary legatees (who do not take jointly or as members of a class) his share goes, not to the others, but to whoever would have inherited the property in case no will had been made. (40 Cyc. 1952, note 59; 28 R. C. L. 338, 339, notes 1 and 2; note, 44 L. R. A. n.s., 811–813.) In one state the court has held to the contrary, but without discussing the cases by which the rule is supported. (Gray v. Bailey, 42 Ind. 349; Holbrook v. McCleary, 79 Ind. 167; West et al. v. West et al., 89 Ind. 529; see, also, Mann v. Hyde, 71 Mich. 278.) In two states the rule has been abrogated by statute. (Woodward v. Congdon, 34 R. I. 316, 323; In re Jackson, 28 Pa. Dist. 943.) Some cases cited in support of the rule are affected by distinctions between lapsed legacies and lapsed devises and some by a failure to make a distinction between a legacy which lapses because of death, which the testator may be regarded as having anticipated, and one which cannot be given effect because void in itself, a condition he can hardly be deemed to have taken into account. The rule has been severely criticized even by judges and text-writers who have felt constrained to follow it. (See note in 31 Yale Law Journal, 782; also Waln's Estate, 156 Pa. St. 194; Prison Ass'n v. Russell's Admr., 103 Va. 563; 2 Jarman on Wills [Sweet's 6th ed.], 1056–1058.) The grounds of such criticism are indicated in these excerpts:

". . . it was held in Skrymsher v. Northcote, 1 Swanst. 566, [1818] that a lapsed portion of a residuary bequest went to the next of kin, and not to the other residuary legatees, on the ground that the latter were given specific portions of the residuum, and could not take more by the intent of the will, and receiving the bequest in common and not jointly, there could be no increase by survivorship. The rule thus established does not commend itself to sound reasoning, and is a sacrifice of the settled presumption that a testator does not mean to die intestate as to any portion of his estate, and also of his plain actual intent, shown in the appointment of general residuary legatees, that his next of kin shall not participate in the distribution at all. The rule is in fact a concession to the set policy of English law, nowhere more severely asserted than in chancery, to keep the devolution of property in the regular channels, to the heir and next of kin, whenever it can be done. If the question were new in this state, speaking for myself I should not hesitate to reject the English rule as wrong in principle and subversive of the great canon of construction, the carrying out of the intent of the testator." (Gray's Estate, 147 Pa. St. 67, 74.) . . .

" There is a well-known rule that where the residue is given to tenants in common, and one of the tenants in common dies in the testator's lifetime, the lapsed share does not go as an accretion to the gift to the other tenants in common, but it is held that there is an intestacy and the share goes amongst the next of kin. That is, there can be no residue of a residue. The arguments by which this rule was arrived at are perfectly intelligible and, one may say, plausible. Nevertheless I think that the effect of it is to defeat the testator's intention in almost every case in which it is applied; but it is a rule by which I am undoubtedly bound." (In re Dunster [1909], 1 Ch. 103, 105.) . . .

This court has not heretofore had occasion to decide whether to follow the rule requiring the lapsed share of one of several residuary legatees to be treated as property undisposed of by the will. We might now avoid deciding that question by holding — as we think the facts justify — that in any event there are special features of the will under consideration which would require a decision in favor of the surviving residuary legatees. One of them is the circumstance that the residue of the estate is larger than the part disposed of by specific legacies, which gives added force to the presumption that the testator refrained from giving all his property to the residuaries only for the sake of the particular legatees. More important, however, is this consideration: Of the ten nieces and nephews to whom specific legacies were given, seven were also made residuary legatees. In the case of each of the other three the language relating to the specific legacy was followed by the express statement that the legatee " is to have no share in the residue and remainder of my estate." Although this provision might be open to interpretation as a mere express statement of what would be implied without it, we regard it as showing affirmatively that the testator did not wish the three legatees referred to to receive more than the specific amount allotted to them. And from his expressly indicating that these three were to receive nothing from the residue it may be inferred that it was not his purpose that any unnamed heirs should be more favored in this regard. But while in our view these specific provisions of the will plainly show the testator intended that the three legatees who were not included among the residuaries should receive no more of his estate than the sums specifically set apart to them, we think if these provisions had been omitted the same purpose would have been sufficiently clear. We prefer to rest our decision upon the general principle rather than upon exceptional features of the particular case.

We regard the rule that lapsed shares of deceased residuary legatees shall be treated as intestate property as in direct conflict with the one to which this court is definitely committed — that the actual purpose of the testator, so far as it can be ascertained, must be given effect. The presumption against intestacy of any part of the estate is a means of carrying out this policy which is disregarded by taking lapsed legacies out of the residue for the benefit of those who would inherit from the decedent in the absence of a will. The reasons for allowing lapsed specific legacies to fall into the residue apply with equal force in favor of allowing all the residue to go to the surviving residuary legatees in the case of the death of one of them, instead of turning over a part of it to persons for whom other provision had been made, or who had not been referred to in the will at all. The statement sometimes made in support of the latter practice — that the share of a deceased residuary legatee cannot fall into the residue because it is itself a part of the residue — appears rather to play upon words than to point out any real difficulty. The result of these views is the approval of the ruling of the court distributing the residue of the estate among the residuary legatees who survived the testator. . . .[10]

SECTION 2.

Ademption and Related Problems.[11]

IN this Section we attempt to solve the problems which arise when unforeseen things happen to the testator's property between the time when he executes his will and the date of his death. The fact that any one of these events was in fact unforeseen in a particular case is often a reproach to the lawyer who drew the will. Careful draftsmen consider the possibility that things of this nature may happen and they make adequate provision in the will with reference to them. Indeed, a study of this Section will serve you well if it undermines the naïve but natural assumption that when a testator dies he is still going to own the property he owns now, and develops a sophisticated foresight as to the kinds of things that are likely to happen to various types of property. You may come to the conclusion that specific legacies of things of substantial value are generally unwise. And you will probably find additional evidence that it is prudent for a testator to reëxamine his will frequently to be sure that it adequately meets changed conditions.

By way of introduction to problems of ademption, it is necessary to distinguish between three types of legacies and devises — specific, general, and demonstrative. This classification is not artificial; for under these three names the courts separate cases in which testators have essentially different dispositive ideas in mind.

If a testator intends to give a particular chattel or piece of real estate to a person, the legacy or devise is specific. If he intends to confer a benefit measured (usually) in money or (rarely) in some other commodity, such benefit to be conferred out of his estate gener-

[10] The result reached by this case is prescribed by statute in some states. Pa. Stat. (Purdon 1930) Tit. 20, § 253; R. I. Gen. Laws (1938) Ch. 566, § 7. The Ohio lapse statute provides that if there is a residuary gift to relatives and one of them predeceases the testator, (a) if he leaves issue surviving the testator, the issue takes, (b) if he leaves no such issue, the other residuary legatees take. Ohio Gen. Code (Page, 1938) § 10504–73.

[11] See generally Mechem, "Specific Legacies of Unspecific Things," 87 U. of Pa. L. Rev. 546 (1939); Page, "Ademption by Extinction: Its Practical Effects," (1943) Wis. L. Rev. 11.

ally, then the gift is general. If he intends to confer a general benefit but intends that the claim of the legatee shall be primarily satisfied out of specific property, then the gift is demonstrative. As will appear, it is frequently no easy matter to determine whether a particular gift is of one or the other of these types.

Specific legacies and devises and their characteristics. A gift of " my mother's portrait painted by Silas Jones " is obviously specific. So also is a devise of " the land and buildings at 35 Oak Street." " My 100 shares of stock of the AB Corporation " is clear enough; but what of " 100 shares of the stock of the AB Corporation " if (1) T owns no stock of this corporation, or (2) T owns 100 shares, or (3) T owns 500 shares? [12] A specific legacy or devise has one advantage and one disadvantage from the point of view of the legatee. The advantage lies in the fact that it is not " abated " until after the residuary and general legacies and devises — that is, if the testator's assets are insufficient to satisfy all the gifts in his will, either because he did not own enough property at his death or because of the shrinkage due to debts, taxes and administration expense, all lands and chattels specifically devised or bequeathed are turned over to the specific devisees or legatees before any of the general legacies are paid. Thus, if a testator dies leaving creditors, the executor is bound to sell assets for the satisfaction of creditors in the following order, except so far as a different order is prescribed in the will:

1. Intestate property,
2. Residuary devises and bequests,
3. General devises and bequests,
4. Specific devises and bequests.[13]

The disadvantage of the specific gift is that it is subject to ademption — that is, if the specific property given is not among the testator's assets at the time of his death, the legatee gets nothing. The problems arising out of this apparently simple rule constitute the subject matter of the cases hereinafter appearing. The difficulty of these problems, and in many cases the unsatisfactory nature of the decision arrived at, may indicate that the apparently simple rule has fundamental defects.[14]

General legacies and their characteristics. A gift of " $1000 " is

---

[12] See Unitarian Society *v.* Tufts, 151 Mass. 76, 23 N. E. 1006 (1890); Re Willcocks, [1921] 2 Ch. 327; Partridge *v.* Partridge, Cas. t. Talb. 226 (1736).

[13] On abatement generally, see Atkinson, Wills (1937) 707.

[14] This has been ably suggested in Note: The Ademption of Legacies of Stocks and Bonds, 41 Yale L. J. 101 (1931) albeit the suggestion is couched in the lush idiom of the missionary days of " realism " and the " functional approach." For example, " Fortunately these technicalities [i.e. the distinction between general, specific and demonstrative legacies] are but the remnants of a conceptualistic mode of thinking that is fundamentally foreign to the modern outlook." 41 Yale L. J. at 106.

the common type of general legacy. Such a gift, when measured in money, is also commonly called a pecuniary legacy. The effectiveness of a gift of $1000 to A is not dependent upon the testator having $1000 in money at the time of his death; it is the duty of the executor to sell property not specifically bequeathed in order to produce the $1000 for payment to A. There can be general legacies which are not pecuniary legacies; but these are not common. Thus, if T bequeaths " 100 shares of U. S. Steel common stock " to A, (in the absence of other indications, from the will or the circumstances in which it was written, that this was a legacy of specific shares of Steel owned by T) it is the duty of the executor to sell assets of the estate not specifically bequeathed, buy 100 shares of Steel with the proceeds, and deliver the certificate to A. The assets of the testator's estate may be insufficient to pay a general legacy, and for this reason the legatee may not get his money; but a general legacy is a claim upon the general assets of the estate, not upon any particular chattel, and hence is not subject to " ademption." Specific legacies and devises are satisfied before general legacies; or, to put it another way, general legacies are sacrificed to creditors ahead of specific gifts.

Demonstrative legacies and their characteristics. Suppose T's will provides, " I bequeath $1000 to A and I direct that my ten shares of U. S. Steel be sold and the proceeds applied to payment of this gift." This is a demonstrative legacy — i.e. a general legacy charged upon specific property. Such a gift, like a general legacy, is not subject to ademption; thus, if T gives away the U. S. Steel stock before his death, A has a general legacy of $1000 payable out of the assets of the estate not specifically given. Similarly, if the U. S. Steel stock is still owned by T at his death but sells for only $600, A is paid the $600 and has a general legacy for $400. In the matter of abatement of legacies (due to insufficiency of T's estate or the claims of T's creditors) a demonstrative legacy ranks with specific legacies to the extent of the specific property upon which it is charged. Thus, in the last supposed case, if the claims of creditors reduce T's estate so that general legatees can only be paid 50 cents on the dollar, A is paid the $600 which is brought in by the sale of the stock, and he also gets $200 from the general assets (being 50% of his claim for a balance of $400 over the proceeds of the specific property).[15]

[15] A demonstrative legacy may often be used to minimize inheritance taxes. Suppose T is domiciled in Massachusetts and owns New York land. He wishes to give a legacy of $100,000 to his sister, S, and another legacy of $100,000 to his grandchild, G. Under the Massachusetts inheritance tax law a legacy of this amount to a sister is taxed at the rate of 8 per cent, but a similar legacy to a grandchild is taxed at 4 per cent. Mass. Gen. Laws (Ter. Ed. 1932) C. 65, § 1. New York has an estate tax law modelled upon the Federal act which imposes a flat rate of tax not dependent upon the degree of relationship of the legatee to the testator. Therefore, T will save taxes if he directs that the

Early history of "ademption" and "revocation by conveyance."[16] As has been pointed out, the passage of personal property upon death was formerly handled by the ecclesiastical courts, and these were dominated by Civil Law ideas. Swinburne, who presided over the ecclesiastical court at York, wrote in 1590 the treatise on wills which was classic for over a century; and this treatise was little more than an anglicization of Roman Law on the subject. Thus the Roman term " ademptio " was transliterated into the English word " ademption " and given its Roman Law meaning. " Ademption of legacies," says Swinburne,[17] " is two folde, *expressed* and *secrete: expressed*, when the testator doth by words take away the legacie before given: *secrete*, when the testator doth by deedes without words take away the legacie, as when he doth give away the thing bequeathed, or doth voluntarily alienate the same before his death." Thus we find that, in its origin as an English word, " ademption " includes what we now call revocation by subsequent document as well as acts with reference to the property bequeathed which prevent the bequest from taking effect. Obviously both of these things were thought of as means by which, *at the time the act of " ademption " was done*, the testator could nullify the legacy.

In the law of real property the Civil Law notions were not accepted; but, in the point which concerns us here, a similar result was reached by other means. The Statute of Wills (1540) provided that " every person . . . having, or which hereafter shall have " any lands could, with restrictions here unimportant, devise the same. The quoted words were construed by the courts as requiring that the testator " have " the lands at the time of the will;[18] whence arose the rule that after-acquired realty could not be devised. The devise was considered as being revocably operative at the time the will was executed. If the land was thereafter alienated and was then re-acquired, this after-acquired title could not pass.[19] The alienation, which made it impossible for the property to pass under the will, was habitually referred to as " revocation by conveyance."

Effect of statutes requiring certain formalities for revocation of wills; necessary change in the concept of ademption. It was all very well, prior to 1677, to say that an alienation of a portrait " adeemed " (i.e., revoked) a specific bequest of the portrait and that an aliena-

---

legacy to S be paid out of the New York land and the legacy to G be paid out of Massachusetts assets. If T makes no direction in the will, the executor cannot thus marshal the assets to produce this lower tax. Kingsbury *v.* Chapin, 196 Mass. 533, 82 N. E. 700 (1907).

[16] See Warren, " History of Ademption," 25 Iowa L. Rev. 290 (1940). As to the domination of Civil Law ideas in the ecclesiastical courts, see Chapter I, Introduction, supra.

[17] Swinburne, Wills (1590) 277.

[18] Brett *v.* Rigden, Plowden 340, 344 (1568).

[19] Harwood *v.* Goodright, 1 Cowper, 87, 90 (1774).

tion of Blackacre " revoked by conveyance " a specific devise of the same; for up to that time a will, whether of realty or personalty, could be revoked without any formalities at all. However, in 1677, the Statute of Frauds prescribed that wills could be revoked only by certain writings and certain specified acts to the document itself, and all modern statutes impose the familiar formal requirements upon revocation.[20] Since that date, it has become necessary to revise the ancient Roman notion of ademption and its common-law counterpart, revocation by conveyance. No longer can these be considered as methods of revocation of wills, for the statutes forbid. They are now merely expressions of the truism that the testator cannot dispose in his will of property which he does not own at his death. " Revocation by conveyance " as a term has passed out of current legal usage, largely because the universal statutes permitting devise of after-acquired property long ago deprived it of its original significance. The term " ademption " is now applied to both realty and personalty, — an unfortunate term because, although it was fairly descriptive of the doctrine it represented before the Statute of Frauds, it is presently misleading.

ELWYN v. DeGARMENDIA.

COURT OF APPEALS OF MARYLAND, 1925.

148 Md. 109, 128 Atl. 913.

BOND, C. J. . . . The case is that in 1913 the testatrix made a will which contained a legacy to the petitioner of " one string of my pearls," and a legacy to a Mrs. Rojestvensky of " the second string of my pearls," and at the time of her death in 1923 she had all her pearls combined in one string or collar. And in a form of will prepared by the testatrix in the year 1922, but never executed (see In re DeGarmendia Estate, 146 Md. 47), she omitted the legacies of pearls to Mrs. Elwyn and Mrs. Rojestvensky, and to the form of bequest to her sister, Mrs. Von Walbrunn, as it appeared in the will of 1913, she added the words " including my pearls." The question to be decided, then, is whether the legacy of one or two strings to the petitioner has been lost by ademption. The executor, in making up his administration account, assumed that the legacy had been adeemed, and stated that the collar made up of all the 164 pearls would be distributed to Caroline Von Walbrunn. The petitioner prayed the orphans' court that this distribution might be changed, and the string of pearls be distributed to her; and the petition was answered by the executor and, after testimony had been taken, dismissed. The petitioner appeals from the order of dismissal.

[20] See Chapter V, Introduction.

At the time of making the will of 1913 the testatrix had a double necklace of pearls, with the two strings united by a jewelled clasp. One string was shorter than the other, so as to lie inside, and both strings were made up in the usual method, with the pearls graduated in size toward the largest in the center. The pearls are now in Paris, where the testatrix last resided. Beyond the facts just stated, there is no description in the record, and apparently no knowledge here, of the number, characteristics or qualities of the pearls; and no estimate of the value, or proportion of value, in each string, is given. It is to be observed that by the provisions of the will neither of the legatees is given one string rather than another. Each is to have one or the other, indifferently. The legacy is a specific one, in that it refers to the pearls which the testatrix owned, and the executor is charged with the duty of dividing the necklace, and allotting the two strings. It was permissible for the testatrix to provide for such an allotment by the executor; such provisions have, indeed, been long familiar, as when a testator bequeaths one of his horses, not naming which, to a designated legatee, and the like. Ward on Legacies, 17.

A specific legacy, that is, a legacy of something distinguished from the rest of the testator's estate, is adeemed or nullified if the thing given does not continue in existence, so distinguished from the rest of the testator's estate at the time of his decease. And the ademption might, of course, result not only from complete loss or destruction of the subject of the gift, but also from changes which involve a loss of its identity as specified.

Ademption, we think, is to be sought for in the facts as to destruction or loss of the thing specified in the legacy, or loss of its identity as specified, rather than in change of intention on the testator's part. Lord Thurlow, who decided the leading case of Ashburner *v.* McGuire, 2 Bro. Ch. C. 110, after two years of study and reflection (Chaworth *v.* Beech, 4 Ves. Jr. 555, 556), concluded that the only rule to be adhered to was to see whether the subject of the specific bequest remained *in specie* at the time of the testator's death, for if it did not, then there must be an end of the bequest; and that the idea of discussing what were the particular motives and intention of the testator in each case, in destroying the subject of the bequest, would be productive of endless uncertainty and confusion. . . . That conclusion did not gain entire acceptance, and many decisions have since treated of ademption as a change of mind. But those very decisions make it evident that, if a question of ademption is approached from that side, the uncertainty and confusion which Lord Thurlow predicted is likely to result, and the courts may be embarrassed with problems of proof of the new intention, possibly of the admission of subsequent parol declarations of the testator (cf. Grogan *v.* Ashe, 156 N. C. 286), and infringements upon the rule restricting the courts to formally executed wills for the ascertainment of the intentions of a decedent with respect to the disposal of property. . . .

This brings the inquiry down to the effect of the reference in the legacies to the two strings into which the pearls were then divided. Does it render the continued existence of those particular strings essential to the gifts, or may the gifts be regarded as independent of that division? The mere designation of the form or locality of a thing given is not always decisive. In Joynes *v.* Hamilton, 98 Md. 665, 683, this Court held that in a legacy of a ground rent redeemable at any time upon payment of $2,000, the testator must have had in mind the possibility of redemption and substitution of the money, and to have intended that the money should pass under the legacy. " When," says 1 Roper, Legacies, 344, " from the nature of the place in which the goods are specified to be, it is considered that the locality of them was not referred to as essential to the bequest, but merely as descriptive of the articles meant to be given, and substituted in lieu of a schedule particularizing them," no ademption should result from a moving of them. . . . So Roper cites illustrations of gifts of the testator's furniture in a designated house, which, being all the furniture the testator owned, was thought to have been intended to pass even if moved from that house. . . .

The question, then, is one of the testator's intention in the designation or description of the articles given. Are we to suppose the testatrix in the will in this case to have intended that her pearls were to go to Mrs. Elwyn and Mrs. Rojestvensky in these two strings or not at all, so that if the strings were broken, even by accident, and the pearls commingled, the legacies were to fail. Or if she had deliberately commingled the pearls for some temporary purpose, so that precisely the same grouping as that in the two strings could not be restored, should we say that by this commingling the exact subjects of the gifts, as they were intended, had lost their identity, or existence, *in specie?* As has been observed, the testatrix did not give either legatee a particular string of pearls, but only one or the other indifferently. She was disposed to treat the legatees equally as objects of her friendship and bounty, although by taking the pearls as they were then strung she could give only equal chances in an unequal division. We think it would be more nearly in accordance with her intention to regard the existing division as one adopted merely because of its convenience; and that we should be giving undue weight to that element in the designation of the subjects of the legacies, and should defeat the testatrix's purpose, if we should hold that the restringing of all the pearls into one necklace worked an ademption. We, therefore, disagree with the view taken by the orphans' court, and hold that the petitioner's legacy in the will of 1913 is still valid and effective despite the commingling of the pearls in the one string.

The effect of this decision is that the executor has in his possession oue collection of pearls bequeathed to two legatees, and the legal situation of the legatees is precisely that of any other two owners of property indistinguishably commingled by a cause beyond the control of either owner; the two are owners in common. . . .

PROBLEM.

1. Margaret owned one-half of the premises at 22 Oliver Street, New York City. In 1884 she executed a will devising this property to her daughter, Lizzie Ametrano. In 1896 the City of New York took the property by eminent domain, Margaret having refused to sell. The compensation awarded for the taking was $4900. Margaret deposited this $4900 in a savings bank and later withdrew all the interest and $400 of principal. She then died. What rights has Lizzie? Ametrano v. Downs, 170 N. Y. 388, 63 N. E. 340 (1902).

IN RE BARROWS' ESTATE.

SUPREME COURT OF VERMONT, 1931.

103 Vt. 501, 156 Atl. 408.

[Mary L. Barrows lived in a house on North Avenue, Burlington. She executed a will which directed her executor to sell the same and to pay one-half of the proceeds to R. G. Malhiot and Mrs. S. M. Malhiot. Later the testatrix became insane and a guardian was appointed. He moved her to a sanitarium and, since the homestead was producing no income, and could not be rented with substantial repairs which it was not prudent to make, sold the homestead under an order of the probate court. He obtained $9000 from the sale and expended $2000 thereof for support of the testatrix. The remaining $7000 was kept in a separate bank account. At all times the testatrix owned $24,000 worth of securities listed on the New York Stock Exchange and readily salable. The guardian had no knowledge of the contents of the testatrix's will.

On the death of the testatrix, the probate court awarded to R. G. Malhiot one-fourth of $9000. The residuary legatees appealed.]

MOULTON, J. Both sides agree that this is a specific legacy, and so it is, for it is a bequest of certain part of the specified fund, i.e., the proceeds of the sale of the identified property. . . . The subject of the gift is not the real estate and furniture, but a designated part of the money received from the sale of it. Since it is specific, it may be adeemed. . . . The intent, on the part of the testatrix, to make it specific, which clearly appears from the nature of the bequest, necessarily includes an intent to render it subject to ademption. . . .

A specific legacy is adeemed and the legatee takes nothing where the particular property has ceased to exist or has been disposed of by the testator during his lifetime. Thayer v. Paulding, 200 Mass. 98, 85 N. E. 868, 869; or where it is so changed in substance that it does not remain in specie at the time the will goes into effect. Ford v. Ford, 23 N. H. 212, 215. But not where the property, although somewhat changed, remains the same in substance. . . .

As to whether, in cases not involving a fortuitous destruction of the subject-matter, there must be an intention on the part of the testator in order to work an ademption, the authorities have not been harmonious. In Roman law, an animus adimendi was necessary. Just. Dig. Lib. 11, tit. 20, para. 12. But, by the decided weight of modern authority, intention is immaterial. Thus, in Re Brann, 219 N. Y. 263, 114 N. E. 404, 405, L. R. A. 1918B, 663, 665, Cardozo, C. J. says: " It was once thought that ademption was dependent on intention, and ' it was, therefore, held in old days that when a change was effected by public authority, or without the will of the testator, ademption did not follow. But for many years, that has ceased to be law.' * * * What courts look to now is the fact of change. That ascertained, they do not trouble themselves about the reason for the change."

There are, however, a number of decisions wherein a question of ademption has arisen from the act of a guardian or conservator of the estate of a testator who has been adjudged insane after the execution of the will containing the specific bequest. Since this question has not heretofore been presented in this state, a somewhat extended inquiry into the facts disclosed in these cases, and the reasoning upon which they have been decided, will be helpful in the determination of the present controversy.

It was held in England that, where the subject of a specific bequest was sold by the committee in lunacy of an insane testator, in the course of his administrative duty as such, the legacy was adeemed, notwithstanding the fact that the proceeds of the sale were earmarked. In re Freer, L. R. 22 Ch. Div. 622, 627, 628; Jones v. Green, L. R. 5 Eq. 555, 559; and see annotation 30 A. L. R. 679 for further citations. . . . The rule, however, is now changed by statute, and the acts of committees in lunacy no longer work ademptions where the proceeds of property specifically bequeathed is not otherwise applied by the committee. 53 and 54 Vict. c. 5, para. 123 (1); In re Walker, [1921] 2 Ch. 63, 65, 66. See annotation 30 A. L. R. 680. Under this statute it has been held that a specific legacy partly used for the support of the lunatic testator was adeemed to that extent. In re Hodgson's Trusts, [1919] Ch. Div. 189, 196. . . .

The doctrine of the English cases was adopted in Hoke v. Herman, 21 Pa. 301, 305. . . .

On the other hand, the test of intention was approved in Wilmerton v. Wilmerton, 176 F. 896, 900, 100 C. C. A. 366, 28 L. R. A.

(N. S.) 405 (cert. den. 217 U. S. 606, 30 S. Ct. 696, 54 L. Ed. 900). The conservator of the estate of a lunatic testator collected in part the proceeds of a certain fund, which had been made the subject of a specific legacy, and used the amount collected for the support of the lunatic, although there were ample assets of other description available for this purpose. The court refused the reasoning of the English and Pennsylvania cases, and held that the conservator was a custodian merely, with no power to change the testator's intention, since the latter, being lunatic, was, at least so far as a disposing mind was concerned, civilly dead. In holding that there was no ademption, "the question, in our judgment," said the court, "is not whether, as a mere matter of accident, or of purpose outside of the testator's purpose, the thing set apart as the corpus of a special bequest has been changed in specie. The real question is whether, all things considered, the testator's testamentary disposition did, or did not, remain, with reference to the particular thing embodied in the specific bequest or its proceeds, the same as it was the last moment he was able to exercise a testamentary disposition. In that way, and in that way only, we think, can the right of the man to dispose of his property according to his own wishes, exempt from the interference, caprice or interest of others, be fully carried out. In that way only can his intention, as embodied in his will, be truly administered." . . .

On the record in the instant case the only issue concerns that part of the fund used by the guardian for the support of the testatrix. The unexpended balance has been kept separate from the other assets, and is intact and identified. Since the proceeds of the property, and not the property itself, was the subject of the bequest, its character was not lost or its substance changed because the sale occurred during the lifetime of the testatrix. Therefore there is no question of an ademption arising from a change in the nature of the property bequeathed. . . .

The guardian has acted in good faith. The sale was authorized, and indeed, in view of the unproductive character of the property, its deterioration, and the expense involved in its retention, from an economic standpoint, this was unquestionably the prudent and proper course to pursue.

It is true that there were other assets, not specifically bequeathed, and readily salable. . . . Furthermore, if there had been no guardianship and the bills for the testatrix's support had remained unpaid at the time of her death, this property, the subject of the residuary bequest, would have been held to respond to the indebtedness, and, if sufficient for that purpose, no abatement of the specific legacies would follow. Kearns v. Kearns, 77 N. J. Eq. 453, 76 A. 1042, 140 Am. St. Rep. 575.

Nevertheless, the fact remains that a portion of the fund composed of the proceeds of the sale was not in the estate at the time the will took effect. The operation of a bequest of personal property is referred to the condition of that property at the death of the testator. In re Foote, 22 Pick (Mass.) 299. The will speaks as of that time. In re Bugbee's Will, 92 Vt. 175, 186, 102 A. 484; In re Walbridge's Will, 102 Vt. 429, 431, 150 A. 126. We consider that the rule, supported by the weight of authority, to the effect that no question of intention is material, but that the test is whether the property remains in specie at the time of the death of the testator, ought to be adopted. It follows as a logical consequence that, when a part of the proceeds were expended by the guardian, the legacies were adeemed to that extent. . . .

Decree reversed, and cause remanded. . . .[21]

WILLIS *v.* BARROW.

Supreme Court of Alabama, 1929.

218 Ala. 549, 119 So. 678.

[Thomas Jefferies executed his will on February 22, 1927. It gave to each of three sisters named Autrey "one-third of the money owned by me on deposit in the Troy Savings Bank of Troy, New York." At that time there was on deposit in that bank $3541.81. Six weeks later Jefferies withdrew the balance in the Troy Savings Bank and deposited the same in a separate account in the First National Bank in Mobile, Alabama. At the time he had another account in the First National Bank, but he did not mingle the two. A month later he died.]

BOULDIN, J. . . . The case is narrowed to a construction of the bequests to each of the three Autrey sisters in these words:

"One-third the money owned by me which is on deposit in the Troy Savings Bank of Troy, New York."

Eminent counsel on both sides treat the case as involving two inquiries, viz.:

(1) Are these demonstrative or specific legacies?

(2) If specific, did the withdrawal of the fund from the Troy Bank work an ademption of the legacies? . . .

We are clear to the conclusion these are specific legacies. . . .

The question then recurs, Were these legacies adeemed by the transfer of the fund from the Savings Bank of Troy, N. Y., to the First National Bank of Mobile, Alabama?

The argument of appellants proceeds thus: A deposit on savings

[21] For comment on this case, see 45 Harv. L. Rev. 710 (1932); 41 Yale L. J. 101 (1931); 17 Va. L. Rev. 584 (1931); 16 Corn. L. Q. 623 (1931); 79 U. of Pa. L. Rev. 990 (1931).

account creates the legal relation of debtor and creditor between banker and depositor; the testator is presumed to know this legal status; he had no specific money in the bank, but a debt against the banker; the bequest was, therefore, merely of the debt owing by the bank; the transfer of his deposit was payment by the Troy Bank; payment of a debt works ademption of a specific bequest of the debt. A will speaks as of the death of the testator; at that time there was no debt from the Troy Bank in existence; hence the subject matter of the gift was no longer in being. We cannot concur in this process of reasoning.

True, of course, the legal relation of debtor and creditor between banker and debtor exists in such case; true, also, this debt was paid upon presentation of a passbook and draft to the Mobile Bank. As a rule, payment of a debt made the object of a specific legacy extinguishes the legacy by ademption.

But a deposit in bank is more than an ordinary debt. Money on deposit in the popular sense is a thing, a fund subject to the depositor's call. Such also is the language of business. It is known as a *deposit*. It is so designated in law, carrying distinct legal qualities. Money is deposited. Money is to be returned. The banker cannot be called upon at any place. His undertaking is to have money at a designated place, ready to pass it through the window when demanded according to banking rules.

That the testator was thinking of this deposit as so much money rather than a mere chose in action is clear. He designates it " the money owned by me." In his thinking, this money was as distinctly a " thing " to be bequeathed as if it had been in a separate package.

We see no indication of a different intent in transferring this fund to another bank. The transfer was within about 6 weeks after making the will; the transferee bank had been named his executor, occupied a distinct position of trust. Significant is the fact that the identical fund was put in a separate savings deposit rather than commingled with a like savings deposit then in the same bank.

The authorities are much in conflict as to whether the intention of the testator in his susequent acts is to be sought in passing upon the question of ademption. See 28 R. C. L. 344, § 338; Elwyn *v.* DeGarmendia, 148 Md. 109, 128 A. 913, 40 A. L. R. 553, 556.

Not now endeavoring to determine which rule is supported by better reason, we limit our inquiry as to the intent of the will itself. Accordingly, we think the fact of his keeping this fund intact as a distinct entity in the bank he had recently chosen as the executor of his will is strongly indicative of his thinking of the fund itself as the object of his gift; and not the place of deposit. The place was merely descriptive; is still descriptive in connection with other agreed facts in identifying the fund bequeathed. . . .

We are at the conclusion that these are specific bequests of a definite fund, which was kept intact, and now fully identified as the same "money" bequeathed. In such case there is no ademption. . . .

PROBLEM.

1. T executed his will in 1912 and made therein a gift as follows: "I bequeath and devise to A, as trustee, the mortgage deed which I hold on property of one Moxon in Boston, the real estate thereby conveyed and the note and claim thereby secured, in trust to either assign or collect the same as soon as convenient and to divide the proceeds between X, Y and Z." Moxon, the mortgagor, paid off the mortgage in 1914 and T deposited the proceeds, $3000, in three savings banks in equal shares, where they remained intact until his death. In 1917 T died, leaving substantially no assets other than these deposits. X, Y and Z were T's only living relatives; the residuary legatee was a lady at whose house T had boarded for some years. X, Y and Z brought a proceeding to obtain the savings deposits. Without objection there was admitted in evidence a letter from T to X, dated 1915, stating that T had $3000 in the bank and that after his death X, Y and Z would get it. What decree should be rendered? Moffatt *v.* Heon, 242 Mass. 201, 136 N. E. 123 (1922). Compare Joynes *v.* Hamilton, 98 Md. 665, 57 Atl. 25 (1904), stated in Elwyn *v.* DeGarmendia, supra, p. 152.[22]

CURTIS *v.* CURTIS.

COURT OF CHANCERY, DELAWARE, 1938.

2 Atl. (2d) 88.

[Bill for instructions to determine whether a legacy of certain bonds was adeemed. The learned Chancellor held that there was no ademption in the following opinion.]

THE CHANCELLOR [WOLCOTT] . . . The testatrix provided in the seventh item of her will as follows:

"Seventh, I give and bequeath unto my said husband, Alfred A. Curtis, any bond or bonds of Curtis and Brother Company, a corporation of the State of Delaware, which I may own, hold or be entitled to, for his own use absolutely." . . .

After the will was executed Curtis and Brother Company was placed in receivership by decree of this court on February 6, 1931. The receivership proceedings eventuated in a practical reorganiza-

[22] Facts stated in this Problem are drawn, not only from the Massachusetts Reports, but also from the original Record on file at the Supreme Judicial Court. Joynes *v.* Hamilton was cited in the specific legatee's brief but ignored by the Court.

SECT. II.]   ADEMPTION   161

tion of the corporation. The reorganization was in accordance with a plan which the receivers formulated and which, on the receivers' petition, this court after full hearing approved as fair and equitable. All the bondholders approved the plan. In furtherance of an opportunity to effectuate the plan of reorganization a sale of all of the corporation's assets was ordered. A new corporation was organized under the laws of this State to bid in and acquire the assets as the plan contemplated. The new corporation took the name of Curtis Paper Company. It became the successful bidder at the sale and thereupon acquired the entire assets of the old corporation. The business of the old company was carried on by the new.

The plan provided that the new corporation should create an issue of $290,000 of bonds to be secured by a first and closed mortgage on the same identical property which had been pledged by way of mortgage to secure the issue of bonds in identical amount of the old company, of which the testatrix held $37,000 worth. Except for the matter of making a temporary five-year arrangement whereby interest up to six per cent was payable only in case it was earned and whereby a requirement for a minimum sinking fund payment of two per cent per annum was provided, the new bonds were identical with the old ones in every substantial respect. The name of the obligor was, to be sure, different. But the amount authorized, the security pledged, the maturity, the rate (except during the temporary period) were identical with the old issue. The business of the new company was likewise the same as was that of the old. No new assets were acquired.

Under the plan the holders of the old bonds were to receive in exchange therefor bonds of the new company on a par for par basis. The testatrix received in exchange for her $37,000 of bonds of the old company a like amount of the bonds of the new company. . . .

What the testatrix bequeathed to her husband was all of the bonds of Curtis and Brother Company which she held, the same being $37,000 in amount. When she died, however, she possessed no bonds bearing the name of that company as the obligor. But she did possess a like amount of bonds of Curtis Paper Company which she had received in exchange for the Curtis and Brother Company bonds under the circumstances recited in the statement of facts. Those circumstances show that the bonds she possessed, regarding them as securities for the payment of money, were in every substantial respect the same securities as she had when she executed the will. The only difference was in the identity of the obligor. But that is a difference which in essence is purely artificial. The new company was the same as the old, except as the law attributes different personalities to the artificial entities of its creation. If it had been practical to accomplish the so-called reorganization by retaining the old company's corporate existence and then changing its name by proper amendment to Curtis Paper Company, we would have in every substantial respect exactly what we have now. . . .

If the alteration in the subject matter of the legacy be purely formal, no ademption is worked. The test which the courts apply is the test of substantial identity. Though the test may be found from an examination of the authorities to be productive of different results when applied to some species of property, yet with respect to corporate stocks and bonds courts are practically unanimous in holding that a legacy of such securities is not adeemed by the circumstance that the bequeathed securities were exchanged by the testator for other securities which he held at death, if the only difference between the two is one in name and form only. . . .

FIRST NATIONAL BANK OF BOSTON v. PERKINS INSTITUTE FOR THE BLIND.

Supreme Judicial Court of Massachusetts, 1931.

275 Mass. 498, 176 N. E. 532.

Carroll, J. This is a petition for instructions by the executor of the will of Amelia G. Dyer who died July 4, 1928. In the sixteenth clause of her will the testatrix gave to her nephew, John Baker, hereinafter referred to as the legatee, " all of my stock in the Standard Oil Company of New York and the Standard Oil Company of New Jersey." Instructions are sought as to the disposition of $7,000 in principal amount of the debentures of the Standard Oil Company of New Jersey, which the legatee contends passed to him under this clause of the will, and the other respondents contend belong to them under the residuary clause.

It was agreed that at the time of the execution of the will the testatrix owned one hundred ten shares of the seven per cent preferred stock of the Standard Oil Company of New Jersey; that this stock was callable at $115 a share and accrued dividend and was called for payment by vote of the directors on November 15, 1926. To meet this call debentures totaling $120,000,000 were to be issued; these debentures were sold to bankers in New York. The bankers agreed to give the holders of the stock a preferential right to subscribe for these debentures. The testatrix sent to the bankers her one hundred ten shares of stock, subscribing for a sufficient number of debentures to absorb the stock. The issue of the debentures was oversubscribed; accordingly, there was allowed to Mrs. Dyer seven of these debentures in payment for sixty-two shares of stock. The remainder of her stock was redeemed by the New Jersey company. At the time of her death Mrs. Dyer owned the $7,000 of debentures.

There was no stock of the Standard Oil Company of New Jersey in the estate of the testatrix when she died. Her stock in that company had been taken up by the payment in cash from the New Jersey company, and the debentures which had been purchased by the bankers and transferred to her by these bankers in exchange for sixty-two of her shares. The debentures came to her, not from the New Jersey company but from the bankers who were the owners of them. In these circumstances the legacy of the stock of the Standard Oil Company of New Jersey was adeemed. The legacy of the specific thing had been disposed of by the testatrix before her death. The case cannot be distinguished from Moffatt v. Heon, 242 Mass. 201, where it was held that the specific legacy of a mortgage which was paid before the death of the testator had been adeemed. . . .[23]

IN RE SLATER.

Court of Appeal, England.

[1907] 1 Ch. 665.

By his will dated February 8, 1904, the testator, J. A. Slater, made the following bequest: " To Catherine Pontin Slater I bequeath the interest during her life arising from money invested in . . . Lambeth Waterworks Company." . . .

The testator died on May 15, 1905.

At the date of his will there was standing in the name of the testator in the books of the Lambeth Waterworks Company 1075£. Lambeth Waterworks 10£. per cent. stock.

By the Metropolis Water Act, 1902, it was provided that as from June 24, 1904, the undertaking of each of the metropolitan water companies (including the Lambeth Waterworks Company) should be transferred to and vested in a water board created by the Act and called the Metropolitan Water Board, and that the Water Board should pay to each company as compensation for the transfer of their undertaking a sum to be determined, in default of agreement, by arbitration under the Act, but the sum so payable might, if the Water Board and the company so agreed, be discharged wholly or partly in water stock. On August 2, 1904, the directors of the Lambeth Waterworks Company prepared a scheme under the Fourth Schedule of the Act for the application and distribution of the compensation awarded to the company under the Act; and under the scheme, on December 27, 1904, there was issued to the testator in respect of his holding the nominal amount of 3739£. 13s. 2d. Metropolitan Water Board stock. The testator was possessed of this stock at the date of his death.

A summons was taken out by the executors of the will for the determination of the question whether the bequest above set out

[23] For comment on this case see Note: Ademption of Legacies of Stocks and Bonds, 41 Yale L. J. 101 (1931).

comprised the sum of 3739£. 13s. 2d. Metropolitan Water Board stock, or whether the same formed part of the testator's residuary estate.

Joyce, J. held that the Water Board stock did not pass under the bequest, but fell into the residue.

C. P. Slater appealed. . . .

Cozens-Hardy, M. R. . . . The testator in this case in February, 1904, made a bequest which certainly has the merit of brevity. It is a bequest which all parties admit to be a specific bequest.[24] . . .

It is contended on behalf of the appellant that that Metropolitan Water Board B stock is to be substituted for the Lambeth Waterworks stock, and that it ought to go to the tenants for life, and to the persons ultimately entitled to the capital of this specific bequest. That view is opposed on two grounds. It is said first that the provisions of s. 24 of the Wills Act [25] require that this bequest should be construed as to the property comprised therein as speaking from the death, and that if so, there being nothing upon which it can operate — there being at that time no Lambeth Waterworks Company stock — the bequest fails. Alternatively it is said that even if you are in effect to read into the language of this bequest words which make it specific, and applicable only to the stock which the testator had at the date of the will, still that which has since happened has adeemed that specific legacy.

Joyce, J. dealt with the case only on the former of those grounds. He held that s. 24 of the Wills Act applied, there being no sufficient contrary intention to exclude the operation of that section, and that the claim of the specific legatee failed.

I agree with the learned judge in that view. It seems to me that this is a will in which there is no contrary intention at all, or at any rate no sufficient intention to exclude the operation of s. 24. . . .

But, supposing I am wrong in that, and that the appellant is right on this point, and that by construction I am to read this bequest as meaning " I bequeath the interest during her life arising from the money invested in the following particulars which I now hold," then you are face to face with the question, Has not this gift, so far as the Lambeth Waterworks Company's stock is concerned, been adeemed by the subsequent transaction? Speaking for myself, although it

[24] This admission may well have been improvident. To save legacies from ademption courts show a strong tendency to construe them as demonstrative rather than specific. Thus, in Mytton v. Mytton, L. R. 19 Eq. 30 (1874), a gift of " the sum of £3000 invested in Indian security " was held demonstrative despite the fact that at the time of executing the will the testatrix had exactly £3000 of East India debentures. Accord, Johnson v. Conover, 54 N. J. Eq. 333, 35 Atl. 291 (1896) (" the sum of $8000 invested in stocks ").

[25] Section 24 of the Wills Act reads as follows: " Every will shall be construed, with reference to the real estate and personal estate comprised in it, to speak and take effect as if it had been executed immediately before the death of the testator, unless a contrary intention shall appear by the will."

may not be absolutely necessary for the decision of this case, I think it has been.

The Lambeth Waterworks undertaking was sold, and sold for cash — sold, that is, for cash in this sense, that the price was ascertained in cash and could only be paid otherwise than in cash if both the vendors and the purchasers agreed to a scheme providing for satisfying the purchase-money otherwise. That agreement was obtained in the present case. A scheme was prepared, and the Water Board B stock was allotted to the testator in respect of his shares in the old company. But can it possibly be said that that is the same thing? Instead of having shares in a company dependent for its profits upon water rates which they, and they alone, were able to demand from the limited area within the ambit of their Act of Parliament, the Water Board B stock is a stock which is payable out of water rates levied not merely upon the Lambeth Waterworks area, but upon the whole of the metropolitan area, and, I think, also on some districts even outside the metropolitan area. But, more than that, in the event of the water rates being insufficient to provide for the interest the present stock has a claim upon the rateable property in London, and any deficiency has to be made good out of the general rates. I cannot bring myself to say that that is the same thing. I feel bound myself to adopt the view taken not in one case only, but in many, that you have to ask yourself, Where is the thing which is given? If you cannot find it at the testator's death, it is no use trying to trace it unless you can trace it in this sense, that you find something which has been changed in name and form only, but which is substantially the same thing.[26]

[26] On this point, contra, Goode v. Reynolds, 208 Ky. 441, 271 S. W. 600 (1925); In re Peirce, 25 R. I. 34, 54 A. 588 (1903). Accord, Horn's Estate, 317 Pa. 49, 175 A. 414 (1934).

As an indication of the changes that may take place with reference to shares of stock owned at the time a will is made, Horn's Estate, supra, is interesting. The gift there was of " my Ohio Fuel Corporation stock." After the will the following things happened:

(1) In 1926, the Ohio Fuel Corporation, an Ohio corporation, was merged with Columbia Gas & Electric Company, a West Virginia corporation, into Columbia Gas & Electric Company, a Delaware corporation. Testator received, for his 209 shares of Ohio Fuel, 32 shares of preferred and 73 shares of common in the Delaware corporation, plus $44.01 in cash.

(2) In 1929, Columbia Gas & Electric issued 2½ shares of common in exchange for each share of common held, thus increasing testator's holding of common to 182.5 shares.

(3) In 1930 a 25% stock dividend increased his holding of common to 228 shares.

(4) Later Columbia Gas & Electric sold its oil and gas properties to a new corporation known as Columbia Oil and Gasoline Corporation, which issued stock which was put under a voting trust agreement, testator receiving 45 certificates of interest in the voting trust.

(5) At several times Columbia Gas & Electric gave its stockholders purchase " rights " and testator always exercised these rights, thereby acquiring new stock in the corporation.

On this ground also I think that the decision of Joyce, J. was right, and that this appeal must be dismissed.

NOTE: IS PROPERTY DESCRIBED AS OF THE TIME OF THE WILL OR AS OF THE TIME OF TESTATOR'S DEATH? RELATED QUESTIONS.

THE first point of decision in In Re Slater, supra, raises the question here stated. Section 24 of the English Wills Act (quoted in footnote 25, p. 164) is declaratory of the common-law presumption that, in describing property, the will speaks as of the death of the testator. But the presumption is rebuttable; and judgments are bound to differ as to whether the language of a will or the circumstances of its formulation are adequate to rebut it. A sampling of the cases which have arisen will suffice to indicate the variations of the problem and point the moral.

(1) T bequeathed " to Florence Hayes my diamond brooch " and " to Mrs. Lomax any jewelry not otherwise disposed of in this will." At the date of the will T owned a brooch worth $1500. She later purchased a second brooch for $500. Still later she turned in both brooches to a jeweler with $350 cash and got a third brooch, which she owned at the time of her death. It was held that Florence Hayes got the third brooch. Waldo v. Hayes, 96 App. Div. 454, 89 N. Y. S. 69 (1904).

(2) T bequeathed " my piano to Beatrice and my table linen, kitchen furniture, cooking utensils, trinkets and jewelry to Beatrice and Alice." At the time of the will T owned a " player piano." She later sold it to Beatrice's husband for £5. Immediately thereafter she purchased another " electric motor player piano " for £228, which she owned at the time of her death. It was held that the second piano did not pass to Beatrice, since the words " my piano " were a sufficient indication of a contrary intention to take the case out of Wills Act, § 24. In re Sikes, [1927] 1 Ch. 364.

(3) T, a native of Germany, executed his will in 1920. He gave his wife $50,000 and gave legacies totaling 475,000 " marks " to relatives in Germany. He died in 1927. At the date of the will the mark was worth $.0153. Thereafter, the mark further depreciated in value until it was practically worthless and was withdrawn from circulation. In 1924 the mark was re-established upon a gold basis and was called the " reichsmark." At T's death there was no value to the old mark and the reichsmark was worth $.2371. It was held that the legacies were payable in reichsmarks. Matter of Lendle, 250 N. Y. 502, 166 N. E. 182 (1929). But compare Matter of

Teed, 120 Misc. 372 (1923) in which T executed in 1914 a will making a gift of " 5,000 marks," T died in 1920, and it was held that the legacy was payable in marks of 1914 value, not the depreciated marks of 1920.

(4) T executed a will in which he bequeathed " to A 25 of my shares in the XYZ Corporation." At the time of the will T owned 50 shares of XYZ stock, par value $100. Later the XYZ Corporation split its stock 5 for 1, reducing the par value to $20. Therefore, T owned at the time of his death 250 shares of XYZ stock, par value $20. It was held that A should get 125 shares of the new stock, not merely 25. Clifford's Estate, 56 Sol. J. 91 (1911); Guardian, Trust, and Executors Co. of New Zealand v. Smith, [1923] N. Z. L. R. 1284.

A somewhat similar problem arises with some frequency where there is a gift to a person described by a marital relationship and the relationship changes between the date of the will and the date of the testator's death. In Matter of Bradley, 119 Misc. 2, 194 N. Y. S. 888 (1922) there was a gift to " Mrs. Eli Ellis, Pleasant Avenue, Walden, New York." After the will was executed the then Mrs. Ellis died and Ellis married again. It was held that the legacy lapsed. In Solms' Estate, 253 Pa. 293, 98 Atl. 596 (1916) a trust was created for Sidney Solms for life and after his death for " the widow of the said Sidney, should she survive him, for and during the term of her natural life." The woman to whom Solms was married at the date the will was executed died, and when the testator died Solms had married again. It was held that the second Mrs. Solms was not entitled to a life interest in the trust. But there is good authority contra. Meeker v. Draffen, 201 N. Y. 205, 94 N. E. 626 (1911). Compare Crocheron v. Fleming, 74 N. J. Eq. 567, 70 Atl. 691 (1908).

In all of these cases the execution of a codicil after the change has taken place may, under the doctrine of " republication," cause the description to apply as of the date of the codicil rather than as of the date of the will. Thus, in In Re Hardyman, [1925] Ch. 287, T executed a will making a bequest to " the wife of A "; then Mrs. A died and A remarried; then T executed a codicil making minor alterations in the will immaterial to the bequest above quoted. It was held that the republication caused the gift to " the wife of A " to be a gift to the woman who was married to A on the date of the codicil. But a republication was not sufficient to produce this result in Matter of Bradley, discussed in the preceding paragraph.

NOTE: ELECTION REQUIRED OF DEVISEE OR LEGATEE WHOSE OWN PROPERTY IS DEVISED OR BEQUEATHED BY TESTATOR TO ANOTHER.[27]

If a testator should say in his will " I devise Blackacre to A, provided that A conveys Whiteacre to B," it is clear that A would have to elect whether he wants to get Blackacre or keep Whiteacre. He could not do both.

Now suppose that the testator erroneously believes himself to be the owner of both Blackacre and Whiteacre (A's land) — an error which is not uncommon, since laymen frequently misunderstand the legal elements which place title in one member of a family rather than another. Thus believing, he dies leaving a will which provides, " I devise Blackacre to A and Whiteacre to B." Of course, the devise of Whiteacre to B is ineffective, since Whiteacre is owned by A, not by the testator. But can A receive the devise of Blackacre without giving up Whiteacre to B? The answer is, No. The testator has indicated an intention (however based on error) that A shall not have both Blackacre and Whiteacre; and the courts hold that, in the absence of indications to the contrary, this is in effect a devise of Blackacre to A, conditional upon his transfer of Whiteacre to B.

Hence the rule that where a testator devises or bequeaths the property of one beneficiary of his will to another beneficiary of his will, the former must elect whether to (1) take under the will and relinquish his own property thus erroneously devised or bequeathed, or (2) take nothing under the will and keep his own property. See generally Atkinson, Wills, pp. 718–719.

PROBLEM.

T, in 1930 executes a will devising Blackacre to A and Whiteacre to B. In 1932, T conveys Whiteacre to A. In 1933, T dies. Can A receive Blackacre and also keep Whiteacre? Hattersley v. Bissett, 51 N. J. Eq. 597, 29 Atl. 187 (1893). But see Atkinson, Wills, p. 719.

SECTION 3.

Satisfaction of Legacies.

SUPPOSE T executes a will in which he bequeaths $20,000 to his son, S, $20,000 to his daughter, D, and the residue to his wife. Later he gives S $15,000 to set him up in business. Upon T's death, can S also get the full $20,000? The answer is, No. The general legacy to S

[27] It is no easy matter to find an appropriate location for this note. The excuse for locating it here is this: Ademption deals with the situation in which T owned the property at the time of his will but not at the time of his death; this note deals with the situation where he never owned it at all.

has been "satisfied" pro tanto by the inter vivos gift. Therefore, at T's death, S gets only $5,000.

The doctrine of Satisfaction is sometimes called "ademption," sometimes "ademption by satisfaction," sometimes "ademption of portions." But it is clear that there is a generic difference between the doctrine of Satisfaction dealt with in this Section and the doctrine of Ademption discussed in the preceding Section of this Chapter. Ademption can take place only with reference to specific legacies and devises; the legacy or devise is *adeemed* when the testator does not, at his death, own the property which is described in the will. Satisfaction takes place with reference to general and residuary legacies; the legacy is *satisfied*, not because the executor is unable to find property with which to confer the benefit described in the will, but because the testator has already conferred the benefit in his lifetime ("has become his own executor," as it is sometimes said) and does not intend to confer it twice.[28]

Certain rules relating to satisfaction are well settled: [29]

1. Any general bequest *can* be satisfied by the testator inter vivos, and whether it *is* satisfied by an inter vivos gift depends upon the intention of the testator at the time the inter vivos gift is made. The intention of the testator can be established by evidence of his oral declarations. (The obvious difficulties with the statutes of wills seem not to have bothered the courts.)
2. There is a *presumption* of satisfaction if the testator stands *in loco parentis* to the legatee and, after the execution of the will, makes an inter vivos gift of the same kind of property to him. This is called the "presumption against double portions."
3. There is no presumption of satisfaction where
    a. the testator does not stand *in loco parentis* to the legatee, or
    b. the property given inter vivos is not of the same kind as that bequeathed. This latter rule is known as the doctrine of *ejusdem generis* — not to be confused with the general canon of construction, known by the same Latin name.[30]

In these situations the intent to satisfy must be affirmatively proved.

There is an obvious kinship between the doctrine of satisfaction

---

[28] For a good statement of the difference between ademption and satisfaction, see Beck v. McGillis, 9 Barb. 35, 56 (1850).

[29] Atkinson, Wills, p. 685 et seq.

[30] "General words in any contract relating to a particular subject matter shall be interpreted as meaning things of the same kind as the particular matters referred to." 3 Williston on Contracts (Rev. Ed. 1936) § 619. For example, in Bers v. Erie R. R. Co., 225 N. Y. 543, 122 N. E. 456 (1919), a bill of lading limited the liability of the carrier on "private or other sidings"; the court declared that this did not mean all sidings but private sidings and sidings that were like private ones; it did not include public sidings.

relating to legacies and the doctrine of advancements relating to intestate shares (Chapter 1, supra). And the same potential difficulty exists with regard to both doctrines — namely, that the testator or intestate may unintentionally bring the doctrine into operation by making an inter vivos gift. Clients should be warned that inter vivos gifts to children may cause their wills and the intestate laws to have an effect quite different from what they appear to say. It is advisable, in making a substantial gift to a child, to make at the same time a written declaration as to whether or not the gift is intended as an advancement against the child's intestate share or a satisfaction of a legacy made to him.

Appeal of Moore, p. 75 supra, deals with the related question whether a testator can reserve the power to charge or un-charge inter vivos gifts against legacies by unattested memoranda which reflect his changes of mind from time to time. As an authority the case should be taken *cum grano salis*.

CARMICHAEL *v.* LATHROP.

Supreme Court of Michigan, 1896.

108 Mich. 473, 66 N. W. 350.

Hooker, J. The will of Henry P. Pulling was executed in June, 1872. After giving his wife the use and enjoyment of all of his property during life, in lieu of dower, it provided that —

"*Second.* All the remainder of the estate of, in, and to my said property, both real and personal, subject to the said life estate of my said wife, I give, devise, and bequeath to my three daughters, Ada M. Lathrop, of Detroit, Michigan, Emily Lloyd, of Albany, New York, and Marilla B. Carmichael, of Amsterdam, New York, and to their heirs forever, share and share alike. . . ."

Mr. Pulling died in July, 1890, and the will was probated August 19, 1890. Joseph Lathrop qualified as executor. The probate records show that at the time of the testator's death he was seised in fee of real estate to the value of $65,000, that there was due to him upon land contracts $45,000, that he owned other personal property to the amount of $30,000, and that there were no debts or claims against the estate. Previous to the death of the testator, he conveyed to each of the defendants a parcel of real estate; that conveyed to Mrs. Lloyd being alleged to be worth $14,000, and that received by Mrs. Lathrop said to be worth $10,000. There is evidence tending to show that he intended to repair the house upon Mrs. Lathrop's property, thereby making the gift to her equal to that of Mrs. Lloyd, and that he intended to do as well by his other daughter, the complainant; but her husband became embarrassed, and finally went to state's prison, and she never received a home, as the others had. Her father, however, gave to her money from time to time, for her support, which aggregated $1,100. Soon after the probate of the will, litigation arose between the widow and children, which was finally adjusted, and the property was divided, the parties executing the necessary deeds and other instruments to carry it into effect. The accounts of Lathrop, the executor, were settled, and he was discharged. There is now some land held in common by the three sisters.

The complainant files the bill in this cause, alleging that the lands conveyed by the testator to her two sisters should be treated as ademptions of their respective legacies, and that they should be required to account to her for her share thereof. She alleges that her father so intended, and that they recognized the justice thereof, and promised to see that she received the same, and, relying upon such promises, she consented to the settlement of the estate, expecting that her sisters would pay her an amount equal to her share of said parcels so received by them. It seems tacitly agreed that this record involves only the question whether the property conveyed to Mrs. Lloyd and Mrs. Lathrop before the testator's death should be applied upon their respective interests under the will, or, in other words, as the counsel for the complainant state it, whether it can be treated as an ademption or a satisfaction *pro tanto* of their bequests. . . .

The case is one where it is claimed that a gift of personal property by will may be satisfied by a conveyance of land, when such is the clear intention of the testator.

If a person should bequeath to another a sum of money, and, previous to his (the testator's) death, should pay to such person the same amount, upon the express understanding that it was to discharge the bequest, the legacy would be thereby adeemed. But, in the absence of an apparent or expressed intention, that would not ordinarily be the effect of the payment of a sum of money to a legatee under an existing will. Generally, such payment would not affect the legacy. To this rule there is an exception, where the testator is a parent of or stands to the legatee *in loco parentis*. . . .

There are cogent reasons in support of the rule stated, — i.e. that payment to a son adeems the legacy, — which is based on the theory that such legacy is to be considered as a portion, and that the father's natural inclination to treat his children alike renders it more probable that his payment was in the nature of an advancement than a discrimination in favor of one, oftentimes the least worthy. Double portions were considered inequitable, and upon this the doctrine rests. Suisse *v.* Lowther, 2 Hare, 424, 433.

While the authorities are a unit that a legacy by one *in loco parentis* will be adeemed by payment, in the absence of an apparent or expressed intent to the contrary, the doctrine was early restricted. Among other limitations was the rule that the presumption could not be applied to a residuary bequest, because the court would not presume that a legacy of a residue, or other indefinite amount, had been satisfied by an advancement, as the testator might be ignorant whether the benefit that he was conferring equaled that which he had already willed. Freemantle *v.* Bankes, 5 Ves. 85; Clendening *v.* Clymer, 17 Ind. 155; 2 Story, Eq. Jur. § 1115. This exception fell with the discarding of the rule that satisfaction must be in full. Pym *v.* Lockyer, 5 Mylne & C. 29; Montefiore *v.* Guedalla, 1 De Gex, F. & J. 93. Again, it was held that it could not be applied unless the advancement was *ejusdem generis* with the legacy. See 2 Story, Eq. Jur. § 1109.

Counsel for the defendants contends that " the conveyance of real estate after the making of a will is held not a satisfaction of any legacy, in whole or in part, *even though that was the clear intent* of the testator," and he cites several authorities to sustain the proposition. . . . [The learned court here reviews the authorities.]

It is apparent that the law looks upon a legacy to a son as a setting off of his portion. Also, it is plain that a subsequent gift, unless it be of real estate, is presumed to be in satisfaction *pro tanto* of the legacy. It is also settled that whether the gift is to be considered an ademption of a legacy must depend upon the intent of the testator alone. A gift of personal property to a son may be shown not to have been so intended, but the burden is upon the legatee. Ford *v.* Tynte, 2 Hem. & M. 324. A gift to a stranger may be shown to have been intended as an ademption, but here the presumption is the other way, the burden being upon the administrator to show such intent.

There can be no doubt that a testator's conveyance of real property may constitute an ademption, if he so intends it, e.g. where he expresses the intent in the conveyance, and possibly in other ways. If so, the only significance of the doctrine *ejusdem generis* is its effect upon the presumption. . . .

We think the testimony shows the testator's intent. There may be testimony in the record that was incompetent to prove it, but there is sufficient that was competent. The widow was conversant with the entire transaction, and the defendants' statements are admissions of their knowledge of such intentions.

It is contended that " the allowance of a conveyance of property as a satisfaction of a devise or legacy would be equivalent to a revocation of the will in part, and it would have to be proven in the manner provided by our statute for the revocation of wills, that is, by the destruction of the will, or the making of a new will." 2 How. Stat. § 5793; Lansing *v.* Haynes, 95 Mich. 16. We think it should not be called a revocation of the will. The defendants' bequests are permitted to stand unquestioned, and matter in discharge of the obligation (i.e. payment) is shown. The will is not overturned or revoked. It is satisfied.

We think the prayer of the bill should be granted, and the record should be remanded to the circuit court for the county of Wayne, in chancery, for further proceedings. Decreed accordingly. . . .

JOHNSON v. McDOWELL.

SUPREME COURT OF IOWA, 1912.

154 Iowa 38, 134 N. W. 419.

LADD, J. The estate left by B. F. Winkleman, deceased, after the payment of debts and costs of administration, amounted to $273.85. By the second clause of his will, executed in 1883, he bequeathed $600 to his niece, Ella McDowell, and by the third clause the residue of his estate to his nephews, James M. and Melvin Winkleman, the interveners. The issues raised by the pleadings were such that unless the legacy to Mrs. McDowell was satisfied prior to the testator's death, the judgment of plaintiff against her was rightly ordered to be satisfied from a legacy to her; but, if satisfied, the entire amount passed to the interveners under the third clause of the will.

That the testator paid her $400 April 9, 1908, is not questioned, but, as he did not stand *in loco parentis*, no presumption arises therefrom that this was intended to be in satisfaction, even in part, of the legacy. . . .

Whether such payment was in satisfaction thereof necessarily depends upon the intention of the testator in making it and extrinsic evidence is admissible to aid in ascertaining such intention. . . .

Such evidence is resorted to not for the purpose of showing an intention of revoking or altering the will, but to establish the purpose of the testator in making the subsequent advance or payment; that is, whether he intended it to operate as a satisfaction of the legacy or as an additional bounty to the legatee. With this is mind, let us turn to the evidence. It appears that in April, 1908, the testator received from one Hunt in final settlement for the purchase of some land, the sum of $750, and out of this handed $400 to Mrs. McDowell, who was then present, and took the following receipt from her: " April 9, 1908. I, Ella McDowell, on the receipt of four hundred dollars ($400.00) in hand paid by B. F. Winkleman, hereby relinquish all claims, now and forever, against the estate of B. F. Winkleman. H. C. Winkleman, Witness. Ella McDowell."

Hunt, who testified, was asked: " Was there anything said as to what that $400 to her was for? A. Now, when I went up there and settled with B. F. Winkleman, it was understood, I presume, by that that she was to get $400, and, before she would receive that, she had to sign her right away; that is, what she should receive out of B. F. Winkleman's estate. Q. That was said there in your presence? A. Oh, certainly; yes, sir."

This was the only evidence bearing on the subject except proof that deceased was unmarried, without children, and then residing at the home of a brother, but immediately thereafter went to live with Mrs. McDowell and husband. There was no evidence indicating that Mrs. McDowell held any claim against the heirs. About twenty-five years prior thereto, he had in his will made her his legatee, and it seems very clear in the light of the oral testimony that both she and deceased intended the amount paid to cover whatever she might take from his estate. It is true that he went to live with the legatee thereafter, but there is no showing of how long he remained with her or of an understanding had with reference thereto, and there is no foundation for the assumption of the appellee that this payment might have been for future support. True, there is no specific reference in the receipt or testimony to the legacy. But the witness testified that she "had to sign the right away; that is, whatever she should receive out of B. F. Winkleman's estate." This was broad enough to cover what she might claim as heir or legatee. It is not to be assumed that he had forgotten the will as suggested by appellee, and though there is no proof of the fact, both parties assume in argument that he was about eighty years old. The evidence discloses that he had a small estate and, in the absence of any showing, we are not ready to infer that he was handing this money over to his niece for some disclosed purpose rather than that established by the evidence. In view of the amount of property he had, it is not reasonable to suppose he intended to make his niece a gift of the $400 in addition to the legacy. Indeed, the receipt would scarcely have been given, had a gift been intended, nor could it have been intended, if the payment of an existing debt, for the claims mentioned are those against the estate and ordinarily such a receipt, if in satisfaction of an indebtedness, would at least refer to it in some way as an existing obligation. The parties were evidently dealing with reference to the future, and though the word "claims" as ordinarily used may mean pecuniary obligations, it often has a much broader meaning, and there is nothing to indicate that it was employed in that restricted sense in the receipt and the testimony of Hunt clearly proves that such was not the purpose.

The appellee contends that the finding of the court should be accorded the conclusiveness of a verdict of the jury. Undoubtedly, such is the rule when there is a conflict in the evidence, but the record is such that only one reasonable inference is deducible therefrom. Mrs. McDowell had an interest in expectancy to relinquish as legatee, and as she was to sign away what she should receive from testator's estate, it ought not to be inferred against the undisputed evidence that, in doing so, she had another purpose, and that the testator in paying her money had another design in mind not expressed. While the evidence is meager, we think the only conclusion to be drawn therefrom is that the money was paid with the design of satisfying the legacy. That it was less in amount than the bequest can make no difference. The legacy was subject to the testator's absolute control, he could satisfy and discharge it by advancing any sum of money in lieu thereof, or he could revoke it entirely without the assent or approbation of the legatee.

We think the evidence conclusive, not only that he intended the payment as a satisfaction of the legacy, but that it was received with that understanding. It follows that the fund in controversy passed to the interveners under the third clause of the will, and the judgment is *reversed*.[31]

[31] See 3 Property Restatement (1940) § 315 (1) (a) and § 316 (a).

CHAPTER IX.

THE ADMINISTRATION OF DECEDENT ESTATES.

This Chapter contains no judicial opinions for study. It is designed to give you, partly in text and partly through Problems, a general body of information upon which you can build a knowledge of the local probate practice under which you will work. As to the Problems, try to figure them out unaided. After you have given them your best, turn to pages 198–202, where you will be able to check your answers against the results of the cited cases. Answers are provided in this Chapter since the Problems raise new issues rather than applications and extensions of rules found in principal cases.

Many of the Problems arise out of serious and costly mis-steps — usually by lawyers — in the conduct of an administration. You have been warned!

SECTION 1.

The Grant of Administration.

The necessity and purpose of administration. When a person dies, he ordinarily owns property, has claims against other persons (a species of property) and owes debts, absolute or contingent, matured or unmatured. A process of liquidation has to be engaged in, similar to that which takes place in the hands of a receiver when a corporation is dissolved or becomes bankrupt. This task is undertaken by the court exercising probate functions in the jurisdiction — a court which is usually called the probate court but may be known by other names, e.g., Surrogate's Court in New York, Orphans' Court in Pennsylvania, Prerogative Court in New Jersey, Court of Ordinary in Georgia. The court acts through an executor or administrator appointed for that purpose. The duty of the executor or administrator (generically known as the "personal representative") is to collect the assets of the decedent, pay his debts or provide for the payment of debts not yet payable, and distribute the remaining assets to the persons entitled thereto either under the will or by intestacy.

If A takes assets of the decedent, D, without an administration, even though A is the sole heir of D, he takes them subject to the claims of D's creditors. These claims may be enforced (a) by the creditor having an administrator appointed for the estate of D who will thereupon bring action against A for the recovery of the assets, or (b) by the creditor bringing direct action against A on the theory that, by intermeddling with D's assets, A has made himself " executor de son tort " — a position in which A has all the liabilities but none of the rights of a de jure personal representative.[1]

Without an administration bank accounts and other choses in action cannot be collected because there is no one who is entitled to give a release or bring suit; [1a] the title to real estate owned by the decedent cannot be made marketable because there is no assurance against the existence of creditors of the decedent with claims against the land.

Types of personal representatives. The personal representative is designated by different terms depending upon the nature of his duties:

1. The *executor* is a person nominated in the will of a decedent to act in that capacity. The court customarily appoints the person so nominated unless he is in some manner disqualified [2] or renounces.

2. The *administrator* is a person appointed to administer the estate of an intestate decedent. Statutes in all jurisdictions determine the person who is entitled to be the administrator of any decedent; and the court grants letters of administration to such person unless he is disqualified or renounces.

3. The *administrator with the will annexed* (also known as administrator cum testamento annexo or administrator c.t.a.) is appointed to administer a testate estate in which no executor is nominated or the named executor is disqualified or renounces at the outset.

4. The *administrator of goods not administered* (also known as administrator de bonis non or administrator d.b.n.) [3] is one who succeeds to the office of an administrator which the original incumbent has not fully performed.

5. The *administrator of goods not administered with the will annexed* (also known as administrator de bonis non cum testamento annexo or administrator d.b.n.c.t.a.) is one who succeeds to the office of an executor or administrator c.t.a. which the original incumbent has not fully performed.

6. A *special administrator* is one who is appointed to handle the affairs of an estate, testate or intestate, for a limited time for some

---

[1] In many jurisdictions the doctrine of "executor de son tort" has been abolished. E.g. New York Decedent Estate Law, Section 112. It has been consistently condemned by writers on the subject. See generally Atkinson, Wills, pp. 546 et seq.

[1a] Statutes frequently permit the next-of-kin to collect wages without administration. N. Y. D. E. L. § 103-a.

[2] As to what constitutes disqualification, see Atkinson, Wills, p. 567.

[3] It is habitual to use the Latin name for the administrator d.b.n. The English name is in common usage for the administrator c.t.a.

special purpose. The most frequent occasions for resort to a special administrator are (a) when the affairs of a decedent need immediate attention and cannot await the appointment of a permanent personal representative, which usually takes several weeks, and (b) when a will is being contested and it is necessary to hold the assets pending the contest. In either of these events the special administrator is often called an *administrator pendente lite*. In all states there is a procedure for having a special administrator appointed without delay.

7. A *public administrator* is a permanent official who undertakes to administer the assets of intestates where no one appears who is entitled to act as administrator.[4]

Jurisdiction to appoint a personal representative. A state has jurisdiction, through its courts, to appoint an executor or administrator of a decedent if (a) the decedent was domiciled in the state at the time of his death or (b) the decedent left property in the state. The second of these two bases of jurisdiction raises the question as to where certain types of property have their situs. Realty and tangible personalty present no problem. A chose in action has its situs wherever the debtor can be served with process. Corporate stock presents a difficult theoretical problem; it may be assets at the place where the stock certificate is found, where the corporation is incorporated or where the corporation does business; the usual practice is for the stock to be administered where the certificate is found.[5]

Enoch Arden & Co. One troublesome thing about the dead is their habit of coming to life under embarrassing circumstances. Enoch Arden returned and was a gentleman about it. " Sir Roger Tichborne " came up out of the sea after twenty years, provided the most celebrated English trials of the nineteenth century, and went to jail as an imposter. In 1909 Kumar Ramendra Narayan Roy of Bhowal was placed on a funeral pyre in Darjeeling and set ablaze; in 1946 after sixteen years of litigation the Judicial Committee of the Privy Council finally put the stamp of truth on his story of a thunder storm, a wandering band of holy men, and a twelve-year comatose Odyssey as a beggar; then three days after the decision he died and

---

[4] Human nature being what it is, it rarely happens that persons with any substantial property die without relatives, proximate or remote. But it often happens that a person of no property dies as a result of an accident caused by some other person. The cause of action thus arising is sometimes of considerable value and a public administrator may have to take care of it. On the night before the Fourth of July, 1925, the building housing the Pickwick Club (a Boston night club not catering to the silk-hat trade) collapsed, killing 41 persons; in the litigation which ensued, 11 of these 41 were represented by the Public Administrator.

[5] See Restatement of Conflict of Laws, § 467, Comment e; § 477. See also, Atkinson, Wills, p. 562.

was conclusively cremated.[6] War, amnesia, jungles, tribesmen who like slaves, and various combinations of these are returning husbands to wives who have married again, and such occurrences will continue for many years to come.

These and other resurrectees pose the question whether the fact that they were not dead vitiates administrations of their affairs (which may have proceeded through all the usual steps to final distribution and allowance of a final account) by depriving the court of jurisdiction to issue the letters testamentary or letters of administration. The desirability of having a corpse — or at least of knowing for certain whether you do have one — is indicated by the following:

PROBLEMS.

1. Moses Scott resided in the Territory of Washington in 1881. In that year he disappeared and was not heard from again until 1891. In 1888 a petition for administration of Moses's estate was presented, alleging that he had disappeared more than 7 years previously and had not been heard from and that diligent inquiry had failed to reveal any information concerning him[7] and therefore concluding

---

[6] References are as follows:

(1) Since I had to look up who wrote "Enoch Arden" I here record that it was Tennyson.

(2) The most recent volume on Arthur Orton, alias Tichborne, is Lord Maugham, The Tichborne Case (London, 1936). Wigmore uses episodes from both Tichborne Cases (the action by the claimant to recover the estate, Tichborne v. Lushington, and the perjury trial, R. v. Castro) to illustrate numerous points. See Wigmore on Evidence (3d ed. 1940) §§ 270, 982, 983. The verbatim testimony appears in Kenealy, The Trial at Bar of Sir Roger C. D. Tichborne (London, 1878). The charge to the jury took twenty days and appears in two volumes entitled "Charge of the Lord Chief Justice of England in the case of The Queen against Thomas Castro, otherwise Arthur Orton, otherwise Sir Roger Tichborne" (London, 1874).

(3) The facts as to the Kumar who played phoenix appear in Srimati Bibhabati Devi v. Kumar Ramendra Narayan Roy, [1946] A. C. 508, 62 Times Law Reports, 549. Throughout the litigation the Kumar was supported by his sister, Jyotirmoyee. The chief opponent was his "widow." The trial lasted 608 days. Bizarre details appear in the opinion.

[7] There is a presumption that one is dead if he is absent from his domicile for 7 years and is not heard from during that period. It is also presumed that the absentee died intestate, unmarried and without heirs, in the absence of a showing to the contrary. In Matter of Feehan, 145 Misc. 837 (1932) there was an application for letters of administration predicated upon a presumption of death through absence. In 1848, Mary Feehan left her home in Kilkenny, Ireland, to take up a residence in India, where she was to be employed as a servant. In 1887 Patrick, a brother of Mary, died in New York, leaving a small legacy to Mary. No word was ever received from Mary by any of the family in Ireland or New York after Mary left for India. In 1932 nieces of Mary petition for administration of her estate in New York, for the purpose of obtaining the legacy given by Patrick. Mary would be 116 years old, if she were still alive. Administration was refused on the ground that the presump-

that the petitioner believed Moses to be dead. Upon evidence of the foregoing facts the probate court entered a finding that Moses was " dead to all legal intents and purposes, having died on or about March 25, 1888," and appointed an administrator. This order of the probate court was made under the ordinary statutes referring to administration of the " estate of any deceased person." Under this statute notice was given by publication that a petition had been filed for the appointment of an administrator for the estate of Moses H. Scott and that a hearing would be held upon said petition at a stated time and place.

The probate court authorized the administrator to sell all Moses's real estate. The administrator sold a parcel to one Ward who in turn sold to McNeal. Moses Scott re-appeared in 1891 and brought the present action of ejectment against McNeal in the courts of the State of Washington. Judgment was for the defendant. Scott now brings the case to the Supreme Court of the United States by writ of error. What judgment? Scott v. McNeal, 154 U. S. 34, 14 Sup. Ct. 1108 (1894). But see Rodrigas v. Savings Institution, 63 N. Y. 460 (1875); s.c. 76 N. Y. 316 (1879); Hamilton v. Grange Savings Bank, 99 N. J. L. 503, 124 Atl. 62 (1924); 34 Yale L. J. 97 (1924).

2. Suppose, in Scott v. McNeal, supra, Scott had brought action against the administrator to recover the proceeds of the sale to Ward, which proceeds the administrator had already distributed to the persons named in the decree for distribution of the probate court. Could Scott have recovered? Beckwith v. Bates, 228 Mich. 400, 200 N. W. 151 (1924).

3. Suppose, in Scott v. McNeal, supra, the administrator had collected a debt owed to Scott by D. When Scott reappeared, could he collect again from D? Could D, if made to pay twice, recover from the administrator? And, if he could, the administrator being insolvent and having distributed all the assets of the estate, could D recover against the sureties on the administrator's bond? National Surety Co. v. Wages, 48 Ga. App. 720 (1933); Restatement of Restitution, § 24, Comment h.

4. A Pennsylvania statute provided that if a person should be absent and unheard from for more than 7 years, administration could be granted upon his estate as an absentee, provided that (a) notice of the application be published in the county for 4 weeks before hearing; (b) after a finding that the legal presumption of death has been made out, a notice of such finding be published in the county where the court sits and at the place where the absentee was last heard from, requiring proof within 12 weeks of the continuance in life of the absentee; (c) a bond be required from each

---

tion of death arises only when one fails to communicate with those at his domicile, not where he fails to communicate with persons at an old home after he has left it to set up a new one.

distributee promising that he will refund the amount received if the absentee returns. Margaret Cunnius disappeared in Pennsylvania; the above statute was complied with and her assets were collected and distributed by an administrator. D was a debtor of Margaret. He paid the administrator the amount of the debt. Margaret now returns and sues D for payment of the debt. Should she recover? Cunnius *v.* Reading School District, 198 U. S. 458, 25 Sup. Ct. 721 (1905).

Territorial limits on the powers of the personal representative; ancillary administration. The executor or administrator is the "hand of the court" which appointed him. He has no powers as personal representative in any state other than that of his appointment, except as these are given by statute of such other state; his representative capacity ends when he crosses the state line. Therefore, when assets exist in more than one state, it is usually necessary that a personal representative be appointed in each state. The administration at the decedent's domicile is the primary administration; the administration in any other state is known as ancillary administration. (The official is known as an ancillary *administrator* even though there is a will.) The personal representative at the domicile is usually appointed ancillary administrator if he applies, but this is impossible in some states which require that the personal representative be a resident of the state. The chief purpose of the requirement of ancillary administration is to see to it that local creditors are satisfied without undue inconvenience. It is the function of the ancillary administrator to collect the local assets, pay the local creditors, and then transfer the balance of the assets to the domiciliary personal representative for distribution.[8]

Considerations of economy and convenience make it desirable to avoid ancillary administration wherever possible, and as a matter of practice it is frequently avoided. The following problems consider the extent to which ancillary administration is necessary, the types of informal arrangements which are designed to avoid it, and some difficulties that may be caused by these arrangements. It will be observed that we pay a heavy price in efficiency for our multiple state sovereignties.

PROBLEMS.

T dies domiciled in New York and E is appointed executor of his will by the Surrogate's court for the proper county.

5. Can E bring an action in the Massachusetts courts to recover T's alleged share in the estate of his father? Cassidy *v.* Shim-

[8] As to the situation where the estate is insolvent, see Restatement of Conflict of Laws, § 497.

min, 122 Mass. 406 (1877); Restatement of Conflict of Laws, § 507.

6. Can E bring an action in the Massachusetts courts under the Federal Employers' Liability Act (providing that common carriers shall be liable for the death of an employee under certain circumstances " to his personal representative for the benefit of the surviving widow and children of such employee ") to recover for the death of T? Brown v. Boston & Maine R. R. 283 Mass. 192, 186 N. E. 59 (1933). But see Ghilain v. Couture, 84 N. H. 48, 146 Atl. 395 (1929); Rose, " Foreign Enforcement of Actions for Wrongful Death," 33 Mich. L. Rev. 545 (1935).

7. E brings an action in the New York courts against D, a debtor of T, and recovers judgment. Can he bring an action on the judgment in the Massachusetts courts? Hare v. O'Brien, 233 Pa. 330, 82 Atl. 475 (1912); De Paris v. Wilmington Trust Co., 7 Boyce (Del.) 178, 104 Atl. 691 (1918); Restatement of Conflict of Laws, § 508, Comment b.

8. E takes possession of an automobile owned by T. D steals it and brings it into Massachusetts. Can E bring trover in Massachusetts to recover the value of the automobile? Restatement of Conflict of Laws, §§ 483, 508. Would the result be different if the automobile were stolen between the death of T and the appointment of E? Brackett v. Hoitt, 20 N. H. 257 (1850).

9. T held an overdue negotiable note made by D, a resident of Massachusetts. Can E bring suit upon the note in the Massachusetts courts? Restatement of Conflict of Laws, § 509. Would the result be different if the note matured after the death of T? Cf. Restatement of Conflict of Laws, § 483, Comment b.

10. At T's death D, a resident of Massachusetts, owed him $100 upon an open account. E demands payment. Is D protected in making payment by mailing check to E if (a) there is a Massachusetts ancillary administration of which D knows? (b) there is a Massachusetts ancillary administration of which D does not know? (c) there is no Massachusetts ancillary administration at the time, but such administration is later granted? Restatement of Conflict of Laws, § 482; Beale, " Voluntary Payment to a Foreign Administrator," 42 Harv. L. Rev. 597 (1929); Atkinson, Wills, 553.

11. At T's death D, a resident of Massachusetts, owed him $100 upon an open account. Is D protected in going to New York and paying E? Beale, " Voluntary Payment to a Foreign Administrator," 42 Harv. L. Rev. at 606 (1929).

It is obvious that in the great majority of cases, the natural and convenient place to have a will contest litigated is the state of the decedent's domicile. Moreover, a judgment in that state is binding with regard to personal property in all states and with reference to all persons, whether they join in the proceedings or not.[9] Yet, obviously, any state in which a will contest is commenced has jurisdiction to decide the issue as to personalty and realty within its own borders; and there often exist reasons why the executor believes it more advantageous to the will to litigate outside of the domiciliary jurisdiction.

PROBLEM.

12. T dies, domiciled in New York. His heirs and next-of-kin are domiciled in New York. The executor and principal beneficiaries under his will are domiciled in Massachusetts, where much of his property is located. The executor petitions in Massachusetts for allowance of the will. What steps should be taken by the heirs and next-of-kin (who believe that it is advantageous to them to litigate in the New York courts) and what action should the Massachusetts court take? Rackemann v. Taylor, 204 Mass. 394, 90 N. E. 552 (1910).

Effect of the revocation of letters testamentary or letters of administration. With some frequency it occurs that a decree granting probate or administration is revoked. After administration has been granted upon the belief that the decedent died intestate, a will is found. Or after probate has been granted, a later will is found, or newly discovered evidence shows that the probated instrument was forged. It seems too obvious for argument that the facilitation of administration of all estates requires that purchasers from the old personal representative and persons who have paid debts to him be protected, although there is no reason why distributees from him should not be required to disgorge provided there is no change of position which puts them on a par with purchasers. And such is the law. But there was an old English notion that an executor (different, in this respect, from an administrator) derived his title directly from the will, and that probate merely confirmed, but did not confer, his title; hence, when administration had been granted but there actually existed an undiscovered will which was later found and probated, the title of the administrator was non-existent from the beginning and purchasers from him were not protected. To make a workable modern law this ghost of the past had to be laid; and it was so laid in the leading case of Hewson v. Shelley, [1914] 2 Ch. 13.

PROBLEMS.

13. T died leaving a will to which one of the witnesses was a person who was an endorser upon the note of X, which note the will directed

[9] Restatement of Conflict of Laws, § 470 (2). A judgment in any other state is binding upon all persons who are served or who appear (§ 470 (3)), but not upon others (§ 470 (4)).

the executor to pay. The probate court granted probate of the will and appointed E as executor. The next-of-kin appealed. Pending the appeal, E sold the assets of the estate to P. The appellate court ruled that the witness was not a proper witness and therefore that the will was invalid. Is P protected?

14. T died and A was appointed administrator of his estate under a petition which alleged that T died intestate. A brought an action against D, a debtor of T. D discovered a will of T which named E as executor. In the action of A against D, D offers the will in evidence, together with the testimony of the attesting witnesses. A objects. What ruling? See Christianson *v.* King County, 239 U. S. 356, 36 Sup. Ct. 114 (1915); Noell *v.* Wells, 1 Lev. 235 (1668).

The title of the personal representative to personalty and realty. The executor or administrator, by virtue of his appointment, obtains title to the personalty of the testator (including leasehold estates in land); but in the absence of statute he does not obtain title to freehold real estate. As to such realty statutes universally give the right, upon petition, to have the land sold if the personal estate is insufficient to pay debts;[10] but, subject to the possibility of such a petition, the real estate passes directly to the heir or devisee. The title of the executor to personalty (and to realty, where statutes of the above type exist) relates back to the date of the testator's death for most purposes; but dealings with the property by a person who is later appointed executor are confirmed by the appointment only to the extent to which they would have been proper after the appointment.[11] It follows that a person who deals with an alleged executor or administrator runs considerable risk unless he sees a certified copy of the decree of appointment. Competent personal representatives habitually have such a copy available to show to persons with whom they deal. Transfer agents of corporations habitually require a copy of the letters testamentary or letters of administration to be attached to the old stock certificate before a new one will be issued.

Whether rights of action pass to the personal representative. "Personal" actions die with the decedent; "non-personal" actions pass to his executor or administrator. At common law the line between personal and non-personal actions was roughly the line between actions ex delicto and actions ex contractu, but there were non-personal torts (e.g. trespass to real estate) and personal contractual claims (e.g. breach of promise to marry). Statutes generally

---

[10] At common law, freehold land was not subject to payment of debts unless the testator provided to the contrary in the will; but courts were astute to find a provision subjecting land to payment of debts.

[11] See Warren, "Problems in Probate and Administration," 32 Harv. L. Rev. at 320 (1919).

broaden the scope of actions which survive. Actions for personal injuries generally survive. Actions for defamation, alienation of affections and breach of promise to marry generally do not.

PROBLEM.

15. T, being about to engage in a hazardous business enterprise, conveyed his home to his daughter without consideration for the purpose of protecting the home from attachment and execution in the event that the enterprise should fail. The enterprise did fail and T died insolvent. Can his executor bring an action against the daughter to recover the property as a fraudulent conveyance? See Atkinson, Wills, 601.

SECTION 2.

Outline of the Steps in an Administration.

The statutes of the several states (there is no Federal probate jurisdiction outside of the District of Columbia and the territories [12]) provide various procedures in the administration of estates. But they all follow the same general scheme.

1. *The petition for probate or administration and action thereon.* The executor or any interested person petitions the appropriate court to probate the will and grant letters testamentary, if a will has been found. Or the heirs or next-of-kin or a creditor petition for a grant of letters of administration. Notice of hearing on the petition is given to all interested persons by service of process, mail or publication as the statutes require. (If immediate action in the estate is necessary, a special administrator is appointed immediately at an ex parte hearing with such safeguards as the court thinks necessary in the circumstances; the special administrator gives bond with sufficient sureties and takes over the assets. In some states probate " in common form " is granted at once upon the affidavit of a witness to the will; but if the will is contested by the filing of a caveat by any interested person, the probate " in common form " amounts to little more than a special administration, and the real issue of probate is decided upon the petition for probate " in solemn form.") After a delay adequate to enable interested persons to appear, usually about three weeks, the hearing is held. If there is no contest, a decree is entered declaring that the will is allowed or administration granted and naming an executor or administrator. If there is a contest, the issue at stake is set down for trial by judge or jury. Frequently there is a preliminary question whether a motion for trial by jury will be allowed, since in many states the granting of a jury trial is discretionary with the court. In some states the jury

[12] But this does not mean that some probate issues may not be litigated in the Federal courts. See footnote 7, Chapter IV, supra.

trial, if any, is held in the probate court; in others the issue is sent to some other court to be tried. After the trial, the probate court enters the appropriate decree.

2. *The issuance of letters; the bond.* The decree of probate or administration names the executor or administrator and fixes the amount of bond which he must give and the sureties thereon which he must provide. The amount of the bond is usually twice the value of the personal property in the estate; the petition for probate or administration is usually accompanied by an affidavit as to the amount of such property and this affidavit is accepted as true unless some person disputes it. Sureties on the bond are required unless the will otherwise provides, or all interested parties consent to a bond without sureties, or the executor is a corporate fiduciary; but in some states one or more of these grounds of exemption from the giving of sureties are not recognized. The sureties must be satisfactory to the court as to their financial responsibility; but ordinarily a surety company is accepted as a sole surety. The traditional form of bond is a promise by the personal representative and the sureties to pay the nominal amount (penal sum) of the bond to the probate judge, with an additional provision that if the personal representative shall perform his duties faithfully this promise shall be void and of no effect. If the form of the bond were followed, it would mean that upon any default the personal representative and sureties would be liable for the entire penal sum; but it is well settled that they are liable only for the amount of loss caused by any misconduct. A suit on the bond is usually brought in the name of the probate judge for the benefit of the damaged parties, the latter controlling the proceeding. When a satisfactory bond with sufficient sureties has been filed the probate court issues to the personal representative a certificate of his appointment, known as letters testamentary (in case of a will) or letters of administration (in case of an intestacy).

PROBLEM.

16. E is nominated executor in the will of T and is appointed by the appropriate probate court, subject to providing a surety on his bond. E owes T's estate a larger amount of money than he can pay. E and T's family ask S to become surety on E's bond. Is there any peculiar danger from S's point of view? Bassett *v.* Fidelity and Deposit Co., 184 Mass. 210, 68 N. E. 205 (1903); Lyon *v.* Osgood, 58 Vt. 707, 7 Atl. 5 (1886).

3. *The publication to creditors; short statutes of limitations.* All states have statutes designed to require prompt presentation and adjudication of claims against decedent estates. These statutes are discussed in Section 3 of this Chapter under the heading " Problems Relating to Creditors." In general the statutes bar claims which

are not presented within a relatively short period (say, six months) and bar actions upon most claims after the expiration of a somewhat longer period (usually one year). To start the running of the short statute of limitations it is usually necessary for the personal representative to give notice of his appointment to the creditors and call upon them to present their claims; this is usually done by publication for a stated period in newspapers of general circulation in the vicinity of the court.

4. *The inventory.* Within a fairly short period after his appointment (say, three months) the personal representative is required to file with the court an inventory of the assets of the estate together with an appraisal of the value of the same by disinterested appraisers. The appraisers usually need not be professionals in that field; and in practice the appraisal is often made by persons who have little qualification for the task.[13] The appraisal is not conclusive upon anyone — e.g., the taxing authorities or residuary legatees, but it gives a rough idea of the value of the estate and serves as a base point for the bookkeeping and accounting of the executor. Thus, if an asset of the estate is sold at a price in excess of its appraised value in the inventory, the executor's account will show the sale as a capital gain; if it is sold at a price below its appraised value, the account will show the transaction as a capital loss. Of course, the executor's books are not conclusive on the taxing authorities in computing gains and losses for income tax purposes.

5. *The collection and preservation of the assets and the payment of claims.* The principal task of the personal representative is to bring into his own hands the assets of the estate, recover sums due from the debtors of the decedent, pay his creditors and hold the balance of the assets for distribution. In the course of this process he may have to bring actions; this he does in the courts of general jurisdiction, not in the probate courts. He may also have to defend actions; at common law this also was done in the courts of general jurisdiction, but many statutes provide for the adjudication of claims against the estate in the probate courts. As to litigation to which the decedent was a party during his lifetime, the personal representative must take the appropriate steps to substitute himself as a party. The circumstances may be such that the personal representative will want to have the permission of the probate court, whose agent he is, to prosecute or defend new or old actions or to compromise claims, whether or not they are litigated; and he frequently petitions for such permission. It is obvious that the personal repre-

---

[13] However, where the estate is subject to the federal estate tax, or where the state taxing authorities impose anything approaching the federal requirements, a careful appraisal by experts must be made for tax purposes and might just as well be made for probate purposes at the outset. See Newhall, Settlement of Estates (3d ed. 1937) § 139.

sentative should not pay creditors who present claims to him until he has satisfied himself that the estate is solvent; for if the estate is insolvent and the personal representative pays a creditor more than he is entitled to receive, the personal representative is liable for the excess.[14] The statutes and practice in the various states differ considerably as to the time when and circumstances under which the personal representative can, with protection to himself, pay creditors who have presented their claims.

6. *The Federal Estate Tax and the personal representative's duties with reference thereto.*[15] The Federal Estate Tax is governed by the Internal Revenue Code, Chapter 3, which consolidates the Revenue Act of 1926, the Revenue Act of 1932, and their numerous amendments. The 1926 and 1932 Acts impose two different taxes, but they may be treated as one for purposes of brief statement.

The tax is imposed upon the "net estate" of the decedent at a rate which increases with the size of the estate; it is a tax upon the estate as a whole, not a series of taxes upon each gift. An exemption ($60,000 as of mid-1949) is allowed — i.e. the first $60,000 of the "net estate" is not taxed.[16] The "net estate" is determined by making certain deductions (e.g. administration expense, debts of the decedent, certain taxes, charitable gifts, property subjected to estate or gift tax within the previous five years) from the "gross estate." The Revenue Act of 1948 authorized a "marital deduction" (see Appendix II A, infra) of assets of the gross estate which are received by the decedent's spouse up to 50% of the "adjusted gross estate."

The "gross estate" includes not only real and personal property which the decedent owned, but also life insurance, property covered by certain powers of appointment,[17] certain interests in property in

---

[14] Of course, the personal representative would be entitled to restitution from the overpaid creditor. Restatement of Restitution, § 20 and page 16 of Explanatory Notes.

[15] Written as of June 1, 1949. For an elementary survey which puts the Federal Estate Tax in its context, see " A–B–C of Taxes for Property Lawyers," an appendix to Casner & Leach, Cases on Property.

[16] The exemption of $100,000 provided in Internal Revenue Code, § 812 (a) is important only in the calculation of the 80% credit provision for state taxes paid as provided in the 1926 Act. See Griswold, Cas. Federal Taxation (2d ed. 1946) 266.

[17] Internal Revenue Code, § 811 (f) includes in the gross estate property over which the decedent had a power of appointment, whether or not exercised, unless the power was one of the two following classes:

    (a) a special power where the objects are limited to the descendants of the donor and the donee, and the spouses of the donor, the donee and their descendants.

    (b) a special power simply collateral — i.e. where the donee has no owned interest in the property.

In Appendix II B, infra, appears a comparison of Federal Estate Tax provisions with reference to powers of appointment in three phases: (1) before 1942, (2) under the Revenue Act of 1942, (3) under the Revenue Act of 1948. Master this material; it is basic to any estate planning for substantial clients.

which the decedent had any kind of joint ownership, and certain transfers made by the decedent during his lifetime. The most important inter vivos transfers which are included in the " gross estate " are transfers made in contemplation of death,[18] transfers intended to take effect in possession or enjoyment upon the death of the decedent,[19] transfers under which the decedent has retained a life interest for himself, and transfers where the decedent has retained a power to alter, amend, revoke or terminate. It is obvious that the term " gross estate " is highly artificial, since it includes not only property which in any ordinary sense is part of the decedent's estate but also property which has been dealt with in such a way that there was a tendency to avoid the estate tax.

The duties of the personal representative under the estate tax law have reference to two papers. If the " gross estate " may exceed $60,000, he must file in duplicate with the collector of internal revenue a *preliminary notice* of the approximate value of the estate; this must be done within two months of the appointment of the personal representative, and the notice must be upon the form provided for that purpose. Then, within 15 months of the date of death, he must file a *return*, giving the very detailed information required by the provided form and computing the amount of the tax. The appraisal of the decedent's property which must accompany the return is governed by regulations and forms prescribed by the Treasury Department; and it is important that, if the estate involves a federal tax, such appraisal should be properly made at an early period in the administration of the estate. The tax is payable 15 months after death, except as extensions may be granted. After the return is made and the tax paid, the return is investigated with great thoroughness by an examining officer of the Treasury Department. Following such investigation the commissioner makes a final determination of the tax due, and the personal representative either accepts his decision or takes the steps provided by law for having it reviewed. Needless to say, negotiations with the tax authorities constitute an important part of the personal representative's duties where the value of the estate is considerable.

[18] Distinguish a " gift *causa mortis* " from a "gift in contemplation of death." The former, a conception of the judge-made law, is a gift in immediate expectation of death. This causes it to be revocable, and to be automatically revoked if death does not ensue. The gift in contemplation of death, a creature of the tax statutes, can be made years before death. Gifts are presumed to be " in contemplation " if made within two years of death.

[19] As of 1946 one of the major causes of heart-burn to the deserving rich and their counsel was Helvering v. Hallock, 309 U. S. 106 (1940) and Treasury Regulation 105 (1946) § 81.17 based thereon. The issue is whether there shall be included in the gross estate property subject to inter vivos trusts where the settlor has retained some reversionary interest, frequently trifling. See Eisenstein, " The Hallock Problem: A Case Study in Administration," 58 Harv. L. Rev. 1141 (1945); Spencer, " The Federal Estate Tax on Inter Vivos Trusts: A Common Sense Rule for Hallock Cases," 59 Harv. L. Rev. 43 (1945).

7. *State death taxes.* Some states (e.g. New York) have estate taxes modelled upon the federal law. Others (e.g. Massachusetts) have an inheritance or legacy tax which imposes a tax upon each gift, the rate of tax depending upon (a) the amount of the gift and (b) the proximity or remoteness of relationship of the decedent to the beneficiary. The practice under these statutes differs so considerably among the several states that it is not profitable here to do more than call attention to the fact that the personal representative must comply with the local requirements.

It should also be noted that the states which have an inheritance or legacy tax also have a subsidiary estate tax. The federal Revenue Act of 1926 allows a deduction from the federal Estate Tax of state taxes paid up to 80% of the federal tax. The state subsidiary estate taxes are aimed to take advantage of this deduction by bringing into the coffers of the state any amount by which the state inheritance tax is less than 80 per cent of the federal tax. These subsidiary estate taxes are known as the " Take up the slack " statutes. (No similar 80 per cent deduction is allowed under the tax imposed by the federal Revenue Act of 1932 as amended.)

8. *Distribution.* After the assets have been collected, the taxes and other debts paid, and the time expired within which creditors can present their claims, the estate is ripe for distribution to the legatees or next-of-kin.[20] The usual practice is for the personal representative to present a petition for distribution, setting forth the disposition of the assets which he proposes to make. After notice to all interested parties and, if necessary, a hearing, a decree of distribution is rendered by the probate court. In some states it is the practice to prepare a final account showing in advance the distribution proposed; the assent of all interested parties to such an account is sufficient protection to the personal representative.

9. *Accounting.* The accounts of the personal representative constitute his reports to the probate court with reference to his stewardship. The statutes usually require him to file periodic accounts (say, at the end of each year of his incumbency) and then at the closing of the estate to file a final account. The allowance of an account establishes the propriety of the action therein disclosed; but, particularly with reference to intermediate accounts, state practices differ as to the conclusiveness of such an adjudication. The hearing upon the allowance of an account presents the opportunity of any

[20] *Income and interest on legacies.* Specific legacies bring to the legatee any income or increase accruing after the death of the testator. General pecuniary legacies usually bear interest commencing one year after the testator's death; but in the case of legacies given for support of a minor child and some few other classes, interest runs from the testator's death. If a legacy is not payable until some future time, interest ordinarily does not run until that time. Contrary indications of intent of the testator on this matter will, of course, control any of the above rules.

interested person to dispute the propriety of the accountant's conduct.

An account contains (a) a debit side, i.e. items of property which the accountant has received and with which, therefore, he charges himself, (b) a credit side, i.e. items which the accountant has paid out, lost or distributed and which he asks be approved as proper payments, losses and distributions, and (c) a balance, showing the assets which are still in his hands.

The debit side of the account commences with the balance shown by the inventory or the last previous account. It then proceeds to list the new property which has come into the accountant's hands since the inventory or last previous account — e.g. assets newly discovered, income on assets previously shown, gains over inventory value upon the sale of assets.

The credit side of the account shows payments to creditors, distributions to legatees, losses by virtue of sale of assets below inventory value, payments of expenses of administration including the compensation of the accountant himself, losses by virtue of bad debts, etc.

When the total of the credit side is deducted from the total of the debit side (including the inventory or the balance from the last previous account), the balance represents the property still in the accountant's hands. It is usually required that this property be listed. Of course, if the account is a final one, no balance will be shown.

10. *Routine of administration.* An executor or administrator has a multitude of miscellaneous tasks to perform in the conduct of his office. It is dangerous for him to assume that he will automatically think of his varied duties at the time when they ought to be performed. Any lawyer should prepare for himself, and for any executor or administrator for whom he acts as counsel, a memorandum which will call to his attention the information he should seek and the steps he should take. Such a memorandum should obviously be geared to the law of the state in which he is acting. The following may serve as a starting point, and a perusal of it by the student will indicate the existence of some problems which the brief outline provided by this Section has not dealt with.

1. *The Decedent.* Date of death? Actual place of death? Domicile at time of death? When established? Possibility of dispute as to domicile and hence possible question as to validity or interpretation of will and taxability of personalty by more than one state?
2. *Spouse.* Married? Prior marriage? Question of validity of prior divorce?
3. *Heirs and next-of-kin. Issue?* Dates of birth of issue? Guardians of minor issue? Necessity of having guardians ad litem appointed?

4. *Legatees and devisees.* Minors? Guardians? Guardians ad litem necessary?
5. *Real estate.* Title in whose name? Mortgages and obligations thereunder? Should insurance be changed as a result of death? Tenants and leases? Time for exercising rights to renew or cancel?
6. *Automobiles.* Registered in whose name? Should registration be changed to permit operation by family? Should insurance be changed?
7. *Location of intangible property.* Safe deposit box? Access thereto? Accounts with bankers and brokers? Pledged property? Agency, custodianship and investment counsel accounts? Checking accounts? Savings accounts? Cooperative banks?
8. *Securities.* Are there securities upon which subscription or other rights exist which must be exercised within a specified time? Other securities problems requiring immediate attention?
9. *Insurance.* As to life insurance, preparation of notice and proofs of loss? As to fire, theft, liability, etc. insurance, have any losses occurred as to which notice or proof of loss should be filed? Cancel or transfer insurance upon realty or tangibles sold or distributed. Is fire, theft and liability insurance in such form that it affords protection after death?
10. *Did decedent have power of appointment?* Terms of instrument? General or special power? [21]
11. *Debts due decedent.* Salary? Royalties? Rents? Commissions? From fiduciaries? Annuities? Pensions?
12. *Cemetery situation.* Funeral bills? Perpetual care provided for?
13. *Fiduciary capacity of decedent.* Executor or administrator? Trustee? Assignee for benefit of creditors? Trustee in bankruptcy? Steps to be taken to secure discharge of decedent and appointment of successor?
14. *Litigation.* Suits pending by decedent? Against decedent?
15. *Ancillary administration.* Probably necessary in what states?
16. *Tax situation of decedent.* Claims for abatement or refund? Tax appeals pending? Current income tax and gift tax returns filed? Should extensions be obtained?
17. *Data for estate tax returns.* Life insurance? Did decedent have right to alter or revoke a trust? Property received by decedent from another estate taxed by Federal Government

---

[21] See Olney *v.* Balch, 154 Mass. 318, 28 N. E. 258 (1891) holding that where a decedent exercises a general power of appointment by will, the property subject to the power should be turned over to the executor to be administered as part of the decedent donee's estate.

within 5 years? Property, goods or money owned jointly with another?

SECTION 3.

Some Problems in the Conduct of the Administration.

An executor or administrator is, like a trustee, a fiduciary; and in general his rights and duties are similar to those of a trustee. Hence, much of the information acquired in a course in Trusts is applicable to the administration of estates. But there are certain obvious differences between the situation of a trustee and that of a personal representative which create different problems and put a different emphasis upon problems which are common to the two functions. (1) A trustee usually receives relatively homogeneous assets — commonly stocks and bonds; but a personal representative receives a mass of property, tangible and intangible, of every kind and description. (2) A trustee usually takes the assets free from the claims of creditors; but a personal representative must satisfy creditors of the decedent out of the property in his hands. (3) A trust usually contemplates custody of the assets for a considerable period of time for investment purposes; but a personal representative is charged with the duty of administering the assets and distributing them as soon as possible, any duty to invest being incidental to this limited purpose. (4) A trustee is usually some person entirely dissociated from individual interest in the trust; but an executor often, and an administrator almost always, is a primary beneficiary with reference to the property and is therefore subjected to the strict requirements of fiduciaries who are to some extent dealing with themselves as individuals.

The purpose of this Section is to discuss some of the problems of administration which cause the most difficulty or which are not analogous to the problems of trustees.

A. Problems Relating to Creditors.

Presentment of claims. The path of the creditor whose debtor dies is beset with pitfalls. He must, of course, observe the general statute of limitations. But, more than that, he must comply with local statutes which (a) fix a time limit within which the claim must be presented to the personal representative or the probate court and (b) fix a short statute of limitations within which actions must be commenced. Sometimes the short statute of limitations runs from the appointment of the personal representative, sometimes from the disallowance of the claim by the personal representative. Moreover, in many states there is a statute forbidding suits against the personal representative before some period (say, six months) has elapsed after his appointment.

A serious pitfall is that unmatured as well as matured claims must ordinarily be presented and are barred if not presented within the prescribed time. This means that the creditor must take steps upon the death of his debtor which he would have no need, indeed no right, to take if his debtor were still alive. The possibilities of loss in this situation are obvious.

Contingent claims (e.g., claims based upon a guarantee or endorsement, claims in the nature of insurance, warranties of title) are treated differently under the practice of different states. In some states the claim must be presented, together with a petition that the personal representative be required to retain assets out of the estate sufficient to pay the claim or, alternatively, take a bond from distributees obliging them to pay the creditor if his claim becomes absolute. In other states the contingent creditor is not required to take action but is allowed to assert his claim against distributees when the claim becomes absolute.

A secured creditor can assert his claim against the security even though his rights against the personal representative are barred by failure to comply with the non-claim statutes. But he can also collect from the personal representative as if he were not secured. Whether the residuary legatee or the distributee of the mortgaged or pledged property bears the burden of the secured creditor's claim is discussed, infra, under "Exoneration of mortgaged property."

Statutes and authorities differ as to whether the personal representative can waive the general statute of limitations. But almost never does he have the power to waive the non-claim statute and the short statute of limitations. All too frequently it happens that an executor voices good will and high purpose with reference to a creditor, lulls him into a sense of security until the time for presentation of the claim and suit thereon has run out, and then loses interest in paying the obligation. This type of quasi-fraud gives no rights to the creditor. The only safe thing for a creditor to do is to comply with the letter of the statutes; but unfortunately the creditor does not usually seek this sound advice until it is too late.

In some states the statutes require that the claim be presented to the personal representative, in others to the probate court.

Priorities in insolvent estates. In many states a special procedure is provided for insolvent estates, including a declaration by the personal representative to the court that the estate is insolvent and the appointment of commissioners to examine and pass upon the claims. In other states insolvency appears only by the fact that there is a deficiency of assets to pay all the claims presented.

In all states there are certain claims which have priority, though within limits the priorities differ from state to state. Universally the widow's allowance, funeral expenses and costs of administration are paid first. A federal statute provides that federal taxes must be paid next and some state statutes have similar provisions as to state taxes. Judgment debts, wages and rent are often given priority. Other creditors share what is left pro rata.

Exoneration of mortgaged property. Where T dies, devising property to A upon which there is a mortgage, the issue naturally arises whether A gets only the equity in the property (i.e. its value in excess of the mortgage) or gets the property free and clear, being entitled to have the personal representative pay the debt secured on the property. The solution of this question depends upon (a) the source of the mortgage, (b) the nature of the property out of which exoneration would come, and (c) the statute law of the jurisdiction, for quite a number of statutes exist declaring that there shall be no exoneration except as provided in the will.[22]

PROBLEMS.

17. T purchases Blackacre subject to a purchase-money mortgage given by T's vendor. T dies, devising Blackacre to A. Is A entitled to have the mortgage paid out of the residuary estate? Stieglitz *v.* Migatz, 182 Ind. 549, 105 N. E. 465 (1914).

18. Same case as Problem 17, except that when T purchased from his vendor he assumed the existing mortgage. Hoff's Appeal, 24 Pa. 200 (1855); Creesy *v.* Willis, 159 Mass. 249, 34 N. E. 265 (1893); Note, " Exoneration of Specific Property from Encumbrances Existing at Death of Testator," 40 Harv. L. Rev. 630 (1927).

19. T purchases Blackacre and then executes a will devising Blackacre to A. Thereafter T borrows $5000 from B and gives a mortgage on Blackacre as security.[23] T dies. Is A entitled to have the executor pay off the mortgage

   a. out of the residue? Smith *v.* Kibbe, 104 Kan. 159, 178 Pac. 427 (1919).

   b. out of general pecuniary legacies? Brown *v.* Baron, 162 Mass. 56, 37 N. E. 772 (1894); In re Smith, [1899] 1 Ch. 365.

   c. out of specific legacies and devises? Thomas *v.* Thomas, 17 N. J. Eq. 356 (1866).

20. T dies domiciled in Connecticut, owning Massachusetts land upon which there is a mortgage given to secure a note of T. T devises this land to A. By Connecticut law a devisee is entitled to have such a mortgage paid out of the residue; by Massachusetts

---

[22] Mass. Gen. Laws (Ter. Ed. 1932) c. 191, § 23; N. Y. Real Prop. Law § 250. The latter statute was amended in 1937 (L. 1937, c. 75) to apply the same rule in the situation where land is devised upon which the purchase price has not been paid. This eliminates some of the bizarre by-products of the doctrine of equitable conversion.

[23] Should it make any difference that the $5000 is used to erect a building on Blackacre rather than being used to provide working capital for T's business or buy a yacht? See Atkinson, Wills, 715.

statute a devisee is not entitled to have such a mortgage paid out of the residue. Should the executor pay off the mortgage debt? Higinbotham v. Manchester, 113 Conn. 62, 154 Atl. 242 (1931); Matter of Blackinton, 158 Misc. 580 (Surr. 1934).

B. Investment and Care of Funds.

In sizable estates there usually comes into the hands of the personal representative, either at once or in the course of administration, the decedent's stocks and bonds and considerable amounts of cash.

Is the personal representative entitled to retain securities which he finds in the decedent's estate?[24] This depends upon (a) the conservative or speculative character of the investments and (b) the probable length of time the administration will take. Holding speculative investments for a considerable number of years will render the personal representative liable for losses suffered. The primary duty of a personal representative (as distinguished from a trustee) is to turn over the estate to creditors and distributees as quickly as possible, and hence he is not obliged, to the extent that a trustee is obliged, to revise the investment portfolio to meet trustee standards. But the longer the administration is likely to take, the more his position approaches that of a trustee and the closer he must conform to trustee requirements. In matters of investment it is wise for the personal representative to protect himself by court order or the assent of interested parties.

What should the personal representative do with funds which come into his hands? (1) The funds should be immediately placed on deposit in a bank selected with due care, in the name of the personal representative in his fiduciary character. Placing the funds in an account which is not designated as a fiduciary account is a breach of duty and creates a liability for any loss that may occur due to the failure of the bank. (2) If the funds are substantial and are not needed for the current affairs of the administration, they should be put in a savings bank. If this is not done, the personal representative may be liable for the interest which could have been earned. (3) The purchasing of investment securities by an executor or administrator is a delicate matter. Many wills provide that the executor shall have the power to invest. Some statutes have a similar provision. But if neither the will nor a statute authorizes investment, the personal representative probably should not purchase investments except as he is permitted to do so by court order or the assent of all parties.

[24] See Atkinson, Wills, p. 638. For the type of statute which may affect this and other investment problems, see N. Y. D. E. L. § 111.

C. *Contracts of the Personal Representative;
Carrying on the Decedent's Business.*

Where any fiduciary — whether he be an executor, an administrator, a trustee, a receiver, or an assignee for benefit of creditors — makes a contract he is personally liable thereon to the other contracting party; and it is no defense that the contract was a proper one for him to make as fiduciary. It is amazing how few laymen are aware of this well-settled rule and how often lawyers find themselves in trouble by overlooking it. Of course, if the contract was a proper one, the fiduciary is entitled to reimbursement out of the estate in his hands; but difficulty arises when the estate is insufficient to provide such reimbursement. Executors and administrators frequently make contracts, the most usual ones being for funeral expenses, tombstones and the engaging of attorneys. Sometimes it is desirable to borrow money for estate purposes, though this should not be done without court authorization.

The personal representative can protect himself against individual liability, but certain formulas commonly used for this purpose are ineffective.

PROBLEMS.

21. E, executor of the will of T, borrowed $1000 from A for a proper estate purpose and gave therefor a note in the usual form except that the note was signed " E, Executor of the Estate of T." The assets of T's estate are not sufficient to pay the note. What are A's rights? Rittenhouse *v.* Ammerman, 64 Mo. 197 (1876).

22. Same facts as Problem 21 except that the note is signed, " Estate of T, by E, executor." What are A's rights? Grafton National Bank *v.* Wing, 172 Mass. 513, 52 N. E. 1067 (1899); Germania Bank *v.* Michaud, 62 Minn. 459, 65 N. W. 70 (1895).

23. Same facts as Problem 21 except that the note is signed, " E, Executor of the Estate of T, but not individually." What are A's rights? Morehead Banking Co. *v.* Morehead, 116 N. C. 413, 21 S. E. 191 (1895).

24. Same facts as Problem 21, except that the note contains a provision as follows: " This note is given by E as Executor of the Estate of T and not individually; it constitutes a promise to pay only to such extent as the assets of said Estate are sufficient for that purpose; and any judgment upon this note shall be satisfiable only out of assets of the said Estate and not out of the individual assets of E." What are A's rights? See Atkinson, Wills, p. 614.

Where the decedent has been engaged in an unincorporated business, it is frequently sound from an economic viewpoint that the business should be carried on. But serious liabilities may be involved unless the executor takes careful steps to protect himself in this activity.[25] It is usually proper for the executor to sell a stock in trade over the counter rather than to make a sale in bulk to a single purchaser. Certain other types of temporary action in the nature of carrying on the business may also be within the executor's inherent powers under some circumstances, but each situation of this type must be examined with the greatest care under the applicable statutes and authorities. If the will authorizes the executor to carry on the business, he is protected in carrying it on; but it should be noted that assets of the estate other than those devoted to the business at the testator's death cannot be used in the business unless the will expressly so provides. A valid court order will protect the executor, but there are cases in which it is held that such an order has no validity unless a statute authorizes it. Assents from all interested parties are also ample protection, but if there are minors who are interested, they usually cannot be bound by this method. If the executor carries on the business without sufficient authorization, or uses assets beyond those authorized, he is personally liable for resulting losses and must account to the estate for any gains.

Problem.

25. T was in business as a custom tailor. He left a will which authorized his executor, E, to carry on the business for two years and gave to T's son, S, an option to purchase the stock in trade of the business at any time within the two years. E bought cloth from A for the business, signing the purchase order "E, executor of estate of T," and undertaking to make payment in the amount of $250 in 90 days. The cloth was made up into suits and sold. During the 90-day period it was discovered that E had made an improper investment of funds of the estate and had lost $600 thereby. E is insolvent. What are A's rights? In re Johnson, 15 Ch. D. 548 (1880); Scott, "Liabilities in the Administration of Trusts," 28 Harv. L. Rev. 725, 735–736 (1915); Scott on Trusts (1940) §§ 244.3, 268.2.

ANSWERS TO PROBLEMS IN CHAPTER IX.

1. Scott is entitled to the land. His estate was administered as a decedent estate. No notice to him was given or directed. The fact of his death was necessary to the jurisdiction of the court. He being alive, the court had no jurisdiction; its proceedings are void and can be attacked collaterally. The action of the Supreme Court of Washington in holding otherwise deprived Scott of his property without due process of law.

The cited New Jersey case reaches the opposite result by construing the New Jersey statute in such a way as to fall within the

[25] See Atkinson, Wills, pp. 621–624.

principle of the Cunnius case cited in Problem 4. The Yale Law Journal thinks it better for the legislature to pass an absentee statute than for the courts to warp a decedent estate statute into the absentee mold.

2. Scott could have recovered. The administrator was a wrongdoer since the decree appointing him was void. He is liable to Scott for money had and received.

3. Scott could collect again from D; the administrator's appointment was void and therefore a payment to the administrator was no defense against Scott. D could have defended an action against him brought by the administrator by proving that Scott was still alive.

When Scott appears D can get restitution from the administrator of the amount paid to him under mutual mistake of fact. But he cannot recover on the administrator's bond, if it is of the usual type, because there has been no breach of the condition of the bond. The usual probate bond is conditioned upon the administrator (a) collecting the assets (b) distributing as ordered by the court (c) accounting as required. All these have been done.

4. Margaret cannot recover. The absentee statute is designed expressly for this purpose. Notice is given to the absentee by publication, and protections of the absentee's interests are provided. These are adequate to satisfy the requirements of due process of law. Scott v. McNeal is distinguished, because there the procedure offered no protection to the interests of the alleged decedent.

5. No. The right of action belonged to the decedent. Authority to bring suit upon it in Massachusetts cannot be given by the New York court.

6. The two cited cases differ as to the answer. The latter permits E to sue, the former does not. Superficially this case seems to present the same issue as Problem 5. But the New Hampshire case points out that the question is: What do the words " personal representative " mean as used in the Federal Employers' Liability Act? That Act designates the " personal representative " as the party to bring suit merely as a convenient and appropriate person to act for the widow and children. He is not suing in his probate capacity as executor or administrator. The proceeds of any such suit are not assets of the estate or subject to the claims of the estate's creditors; the proceeds go to the widow and children directly. Hence, concludes the New Hampshire court, where no local personal representative has been appointed, the domiciliary personal representative can bring the action.

7. Yes. The original right of action upon which E brought suit in New York was derivative from T and could be brought only in the state of E's appointment. However, the judgment in that action ran to E and is not derived from T. Hence E can bring an action on that judgment anywhere.

8. E can bring trover for the theft occurring after his appointment. By virtue of his appointment in New York E acquired title to the automobile which was then located in New York. The tort was committed against him and the right of action was his. The right of action was not derivative from T. . . . The same result would follow if the theft took place after T's death but before the date of the decre appointing E, for E's title to the goods of T relates back to the moment of T's death.

9. No. Whether the note matures before or after the death of T, E is suing in his representative capacity upon a right of action derived from T. There is an obvious difference between an accrued right of action (where the note is overdue) and an inchoate right of action (where the note has not matured at T's death) but the same result is reached in the two types of cases.

10. The Restatement says that D is protected if no ancillary administrator has been appointed in Massachusetts or if, one being appointed, D has no knowledge of that fact. But the cases are in substantial conflict. D would be well advised to sit tight until a Massachusetts administrator is appointed unless E will make a satisfactory arrangement as to saving D harmless from further claims.

11. Yes. When D is in New York E could serve him with process and get a judgment against him. D is protected in making voluntary payment where he could be forced to pay by legal action.

12. The heirs should move for a stay of proceedings pending a determination of the contest at the domicil. The court should allow the motion.

13. P is not protected. The appeal suspended the operation of the decree. Persons dealing with an executor or administrator are not protected unless he has been appointed and the period for appeal from the appointment has expired. The personal representative's certificate of appointment should specify that the appeal period has expired without any appeal being entered. Persons dealing with the personal representative should require such a certificate.

14. Evidence excluded. The decree of the probate court cannot be collaterally attacked except for lack of justification (Compare Scott *v.* McNeal, Problem 1 supra). D must bring a petition to have A's appointment revoked, and this must be done in the court that appointed him.

15. Most states allow the personal representative to bring actions to set aside fraudulent conveyances, but some require that the creditors do so. If the personal representative brings the action he must return to the conveyee any amount not needed for payment of debts; the property recovered cannot be made a part of the estate for transfer to legatees or distributees.

16. There certainly is. The Massachusetts case holds that E's debt to T is an item with which E must charge himself upon his

account, and the failure to pay it constitutes a breach of the bond upon which S is liable as surety. However, the Vermont case holds that S is liable only to the extent that E was able to pay the debt when appointed.

17. Of course not. The mortgage note is not an obligation of T, and the executor or administrator is therefore not justified in paying it.

18. The authorities are in conflict. The Pennsylvania case holds that the mortgage should be paid off out of the residue; the Massachusetts case contra. The issue is plainly one of the intention of T. Did he mean to give A land free-and-clear or encumbered land? Where the encumbrance was on the land at the time T bought it there is obvious plausibility in the argument that he was thinking of this property as an equity of redemption, not unencumbered land.

19. Where the debt secured by the mortgage was originally contracted by T, A is entitled to have the debt paid and the mortgage discharged out of the residue. If the residue is insufficient and general (pecuniary) legacies would have to be abated to pay off the mortgage the authorities are in conflict; the English case favors the pecuniary legatee, the Massachusetts case the devisee of the mortgaged land. It is clear that specific legacies and devises will not be abated to clear the land of the mortgage. Some consideration should properly be given to the use to which the borrowed money was put. One argument for exoneration of the mortgaged land is that the personal estate was augmented by the money borrowed; if this is not true, and the money in fact went into improvements on the land, the case against exoneration is much stronger.

20. This is a difficult, perhaps insoluble, problem. So far as land is concerned a will is interpreted according to the law of the situs of the land — i.e. Massachusetts. So far as personalty is concerned, the controlling law is that of T's domicil — i.e. Connecticut. Restatement of Conflicts, §§ 251, 308. The Problem concerns a relationship between land and personalty. The Connecticut court held that Connecticut law should govern, giving as a reason that the question concerned the action of the executor and that this was governed by the domiciliary law. However, the matter is not quite so simple, since arguably the duty of the executor is determined by the proper interpretation of what was devised, which is a matter for Massachusetts law. As would be expected the New York case takes the latter view.

21. A can recover against E personally. The phrase " Executor of the Estate of T " is merely descriptive; it does not limit A's rights.

22. The Massachusetts case held that no one was liable since there was no such entity as the " Estate of T " and E did not purport to bind himself but only to represent a principal. The Minnesota case holds E personally liable.

23. The cited case held that E could not be held liable except as the assets of the Estate were capable of meeting the claim. But there are cases contra.

24. This clause protects E. The difficulty is that the other party to the transaction may be loath to accept such a provision.

25. A can obtain a personal judgment against E, but this is worthless. In ordinary circumstances he would be able to reach by equitable execution E's right of indemnity against the estate. But since E owes the estate an amount in excess of E's claim for indemnity with reference to A's note, nothing can be obtained from the Estate. It is just too bad.

CHAPTER X.

PERPETUITIES IN A NUTSHELL *

The Rule Against Perpetuities is the *sanctum sanctorum* of the law, complete with its bearded and incomparable high priest, John Chipman Gray, and a coterie of acolytes. The Rule is all things to all men — to the legal historian, a museum specimen of a judge-made rule gradually evolving and crystallizing through a century and a half (1680-1833); to the analyst, a series of intricate applications, mathematical in their precision; to the theoretician, an opportunity to spin out his webs, hoping that there is more jurisprudence than pedantry in the spinning;[1] to the innovator, a challenge to legislative improvement; and to the troubled spirit, a blessed sheltering realization that lives-in-being-and-twenty-one-years have the same validity after two world wars and four Democratic administrations that they had when Queen Victoria ascended the throne. If, for one of these reasons or some other, you do not develop an affection for the Rule, you are indeed unfortunate.

The greatest importance of the Rule in the practice of the profession does not lie in the argument of cases. It lies in the drafting of the instruments which must measure up to the requirements of the Rule or fail. And for this purpose it is less important that the law of perpetuities be elaborated in the magnificent detail of Gray's treatise than that it be stated in so small a compass that the elements of the Rule can be grasped as a whole and retained as a background of knowledge against which effective dispositive instruments can be created. This chapter seeks to perform this function of simplified statement.

For students who are to take a course in future interests this chapter offers the groundwork upon which a more advanced treatment of perpetuities problems can be built. For other students, this or some other survey is an essential piece of equipment for the profession.

---

* This chapter originally appeared in 51 Harv. L. Rev. 638 (1938). It is revised and reprinted by permission of the Harvard Law Review. If it fails of its purpose it has, at least, eminent company. Lord Thurlow undertook to put the Rule in Shelley's Case in a nutshell. "But," said Lord Macnaghten, "it is one thing to put a case like Shelley's in a nutshell and another thing to keep it there." Van Grutten v. Foxwell, [1897] A. C. 658, 671.

[1] I plead guilty on this count. See Leach, *Powers of Sale in Trustees and the Rule against Perpetuities* (1934) 47 Harv. L. Rev. 948; Leach, *Rule against Perpetuities and Gifts to Classes,* 51 Harv. L. Rev. 1329 (1938).

COMMON LAW AND STATUTE

We here deal with the common-law Rule against Perpetuities. This is applicable uniformly throughout the United States except as modified by statute in Arizona, California, District of Columbia, Idaho, Kentucky, Louisiana, Minnesota, Mississippi, Montana, New York, North Dakota, Oklahoma, South Dakota, Wisconsin and Wyoming. In nearly all of the states just enumerated the principles of the common-law Rule have substantial application; in some of them (*e.g.*, the District of Columbia, Kentucky) it is possible that the statutory rule merely re-enacts the common-law Rule; and in others (*e.g.*, Mississippi) the statute applies only to real estate, leaving the common-law Rule applicable to personalty.[2]

I. STATEMENT OF THE RULE

Gray's statement of the Rule, adopted by practically every court which has dealt with the subject, is as follows:

No interest is good unless it must vest, if at all, not later than twenty-one years after some life in being at the creation of the interest.

The whole law of perpetuities cannot be put in a single sentence. Gray's formulation would be more realistic if it were preceded by the words *Generally speaking* and if the word *vest* were put in quotation marks. But this formulation has proved workable, solves the great bulk of cases that arise and serves as a convenient starting point for the solution of those which it does not solve.

II. NATURE OF THE RULE

The Rule against Perpetuities is a rule invalidating interests which *vest* too remotely. Indeed, it is often called the rule against remoteness of vesting.

It is *not* a rule invalidating interests which *last* too long. Thus a gift to A for life, remainder to B in fee is entirely valid, although the remainder may last forever. Similarly a gift to A for life, re-

---

[2] The statutory situation in all the above states is dealt with, including citation of cases, in the Appendix to Volume 4 of the PROPERTY RESTATEMENT (1944). Louisiana, Mississippi and Wyoming, which have statutes basically different from the common law are treated only by references to the statutes and their legislative backgrounds (pp. 2628–2629). The New York statutes and judicial interpretations thereof are extensively considered (pp. 2632–2711). Statutes and judicial interpretations of the remaining states are considered alphabetically beginning at p. 2712. Perpetuities statutes are also treated in 2 SIMES, FUTURE INTERESTS (1936) c. 32; Gray, Perpetuities (4th ed. 1942), §§ 728–752.1. Indiana has re-adopted the common-law Rule since the Restatement was published. Ind. Acts, 1945, c. 216, § 1. Michigan's statutory rule, applicable to realty only, was repealed by Public Act 38 of 1949.

mainder to A's children for their lives, remainder to B in fee is valid, although the life estates in A's children may last longer than the period of perpetuities; B's remainder is vested at once, though it may not become possessory until beyond the period of perpetuities.[3]

The Rule against Perpetuities is *not* a rule against suspension of the power of alienation of property through the creation of interests in unborn or unascertained persons; and it is not satisfied by the fact that there are persons in being who can together give a complete title to a purchaser. Thus, where land is given to A in fee, but if liquor shall ever be sold on the premises then to B in fee, the executory interest in B is bad even though A and B together can give a complete title to the land.[4]

The Rule against Perpetuities must be distinguished from the rules against restraints on alienation, though, like these rules, it stems from the general policy against withdrawal of property from commerce. A restraint on alienation is some provision which, even after an interest has become vested, prevents the owner thereof from disposing of it at all or from disposing of it in particular ways or to particular persons — the most common example being the spendthrift trust. An interest which is void under the Rule against Perpetuities fails because it vests too remotely; it may be, and usually is, freely alienable at all times.

III. Elements of the Rule

A. The Period of Perpetuities

The period within which interests must vest or fail is: twenty-one years after any reasonable number of lives in being at the creation of the interest, plus actual periods of gestation. Rules to be noted with reference to this period are the following:

A. The 21-year period may be in gross as well as connected with the minority of any person. Thus the following are valid:

1. Bequest "to all descendants of mine who shall be born within 21 years after my death."

---

[3] Seaver v. Fitzgerald, 141 Mass. 401, 6 N. E. 73 (1886). But it is unwise to create trusts which last beyond the period of perpetuities. See heading X-C, *infra*.

[4] Brattle Square Church v. Grant, 3 Gray 142 (Mass. 1855). Statutes which follow the New York model require that the "absolute power of alienation" shall not be suspended for longer than the locally prescribed period of perpetuities. N. Y. REAL PROP. LAW § 42. This is a different test from that of the common-law Rule against Perpetuities. It is generally construed to be in addition to the common-law test, not in substitution for it. Matter of Wilcox, 194 N. Y. 288, 87 N. E. 497 (1909). See Updegraff, *The Rule Against Perpetuities in the District of Columbia* (1926) 14 GEO. L. J. 336; Roberts, *Kentucky's Statute Against Perpetuities* (1928) 16 KY. L. J. 97.

2. Bequest to a trustee " to pay the income to A for life and then to pay the principal to such children of A as reach the age of 21."

B. The 21-year period cannot precede the measuring lives; or, to put it more exactly, the measuring lives must be in being at the creation of the interest (*i.e.*, the death of the testator in a will, the delivery of a deed); it is not sufficient that they come into being within 21 years.

3. Bequest " to accumulate the income for 21 years and then to pay the income to such of my grandchildren as shall then be living for life and upon the death of the survivor to pay the principal to my great-grandchildren then living." The life estates to the grandchildren are valid, since they vest within 21 years; but the remainders to great-grandchildren are invalid.[5]

C. The measuring lives need not be mentioned in the instrument, need not be holders of previous estates, and need not be connected in any way with the property or the persons designated to take it.[5a]

4. Bequest " to my grandchildren who shall reach the age of 21." This is valid, since all grandchildren must be born in the lives of the testator's (T's) children and these must perforce be lives in being at T's death.

5. *Inter vivos* trust for " my grandchildren who shall reach the age of 21." This is bad, since (unlike the case of a bequest) other children may be born to the settlor and the children cannot, therefore, be taken as the lives in being.

6. Bequest " to A's grandchildren who shall reach the age of 21." This is bad since, A still being alive and presumptively capable of having more children, his children cannot be taken as the lives in being.

7. Bequest " to such of my children and more remote issue as shall be living 21 years after the death of the survivor of R, S, T, U, V, W, X, Y and Z " (these being nine healthy babies selected at random). This is valid.

D. Any number of lives may be selected,[6] provided they are not so numerous as to make it impossible to ascertain their termination.

8. Bequest in 1926 to " my descendants who shall be living 21 years after the death of all lineal descendants of Queen Victoria now living." There were 120 such descendants. The gift was held

---

[5] It is, of course, assumed that the testator (T) had children living at his death and that, consequently there was a possibility that other grandchildren would be born. If this is not so, the grandchildren are themselves the lives in being and the gift to great-grandchildren is valid.

[5a] McArthur *v.* Scott, 113 U. S. 340, 383 (1885); Fitchie *v.* Brown, 211 U. S. 321, 329 (1908).

[6] For " let the lives be never so many, there must be a survivor, and so it is but the length of that life; for Twisden used to say, the candles were all lighted at once." Scattergood *v.* Edge, 1 Salk. 229 (K. B. 1699).

valid, but it has been clearly indicated that such a contingency would be held too remote in a will taking effect as late as 1943.[7]

E. Actual periods of gestation are included in the period of perpetuities.

9. Bequest " to my children for their lives, remainder to my grandchildren who shall reach 21." The testator (T) at his death has one living child, C1, and one child *en ventre sa mere*, C2, who is born 8 months later. C2 at his death leaves a child *en ventre sa mere*, G, who is born 8 months later. G reaches 21. The gift to grandchildren of T is valid and G takes a share in it.[8] But,

10. A bequest to " such of my descendants as shall be living 21 years and 9 months after the death of A " is invalid. Periods of gestation are included in the period of perpetuities only so far as they actually occur.[9]

B. *The Required Certainty of Vesting*

A future interest is invalid unless it is absolutely certain that it must vest within the period of perpetuities. Probability of vesting, however great, is not sufficient. Moreover, the certainty of vesting must have existed at the time when the instrument took effect (*i.e.*, the testator's death in the case of a will; the date of delivery in the case of a deed or trust). It is immaterial that the contingencies actually do occur within the permissible period or actually have occurred when the validity of the instrument is first litigated.

It is at this point that the rule becomes a trap to the draftsman. Many perfectly reasonable dispositions are stricken down because on some outside chance not forseen by the testator or his lawyer it is mathematically possible that the vesting might occur too remotely. Mistakes of this sort are readily classifiable into frequently recurring types. Such possibilities of salvation as exist are discussed under each type.

First comes the " fertile octogenarian " type.

11. T has a widowed sister, A, aged 80. He leaves property in trust to pay the income to A for life, then to pay the income to the children of A for their lives, then to pay the principal to the children of such children.

By the traditional English view the gift of the principal is bad; for the *children* of A include after-born children and A is conclusively presumed to be capable of having children until death.[10] Plainly this is silly on two grounds: (1) When T used the word *children* he never intended to include after-born children of A because he never

---

[7] *In re* Villar, [1929] 1 Ch. 243; *In re* Leverhulme, [1943] All E. R. 274.

[8] Thellusson *v.* Woodford, 11 Ves. Jr. 112 (Ch. 1805).

[9] Cadell *v.* Palmer, 1 Cl. & F. 372 (H. L. 1833).

[10] Jee *v.* Audley, 1 Cox Eq. Cas. 324 (1787); Johnston *v.* Hill, 39 Ch. D. 155 (1888); Ward *v.* Van Der Loeff, [1924] A. C. 653.

considered that after-born children were within the realm of possibility. Hence, although *children* usually means *children whenever born*, it should mean *children now living* when used by T in these circumstances. Two American courts have adopted this view.[11] (2) It is physically impossible for A to have children and a conclusive presumption to the contrary flies in the face of medical knowledge; thus the certainty required by the Rule against Perpetuities exists except so far as the court chooses to blind its eyes. But of all courts in the English-speaking world only the Irish Court of Chancery has refused to follow the presumption in a perpetuities case.[12] The draftsman plainly should restrict class designations (children, nephews, nieces, etc.) to living persons where this coincides with the testator's desires.

Second comes the " unborn widow " type of case.

12. T has a son, A, 45 years old. The son has a wife and grown children. T leaves property in trust " to pay the income to A for his life, then to pay the income to A's widow, if any, for her life and then to pay the principal to the children of A then living."

Incontestably the gift of principal is invalid.[13] A may marry again and his second wife may be a person who was unborn at T's death. Hence the gift to children of A (including after-born children) contingent on their surviving the widow is too remote. Of course, everyone knows that A will not marry a woman 45 years his junior; but it is a mathematical possibility. A provision in the will that the life estate to the widow is dependent upon her being born in the life of T saves the remainder.

[11] Wright's Estate, 284 Pa. 334, 131 Atl. 188 (1925); Worcester County Trust Co. *v.* Marble, 316 Mass. 294, 300, 55 N. E. (2d) 446 (1944).

[12] Exham *v.* Beamish, [1939] I. R. 336. The argument for ignoring the old cases on this point is overwhelming. When the presumption of fertility arose — certainly prior to 1787, the date of Jee *v.* Audley, 1 Cox Eq. Cas. 324 (1787), *supra*, — common experience, unsupported by statistical data, was pretty well mixed with wonder stories, chiefly from the East, including the birth of Isaac to Sarah at the age of ninety. Genesis, xvii, 15 *et. seq.* The wonder stories still come in (*e.g.*, a birth of twins to a Mexican woman of 70 reported in the Boston American for May 24, 1934) but we now have records of the U. S. Department of Commerce showing that in over twenty million births between 1923 and 1932 none was to a woman over 55 and .0001% were to women over 50. See City Bank Farmers' Trust Co. *v.* United States, 74 F.(2d) 692, 693 (C. C. A. 2d, 1935).

[13] *In re* Curryer's Will Trusts, [1938] Ch. 952; Loring *v.* Blake, 98 Mass. 253, 259 (1867); Perkins *v.* Iglehart, 183 Md. 520, 39 A. (2d) 672 (1944). In Helvering *v.* Bullard, 303 U. S. 297 (1937) a settlor used the fact that her counsel had made the unborn-widow mistake as a means of forcing a compromise by which she resettled the property upon trusts she liked better — and as a result of this success got into litigation with the tax authorities ending in an additional tax of $17,271.46. She probably got a new lawyer.

Case 12 can be saved if " widow " can be construed to mean only A's present wife. This construction was approved in Matter of Friend, 283 N. Y. 200, 28 N. E. (2d) 377 (1940); *In re* Solms' Estate, 253 Pa. 293, 98 A. (2d) 596 (1916). But see Meeker *v.* Draffen, 201 N. Y. 205, 94 N. E. 626 (1911).

Third comes the "administration contingency" type. In this class of case a provident and thoughtful testator foresees the possibility that some of the objects of his bounty will die during the relatively short time that is required for the administration of his estate or for the carrying out of very short trusts which he sets up for specific purposes; and, desiring to avoid the additional shrinkage which is bound to attend the passage of his property through another decedent estate, he provides that the property shall pass only to persons who are living at the time when administration is completed and distribution is made. What he fails to observe is that, although everyone expects the administration of his estate or of the trust to be completed within a very short time, it is mathematically possible that it will take more than the period of perpetuities (which, in the absence of an available measuring life, is 21 years). For example:

13. T was in the sand and gravel business. He owned gravel pits which, at the time of his death, would have been exhausted in 4 years if worked at the rate which was habitual with T. T died, leaving a will which devised to trustees the gravel pits in trust to work until the same were exhausted, then to sell the pits and divide the proceeds among T's issue then living. The pits were actually exhausted in 6 years. But the gift to issue was held bad on the ground that they might not have been exhausted within 21 years.[14]

14. T owned Blackacre subject to a mortgage upon which a balance of £1000 was still due, payable £200 per year. The rents from the property were sufficient to meet this payment, plus interest, taxes and insurance with a substantial margin. T devised Blackacre to trustees to pay off the mortgage out of the rents and then to transfer the property to his issue then living. The gift was held bad, since it was possible that the income from the property would decrease so that the mortgage would not be paid off within 21 years.[15]

15. T devised Blackacre to A "from and after the date of probate of this will." The devise was held bad on the ground that " it cannot be said that it [probate] is a condition that must inevitably happen within 21 years from the death of the testatrix.[16]

---

[14] *In re* Wood, [1894] 3 Ch. 381. Valid gift: "... to work the pits for 20 years or until they are exhausted, whichever happens first, and then to sell the property and divide the proceeds among such of my issue as shall be living 20 years after my death or at the exhaustion of the pits, whichever happens first." Observe also that if the gift had been to T's *children* living at the time of sale, it would have been valid; for the children are lives in being at T's death, and the gift to them will vest *if at all* in their lives.

[15] *In re* Bewick, [1911] 1 Ch. 116. Valid gift: "This trust shall continue until 20 years from the date of my death or until the mortgage is discharged, whichever shall happen first. The property shall, at the termination of the trust, be transferred to my issue then living."

[16] Johnson *v.* Preston, 226 Ill. 447, 80 N. E. 1001 (1907); Miller *v.* Weston, 67 Colo. 534, 189 Pac. 610 (1920).

16. T left his property to such of his issue as should be living when his debts were paid and his estate settled. The gift was held bad.[17]

It is less relevant to discuss whether these cases prove Mr. Bumble's proposition that " the law is a ass, a idiot " than to recognize that this is the law with which a draftsman must deal and against which he must protect the instruments which he draws. There is, however, some solace in the approach of the Connecticut court to this type of problem. In *Belfield v. Booth*,[18] a gift which was to vest 14 years after the settlement of the testator's estate was held valid. The court reasoned that the holder of the will was in duty bound to produce it promptly and that the executor had a fiduciary obligation to settle the estate promptly; that the testator expected both of these things to be done; and therefore that, as a matter of construction, the 14-year period " will commence at the time when the accounts of the executor or administrator of his estate are, or should be, settled in the due course of administration; and that this time cannot be delayed so long as seven years from his decease." Such an approach would have saved all the gifts in this group except Case 14.

The certainty required by the Rule against Perpetuities may be produced by the fact that, at the testator's death, relevant persons have died or reached particular ages. Thus,

17. T makes a bequest " to such children of A as shall reach the age of 30." Prima facie this gift is bad. But (1) if A is dead at the death of T, the gift is good, since the children of A may themselves be treated as the lives in being; and (2) even though A is alive, if one of the children has reached 30 at the death of T, this closes the class to future born children, and again the children of A can be treated as the lives in being.[19]

18. T makes a bequest in trust " for B for life and then for such children of A as shall reach the age of 30." Prima facie the remainder is bad. But (1) if A is dead at the death of T, the gift is good, on the same grounds as in Case 17(1). Or (2) if B is dead and a child of A has reached 30 at the death of T the gift is good on the same grounds as in Case 17(2). However (3) if B is living, the fact that a child of A has reached 30 at T's death is

---

[17] See Kales, *How Far Interests Limited to Take Effect " When Debts are Paid " or " An Estate Settled " or " A Trust Executed and Performed " are Void for Remoteness* (1912) 6 ILL. L. REV. 373. In *Trautz v. Lemp*, 329 Mo. 580, 46 S. W. (2d) 135 (1932) a gift of similar type was saved by an unusual construction of the will.

[18] 63 Conn. 299, 27 Atl. 585 (1893).

[19] *Picken v. Matthews*, 10 Ch. D. 264 (1878). The "rule of convenience" as to class gifts, universally recognized, is that the class closes to later born members at any time when a class member is entitled to require a distribution of principal. 2 SIMES, FUTURE INTERESTS (1936) § 373 *et seq*.

immaterial, for the intervening life estate of B keeps the class open to unborn children of A until B's death;[20] the children of A cannot therefore be treated as the lives in being; and the gift is still bad.

C. "Vesting" in Interest

The metaphysical common-law notion that a future estate can vest in interest before it vests in possession is incorporated into the Rule against Perpetuities. A remainder complies with the requirements of the Rule as soon as it becomes vested, regardless of when it becomes possessory. Thus in a devise to A for life, remainder to A's children for their lives, remainder to B, B's interest is good; it is presently vested, though clearly it may not come into possession until the death of a child of A yet unborn — a point well beyond the period of perpetuities.[21] Again,

19. T bequeaths a fund in trust to pay the income to A for life, then to pay the income to A's children for their lives, then to pay the principal to his residuary legatees (B, C, D and E) if they should then be living but, if not, to the heirs of the residuary legatees. The remainder is good. It is not presently vested; but it must become vested within the lives or upon the deaths of the residuary legatees, who are lives in being. If, at the death of the children of A, a residuary legatee is living, his share then becomes vested in possession; if he dies before that time his heirs are ascertained at his death and as to them the gift is thenceforth vested in interest.[22]

The fact that a remainder satisfies the Rule if it "vests in interest" within the period of perpetuities gives great importance to one of the most esoteric distinctions in property law. This is the distinction between (a) remainders which are contingent — i.e. subject to a condition precedent, and (b) remainders which are vested subject to divestment — i.e. subject to a condition subsequent. Assuming that the stated condition (for example, children now unborn reaching 25) is too remote, (a) if the remainder is contingent, the remainder is void; (b) if the remainder is vested subject to divestment, the divesting gift is void and the remainder is indefeasibly vested.

[20] 2 SIMES, FUTURE INTERESTS (1936) § 383.
[21] Evans v. Walker, 3 Ch. D. 211 (1876); Loring v. Blake, 98 Mass. 253 (1867); Gray, Perpetuities (4th ed. 1942) § 232.
[22] But the remainder was held bad in Feeney's Estate, 293 Pa. 273, 142 Atl. 284 (1928). The only possible way of justifying the decision is to say that as a matter of construction "heirs" does not have its technical meaning of persons who are entitled to the residuary legatee's property upon his death, but means persons who would have been the residuary legatee's heirs if he had died at the death of A's children. There is no indication in the opinion that this construction was considered, and no substantial justification for adopting it.

19a. T bequeaths a fund in trust for A for life and then for such children of A as shall reach the age of 25. A has no children at T's death. Reaching 25 is a condition *precedent* on the remainder to the children. Thus the children have a contingent remainder given upon a remote contingency, and it is void.

19b. T bequeaths a fund in trust for A for life and then for A's children, but if any child of A shall die under the age of 25, his share shall pass to the survivors. A has no children at T's death. Failing to reach 25 is a condition *subsequent* on the remainder to each child. Each child takes a vested interest at birth. T intended that each child's interest should be divested if he failed to reach 25. But the intended divestment is too remote and therefore fails, leaving each child's gift indefeasibly vested.[22a]

The distinction is obviously one of words. There is no difference in the thought of the two testators in Cases 19a and 19b. Thus, in perpetuities cases, it frequently happens that great ingenuity is expended in establishing that the condition attached to a remainder is precedent or subsequent. Fortunes can, and do, turn on this point.[22b]

Possibilities of reverter are not subject to the Rule against Perpetuities in the United States. It is sometimes said that this is because they are reversionary interests and hence, in common-law theory, vested. Thus,

20. T devises Blackacre " to the A Church so long as the premises are used for church purposes." Upon the cessation of the prescribed use the property reverts to T and his heirs, even if this occur centuries later.[23]

This exemption of possibilities of reverter from the Rule theoretically makes possible fantastic dispositions. For instance,

21. T leaves the residue of his estate " to the A Trust Company so long as it pays to my oldest living descendant for the time being annual amounts equal to 80% of the amount which a fund of this size would earn at the average current rate of return on investments " as determined by a specified index. The balance of 20% of the income would presumably constitute a sufficient inducement to assure the payment of the amounts stipulated.[24]

However, executory interests do not have the capacity of vesting

---

[22a] Sears *v.* Putnam, 102 Mass. 5 (1869).

[22b] Gray, Perpetuities (4th ed. 1942) § 108. There is a strong constructional tendency to construe gifts as vested. Gray, § 103.

[23] Institution for Savings *v.* Roxbury Home for Aged Women, 244 Mass. 583, 139 N. E. 301 (1923); Leonard *v.* Burr, 18 N. Y. 96 (1858). *Contra*, Hopper *v.* Corporation of Liverpool, 22 Sol. J. 213 (Chancery Court of Lancaster, 1944), criticized in 62 L. Q. Rev. 222 (1946).

[24] This case has never arisen; but it is foreshadowed by *In re* Chardon [1928] Ch. 464; *In re* Tyler, [1891] 3 Ch. 252; and Matter of Terry, 218 N. Y. 218, 112 N. E. 931 (1916).

in interest before they vest in possession. Thus the Rule against Perpetuities requires that executory interests become possessory within lives and 21 years.

22. T devises Blackacre to A, but if liquor shall ever be sold on the premises then to B. B's interest is a shifting executory devise; it may not become possessory within the period of perpetuities; and it therefore fails.[25]

23. T grants Blackacre " to B at such time as lime shall cease to be burned on the premises." B's interest is a springing executory devise; it need not become possessory within the period of perpetuities; and it therefore fails.[26]

IV. APPLICATION OF THE RULE TO GIFTS TO CLASSES

In England the rule became settled that a gift of property to be divided among a class of persons was totally invalid if it was possible that the interest of any member of the class would vest beyond the period of perpetuities.[27] Or, to put it differently, a class gift is not "vested" within the meaning of that word as used in the Rule against Perpetuities until the interest of each member of the class is vested. Thus,

24. T bequeaths a fund in trust for A for life and then in trust for A's children who shall reach the age of 25. Four children of A are living at the death of T. Standing alone, the gift to these children is valid, since they must reach or fail to reach 25 within their own lives. Yet the fact that a later child of A might be born and might reach 25 more than 21 years after the death of all persons in being at T's death invalidates the whole gift.[28]

No satisfactory rationalization of this application of the Rule has ever been advanced. Yet, as is too often the case with regard to problems of future interests, the English cases have been followed in the United States where the issue has arisen without independent examination of the question involved.[29]

[25] Brattle Square Church v. Grant, 3 Gray 142 (Mass. 1855).

[26] Walker v. Marcellus & Otisco Lake Ry., 226 N. Y. 347, 123 N. E. 736 (1919). But suppose the gift is upon a certain event as well as to a designated person, e.g., " to A 25 years after my death." Analytically this also is bad; but such a result is incongruous, since a gift " to X for 25 years, remainder to A " would be vested and valid. The authority is slight. Mann v. Registrar, [1918] 1 Ch. 202; GRAY, PERPETUITIES (4th ed. 1942) §§ 114, 317.

[27] Leake v. Robinson, 2 Mer. 363 (Ch. 1817). See 2 SIMES, FUTURE INTERESTS (1936) §§ 526-28.

[28] Leake v. Robinson, 2 Mer. 363 (Ch. 1817), *supra*. The same result would follow even though all four of the living children had already reached 25 at T's death ! See Case 18, *supra*.

[29] See GRAY, PERPETUITIES § 374; 2 SIMES, FUTURE INTERESTS (1936) § 528. The jurisdictions in which this issue has arisen are, however, relatively few. There is no reason why a court before which the problem arises *de novo* should

Two important limitations on the class-gift rule must be mentioned.

First is the rule that where there is a gift of a specific sum to each person described by a class designation (as distinguished from a gift of a fund or piece of land to be divided between the class) some members may take their gifts though the gifts to others are void. Thus,

> 25. T bequeaths $100 to each child of A who reaches the age of of 25. Four children of A are living at the death of T. Each of these children is entitled to receive $100 if he reaches 25, although the gifts of $100 each to children of A born after the death of T are too remote.[30]

Second is the rule that where there is a gift to a class of sub-classes the gift to a particular sub-class can be valid even though the gift to another sub-class is too remote. Thus,

> 26. T bequeaths a fund in trust to pay the income to A for life, then to pay the income to the children of A for their lives, and upon the death of any child of A to pay the principal upon which such child was receiving the income to the children of such child. A has two children: C1, who was born before the death of T, and C2, who was born after the death of T. Plainly the life estates to both C1 and C2 are valid. Equally plainly the remainder to the

---

not reach an opposite conclusion. Properly the problem is one of separability, not of perpetuities; a question of construction, not of application of a rule of law. Where there is a gift to the children of A who reach 25 and one reaches 25, such child has a vested interest subject to partial divestment in favor of other children who later attain the prescribed age. If the other children are unborn it is the divesting contingency which is remote, not the gift to the child who was living at T's death and has reached 25. As in other cases of partial invalidity the valid portion should be allowed to stand unless T's dispositive intent will be better carried out by declaring the whole gift bad. See heading VII, *infra*.

These ideas are elaborated in Leach, *The Rule against Perpetuities and Gifts to Classes*, 51 Harv. L. Rev. 1329 (1938). Two courts have cited the article courteously, and declined to follow it. Beverlin v. First National Bank, 151 Kan. 307, 98 P. (2d) 200 (1940); *In re* Koellhoffer, 20 N. J. Misc. 139 (1942). It gives me some negative pleasure to note that an equally bright, earnest idea of my colleague Professor Casner also got the judicial bird at about the same time. *In re* Battell's Will, 173 Misc. 273, 17 N. Y. S. (2d) 447, 450 (1940).

A result probably opposed to the English rule was reached in Story v. First Nat. Bank & Trust Co., 115 Fla. 436, 156 So. 101 (1934), but upon grounds which leave it an open question whether the cure is not worse than the disease.

A free-swinging decision from the pen of Chief Justice Doe reduced to 21 void age contingencies in excess of 21. Edgerly v. Barker, 66 N. H. 434 (1891). See Gray, Perpetuities §§ 857–893. This case, if followed widely, would have revolutionized the law of perpetuities; but the promise (or threat) has not been fulfilled. England reached this result by legislation 35 years later. Law of Property Act, 1925, 15 Geo. V, c. 20, § 163.

[30] Storrs v. Benbow, 3 De G. M. & G. 390 (Ch. App. 1853); *In re* Helme, 95 N. J. Eq. 197, 123 Atl. 43 (1923).

children of C2 is invalid. The question concerns the remainder to the children of C1. The share which is to be divided between them will be known at the death of A, since thereafter no children of A can be born; the fraction which each of the children of C1 is to take in the share will be known at the death of C1; therefore all interests will vest within the life of the survivor of A and C1, both of whom were in being at T's death, and the gift is, of itself, valid. The fact that the contemporaneous gift to the children of C2 fails is immaterial.[31]
However, this limitation applies only if the testator separates the ultimate remainder into sub-classes.

27. T bequeaths a fund in trust to pay the income to A for life, then to pay the income to the children of A for their lives and then to pay the principal to the grandchildren of A. The remainder to grandchildren is void.[32]

V. Powers of Appointment

In any discussion of powers of appointment the distinction between general and special powers is so vital that it is well to define the terms at the outset. A *general* power is one which permits appointment to anyone including the donee of the power or his estate — e.g., a devise " to A for life and then to such person or persons as A shall appoint." [33] A *special* (sometimes called limited) power is one which permits appointment only to a designated class — e.g., a devise " to A for life, and then to such of A's children as A shall appoint." The donor of any power, general or special, can provide that it shall be exercised by will only, in which case it is called a *testamentary* power.

[31] Smith's Estate v. Commissioner, 140 F. (2d) 759 (3d CCA, 1943); Cattlin v. Brown, 11 Hare 372 (Ch. 1853); Shepard v. Union & New Haven Trust Co., 106 Conn. 627, 138 Atl. 809 (1927); Dorr v. Lovering, 147 Mass. 530, 18 N. E. 412 (1888).

The last of these cases is exceedingly interesting as an example of the fruits of competent advocacy. The situation was precisely similar to that of Cattlin v. Brown, *supra*. In Lovering v. Lovering, 129 Mass. 97 (1880), one group of grandchildren whose parent was living at the testator's death sought to have the validity of their shares established. Counsel conceded that if the class of children included those born after the testator's death, all gifts to grandchildren were bad !!! Cattlin v. Brown had been decided seventeen years earlier but was not noticed either by counsel or by the court. It was perfectly clear that after-born children were included in the class; and the court therefore held the gift to the petitioning grandchildren void. In Dorr v. Lovering, eight years later, the same court reached precisely the opposite result upon the same will with reference to another group of grandchildren identically situated. In the latter case counsel cited, and the court followed, Cattlin v. Brown.

[32] Pearks v. Moseley, 5 App. Cas. 714 (1880).

[33] In Maryland a power couched in general terms, as in the text, is construed not to permit appointment to the donee or his estate or his creditors. See Balls v. Dampman, 69 Md. 390, 16 Atl. 16 (1888).

As a practical matter, in the creation of powers testators have habitually made them testamentary — that is, exercisable by will only. Following the Revenue Act of 1942 most powers were made special, either in original creation or by partial release; but the Act of 1948 made general powers usually desirable when given to the spouse of the donor. (See Appendix II B.)

With reference to the Rule against Perpetuities two problems arise: (1) Is the power valid? (2) Assuming the power to be valid, is the interest which has been appointed in the exercise of the power valid? The first of these problems is fairly simple, the latter quite complex.

A. *The Validity of the Power*

A special power is void if it is capable of being exercised beyond the period of perpetuities. Thus any special power given to an unborn person is invalid unless the time of exercise is specially restricted.

> 28. T bequeaths a fund in trust to pay the income to A for life, then to pay the income to A's children for their lives and then to pay the principal to such of A's grandchildren as the oldest child of A shall appoint. A's oldest child, born after T's death, makes an appointment in A's lifetime to grandchildren of A then living. The appointment has no effect because the power is void *ab initio*.[34]

This type of case is rather fantastic; but there are two types which involve the same principle and which are at once much more likely to occur and much more deceptive. The first type consists of cases in which a power is created in the exercise of a special power or a general testamentary power.

> 29. T bequeaths a fund in trust for A for life and then in trust for A's issue as A shall appoint, with power to create new powers. A by will appoints to his son, B, for life, remainder to such of B's children as B shall appoint. B was born after T's death. As will later appear, A's appointment has to be "read back" into T's will; and, thus read back, it gives a special power to B, a person unborn at T's death. This power is void.

The second type consists of cases in which a "discretionary trust" is created to last during unborn lives. Such a trust is in essence a power of appointment and the discretionary power is void if it can be exercised too remotely.

> 30. T bequeaths a fund in trust for A for life and then for the children of A for their lives, with power in the trustees to determine how much of the income shall be applied to each of the children of A. This power is void.[35]

---

[34] GRAY, PERPETUITIES § 477.
[35] Bundy v. United States Trust Co., 257 Mass. 72, 153 N. E. 337 (1926).

CHAP. X.]   PERPETUITIES IN A NUTSHELL   217

A general testamentary power stands on the same footing as a special power. It is void if it is given to a person unborn at the creation of the power.

A general power exercisable by deed or will, however, is different. It is the equivalent of ownership since it enables the donee of the power to become the owner at any time by appointing to himself. Therefore a general power exercisable by deed or will is valid if the donee must *acquire* the power within the period of perpetuities.

31. T bequeaths a fund in trust to pay the income to A for life, then to pay the income to the children of A for their lives, then to pay the principal to such person or persons as the eldest child of A (unborn at T's death) shall appoint. The power is valid.[36]

B. *The Validity of Appointed Interests*

Where an appointment is made under a special power, the appointment is read back into the instrument creating the power (as if the donee were filling in blanks in the donor's instrument) and the period of perpetuities is computed from the date the power was created.[37] Thus,

32. T (the donor) bequeaths a fund in trust for A for life and then in trust for such issue of A as A shall appoint. A appoints to his child, B (unborn at T's death), for life, remainder to B's children. The gift to B's children, when read back into T's will, is a gift to the children of an unborn person and hence too remote.[38]

However, facts and circumstances existing at the date the appointment is made must be considered in determining the validity of the appointment. Thus if, in Case 32, B is in fact a child of A who was

[36] And, as later appears, the period of perpetuities with reference to the appointment is computed from the time the power is exercised, not from the time it is created.

[37] Except in Delaware. Del. Laws 1933, c. 198. This statute, computing the period of perpetuities from the exercise of special powers rather than from their creation, has amazing possibilities. Suppose that A, an economic royalist (and there are such in Delaware), leaves his estate to his son, B, for life, remainder to such of B's issue as B shall by will appoint, with full power of delegation; then B exercises the power by giving a life estate to his son, C, for life, remainder to such of C's issue as C shall by will appoint with full power of delegation; then C exercises the power in the same way and so on ad infinitum. Property can thus be tied up in a family *forever* — a result which has not been possible in Anglo-American law since Taltarum's Case, Y. B. 12 Edw. IV, pl. 25 (1472), emasculated the Statute De Donis. Creditors could never reach such property. Moreover, under the pre-1942 version of I. R. C. § 811 (f) the property would escape all federal estate taxation subsequent to the tax imposed on the estate of A. See Leach, *Powers of Appointment,* 24 A. B. A. J. 807 (1938). In the Revenue Act of 1942, § 811 (f) was appropriately amended to eliminate this potential abuse.

[38] Boyd's Estate, 199 Pa. 487, 49 Atl. 297 (1901). See 2 SIMES, FUTURE INTERESTS (1936) § 537.

born within the life of T, then the appointment to his children is valid.[39]

Where an appointment is made under a general testamentary power the same rules apply: the validity of the appointment is determined by reckoning the period of perpetuities from the date of creation of the power.[40]

Where an appointment is made under a general power exercisable by deed or will the validity of the appointment is determined by reckoning the period of perpetuities from the date of the appointment. The fact that the donee of the power can appoint to himself makes him in substance the owner and makes it reasonable to treat his appointments as dispositions of owned property.[41]

VI. Severability of Invalid Conditions and Modifying Clauses

Where a testator makes a gift to A upon either of two expressed contingencies, one being remote and one not, the gift takes effect if the valid contingency occurs. Thus,

> 33. T bequeaths a fund in trust to pay the income to A for life, then to pay the income to any surviving wife of A for life; then, upon the death of A, or upon the death of A's wife if he leaves one surviving, to pay the principal to A's children then living. At A's death no wife survives. Although the gift to the children would have been too remote if A had left a surviving wife,[42] it was not too remote if he left none. Therefore the children take.[43]

However, if the testator has *expressed* only one contingency and this may occur too remotely, the gift is invalid, even though two or more contingencies are implicit in the expressed contingency and the one of them that occurs is not too remote. Thus,

> 34. T bequeaths $1000 to the first son of A who shall become a clergyman; but if no son of A becomes a clergyman, then to B. [The gift over to B " if no son of A becomes a clergyman " plainly

---

[39] Wilkinson v. Duncan, 30 Beav. 111 (Rolls Ct. 1861); Warren's Estate, 320 Pa. 112, 182 Atl. 396 (1936), overruling Smith's Appeal, 88 Pa. 492 (1879). Contra: Brown v. Columbia Finance & Trust Co., 123 Ky. 775, 97 S. W. 421 (1906). See (1936) 49 Harv. L. Rev. 1011.

[40] Minot v. Paine, 230 Mass. 514, 120 N. E. 167 (1918). This was formerly a much mooted question. See Gray, Perpetuities § 948; Kales, *General Powers and the Rule against Perpetuities* (1912) 26 Harv. L. Rev. 64.

[41] Mifflin's Appeal, 121 Pa. 205, 15 Atl. 525 (1888).

[42] The wife might be a person unborn at T's death. See Case 12, *supra*.

[43] In re Curryer's Will Trusts, [1938] Ch. 952; Gray v. Whittemore, 192 Mass. 367, 78 N. E. 422 (1906). The fountain-head of authority on this point is Longhead v. Phelps, 2 W. Bl. 704 (K. B. 1771). The gift of principal in Case 33 would have been bad if T had said, " then upon the death of the survivor of A and his wife, to the children of A then living." See next case.

includes at least two contingencies: (a) A having no son — which must occur, if at all, at A's death; (b) A having one or more sons, none of whom becomes a clergyman — which cannot be known until the death of A's sons, a time well beyond the period of perpetuities.] A dies without ever having had a son. Nevertheless the gift to B fails.[44]

This distinction is all a matter of the form of words and of chance expressions used by the testator. It has been widely criticized but almost invariably followed.[45]

Another matter of form is the doctrine of "modifying clauses." This permits a gift to be valid in spite of the imposition of an invalid qualification thereon, if the gift and qualification are verbally separable. The fact that such separation rarely occurs does not diminish the usefulness of this doctrine in those few cases to which it can apply. Thus,

35. T bequeaths a fund in trust to pay the income to A for life " and upon the death of A to pay the principal to A's children. As to the share thus given to any daughter I direct that it shall be held in trust for her until her age of 25 and then paid to her if and when she reaches that age; but if she dies under that age, then to A's other children then surviving." Upon the death of A the principal is paid outright to all children including daughters. The modifying clause which imposes the invalid condition is ignored.[46]

VII. Effect of Invalidity of an Interest Under the Rule

Where an interest is void under the Rule against Perpetuities, it is stricken out; and (apart from the principles of infectious invalidity, considered in the four succeeding paragraphs) the other interests created in the will or trust instrument take effect as if the void interest had never been written. Thus,

36. T bequeaths the residue of his estate in trust to pay the income to A for life *and then to pay the principal to such children of A as shall reach the age of 25.* The remainder is void. Thus the italicized words are ignored; the trustee pays the income to A for life and then holds the principal upon a resulting trust for the next-of-kin of T.[47]

[44] Proctor *v.* Bishop of Bath, 2 H. Bl. 358 (C. P. 1794). The gift would have been good if T had said " but if A have no son, or none of the sons born to A becomes a clergyman, then to B." See previous case.

[45] See 2 SIMES, FUTURE INTERESTS (1936) §§ 521–24.

[46] Ring *v.* Hardwick, 2 Beav. 352 (Rolls Ct. 1840). See GRAY, PERPETUITIES §§ 423, 427, 431.

[47] Lovering *v.* Worthington, 106 Mass. 86 (1870); GRAY, PERPETUITIES §§ 248, 249a.

37. T devises land to A and his heirs, *but if the premises shall be used for the sale of liquors, then to B and his heirs.* The executory devise is void. Thus the italicized words are ignored; A has a fee simple absolute.[48]

38. T devises land to A and his heirs so long as no liquor is sold on the premises, *but if liquor shall be sold on the premises then to B and his heirs.* The executory devise is void. Thus the italicized words are ignored; A has a fee simple determinable and the heirs of T have a possibility of reverter.[49]

If an ultimate interest is void under the Rule against Perpetuities, does this cause the failure of prior interests which, standing alone, are not too remote? This is properly a problem of severability whose solution depends upon the answer to the question: Will the general dispositive ideas of the testator or settlor be better carried out by holding the prior limitations valid or by striking them down? Or, to put the question in another way: Is the invalid limitation so essential to the dispositive scheme of the testator or settlor that it can be inferred that he would not wish the prior limitations to stand alone?[50] Generally, courts are very reluctant to strike down a portion of the disposition which is, of itself, valid;[51] but in Illinois and (at least formerly) in Pennsylvania the decisions have given evidence of a punitive spirit which invalidates many entire wills and trusts which would be given partial effect in other states.[52]

If one of two alternative interests is too remote, does that necessarily cause the other alternative interest to be void? The answer is No. If the contingency occurs upon which the second limitation is to take effect, and if the second limitation is of itself valid, it will be given effect.

39. T bequeaths a fund in trust for A for life and then, if children of A survive him, to such of the children as reach the age of 25, but if no children of A survive him, then to B. If, but only if, A dies without surviving children, B takes.[53]

If a limitation is too remote, do subsequent limitations necessarily fail? This question has not arisen in the United States and the cus-

---

[48] Brattle Square Church v. Grant, 3 Gray 142 (Mass. 1854).

[49] First Universalist Society v. Boland, 155 Mass. 171, 29 N. E. 524 (1892).

[50] The principle is well stated in Estate of Whitney, 176 Cal. 12, 19, 167 Pac. 399, 402 (1917).

[51] See 2 SIMES, FUTURE INTERESTS (1936) § 529.

[52] See, for example, Barrett v. Barrett, 255 Ill. 332, 99 N. E. 625 (1912); Kountz's Estate, 213 Pa. 390, 62 Atl. 1103 (1906). The situation has certainly improved in Pennsylvania. See the superb opinion of Goodrich, C. J. in Smith's Estate v. Commissioner, 140 F. (2d) 759 (3d C. C. A. 1943). Judge Goodrich denies that the imputation of a "punitive spirit" in the text was ever justified.

[53] Quinlan v. Wickman, 233 Ill. 39, 84 N. E. 38 (1908). See 2 SIMES, FUTURE INTERESTS (1936) § 531.

tomary American types of dispositions are unlikely to raise it. The English law seems to be that all limitations subsequent to a void limitation are necessarily void; but this result has been severely criticized.[54]

In states which apply the common-law period of perpetuities to personalty and a statutory period to realty another problem arises. Suppose a residue of realty and personalty is left upon trusts which comply with the common-law requirement but violate the statute. The gift is void as to the real estate; but it should be valid as to the personalty unless, as will rarely be the case, the testator's general scheme of disposition would be more nearly effectuated by invalidating the whole trust. Michigan cases on the point, however, strike down the whole trust even though the amount of real estate is trifling.[54a]

VIII. CONSTRUCTION AND PERPETUITIES

The question is: As between two possible constructions of a gift, how far is it proper to select one of the constructions on the ground that it is valid under the Rule against Perpetuities while the other is invalid?

Gray said, " Every provision in a will or settlement is to be construed as if the Rule did not exist, and then to the provision so construed the Rule is to be remorselessly applied."[55] But he added, " When the expression which a testator uses is really ambiguous, and is fairly capable of two constructions, one of which would produce a legal result, and the other a result that would be bad for remoteness, it is a fair presumption that the testator meant to create a legal rather than an illegal interest."[56] This distinction is rather

---

[54] GRAY, PERPETUITIES §§ 251-58; 2 SIMES, FUTURE INTERESTS (1936) § 532. The problem usually arises with reference to a life estate to a living person which is subsequent to a void limitation. Such life estate must vest, if at all, within the life of the taker. For example: A portrait to A for life, then to A's first born son for his life, then to the first born son of such first born son for his life, then to B for life, etc. The gift to A's grandson is too remote; but the gift to B is, of itself, valid.

[54a] Gardner v. City National Bank, 267 Mich. 270, 255 N. W. 587 (1934); In re Richards' Estate, 283 Mich. 485, 278 N. W. 657 (1938). In the latter case a bad gift of realty worth $800 knocked out an otherwise valid trust of $56,045 of personalty. Some repentance of this extraordinary doctrine is suggested in Dodge v. Detroit Trust Co., 300 Mich. 575, 598, 2 N. W. (2d) 509, 518 (1942), where trusts of $37,000,000 were threatened by the inclusion of $40,000 of real estate. The Law Reviews have fallen down badly on this matter; no word of criticism or even comment appears. Gray (4th ed. 1942) does not even refer to the problem. Simes (vol. 2, § 576) states the rule without comment; but when he wrote in 1936 there was no reason to believe that the rule would be extended to situations like the Richards Case. The Restatement (vol. 4, p. 2774) slightly lifts one eyebrow.

[55] GRAY, PERPETUITIES § 629.

[56] Id. § 633.

nebulous but it plainly leans in the direction of severity. It is the accepted formula in England, violated at convenience.[57]

But in the United States we have a precedent which is lacking in England. It has become well settled that, in the construction of a statute, that interpretation will be selected which renders the statute constitutional rather than unconstitutional, even to the extent of a warping of words which cannot be described otherwise than as violent.[58] The rationale of this rule is directly applicable to the construction of wills and trusts under the Rule against Perpetuities. One starts with the inference that the testator (like Congress) intended to do a legal act rather than an illegal one, and one permits this basic intention to overcome inferences as to minor intentions, which would ordinarily be drawn from particular words, unless those words are clear. Such an attitude seems increasingly to represent the trend of American authority.[59]

Almost invariably problems of construction in which the Rule against Perpetuities can play a part involve the question whether references to *children* or *grandchildren* in a will include persons who are born after the testator's death. The ordinary rule of construction is that class designations such as *children* or *grandchildren* include all who are born prior to the period of first principal distribution.[60] But this ordinary meaning (itself a product of a "rule of

[57] For the formula, Pearks v. Moseley, 5 App. Cas. 714, 719 (1880). For the violations, Kevern v. Williams, 5 Sim. 171 (Ch. 1832); In re Powell, [1898] 1 Ch. 227. See In re Carter, 30 N. Z. L. R. 707 (1911).

[58] United States v. Delaware & Hudson Co., 213 U. S. 366, 407 (1909). For a striking example, see the concurring opinion of White, C. J., in the Pipe Line Cases, 234 U. S. 548, 562 (1914).

[59] See, for example, Wheeler, C. J., in Shepard v. Union & New Haven Trust Co., 106 Conn. 627, 635, 138 Atl. 809 (1927); Trautz v. Lemp, 329 Mo. 580, 46 S. W. (2d) 135 (1932); 3 PROPERTY RESTATEMENT § 243, comment n; 4 PROPERTY RESTATEMENT § 375. One can adopt this view without accepting the particularized inferences of two noteworthy cases. In Forman v. Troup, 30 Ga. 496, 499 (1860), the will of Governor George M. Troup was held valid largely on the ground, stated by Lumpkin, J., that "never would I impute such an intention to violate the laws of his State to a man who loved her, and every letter of her laws and every inch of her soil with an energy and devotion that no soul could inspire but that of George M. Troup." In Colt v. Industrial Trust Co., 50 R. I. 242, 246–47, 146 Atl. 628, 630 (1929), the court considered it relevant to the question whether the word "grandchildren" in the will of Colonel Samuel Pomeroy Colt included those after-born (in which case it would have violated the Rule against Perpetuities) to remark that Colonel Colt was "a man of vision, big deeds and generous impulses. . . . was devoted to his family. . . . lived in the homestead where his mother was born. . . . in memory of his mother he erected The Colt Memorial High School. . . . extended and developed the Colt Farm on the shores of Narragansett Bay and as a part of the development constructed a beautiful motor drive through the Farm and along the shore of the Bay and at the entrance to the drive erected a sign ' Colt Farm, Private Property. Public Welcome.'"

[60] See Casner, *Class Gifts to Others than "Heirs" or "Next of Kin"— Increase in the Class Membership* (1937) 51 HARV. L. REV. 254.

construction " of the courts) should yield to a more restricted meaning where there is nothing in the words used by the testator or in the circumstances of the execution of his will which would indicate that the restricted meaning was not intended. Thus,

40. T devised his homestead to trustees to allow his " children and grandchildren " to live in the house until there was only one survivor, and then to convey the house to such survivor. At his death T had two sons and four grandchildren. It was held that " grandchildren " meant grandchildren living at T's death. Thus construed, the devise was valid.[61]

41. T bequeathed the residue of his estate " to the grandchildren of my brother Charles, to be by them received when they and each of them shall attain the age of 25." At T's death 7 grandchildren were living. It was held that the gift included only these 7 grandchildren. Thus construed, the bequest was valid.[62]

IX. Application of the Rule to Various Types of Interests

Thus far we have been considering the application of the Rule against Perpetuities to remainders and executory interests created in the course of gift transactions, with or without the use of powers of appointment. This was the field in which the Rule grew up and in which it has its usual application. We now turn to a consideration of the Rule with reference to types of interests which are more or less off this beaten track.

A. Contracts, Particularly Options

The Rule against Perpetuities is a rule of property law, not a rule of the law of contracts. It is no objection to the enforceability of a contract that the liability thereunder does not accrue until a time beyond the period of perpetuities. Thus insurance and suretyship contracts (both contingent obligations) are valid without reference to the time when the contingency may occur or payment may be required.[62a]

---

[61] Colt v. Industrial Trust Co., 50 R. I. 242, 146 Atl. 628 (1929).

[62] Kevern v. Williams, 5 Sim. 171 (Ch. 1832). Though the court did not seem to observe it, the gift was valid upon any construction, due to the fact that one grandchild was over four years old at T's death. See Gray, Perpetuities, § 638.

[62a] But some contracts for the benefit of third persons partake of many practical characteristics of a trust. Suppose A takes out a policy with the B Life Insurance Company and makes the policy payable as follows: interest on the principal sum to C for life, then to D and E for their joint lives and the life of the survivor until both D and E have attained 35, then the principal to be paid to D and E or the survivor, or if neither D nor E reaches 35 to pay the

However, if a contract for the transfer of property is specifically enforceable, there is created in the promisee an equitable interest in the property; and the question arises whether this equitable interest, based upon the specific enforceability of a contract, is subject to the Rule against Perpetuities. At the outset it should be stated that this question *ought* to be answered in the negative. Assuming that it is desirable to have some restriction upon the equitable interests created by specifically enforceable contracts, the Rule against Perpetuities does not offer an appropriate limitation. The period of lives in being and 21 years, which works admirably with regard to gift transactions for family purposes, has no significance in the world of commercial affairs.

Options to purchase in gross. It has been held both in England and the United States that an option in gross [63] to purchase land is void if it can be exercised beyond the period of perpetuities.[64] The objection to this rule is not in the options that it strikes down but in those that it permits. An option in gross is an effective preventative of the improvement of the land over which it exists, unless (as is rarely, if ever, the case) the purchase price under the option fluctuates in accordance with the improved value of the land. As long as the option lasts the owner in possession cannot afford to make improvements which can be snatched away from him without compensation by the exercise of the option. To allow such a restraint to last for the period of perpetuities is monstrous. However, the common sense of land owners suffices to prevent this problem from being particularly important.

Options to purchase in leases. In England it was held that an option to purchase by a lessee stood on the same footing as an option to purchase in gross: it was void if it could be exercised beyond the period of perpetuities. Thus an option to purchase at any time during a lease for 30 years failed.[65] It was not observed that the situation was the exact opposite of that which exists where there is an option in gross. The improvement of the land is stimulated, not retarded, by the existence of an option in the lessee. If the lessee has an option to purchase he can safely improve; for, by the exercise of the option, he can preserve to himself the benefit of the improve-

---

principal to the estate of the survivor of A, C, D and E. In New York, under the rule limiting trusts to two lives in being, a trust of this duration would be void. Yet such a contract was held valid in Holmes *v.* John Hancock Mutual Life Ins. Co., 288 N. Y. 106, 41 N. E. (2d) 909 (1942). Does this mean that a contract with a trust company, in consideration of payment of $100,000, to pay $2,500 annually forever to my oldest living descendant for the time being, would be valid?

[63] *I.e.*, an option not appurtenant to a leasehold or other interest.

[64] London & Southwestern Ry. *v.* Gomm, 20 Ch. D. 562 (1882); Barton *v.* Thaw, 246 Pa. 348, 92 Atl. 312 (1914).

[65] Worthing Corp. *v.* Heather, [1906] 2 Ch. 532.

ment. If he has no option he cannot economically make an improvement which will still have a substantial value at the termination of the lease. Thus, a rule which invalidates options in lessees for the full term of their leases defeats the policy favoring free alienation and full use of property which the Rule against Perpetuities was designed to further. Several American jurisdictions have recognized this fact and have held valid such options; but the English cases still have some following in the United States.[66] The English rule is particularly surprising in view of the fact that it is well settled that perpetual options to *renew* leases have always been held valid.[67]

Stock option warrants and conversion privileges in bonds. As contracts, options to purchase stock have nothing to do with the Rule against Perpetuities. However, if (1) such an option should refer to particular shares and (2) the stock should be so unique that specific performance of the option would ordinarily be granted, an equitable interest in the stock would arise. The Rule, as above suggested, is no fit instrument to apply to business transactions; but, if the reasoning of the real estate cases is carried to an aridly logical conclusion, options to purchase stock may be subjected to it.[68]

[66] Holding the option invalid if it exceeds the period of perpetuities, Eastman Marble Co. *v.* Vermont Marble Co., 236 Mass. 138, 128 N. E. 177 (1920). Holding the option valid regardless of the length of the lease, Hollander *v.* Central Metal & Supply Co., 109 Md. 131, 71 Atl. 442 (1908); 4 PROPERTY RESTATEMENT § 395. See Abbot, *Leases and the Rule against Perpetuities* (1918) 27 YALE L. J. 878; Langeluttig, *Options to Purchase and the Rule against Perpetuities* (1931) 17 VA. L. REV. 461.

Suppose the equitable interest created by the option is held invalid as a violation of the Rule against Perpetuities, is the holder of the option entitled to maintain an action for damages for the breach of contract? The English courts answer this question in the affirmative on the ground that, as a contract, the option is not concerned with the Rule against Perpetuities. Worthing Corporation *v.* Heather, [1906] 2 Ch. 532, *supra* note 65. The Massachusetts courts agree that the Rule against Perpetuities has no application to contracts as such; but they hold that "the tendency of mulcting one for breach of a covenant to convey land . . . has as much deterrent force and effect in arresting the free circulation of property as would the specific enforcement of such contracts" and that for that reason recovery of damages should be denied. Eastman Marble Co. *v.* Vermont Marble Co., 236 Mass. 138, 128 N. E. 177 (1919); 4 PROPERTY RESTATEMENT § 393, comment h.

[67] Bridges *v.* Hitchcock, 5 Bro. P. C. 6 (1715); London & Southwestern Ry. *v.* Gomm, 20 Ch. D. 562, 579 (1882).

[68] No case has yet held the Rule applicable to such options. One case says the Rule is inapplicable to them. Kingston *v.* Home Life Ins. Co., 11 Del. Ch. 258, 101 A. 898, aff'd in 11 Del. Ch. 428, 104 A. 25 (1918). See 2 DODD & BAKER, CAS. BUSINESS ORGANIZATIONS (1934) 496n. The position of the RESTATEMENT appears in Vol. 4, § 393, comment e and § 400. Of course, if such an option should be held subject to the Rule and thus not specifically enforceable, it would seem to follow that it could not be made the basis for an action for damages. Note 66, *supra*.

B. Revocable Trusts; Insurance Trusts

The question with regard to revocable trusts and insurance trusts is whether the period of perpetuities is computed from the creation of the trust or from the death of the settlor.

Suppose A creates a trust to pay the income to himself for life, then to pay the income to his children, then to pay the principal to his grandchildren, reserving to himself the power to revoke the trust at any time during his life. If the period of perpetuities is computed from the creation of the trust, the possibility that A will have further children causes the gift to the grandchildren to be too remote; but if the period is computed from the death of A, the impossibility of further children of A being born allows them to be taken as the lives in being and causes the gift to grandchildren to be valid.[69] The existence of the power of revocation should cause the period of perpetuities to be computed only from the expiration of the power — i.e., from the death of A — and it has been so held.[70] So long as one person has the power at any time to make himself the sole owner, there is no tying-up of the property and no violation of the policy of the Rule against Perpetuities. If the power is not exercised the future interests which could have been destroyed by the exercise of the power are in substance gifts made by the holder of the power at the time of the power's expiration, and they should be so treated under the Rule against Perpetuities. The situation is analogous to future interests after an estate tail, where the period of perpetuities is computed from the date of expiration of the estate tail; the power to disentail makes the tenant in tail the substantial owner and causes interests after the estate tail to be in substance gifts by the last tenant in tail at the time of expiration of his estate.[71] The situation is also analogous to gifts in default of the exercise of a general power by deed or will, the period of perpetuities being computed from the expiration of the power — i.e., the death of the donee.[72]

With regard to insurance trusts, the problem of deciding whether the period of perpetuities is computed from the creation of the trust or from the death of the assured-settlor is complex. There is substantially no authority. If the trust is revocable, the decision should be the same as in the case of any other revocable trust; and it has been so held.[73] But if the trust is irrevocable, variations in the terms of the policies (notably, whether they are " assigned " or " unas-

---

[69] Compare Cases 4 and 5, *supra*.

[70] Equitable Trust Co. *v.* Pratt, 117 Misc. 708, 193 N. Y. Supp. 152 (1922), aff'd, 206 App. Div. 689, 200 N. Y. Supp. 921 (1st Dept. 1923); Manufacturers Life Ins. Co. *v.* Von Hamm-Young Co., 34 Hawaii 288 (1937).

[71] GRAY, PERPETUITIES §§ 443-50.

[72] Ortman *v.* Dugan, 130 Md. 121, 100 Atl. 82 (1917).

[73] Manufacturers Life Ins. Co. *v.* Von Hamm-Young Co., 34 Hawaii 288 (1937).

signed ") and in the trust instrument (notably, whether the trust is "funded" or "unfunded") may produce one or the other result.[74] Any settlor should be advised to create a trust which is valid under a computation of the period of perpetuities from the creation of the trust.

C. Rights of Entry for Condition Broken; Possibilities of Reverter

It is the settled American law that both of these types of interests are exempt from the operation of the Rule against Perpetuities. Thus, a gift "to the A church so long as the premises are used for church purposes" creates a possibility of reverter in the grantor which will become possessory whenever the contingency occurs.[75] Similarly, a gift "to the A church in fee simple, but if the premises are ever used other than for church purposes the grantor and his heirs may re-enter and repossess the premises as of their former estate" creates a right of entry for condition broken in the grantor, and this right of entry can be exercised whenever the named contingency occurs.[76]

D. Powers of Sale in Trustees and Mortgagees

We have seen that a power of appointment (unless it is a general power exercisable by deed or will) is void if it can be exercised beyond the period of perpetuities.[77] There is no such restriction upon powers of sale in trustees during the continuance of a trust. Such powers facilitate rather than hinder the free circulation of property, and to strike them down frustrates the policy of the Rule against Perpetuities.[78] Likewise, there is no such restriction upon powers of sale in mortgagees. Such powers are ancillary to the security title of the mortgagee, are administrative rather than dispositive in character, and do not give rise to the abuses which the Rule against Perpetuities was designed to remedy.[79]

---

[74] These matters are discussed in Note, *The Rule against Perpetuities and Insurance Trusts* (1932) 45 HARV. L. REV. 896; Morris, *The Rule against Perpetuities as Applied to Living Trusts and Living Life Insurance Trusts* (1937) 11 CIN. L. REV. 327.

[75] See Case 20, *supra*, and authorities cited.

[76] Strong *v.* Shatto, 45 Cal. App. 29, 187 Pac. 159 (1919). The rule is otherwise in England. *In re* Trustees of Hollis' Hospital, [1899] 2 Ch. 540.

[77] Cases 28–30, *supra*.

[78] Melvin *v.* Hoffman, 290 Mo. 464, 235 S. W. 107 (1921); Leach, *Powers of Sale in Trustees and the Rule against Perpetuities* (1934) 47 HARV. L. REV. 948. The rule is otherwise in England. *In re* Allott, [1924] 2 Ch. 498.

[79] GRAY, PERPETUITIES §§ 565–71; Leach, *supra* note 78, at 949.

X. Associated Rules

In addition to the Rule against Perpetuities (*i.e.*, the rule invalidating interests which vest too remotely) there are a few other bodies of legal doctrine relating to the imposition of time limitations for the purpose of preventing property from being tied up. The rules forbidding restraints on alienation might be considered as "associated rules," since they, like the Rule against Perpetuities, are designed to foster the free circulation of property; but they are not here treated, because most of such rules invalidate a restraint *in toto* without reference to the time during which it is imposed. So far as the validity of a restraint is dependent upon a time duration analogous to the period of perpetuities, it is hereinafter treated.

A. *Restrictions on Accumulations*

In the famous case of *Thellusson v. Woodford*,[80] it was held that a trust to accumulate the income of property for the period of perpetuities is valid. Despite some understandable grumbling about excessive use of the dead hand, this is also the American rule.[81]

Statutes commonly prescribe more stringent limits for periods of accumulation — the commonest provision being that the accumulation "must be made for the benefit of one or more minors" and must terminate before their majority.[82] This is not the place for an extended discussion of these statutes; but it is desirable that two warnings should be given. (1) The requirement that the accumulation be "for the benefit" of the minor and terminate at majority means that when the minor reaches 21 the accumulations must be paid over to him outright; and if the instrument does not so provide, the accumulation provision is void. Thus,

[80] 11 Ves. Jr. 112 (Ch. 1805).

[81] Gertman *v.* Burdick, 123 F. (2d) 924 (C. A. D. C. 1941); cert. denied, 315 U. S. 824 (1942). If there ever was a case for the overthrow of Thellusson *v.* Woodford, this was it. There was a $1,600,000 estate of which the income, apart from small annuities, was to be accumulated for two named lives and 21 years thereafter. The accumulation provision seems to have been sheer vanity. A trust lasting 55 years was foreseeable with an ultimate value of about $10,800,000. Pine, J., newly appointed to the District Court, held the accumulation bad, giving such clauses the idealogical works: "concomitants of aristocracy . . . inconsistent with the principles of democracy . . . relics of a feudal society, obsolete and repugnant to our institutions and conditions." 33 F. Supp. 921, 928 (1940). But in the Court of Appeals, the present Chief Justice of the United States ruled that the Thellusson Case stated the common law and that, if accumulations were to be restricted to less than the period of perpetuities, the legislature would have to do it. Even with Pine, J.'s clarion call in the record, the Roosevelt Court denied certiorari. The legislatures surely ought to go to work; from any conceivable point of view such provisions are outrageous.

For further grumbling, see Moeller *v.* Kautz, 112 Conn. 481, 152 A. 886 (1931).

[82] E.g., N. Y. Real Prop. Law § 61.

42. Under such a statute T bequeaths his estate in trust to pay to his minor child, A, so much of the income as should be needed for his support and education during minority; to accumulate the balance of the income during A's minority and add the same to principal; upon A's majority to pay to him the whole income of the combined fund of principal and accumulations during his life; and upon A's death to pay the combined fund of principal and accumulations to A's children. The provision for accumulation is void, and A is entitled to the full income of the fund during his minority.[83]

(2) Many usual and harmless provisions in wills and trusts create "accumulations" without superficially appearing to do so. For example, a provision that trustees shall use income to discharge a mortgage on real estate in the trust,[84] a provision that, if the market value of the principal of the trust falls below its market value as of the date of creation, income shall be used to make up the deficiency,[85] a provision that stock dividends shall all be treated as principal in a jurisdiction where some of them would otherwise be treated as income,[86] have all been held to create invalid accumulations.

B. *Time Restrictions upon Restraints Otherwise Valid*

The rules as to restraints upon alienation strike down certain attempts to prevent the free circulation of property, regardless of the time element. Thus a provision in a conveyance in fee simple from A to B declaring that the property shall not be conveyed by B is wholly ineffective, and it generally makes no diffeernce that the restraint is limited in time — say, to ten years.[87] But some important types of restraints do not fall within the general prohibitions of these rules. For example:

a. Restraints upon alienation of equitable life interests in trusts — the familiar "spendthrift trusts" — are held valid almost everywhere.[88]

---

[83] Pray v. Hegeman, 92 N. Y. 508 (1883). When income is undisposed of and no valid direction for accumulation is given, the income passes to the "persons presumptively entitled to the next eventual estate." N. Y. REAL PROP. LAW § 63. This is the usual statutory provision.

[84] Hascall v. King, 162 N. Y. 134, 56 N. E. 515 (1900).

[85] Bankers' Trust Co. v. Moy, 148 Misc. 38, 265 N. Y. Supp. 77 (Sup. Ct. 1933).

[86] Maris's Estate, 301 Pa. 20, 151 Atl. 577 (1930). But see N. Y. PERS. PROP. LAW § 17a.

[87] See Manning, *The Development of Restraints on Alienation Since Gray* (1935) 48 HARV. L. REV. 373; Schnebly, *Restraints on Alienation of Legal Interests* (1935) 44 YALE L. J. 961, 1186, 1380. For a short summary, see GRAY, RESTRAINTS (2d ed. 1895) 278.

[88] See GRISWOLD, SPENDTHRIFT TRUSTS (2d ed. 1947) §§ 150–235.

b. Restraints upon anticipation of equitable fee interests in trusts — *e.g.,* " To A trustee in trust to pay the income to B until he reaches the age of 40 and then to pay the principal to him " — are recognized in most states.[89]

c. Restraints upon alienation of legal life estates seem to be finding greater favor in the courts.[90]

It is probable, though there is no clear American authority on the point, that any one of these restraints which escapes the general rules as to restraints upon alienation is nevertheless invalid if it may last longer than the period of perpetuities.[91] Thus,

43. T bequeaths the residue of his estate in trust for A for life, remainder for such issue of A and in such manner and for such estates as A shall by will appoint. A by will appoints one-half of the fund to his son B (living at T's death) for life and one-half of the fund to his son C (unborn at T's death) for life, with survivorship between the sons for life, remainder to such of B's and C's children as shall be born within 21 years after the death of all descendants of T who were living at T's death. A's will contains a clause as follows: " No interest of any beneficiary of this trust, whether in principal or in income, shall be assignable or subject to the claims of creditors of such beneficiary." All interests created by the trust are valid: the interests of B and C vest at the death of A, who was a life in being at T's death; the interests of the remaindermen vest within 21 years after the termination of a reasonable number of lives in being at T's death. The restraint on alienation of B's interest is valid because he was in being at T's death. But it is *probable* that the restraints on C's life estate and upon the remainders is invalid, since they may last longer than the period of perpetuities.[92]

C. *Time Limitations on the Duration of Trusts*

There is no objection, upon principle or by the great weight of authority, to a trust which lasts longer than the period of perpetuities. Thus a trust for A for life, and then for A's children for their lives and then for Harvard College is perfectly good.[93] However,

[89] See Griswold, Spendthrift Trusts (2d ed. 1947) § 513. Also, in a few states, restraints upon alienation of equitable interests in fee are recognized. See *id.* § 88.

[90] Hiles v. Benton, 111 Neb. 557, 196 N. W. 903 (1924).

[91] *In re* Ridley, 11 Ch. D. 645 (1879). See Colonial Trust Co. v. Brown, 105 Conn. 261, 279–80, 135 Atl. 555, 562–63 (1926); Griswold, Spendthrift Trusts (2d ed. 1947) §§ 290–96.

[92] *In re* Ridley, 11 Ch. D. 645 (1879), *as modified by* Herbert v. Webster, 15 Ch. D. 610 (1880).

[93] Seaver v. Fitzgerald, 141 Mass. 401, 6 N. E. 73 (1886). Other authorities are collected in Gray, Perpetuities § 232; Simes, Future Interests (1936) § 557. And see Case 19, *supra.*

at least one court formerly held trusts bad if they exceeded the period of perpetuities in duration; [94] and a few others have rendered decisions or uttered dicta which tend in the same direction.[95]

Assuming, however, that in the particular jurisdiction there is no objection *per se* to a trust which lasts beyond the period, there are still disadvantages to such an arrangement. If the trust instrument contains restraints on alienation (*e.g.*, spendthrift provisions), these may be invalidated by lasting too long. If the trustees are given a power to allocate income among A's children, this power is void.[95a] If the instrument contains provisions for accumulations, these also may fall with resulting litigation as to the disposition of the income thus set free. If the English cases on the application of the Rule against Perpetuities to powers of sale and lease in the trustees [96] should be followed, such powers would be invalid.

For these reasons the preferable draftsmanship practice is to limit the duration of trusts to the period of perpetuities — *i.e.*, to lives in being and 21 years from the death of the testator or creation of the trust, or, if a special power or a general testamentary power is being exercised, from the creation of the power. This is no great hardship because, as has been heretofore indicated, a little care in the selection of the lives in being will cause any trust to last approximately a century.

XI. Charities

There is some relaxation of the Rule against Perpetuities in favor of charities, but not much. Where there is a gift to the A charity, with a gift over to the B charity upon a remote contingency, the disposition is wholly valid. But if either the first or second of these gifts is to a noncharity the second gift fails. Thus,

44. T bequeaths a fund to the municipality of Reading for certain charitable purposes in that town with a direction that, if the said municipality shall for one year omit to perform the directions, the property shall pass to the municipality of London for the benefit of Christ's Hospital. The entire gift is valid.[97]

45. T devises land to the A church for use as a residence for its minister, but if the land shall ever cease to be used for such purpose, then to T's nephew, B. The executory devise to B is invalid.[98]

[94] Barnum *v.* Barnum, 26 Md. 119 (1866). The case is now overruled. Gray, Perpetuities § 245.2.
[95] The cases are cited and discussed in Gray, Perpetuities §§ 234–246.
[95a] See Case 30, *supra*.
[96] In re Allott, [1924] 2 Ch. 498.
[97] Christ's Hospital *v.* Grainger, 16 Sim. 83 (Ch. 1848). See Odell *v.* Odell, 10 Allen 1, 8, 9 (Mass. 1865).
[98] Brattle Square Church *v.* Grant, 3 Gray 142 (Mass. 1854).

46. T devises land to his nephew, A, until Gloversville shall be incorporated as a village, and then to Gloversville for the purpose of establishing a library. The gift to Gloversville is invalid.[99]

An *accumulation* for charity is not limited to the period of perpetuities; but the courts have frequently stated that they have power to strike down an accumulation for charity which exceeds the bounds of reason.[100]

XII. Some Suggestions as to Draftsmanship

Practically anything a testator is likely to want can be done within the limits of the Rule against Perpetuities. Wills fail because of inept work of lawyers, not because of excessive demands of testators. For example, suppose T wants to bequeath his property in trust for his children for life, then for his grandchildren for their lives and then for his great-grandchildren; and suppose that his children are still young enough to procreate further. The gift to great-grandchildren is void unless restricted in some way; but if it is drafted as a gift " to such of my great-grandchildren as shall be born within 21 years after the death of A, B, C, etc." (selecting a dozen or so healthy babies from families noted for longevity), the gift is good and there is small chance that any great-grandchildren will be excluded. But most testators have the good sense to want no such extended dispositions. They want to benefit those whom they know and the children of those whom they know — desires which can be satisfied by simple care of draftsmanship without resort to the artificial device suggested in the quoted limitation. In drafting instruments for such testators the following suggestions are worth noting:

1. Examine *every* will for possible violations of the Rule. The cases dealt with under heading III–B, *supra*, are sufficient proof that the most innocent limitations may fail to comply with the requirement of absolute certainty of vesting within lives and 21 years.

2. Investigate fully the question whether the will disposes of property which is subject to a power of appointment; for, as indicated under heading V–B, *supra*, the period of perpetuities is computed from the creation of the power where the power is either special or testamentary.

3. Describe beneficiaries by name rather than by a class designation wherever that is possible; for this will eliminate many of the casualties of the " fertile octogenarian " type.[101] Where T wishes to benefit an aged sister and her children and grandchildren, say " To my sister, Mary, for life, remainder to John, Henry and William,

[99] Leonard *v.* Burr, 18 N. Y. 96 (1858).
[100] Frazier *v.* Merchants' Nat. Bank, 296 Mass. 298, 5 N. E. (2d) 550 (1936).
[101] See Case 11 *et seq., supra.*

children of my said sister, for their lives; and upon the death of any one of these three the share of the property in which he had a life estate is to pass in fee simple to his children him surviving, or if no children survive him, then to such children of his two brothers as shall then be living per capita." Do not say " To my sister, Mary, for life, remainder to her children for their lives, remainder to her grandchildren in fee."

4. Regard with particular suspicion any gift which is contingent upon the taker attaining an age in excess of 21. Such gifts constitute the largest single group of invalid limitations.

5. Discourage gifts which are contingent upon the taker being living at the time when the estate is settled, or the will probated, or the debts paid.[102] Such gifts can be drafted so that they are valid; but they do little good and often run substantial risks. It is not sufficient that a gift be valid; it is necessary that it be so clearly valid that litigation cannot develop.

6. Limit the duration of trusts to the period of perpetuities. Longer trusts may be valid; but they involve substantial difficulties with certain doctrines related to the Rule against Perpetuities.[103]

The competent drafting of wills is a difficult business which offers only austere rewards. The monetary compensation in this type of practice is usually not adequate to the training and effort required. Often enough the virtues or vices of a will do not appear until the draftsman has long been under the sod. No beneficiary of a well-drawn will is likely to strew orchids upon his grave, whereas defeated claimants under ill-drawn wills are sure to heap imprecations upon his memory. But the counsellor who leaves behind him a will book which succeeds in placing property where his clients wished it without those uncertainties as to validity and ambiguities as to meaning which breed litigation, can sleep the eternal sleep in the comforting knowledge that he has upheld the finest traditions of his craft.

[102] See Cases 13–16, *supra*.
[103] See heading X-C, *supra*.

CHAPTER XI.

PLANNING AND DRAFTING A WILL.

For a Particular Middle-Aged Man With a Family and Considerable Wealth.

There is no such thing as a satisfactory " form " of will in vacuo, and the title of this Chapter is designed to emphasize this basic truth. A proper will is a highly individualized instrument, tailored to the family needs and economic realities of a particular testator's situation and adapted to the laws of the state or states in which the estate will be administered. " Forms " of wills are often useful as a check-list of ideas and a thesaurus of methods of expression; but this is the limit of their proper utility. The following precept would seem axiomatic but it is so frequently violated that it is here placed in italics: *No clause should appear in any will drawn by you unless you individually know precisely what it means, what object it is designed to accomplish, what doctrine (if any) of the law it grows out of, and how it furthers the testamentary intentions of this particular client.*[1]

We consider here the testamentary problem of J. Albert Thomas. He is one type of client whom you will meet — a successful businessman with a grown family and a substantial estate stopping short of great wealth. Other common types — for example, the promising young man, the elderly spinster with inherited property, the man with a small personal business — involve other common problems quite different from those of the Thomas family. But the study of this one hypothetical client is designed to provide basic training for all others.

Drawing wills consists of hard thinking and patient labor, with a sound understanding of the legal rules in the background. There is nothing esoteric about the process, and consequently it is not a monopoly of specialists, as patent law is a monopoly. Conversely, there are no short cuts which permit a practitioner, however experienced, to put the making of wills on a production-line basis. The process is tripartite:

(1) *Investigation.* You must learn the facts about the testator, his family and his property. Most testators will be appalled

---

[1] Most violations of this precept are tragic, but occasionally one is good for a chuckle:

In Matter of Curtis, 64 Misc. 425 (N. Y. Surr. 1909) the will made a gift to the heirs of testator's sisters " per capita as well as per stirpes, equally and in all respects, share and share alike."

at the amount of information you must have if you are to prepare a will adequate to serve as the economic basis of the family life. Yet such things as the trustworthiness of a son-in-law, the probable marriageability of a daughter, the health and wealth of a father-in-law, the exact state of testator's investments particularly with reference to liquidity, the prospects of his business when he shall have been removed from the scene by retirement or death — these and many other quite intimate details may be of the greatest importance in working out an adequate plan.

(2) *Planning.* The testator will have what he considers a plan when he comes to you, but there is no chance at all that he has really thought the matter through. It is your second job, in the light of the facts brought forth in your interviews with him, to help him develop an adequate plan. You must foresee the problems, suggest the alternative solutions, and indicate the desirable or undesirable features of each choice. You must realize that you have gone through this process many times; he, only once. In study and in practice you have seen many types of plans and devices work or fail; you must place this experience, personal and vicarious, at his service. Among other things, you must consider and discuss with him whether, to attain some of his desires, an *inter vivos* trust, an annuity, co-ownership, or insurance are not better instruments than a will. It frequently will occur that, in the planning stage, you will want to consult your client's accountant on some business matters, his insurance man, and an investment counsellor.

(3) *Drafting.* Once the plan has been fixed, yours is the job of couching it in words which (a) transmit to the minds of all who read precisely the plan which lies in your mind and the testator's, (b) provide for a workable administration of the estate, (c) avoid the pitfalls and booby traps which the law on this subject sets for the unwary — surviving antiquities of property law and the changing intricacies of the tax laws being the principal offenders. Success is achieved only if no litigation develops out of this instrument. You have failed if the instrument has to be litigated, even though the litigation sustains your plan. You have shamefully failed if litigation defeats your plan.

Any will should have two types of provisions: (a) dispositive provisions, which indicate the beneficiaries and exactly what each is entitled to receive, (b) administrative provisions, which set the rules by which the executor and trustee (if any) are to be governed in the management of the assets. In most law schools the student becomes acquainted with the law of dispositive provisions in courses on Wills and Future Interests, and with the law of administrative provisions in a course on Trusts. Hence, the drafting of a will — including the will of J. Albert Thomas, which follows — normally draws upon materials found in courses on all three of these subjects.

As you read into the Thomas Estate you will observe that, on the whole, its problems are simple. For example, there are no *inter vivos* trusts to complicate the picture, no substantial inheritances from other estates to distort the family finances on various contingencies, no individual business enterprises or partnerships to carry on or liquidate, no heavy obligations overhanging the estate, no family strife to contend with and provide against. Thomas is as nearly the commonplace testator of his class as you will find. But, despite that fact, observe the large number of highly individual provisions that have to be made for his property.

Get to know J. Albert Thomas, his family, and his problems. Live through this little segment of law practice as your novitiate.

The material to follow comprises:
  a. A summary of a series of conferences held with the client.
  b. The will drawn for the client (left-hand pages beginning with p. 248).
  c. Commentary on the will (right-hand pages beginning with p. 249).

SUMMARY OF CONFERENCES WITH CLIENT.

The following memorandum summarizes several conferences taking place between February 3 and April 15, 1947.

Joseph Albert Thomas, age 56, is the testator. He signs and is generally known as J. Albert Thomas. He now resides at 15 Elm Street, Cambridge, Massachusetts. His business address is Parsons & Eldridge, Inc., 185 Summer Street, Cambridge, Massachusetts. He is Vice President of this corporation.

Domicil.

Testator was born in Connecticut, but took a job in Boston immediately after graduating from Brown and has ever since resided in the vicinity of Boston. He owns a summer place at Alton Bay, New Hampshire, but has never been there longer than 3 months in any year. He has always paid income taxes and voted in Massachusetts and no other state. In the deeds of Massachusetts and New Hampshire real estate, in his insurance policies, and in his former will Testator is described as " of Cambridge, Massachusetts." There, therefore, seems to be no possibility that any state other than Massachusetts will claim his domicil for tax purposes.

Family.

1. Testator has a wife, Winifred Wentworth Thomas, age 52. Neither he nor she was ever married before. They have had three children, all married, as follows:

  a. Samuel Arthur Thomas, age 29. Now married to Dorothy Lawton Thomas, age 23. They have one son, Gerald, age 1. Samuel was married previously to Eva Wilson Thomas; they were divorced in Reno in 1941. Eva got the divorce, Samuel appearing by his attorney. Eva remained in Reno only the necessary 6 weeks, returned to Massachusetts, and has married again. Samuel had no children by Eva. Samuel is a metallurgist and is doing well with a company in Springfield, Massachusetts.

b. Sheldon Thomas married at the age of 23 and was killed in the war at the age of 25. His widow, now aged 24, is Della Langhorn Thomas. She lives in Boston with her infant daughter, Gertrude. She has a small income from insurance which Testator supplements by a monthly allowance of $150. She also has a part-time job. It is expected that she will remarry, although she has no immediate prospects.

c. Deborah Thomas Langenbach, age 25, is married to Spencer Langenbach and lives in Detroit. Langenbach has shown no particular aptitude for business and has no specialized training. Currently he is in a stock brokerage office and Deborah has a job as a stenographer in a lawyer's office. They have no children.

2. Testator's widowed mother is living, age 76. She resides in Hartford, Connecticut, with Testator's sister and the sister's husband. The mother is supported by an annuity taken out for her by her late husband.

3. Testator's sister is Sarah Thomas Beal, age 48. She and her husband, Belford Beal, of Hartford, are in moderate circumstances. It is possible that, if her husband should die, she would be in financial difficulty. She has two children, one working and one in college. Beal owes Testator $2,500 on a note.

Income.

Testator has a salary of $24,000 from his company, plus a bonus which has been as low as $500 in the early 1930's and as high as $20,000 in 1940.

Testator's expenditures have consistently run at a lower figure than his income, even under the present income tax rates, since his children left the home. The surplus last year was about $4,500. He is therefore in a position to make some gifts out of income, if he so desires.

Testator's Property.

1. Stocks and bonds with a current value of $420,000. This is made up as follows:

$100,000 — 800 shares of Parsons & Eldridge, valued at $125 per share. This is the company of which Testator is vice president. The shares are not quoted anywhere. They are rarely sold, being held by about 25 people in all. When sold, they are usually bought within the personnel of the company at book value, which at present is about $125 per share.

$240,000 present market value of common stocks which are either listed on exchanges or traded over the counter.

$80,000 market value of bonds (governments, municipals and industrials) listed or traded over the counter.

2. Testator's house in Cambridge is held by him and his wife as tenants by the entirety. It is subject to a mortgage of $12,000 held by Harvard Trust Co. The note is signed by him alone. Deed has been examined. At the current market the equity is worth $28,000. He built the house in 1928.

3. Furnishings of the house, including antique furniture, are worth about $18,000.

4. Buick Sedan, traded every two years.

5. Checking balance (joint account with wife) running an average of $2,500. Savings accounts (his name only) running an average of $10,000.

6. No jewelry, portraits, etc., of substantial value.

7. Real estate and furnishings of Testator's summer place, called "Baybrook" in Alton Bay, New Hampshire, are held in his name and is worth $27,000. Deed has been examined. He has no other real estate, besides the New Hampshire and Cambridge properties.

Further Details on Parsons & Eldridge, Inc.

This company has 10,000 common shares outstanding and no bonded indebtedness. Thus Testator's 800 shares represent a small minority interest. However, the corporation is closely held by the half dozen men who founded it in 1921 and their relatives. The fact that insiders have always been willing to take any amount of stock offered at book value indicates that the true value of the stock is somewhat higher. In the estate of one officer of the company who died in 1943 the Internal Revenue people claimed a valuation of $190 per share and compromised at $165. The latest sale of stock occurred about six months ago (November 1946) at $125 per share.

Testator acquired the Parsons & Eldridge stock as follows: 200 shares at $100 per share in 1921; 200 more as a 100% stock dividend in 1925; 400 more as another stock dividend in 1928. Thus the stock stands him $25 per share and any sale thereof represents an almost total capital gain.

Testator's position with the company is secure, up to his age of 70, as long as the shares continue to be held as at present. However, if outsiders should obtain control of the company (and outfits in the same line of business have indicated an interest in the company) Testator, in view of his high salary and age, might not be considered indispensable. If Testator's connection with Parsons & Eldridge should be severed he would retire from active business except for his directorships in two small banks. From this it is apparent that

Testator is not in a position where he would be justified in making large gifts out of principal.

Other Property in the Family.

1. Testator's mother has perhaps $15,000 besides her annuity. This will go to Testator's sister when the mother dies. Nothing substantial will come to Testator.

2. Testator's wife's father died leaving a trust of about $80,000 for his widow for life, with full power to use principal, remainder to Testator's wife and her brother and sister. Will has been examined. Testator's wife will probably get about $50,000 from this trust and property owned outright by her mother.

3. The families of Testator's two daughters-in-law and son-in-law are not so well fixed financially that there is any chance of substantial inheritance.

Insurance.

Testator carries $40,000 of straight life insurance, payable to his widow if she survives him, otherwise to his estate. He has the right to change beneficiaries. Testator pays the premiums. Neither Testator nor his wife has taken out any annuities.

Former Wills.

Testator made a will in 1933 by which he left the residue of his property in trust to his wife for life, remainder to the children and issue of deceased children, with a full power of using principal in the wife.

Various Facts Relevant to the Tax Situation.

Testator has created no *inter vivos* trusts.

Testator has made no substantial gifts to his children. Gifts have been limited to usual birthday, Christmas and wedding presents. He makes no periodic payment to children except the $150 monthly to Sheldon's widow.

Testator has made no substantial gifts to his wife other than making her tenant by the entirety of the real estate when he bought and built their home prior to enactment of Gift Tax in 1932. Gifts of jewelry to his wife have totalled about $9,000, never more than $3,000 in any year.

Testator has no power of appointment under any will or trust and does not expect to have any.

Advice Given to Testator on Taxes.

A memorandum has been given to Testator which points out the following facts about his tax situation:

1. If he should sell the Parsons & Eldridge stock during his lifetime he will have a taxable gain of the selling price, less $25 per

share. The income tax on this gain would be 25%. If, however, he should hold this stock until his death and his executor or trustee should sell it, they would pay an income tax only on the amount, if any, by which the sale price exceeded the value on the date of his death. Internal Revenue Code, § 113(a)(5). There are, therefore, tax reasons for retaining this stock during Testator's lifetime. However, where securities in a decedent estate have no established market, there is a fairly wide range for difference of judgment as to valuation; and there is a possibility that the tax authorities may put upon those securities a valuation greater than the price which can actually be realized by selling them. Additional estate taxes assessed by reason of such a valuation will obviously tend to neutralize income tax savings accruing from Testator holding the securities until his death.

2. If Testator should die in the immediate future, his gross estate, under the provisions of the Federal Estate Tax, would be as follows:

Parsons & Eldridge (at 125)	$100,000
Other stocks	240,000
Bonds	80,000
Cambridge house (at full value of equity since Testator provided funds for purchase and building. I.R.C. § 811(e))	28,000
Furnishings	18,000
Bank accounts	12,000
Auto	2,000
New Hampshire property	27,000
Life insurance	40,000
Total	$547,000

Deducting the $60,000 exemption gives a net estate of $487,000. On this estate the present law imposes a tax of $141,540, with a top rate of 32%. If the Parsons & Eldridge stock should be valued at 165 (at least a possibility) the net estate would be increased by $32,000 to $519,000. This would make the tax $152,350, with a top rate of 35%.

3. The Federal Gift Tax has certain provisions of which Testator may wish to take advantage:

a. There is excluded from the Gift Tax gifts up to $3,000 per year to each one of any number of individuals. I. R. C. § 1003(b). Thus, if Testator desired, he could make a tax-free gift in each year of any amount not in excess of $3,000 to any one or more of his relatives. Since such a gift is tax-free and since testamentary gifts would pay a tax of 32% to 35% at present rates, a present gift of $3,000 gives to the donee a benefit equivalent to a gift of $4,500 by will.

b. In addition to the " exclusions " of $3,000 per person per year just stated, the Gift Tax Law permits a total of $30,000 to be given during the Testator's lifetime tax-free. I. R. C. § 1004(a)(1). A return has to be filed with reference to such gifts, but no return has to be filed with reference to the $3,000 " exclusions." For the reasons above stated, an *inter vivos* gift of $30,000 gives to the donee or donees a benefit equivalent to a testamentary gift of about $45,000.

The trend of legislation is toward higher rates of tax and lower exemptions. The Gift Tax rates are about two-thirds of the Estate Tax rates. Hence, to whatever extent Testator feels that he is willing to transfer his property during his lifetime, it is desirable taxwise that he should do so, and the earlier the better.

Inter vivos gifts made " in contemplation of death " are included in Testator's decedent estate; but it is not to be expected that gifts by a man of 56 in good health would be held to be in contemplation of death in the absence of unusual circumstances.[2]

4. If Testator should leave all his estate to his wife, and she should then die more than 5 years after him, the entire estate she received would be subjected to another full Federal Estate tax. On the other hand, if Testator leaves the property in trust to pay the income to the wife for life with remainder to his children and their families, no tax would be payable on the wife's death under present tax laws. Hence it is desirable to limit the wife to the income from Testator's estate, plus such amounts of principal as she would expect to use up during her life.

5. If Testator contemplates making a gift, *inter vivos* or testamentary, to a married son who is making a substantial income, Testator may wish to consider substituting a gift to the son's wife, if she has little income of her own. This has income tax advantages for the son and his family. If the gift is made to the son, the income on this gift will have to be returned by the son, and the rate of tax will begin at the top bracket already being paid by the son. However, if the gift is made to the son's wife, the income on the gift will be returned by the wife and will pay a very low rate of tax since, by hypothesis, she has substantially no other income.

6. In view of a probable Estate tax of $125,000 to $150,000, Testator should be continually sure that his affairs are in such shape that this amount (payable 15 months after death), plus any amount that his widow will need within a year or two after his death, can be realized without harmful forced liquidation.

---

[2] Farmers Loan & Trust Co. v. Bowers, 98 F. (2d) 794 (1938), *cert. den.*, 306 U. S. 648 (1939) should be read. This case is one of a considerable line holding that, if a substantial motive for a gift is the avoidance of estate taxes, the gift is " in contemplation of death." In view of this holding there are obvious dangers in memoranda reciting advice to clients as to the tax advantages of *inter vivos* gifts over testamentary dispositions.

7. The Massachusetts State Inheritance Tax can, as a matter of estate planning, be ignored. This tax is substantial, but it is deductible from the Federal tax in such a way that it represents no increased burden in this case.

Testator's Scheme of Disposition.[3]

Testator's wife is to have the following if she survives Testator:

1. The house and furnishings of their principal home outright. She may want to sell the place and move into something smaller, and he wants her to be free to do so.
2. The automobile.
3. A life estate in the New Hampshire house. He originally thought he wanted her to have a life estate in the furnishings; but they are of small value and, being advised that it would be simpler if he gave her these things outright, he agreed.
4. The income of a trust of the residue, plus payments of principal in each year as follows:
   a. Any income or real estate taxes she has to pay.
   b. Any bills for doctors, nurses, hospitalization, or other medical care or services which she incurs.
   c. Any further amount which in the judgment of the trustees should be paid to her to enable her to live on the same scale as she lived during Testator's life.

Testator's sister is to have $25,000 outright if she survives. Otherwise $5,000 to each of her children who survive. If this latter happens, Testator wants the protection of guardians, for he has no confidence in Belford Beal.

Testator's brother-in-law, Belford Beal, is to be forgiven his note of $2,500.

Testator's secretary, Miss Marion B. Tweedy, of Arlington, Massachusetts, who has been with him since 1922, is to receive $100 for each year she has served as his secretary.

Testator's children and the daughter of the deceased child are to receive $5,000 each at Testator's death. The $5,000 for Gertrude is to be paid to her mother without requiring guardianship.

The remainder in the trust is to go as follows:

1. One-half to be divided equally between (a) Samuel, (b) Deborah, (c) Gertrude and Della.
2. The other half among these three in such amounts as Testator's wife may direct, and if she makes no direction then equally.

[3] The Scheme of Disposition here stated represents the Testator's original plan, plus modifications and additions resulting from conferences with counsel. Of course, the full development of the scheme appears only in the Will itself. After a draft of the will has been prepared many details of the plan will come under discussion, and some revision of the draft is probable on the basis of Testator's preferences.

If Samuel should die, his interest should go by his will, otherwise to his heirs. If Deborah should die, her share should go by her will, otherwise to her heirs. Della should get one-third of her dead husband's share; Gertrude should get the rest but not the principal until she reaches 25. Testator does not want any substantial part of the residuary trust to be paid to anyone who is under 25, but wants the sum held in trust until such person is 25.

If Testator's wife should predecease him, the tangible personalty and the New Hampshire house should go to the children and Della. The Cambridge house should be sold and the proceeds added to the residue. Otherwise the residuary gift remains the same.

The remainder in the New Hampshire property, after the death of Testator's wife, should go to their issue and spouses of same as she appoints and in default to the children and Della. This is a family summer place and should be enjoyed by all of them.

There are *two portraits* of Testator's grandparents which are to go to Testator's sister for her life; at her death one is to go to her eldest surviving child, and the other to Testator's eldest surviving child. Testator's child should get the picture of his grandfather.

Being reminded that Testator's death will cut off the $150 monthly he is paying to Della, Testator stated that he wanted his wife to have power to appoint to Della out of principal a monthly amount not in excess of $250. If his wife makes no appointment then Della is to get $150 a month out of principal. After Testator's wife dies Della and Gertrude will be adequately taken care of by the remainder interests in the trust.

Being reminded that he has provided for pecuniary gifts of $42,500 or more and that the amount of Testator's property at his death is uncertain, Testator declared that he does not want the pecuniary gifts to exceed 20% of the residuary trusts, and desires all gifts to be cut down ratably if they should exceed that amount.

Testator wants taxes to be paid out of the residue.

It was pointed out to Testator that he had made no gift to any member of his wife's family, any charity, or any servant. He stated that these omissions were international and that he had made other provisions for these matters.

Executors and Trustees.

Testator has a faithful employee who is a man of sound judgment thoroughly familiar with Testator's personal and business affairs and who has the confidence of Testator and his family. This is Francis Embree of Belmont. He wants him to be executor. If Embree should predecease Testator, then City Trust Company of Cambridge should act as executor.

City Trust Company should be trustee under the will. (The relative merits of a corporate trustee, an individual trustee, and joint corporate-and-individual trustees were discussed with Testator.)

Testator has particular confidence in his son Samuel. He at first wanted Samuel to be a co-trustee but, on being warned that where a trustee has an interest in the estate certain discretionary trust powers might cause the trust property to be taxed as assets of Samuel's estate when he dies (I. R. C. § 811(f)), concluded not to make Samuel a trustee. However, he wants it expressly stated that Samuel is to be consulted by the executor and the trustee.

Testator at first wanted Embree to be exempt from providing bond with sureties, but after discussion he deems it wise to permit his wife or any of his issue over 21 to require bond and sureties if this seems desirable at any time in the future.

Testator wants both executor and trustee to have broad discretionary powers.

Testator wants the Parsons & Eldridge stock sold within two years after his death. The value of this stock depends wholly upon the identity and skill of the management for the time being; he can keep an eye on this during his life, but is unwilling to take chances after his death. It was pointed out to him that, since the market for this stock is limited, a fixed period of sale would make it possible for those who constitute the market to sit back and wait for the executors and trustees to reduce the price to a ruinous figure, well knowing that they had to sell. Testator agreed that sale might be longer postponed if his wife and children then living assented in writing.

Immediate Pecuniary Needs of Family During Administration.

Della needs continuity of her $150 monthly payments. The widow's allowance made to Testator's wife under Gen. Laws C. 196 § 2, plus the life insurance proceeds and the house should adequately take care of her.

Check with Corporate Fiduciary.

Testator accepted the recommendation that the will be submitted to City Trust Company for comment and suggestion.

Possibility of Wife Electing Against Will.

Under Gen. Laws, Ch. 191, § 15, Testator's widow, by electing to take against the will, would have one-third of his estate set aside for her. Of this she would get $10,000 outright, and the life income on the balance. Since the will gives her substantially greater rights than this, there is no reason to take precautions against waiver of the will by her.

Possibility of Contest of Will.

Testator anticipates no dissatisfaction with this will by any member of his family. He does not desire any clause in the will which declares that any person contesting the will loses the gifts made to him therein.

Disposition of This Will and Previous Wills.

It was recommended to Testator that:

1. He remove his previous will from his safe-deposit box where it now is, have the will photostated, deliver the photostat to this firm for its files, and destroy the original will; [4]

2. He have two photostat copies of the new will made, deposit the original will with the Probate Court for Middlesex County under Gen. Laws Ch. 191, § 10, retain one photostat for his own use, and leave one photostat with the files of this firm.

Testator accepted these recommendations.
There are no other wills of Testator in existence.

Review of This Will.

It was recommended to Testator that on each anniversary of the execution of this will:

1. This office write to Testator, asking what changes in the family and property of Testator have taken place in the previous year and whether Testator desires any changes in the dispositions of the will;

2. This office review the will in the light of changes in the tax laws and other laws with a view to recommending changes which are advisable for legal reasons.

Testator accepted these recommendations. Appropriate notations have been made in the memorandum book of the partner in charge and in the records of the file clerk.

Other Wills in the Family.

Testator's wife has never made a will. It was pointed out that, if she survives testator and her own mother, she will have in her estate the Cambridge house and furnishings ($58,000), the life insurance

---

[4] The old will should be destroyed so that there is no possibility of two wills being offered for probate. An executor into whose hands both should come might feel that he should offer both. A photostat should be made and retained so that proof of the contents of the preceding will could be made. If the present will should be declared void by reason of mental incapacity of Testator or undue influence, this same defect would probably vitiate the revocation of the preceding will. If no proof of the contents of the preceding will were available in honest hands, some designing person might concoct a copy of an alleged will and, with a little persuasive perjury, get it probated.

proceeds ($40,000), and her expected inheritance from her own family ($50,000), plus various incidentals (say, $10,000) — making a total probable estate of some $158,000. It was recommended to Testator that:

1. He should discuss with his wife the desirability of making a will, in view of the complicated and unsatisfactory situation which would result if she should die intestate;

2. This office, upon the death of Testator, should get in touch with Testator's widow and recommend that she then re-examine her property and family situation with a view to making a new will at that time. Testator accepted both of these suggestions.

It is not known whether Samuel, Deborah and Della have made wills, and Testator is not inclined to inquire into that matter.

It is not known whether Testator's sister has a will. Testator will write to his sister, informing her that she is receiving a substantial legacy if she survives him and that she probably would be well advised to make a will providing for her children if she should die soon after Testator. Testator will also inform her, to ease her mind, that if she predeceases Testator he has made some provision for her children who survive him.

IMPORTANT NOTE: The Revenue Act of 1948 requires significant changes in the Estate Plan of J. Albert Thomas. These are discussed in Appendix II C, infra.

Here follows
THE WILL OF J. ALBERT THOMAS
and
COMMENTARIES THEREON

WILL OF JOSEPH ALBERT THOMAS

I, Joseph Albert Thomas, usually known as J. Albert Thomas, of Cambridge, Massachusetts, hereby make my last will, revoking all previous wills and codicils.

I

My wife, Winifred Wentworth Thomas, and I now have a usual principal place of abode at 15 Elm Street, Cambridge, Massachusetts. This property is owned by us as tenants by the entirety, and will therefore become her sole property if she survives me. If at the time of my death I own any interest in our then usual principal place of abode (whether it be said 15 Elm Street or any successor thereto) and if my said wife survives me, then I devise such interest to my said wife. If my said wife survives me, I direct my executor to pay off and discharge any mortgage or other encumbrance or lien upon all the interest or interests in our usual principal place of abode which my said wife shall own at my death, or which she shall acquire on my death as a result of some form of co-ownership or by operation of this Paragraph, and to pay any interest which is due or may become due thereon.

II

If my wife, Winifred Wentworth Thomas, survives me, I bequeath to her all tangible personal property which I shall own at the time of my death; and I hope, but do not require, that out of this property she will give to each of my children, children-in-law, and grandchildren some token of my affection for them. If my said wife does not survive me, I bequeath such tangible personal property in three equal shares as follows:

(a) One share to my son, Samuel Arthur Thomas, of Springfield, Massachusetts, if he survives me; or if he does not survive me to his present wife, Dorothy Lawton Thomas, if she survives me; or, if neither survives me, to such children of said Samuel as survive me.

COMMENTARY ON WILL OF JOSEPH ALBERT THOMAS

Introductory and Revoking Clause

State Testator's full name; also the name by which he signs himself. This latter identifies him easily with reference to deeds, stock certificates, bank accounts and the like. State Testator's domicil.

Paragraph I

Testator is undertaking to see that after his death his widow has their home, whatever it may be, free and clear. It is, of course, necessary to anticipate that they will move to some other house, and that the other house may be in his name, in her name or in both. It is also a possibility that they will be living in rented quarters when he dies. In this event Testator might consider making a monetary gift—say $25,000—in lieu of the provision of permanent quarters. But it is unlikely that the widow, if living in an apartment when her husband dies, would want then to buy and operate a house. So probably the best expedient, if they should be living in rented quarters, is to allow her to be taken care of by the power to invade principal as given in Paragraph VII.

If the widow is to get the property free of mortgage, this must be expressed in the will. See *Mass. Gen. Laws (Ter. Ed.) Ch. 191, § 23*. If a testator specifically devises property subject to a mortgage he should invariably state whether the executor is to pay off the mortgage as a debt of the estate.

Paragraph II

The amount of tangible personality in this estate is substantial—$18,000 worth of furnishings in Cambridge, plus an automobile and the New Hampshire furnishings. Frequently, for reasons of sentiment, a testator will want to bequeath certain specific things to various members of his family. Be cautious about the idea, which will occur to many testators, of allocating particular chattels to various persons by a list which the testator will later make up and change from time to time. If such a list is unattested it can have no legal effect. Thus warn testator either:

(1) To have any such list attested as a codicil or
(2) To indicate that such a list is only a request to the widow to make gifts (which, if substantial, may create a Gift Tax liability in her).

(b) One share to my daughter, Deborah Thomas Langenbach, wife of Spencer Langenbach of Detroit, Michigan, if she survives me; or if she does not survive me to such children of hers as survive me.

(c) One share to my daughter-in-law, Della Langhorn Thomas, of Boston, Massachusetts, if she survives me; or if she does not survive me to my granddaughter, Gertrude Thomas, if she survives me.

If all persons named in any one or two of Clauses (a), (b) and (c) of this Paragraph shall not survive me, the share given in such Clause or Clauses shall be added to the other share or shares, equally if more than one. I intend that no portion of the property dealt with in this Paragraph shall pass into the residue unless all persons designated as legatees in this Paragraph fail to survive me.

In the interest of family harmony I hereby state that I have not promised any particular thing to any person. If my wife does not survive me and the tangible personalty is, therefore, to be divided among the persons named in Clauses (a), (b) and (c), I recommend but do not require that all items of this property be appraised by a professional appraiser and that those who are to participate in the division then select in rotation items at the appraised values, the order of choice to be determined by lot. It seems to me improbable that the legatees named in this Paragraph will desire to own any large portion of the tangible personalty which I leave. I recommend, but do not require, that whatever articles are not desired by any legatee shall be sold by my executor and the proceeds thereof divided, after charging against each legatee the appraised value of items which he has elected to take in kind.

III

I devise the land and buildings on Meredith Road, Alton Bay, New Hampshire, commonly known as Baybrook, to my wife, Winifred Wentworth Thomas for her life, without liability for waste, and upon her death to such of my issue and spouses of my issue as she shall by will appoint, and if

There are several things which ought to be called to Testator's attention about these gifts, if his wife predeceases him:

(1) Samuel and his wife, Dorothy, can be divorced. Would he want her to get this property, under that circumstance, if Samuel predeceased Testator?

(2) Deborah could have a child and then die, either in childbirth or shortly thereafter. Would he want $6,000 of tangible personalty to go to this infant, bearing in mind Testator's lack of enthusiasm for Deborah's husband?

(3) Della can, and probably will, marry again. If she does, and Gertrude grows up, leaves home and marries, wouldn't Testator prefer Gertrude to take this property rather than Della?

Testator, after considering these things, would probably be wise to leave the will as it is. Then if any of these events happens he can alter his will to fit the new situation.

The recommendation of sale by the executor is obviously wise. Eighteen thousand dollars worth of furniture is a large amount. The people who are getting this gift will already have fully furnished houses and will desire only a few items for their personal use. Moreover, one of them lives in Springfield, Mass., and one in Detroit, Mich.; and they might not want to pay moving charges on many bulky chattels. Testator could, of course, leave the legatees to work out this problem for themselves, but a practical suggestion in the will frequently tends to eliminate controversy as to the method of division.

Paragraph III

The life estate with remainders has several advantages over an outright gift either to the widow or to the children. It allows the widow to control the property during her life, although the children and their families will probably be the primary users. It also prevents the property from being assets of her estate on death for tax purposes. The power of appointment given to her over the remain-

she shall make no appointment or if she shall predecease me then in three equal shares as follows:

(a) One share to my son, Samuel Arthur Thomas, if he survives my wife and me; or if he does not survive my wife and me to his present wife, Dorothy Lawton Thomas, if she survives my wife and me and has not remarried; or, if neither of the two previous gifts in this Clause takes effect, to such children of said Samuel as shall survive my wife and me.

(b) One share to my daughter, Deborah Thomas Langenbach, if she survives my wife and me; or if she does not survive my wife and me to such children of hers as shall survive my wife and me.

(c) One share to my daughter-in-law, Della Langhorn Thomas, if she survives my wife and me; or if she does not survive my wife and me to my granddaughter, Gertrude Thomas, if she survives my wife and me.

If all persons named in any one or two of Clauses (a), (b) and (c) of this Paragraph shall not survive my wife and me, the share given in such Clause or Clauses shall go to the takers designated in the other Clause or Clauses. I intend that no portion of the property dealt with in this Paragraph shall pass into the residue unless all persons designated as devisees in this Paragraph fail to survive my wife and me.

During my wife's lifetime she shall have power to sell the fee simple in the said premises with the assent of those persons, over the age of 21, who would be entitled to said property under the terms of this Paragraph if my wife were to die, without making any appointment, immediately before such sale. In the event of such sale the proceeds thereof shall be divided as follows: to my wife an amount equal to the value of her life estate as determined by the American Experience Tables, and the balance to those persons who would have been entitled to said property under the terms of this Paragraph if my wife had died, without making any appointment, immediately before such sale. The purchaser at such sale may make payment to my said wife and shall not be required to see to the application of the purchase money.

der is an exempt power within the provisions of *Internal Revenue Code § 811 (f)* as amended by the Revenue Act of 1942.

The remainders in default of appointment are designed to go only to living persons. Note that, for this purpose, they must be contingent on surviving both the life tenant and the testator.

The power of sale is desirable to take care of the situation where:
(1) The character of the property changes, or
(2) The family loses interest in this particular location. Testator could make the property saleable by putting the property in a trust and giving a power of sale to the trustee, but this is cumbersome; the power of sale in the life tenant, subject to assent by the grown members of the family, is a simpler practical expedient. Suppose, as sometimes happens, the widow is *non compos* during the last years of her lifetime. Is the property then frozen? It ordinarily would be unless specific provision is made for exercise of this power by a guardian. It would be mildly insulting to include mention of a guardian in this immediate context, so the necessary clause is tucked in at a later point — Paragraph IX (m). It is important to facilitate the sale by allowing the purchaser to deal for all purposes with the wife; hence the last sentence in this **Paragraph.**

IV

I bequeath the two oil portraits of my grandfather and my grandmother, which I received from my father's estate, to my sister, Sarah Thomas Beal, wife of Belford Beal, of Hartford, Connecticut, for life; and after her death (or at my death if she shall predecease me):

(a) The portrait of my grandfather shall go to the first named in the following list who shall survive me and my said sister: my son Samuel, my daughter Deborah, my grandson Gerald, my granddaughter Gertrude, the oldest descendant of my said sister.

(b) The portrait of my grandmother shall go to the oldest descendant of my said sister who survives me and her; if no such descendant survives me and her, to the first named in the following list who shall survive me and my said sister, excluding (unless all others in the list be dead) that person who is entitled to receive my grandfather's portrait: my son Samuel, my daughter Deborah, my grandson Gerald, my granddaughter Gertrude.

My said sister shall not be required to furnish any bond with regard to said portraits, or to insure the same; and she shall not be liable for any damage to or loss of the same.

V

I bequeath the following amounts to the following persons:

(a) To my sister, Sarah Thomas Beal, if she survives me, Twenty-five Thousand Dollars ($25,000).

(b) If my said sister does not survive me, Five Thousand Dollars ($5,000) to each child of my sister who survives me. As to any such children who are under the age of 21, I direct that these amounts be paid only to a legally appointed guardian for said children.

(c) Five Thousand Dollars ($5,000) to my son, Samuel Arthur Thomas, if he survives me; or, if he does not survive me, and his present wife Dorothy Lawton Thomas survives me and has not remarried, then to said Dorothy Lawton

Paragraph IV

This Paragraph deals with items of small value but considerable sentimental interest. One important thing, in the interest of family harmony, is to make a disposition which the family will consider fair; this justifies the care taken in drafting the rather cumbersome Clause (b). Another important thing is to be sure that the life tenant is not subjected to liabilities or to the requirement of producing a forthcoming bond. See *3 Simes, Future Interests (1936) §§ 638-649.*

Paragraph V

Clause (a). Testator's sister presents quite a problem. There would be several ways of taking care of her with $25,000:

(1) Direct the executor to purchase an annuity. This would give a small fixed annual income ($1,350 at 1947 rates) which is better than nothing but quite inflexible. Besides the annuitant can elect to take the principal sum instead of the annuity. *Parker v. Cobe,* 208 Mass. 260, 94 N. E. 476 (1911); *3 Scott on Trusts, § 346. Contra,* in New York, by statute. *Decedent Estate Law § 47-b.*

(2) Set up a trust, with power to invade principal. This seems to be the best solution, though there may be some difficulty in finding a really competent trustee for an amount as small as $25,000. The trust gives protection to the sister, and this is the primary objective.

(3) Give a principal sum and rely on her wisdom and discretion. This runs some risk that the sister's husband will influence her to

Thomas; or if neither of the two previous gifts in this Clause takes effect, then equally to such children of my said son as survive me. As to any such children who are under the age of 21, payment shall be made only to a legally appointed guardian for said children.

(d) Five Thousand Dollars ($5,000) to my granddaughter, Gertrude Thomas, if she survives me. This sum shall be paid to her mother, Della Langhorn Thomas, if Gertrude is still under the age of 21 at the time of my death and said Della survives me; and in that case my executor shall not be bound to see to the proper application of said sum. If said Gertrude is under the age of 21 at my death, and her said mother does not survive me, then payment shall be made only to her legally appointed guardian.

(e) Five Thousand Dollars ($5,000) to my daughter, Deborah Thomas Langenbach, if she survives me; or if she does not survive me, equally to such of her children as survive me. As to any of such children who are under the age of 21, payment shall be made only to a legally appointed guardian for said children.

(f) To my present secretary, Marion B. Tweedy of Arlington, Massachusetts, if she survives me, Two Thousand Five Hundred Dollars ($2,500), plus One Hundred Dollars ($100) for each year or fraction of a year during which she is employed by me between the date of this will and the date of my death. My executor's determination of the number of such units of One Hundred Dollars ($100) shall be conclusive.

If the total of gifts made in this Paragraph shall exceed twenty per cent (20%) of the amount available for distribution to my trustee, then all gifts in this Paragraph shall be ratably reduced so that the total of such gifts does not exceed such twenty per cent (20%). In determining the value of the property distributed to my trustee, any stock of Parsons & Eldridge, Inc., shall be taken at its book value as shown on the books of the company at a date one year after my death, and the decision of my executor as to the value of any other assets available for distribution to my trustees shall be conclusive.

use the property unwisely; but in this case Testator feels that this risk is not substantial. This is a typical problem for Testator to decide after you have laid the alternatives before him.

Clause (c). Daughters-in-law should not be neglected where they have become close members of the family. But Testator's attention should be drawn to the question whether he wants to make gifts under circumstances where the chief beneficiary may well be a second husband.

Clause (d). In giving money to a minor you can do any of the following:

(1) Direct that the money be held in trust during minority. This is appropriate where the sum is substantial or where there is a trustee who will be handling other funds anyway, — e.g. Paragraph VII (f) (2) (iii). The investments of a trustee are usually less restricted than those of a guardian, and a more efficient administration is usually possible. But as to amounts as small as $5,000 a trust is too cumbersome.

(2) Direct that the money be paid to a parent, without obligation on the executor to see that it is properly applied to the use of the minor. This is appropriate as to relatively small sums where Testator has confidence in the parents,—e.g. Clause (d) of this Paragraph.

(3) Require the appointment of a guardian. This is inconvenient to some extent; but it is the best choice where the sum is small and Testator does not have confidence in the parents of the minor,—e.g. Clause (b) of this Paragraph. But give careful consideration to relieving the guardian of the obligation to provide sureties on his bond. The premium required by a corporate surety may eat up a big slice of the income; be sure you inform Testator what this premium would be. If your testator is surety-conscious, note that, if there are several small funds given to minors, several sureties would be required for several guardians; but only one surety would be required for a single trustee.

The final provisions of this Paragraph are all too frequently omitted from wills. Testators habitually and properly make pecuniary legacies appropriate to the *probable* size of their estates. But they should recognize that the *actual* estates may be much smaller than they now anticipate, due to unexpected tax impositions, heavy business losses, or other factors. The residuary gift—which is ordinarily made to those persons closest to the testator in relationship and obligation—must be protected if the estate should prove to be unexpectedly small. A sliding scale arrangement, providing for pro rata reductions, is one desirable way of giving protection to the residue. This necessarily raises questions of valuation; it is desirable for testator to express his desires on particular items (e.g. the Parsons & Eldridge stock) and then make the executor's determination conclusive as to any remaining questions.

VI

I forgive the obligation of Twenty-five Hundred Dollars ($2,500) owed to me by Belford Beal of Hartford, Connecticut, evidenced by his note for that amount, dated April 14, 1946.

VII

If my wife, Winifred Wentworth Thomas, survives me, all other property which I shall own at the time of my death or over which I shall then have any power of appointment I devise, bequeath and appoint to City Trust Company of Cambridge, Massachusetts, in trust for the following purposes:

(a) To pay the income to my said wife for her life.

(b) To pay to my said wife out of principal in each year an amount equal to all income taxes, real estate taxes, and personal property taxes paid by her in that year and all bills for her own treatment and care by doctors, nurses, and hospitals paid by her in that year. My trustee shall make payments under this Clause upon such evidence as it deems sufficient.

(c) To pay to my said wife out of principal from time to time such further amounts as in the discretion of my trustee shall be adequate to enable her to maintain the standard of living to which she was accustomed during my lifetime. As a guide to my trustee in exercising this discretion but without imposing any obligation whatever, I declare that, in the event that my said wife should marry again, I still wish to provide for her support in her accustomed manner of living, but I do not wish to provide for the support of her husband. If my said wife shall provide financial assistance to any relatives of hers or of mine or to their spouses, I point out that providing such assistance has been one aspect of our standard of living, and the fact that my wife has used funds

Indeed it is a good general rule that, where the amount of a gift depends upon facts involving some element of investigation and judgment, you should at least consider making the executor's decision conclusive — e.g. the number of years Miss Tweedy has worked, in Clause (f).

Paragraph VI

This forgiveness of indebtedness is a gift to Beal. He will have to pay taxes on it unless the contrary is provided. See Paragraph X(a).

Paragraph VII

Note that the residuary clause expressly exercises powers of appointment even though Testator is not aware that he has any. A residuary *bequest* exercises powers in Massachusetts and some other states by decision or statute. *1 Simes, Future Interests (1936) § 270; 3 Property Restatement § 343.* But this should not be relied upon in drafting wills.

Clauses (b) and (c) raise the whole problem of powers in the life tenant (usually the widow) to invade principal. Formerly it was common to give the life tenant the right to call for any part of the principal she desired. But such a power, under the Revenue Act of 1942, causes the whole trust to be included in the life tenant's gross estate for Federal Estate Tax purposes. *I. R. C. § 811(f); Paul, Federal Estate and Gift Taxation (1946 Supp.) § 9.34.* Moreover, an unrestricted power in the life tenant gives the remaindermen no protection, especially against a second husband. *Colburn v. Burlingame,* 190 Cal. 697, 214 Pac. 226 (1923). If the power to invade principal is to be restricted — and this seems wise — the amount should be fixed on a realistic basis. Non-discretionary items to be taken out of principal, such as taxes and expense of sickness, should be specified (Clause (b)). Where discretion is given to the trustee, some guideposts are desirable (Clause (c)). Some testators, to guard against inflation, have provided that the life tenant shall always receive the equivalent in purchasing power of a fixed amount as of the date of the will. If such a " rubber dollar " clause is used the trustee's decisions in applying it should be made conclusive. A discussion of this whole problem will be found in Leach, *Drafting of Wills and Trusts,* 9 Am. Law School Review, 902 (1941).

Clause (b) may cause an addition to Mrs. Thomas's gross estate in the amount of the estimated value of her rights under Clause (b) for her life expectancy at the moment of death. See Paul, Federal Estate & Gift Taxation (1946 Supp.) 266.

for that purpose is a factor which my trustee may consider in exercising discretion under this Clause.

(d) During the life of my said wife to pay out of principal One Hundred Fifty Dollars ($150) in each month to my daughter-in-law, Della Langhorn Thomas, if she is living, or to my granddaughter, Gertrude Thomas, or her guardian, if said Della is not living and said Gertrude is living, subject to the following:

(1) Said payments shall be increased, decreased, stopped, or resumed as my said wife may from time to time direct in writing addressed to my trustee, but in no event shall the payment for any month exceed Two Hundred and Fifty Dollars ($250). It is my hope that my wife, in consultation with other members of the family, will review the financial needs of said Della and said Gertrude annually and make appropriate adjustment upward or downward in the amount of these payments.

(2) No payment shall be made after both of the following have happened:

(i) Said Della has married or died;

(ii) Said Gertrude has married, reached the age of 25, or died.

(e) At the death of my said wife, as to one-half of the principal, to pay the same to or hold the same further in trust for such of my issue or their spouses as my said wife shall by will appoint, and in default of appointment to the persons who take the other half of the principal of this trust under Clause (f) of this Paragraph.

(f) At the death of my said wife, as to the other one-half of the principal, to divide the same into equal shares and dispose of said shares as follows:

(1) If my son, Samuel Arthur Thomas, survives my said wife, is married, and is living with his wife, to pay one share to the wife of said Samuel; or if said Samuel survives my said wife and either is not married or is not living with his wife, to pay said share to said Samuel; or if said Samuel does not survive my said wife then to pay such share to or hold such share further in trust for such of his wife, or issue, or spouses of his issue, or my issue

Clause (d). The working out of this gift is a bit tricky. The gift is needed only so long as Testator's wife lives, for after her death Clause (f) (2) of this Paragraph will become operative. The payments should be continued even after Della marries (as is probable) until Gertrude is is a position to take care of herself. And some flexibility is desirable to take care of fluctuation in need.

Note that, if Testator's widow becomes *non compos*, she will be unable to exercise the power given to her here; but this is probably not the sort of thing that should be entrusted to anyone else.

If provision is being made for Della in this way, what about providing for Samuel's wife and for Deborah, if their husbands should die during the life of Testator's widow? These possible, but improbable, events are adequately covered by the provision as to family gifts in Clause (c) of this Paragraph and the provision for family loans in Paragraph XII(d).

Clauses (e) and (f) reflect the state of mind of a testator who wishes the life tenant to have some power over the principal but does not want any line of his family to be left out. In some wills this has been done by giving the life tenant a "non-exclusive" power, i.e. a power to allocate shares but not to exclude any member of the benefited class. This raises complex and controversial problems and is a fertile source of litigation. To handle this situation properly Testator should make an outright gift to whatever extent he desires and then, as to the balance, give the life tenant a special power to appoint to any one or more of the group as she elects. See *3 Property Restatement § 360, Comment d.*

Clause (f). Note that it is not necessary to provide that the legatees shall " survive me and my said wife " because this entire Paragraph of the will is contingent upon Testator's wife surviving him.

Clause (f) (1). Note that Testator has accepted the suggestion designed to minimize income taxes of Samuel and his family by giving the legacy to Samuel's wife so that she, and not he, will return the income on this fund. Such a provision should not, of course, be made without consultation with Samuel.

The gift in default of appointment is to persons whom Testator (other than himself) or their spouses, as he shall by will appoint; and in default of appointment to pay said share to those persons who would have taken his personal property if he had died at the death of my said wife, intestate and domiciled in Massachusetts, under the laws of Massachusetts in force at that time, and the shares and proportions of taking shall be determined by said laws. The determination of my executor as to whether, if said Samuel survives my wife, he is married and is living with his wife shall be conclusive upon all parties.

(2) As to one share, pay one-third of it to my daughter-in-law, Della Langhorn Thomas, if she survives my said wife. The balance of this share (or all of it, if said Della Langhorn Thomas does not survive my said wife) shall be paid as follows:

    (i) If my granddaughter, Gertrude Thomas, survives my said wife and has reached the age of 25, then to said Gertrude.

    (ii) If said Gertrude does not survive my said wife, but leaves issue who survive my said wife, then to such issue.

    (iii) If said Gertrude survives my said wife but is under the age of 25, then this interest shall be held by my trustee in trust to pay to said Gertrude the income and such part of the principal as my trustee in its uncontrolled discretion shall determine until said Gertrude reaches the age of 25 or dies under that age; if said Gertrude reaches the age of 25, to pay the principal to her; if she dies under the age of 25 leaving issue, to pay the principal to such issue; if she dies under the age of 25 not leaving issue, to pay the principal to my issue.

    (iv) If said Gertrude does not survive my said wife and leaves no issue who survive her, then one-half shall be paid to the persons entitled to receive the share given in clause (f) (1) of this Paragraph, and one-half shall be paid to the persons entitled to receive the share given in Clause (f) (3) of this Paragraph.

(3) Pay one share to my daughter, Deborah Thomas Langenbach, if she survives my said wife. If she survives

will describe to you as " heirs." But this word should never be used in a will — unless, of course, it is clearly defined. The best way to eliminate all the problems of construction inherent in the use of the word " heirs " is to define the takers with reference to the provisions of a certain statute.

Clause (f) (2). Testator at first wanted to give one-third to Della only if she had not remarried. But why? No such string would be attached to the gift if Della's husband had got his share of the family estate and had then died. Does Testator really want to penalize Della for remarrying? Della is living through difficult years now. Should she not be entitled later to that security which a little money in her own name can give to a woman in middle life? On the basis of these suggestions Testator changed his mind and eliminated the requirement that Della still be unmarried.

The provisions for Gertrude seem cumbersome, but this Clause may be disposing of $50,000 to $100,000 of property. This is worth some thought and a page of typewriting. Provisions like this for a legatee who is now a baby may meet sales resistance on the part of the Testator, but he must be made to realize that the whole will is meant to operate at Testator's death (probably a fairly distant future date) and that the remainder interests in this trust are to take effect at the death of Testator's wife (still more remote by a few years to a couple of decades). Splitting the gifts to Gertrude into several sub-clauses is a wise precaution to ensure that you have covered every possible contingency; it also makes the provision simpler for Testator to grasp. The gift to " issue " in various sub-clauses would raise litigable constructional problems if this word were not defined in Paragraph IX(e).

me but does not survive my said wife, pay said share or hold the same in trust for such spouse or issue or spouses of issue of said Deborah as she shall by will appoint. If she does not survive me, or to whatever extent she (having survived me but not my said wife) fails to appoint, pay said share to those persons who would have taken the personal property of said Deborah if she had died at the death of my said wife, intestate and domiciled in Massachusetts, under the laws of Massachusetts then in force, and the shares and proportions of taking shall be determined by said laws.

VIII

If my said wife does not survive me then all other property which I shall own at the time of my death or over which I shall then have any power of appointment I devise, bequeath and appoint in equal shares as follows:

(a) One share to my son, Samuel Arthur Thomas, if he survives me; or, if he does not survive me, to those persons who would have taken his personal property if he had died at the time of my death, intestate and domiciled in Massachusetts, under the laws of Massachusetts then in force, and the shares and proportions of taking shall be determined by said laws.

(b) As to one share, one-third of it shall be paid to my daughter-in-law, Della Langhorn Thomas, if she survives me. The balance of this share (or all of it if said Della Langhorn Thomas does not survive me) shall be paid as follows:

(1) If my granddaughter, Gertrude Thomas, survives me and has reached the age of 25 then to said Gertrude.

(2) If said Gertrude does not survive me, but leaves issue who survive me, then to such issue.

(3) If said Gertrude survives me but is under the age of 25, then this interest shall be held by my trustee in trust to pay to said Gertrude the income and such part of the principal as my trustee in its uncontrolled discretion shall determine until said Gertrude reaches the age of 25 or dies under that age; if said Gertrude reaches the age of 25, to

Paragraph VIII

Clause (b) (3). If, at Testator's death, his wife has died and Gertrude is under 25, Testator feels that a trust of Gertrude's share should be set up, even though it will be the only trust existing. The amount will be very substantial and, even though Testator has confidence in Della, money of the order of $100,000 is too much to place in the hands of an inexperienced woman to manage. Note that the terms of the trust are written out, even though they are identical to

pay the principal to her; if she dies under the age of 25 leaving issue, to pay the principal to such issue; if she dies under the age of 25 not leaving issue, to pay the principal to my issue.

(4) If said Gertrude does not survive me, and leaves no issue who survive me, then one-half of this interest shall be added to the share specified in Clause (a) of this Paragraph, and one-half to the share specified in Clause (c) of this Paragraph.

(c) One share to my daughter, Deborah Thomas Langenbach, if she survives me. If she does not survive me, said share shall pass to those persons who would have taken her personal property if she had died at the time of my death, intestate and domiciled in Massachusetts, under the laws of Massachusetts then in force, and the shares and proportions of taking shall be determined by said laws.

IX

(a) No principal or income payable or to become payable under any trust created by this will shall be subject to anticipation or assignment by any beneficiary thereof or to attachment by or to the interference or control of any creditor of any such beneficiary, or be taken or reached by any legal or equitable process in satisfaction of any debt or liability of such beneficiary prior to its actual receipt by the beneficiary.

(b) In the exercise of any power of appointment created by this will, unless the contrary is stated, the donee of such power may appoint life estates to one or more objects of the power with remainders to others, appoint to grandchildren or more remote issue even though the parents of such appointees are living, impose lawful conditions upon any appointment provided no one other than an object of the power is benefited thereby, impose lawful spendthrift restrictions upon any appointment, make appointments outright to an object or in trust for the object, create in any object a general power of appointment or a special power to appoint among objects of the original power, appoint by a

those of Paragraph VII(f)(1)(iii). Instead of repeating these terms the Clause could have made the gift " upon the trust provided in Paragraph VII(f)(1)(iii)." But this is not recommended; it is inconvenient to read and makes it difficult for you and Testator to examine the trust provisions in their own context.

Paragraph IX

Clause (a). This is the " spendthrift " clause. It is effective in Massachusetts, both as to income and principal. In some states (e.g. New York) it is effective as to income but not as to principal. In a few states (e.g. New Hampshire, Rhode Island) it is ineffective as to both income and principal. See *Griswold, Spendthrift Trusts (2d ed. 1947); 1 Scott on Trusts §§ 151–153.3.* In the absence of such a clause, or to whatever extent such a clause is ineffective, a beneficiary can sell his interest; from the beneficiary's point of view this is usually extremely improvident, for the price available for such interests is usually of the mess-of-pottage type.

Clause (b). Some litigation has arisen as to whether the donee of a power of appointment may do the things enumerated in this clause where they are not specifically authorized. See *Leach, Cas. Fut. Int., Ch. XVIII, Note: Certain Aspects of the Exercise of Powers of Appointment.* This Clause is designed to eliminate this source of controversy. Note that where the donee of a power of appointment appoints by creating a new power of any type, the property subject to such new power becomes part of his gross estate under *I. R. C.* § 811 (f). *Paul, Federal Estate and Gift Taxation (1946 Supp.)* § *9.33.*

will executed before my death. These powers of the donee of a power of appointment are in addition to, and not in restriction of, powers he would otherwise have.

(c) Under any power of appointment created by this will, no person to whom an appointment is made may share in the gift in default of appointment unless he contributes the property appointed to him to the fund to be distributed in default of appointment.

(d) All powers created by this will are releasable in whole or in part. In addition to any other method of release recognized by law, any such power may be released by an instrument in writing, filed with any court which has granted probate of this will, declaring the donee's intention to release.

(e) Where in this will any gift is made to issue of a person, those children and more remote descendants of such person shall take who would have taken the personal property of such person if he had died at the time said gift becomes possessory, unmarried, intestate, domiciled in Massachusetts, under the laws of Massachusetts in force at the time such gift becomes possessory, and the shares and proportions of taking shall be determined by said laws. Where a power is given to appoint among the issue of a person, appointment may be made to any children or more remote issue of such person.

(f) In construing this will, where a decree of divorce has been rendered by a court of record, and the spouses named therein have not thereafter lived together openly as husband and wife, such divorce shall be considered as valid for all purposes, including the following purposes but without limiting the generality of the foregoing language:

(1) The spouses shall no longer be considered as husband and wife of each other and shall not be considered as heir or next-of-kin of each other upon death.

(2) If a spouse contracts a subsequent purported marriage which, apart from prior marriages, would be valid, such subsequent purported marriage shall be considered as valid; the parties thereto shall be considered husband and wife of each other and heir and next-of-kin of each

Clause (c). This is the "hotchpot" clause. It is designed to prevent incongruous distributions of the fund where an appointment is partially ineffective, due to the lapse of one appointed interest or a violation of the Rule against Perpetuities or otherwise. See *3 Property Restatement § 368*, especially *Comment b.*

Clause (d). On principle special powers should not be releasable. *3 Property Restatement § 335.* However, the tendency of the taxing authorities to impose serious additional taxes where certain types of powers exist (e.g. the 1942 amendment to *I. R. C. § 811 (f)*) makes it desirable to enable the holder of any power to release it. Releasability "in whole or in part" is desirable so that the donee can reduce a broad power (which would cause additional taxes) to a narrower power (which would not) without giving up the power entirely. Since the law as to what constitutes a release is not well developed, it is desirable to specify one type of act which will be effective as a release. In Massachusetts *Gen. Laws, Ch. 204, §§ 27–33* deals with release of powers; these sections were passed in 1943 to cope with the situation created by the Revenue Act of 1942. Many other states have similar statutes.

Clause (e). Where gifts are made to "issue" of a person, A, there is a constructional problem as to who shall take. Suppose A has a living child (C_1) who has two children (G_1 and G_2); then there is one other grandchild (G_3) who is the son of a deceased child (C_2). All four are descendants of A. Do they each take one-fourth, thus causing C_1's side of the family to get three-fourths of the property and C_2's side one-fourth? Or should the property be distributed, as A's property would go upon intestacy, one-half to C_1 and one-half to G_3? The former method is known as distribution *per capita*, and is given a constructional preference at common law. The latter method is known as distribution *per stirpes*, and is what most testators want and what the statutes call for in case of intestacy. Clause (e) ties the definition of "issue" to a specific intestacy statute. Why not merely say "Gifts to issue shall be distributed *per stirpes*"? There are several situations (too complex for discussion at this point) where this provision is ambiguous. See Eagleton, "*Introduction to the Intestacy Act and the Dower Rights Act*," 20 IOWA L. REV. 241, 246 (1935); *Leach, Cas. Fut. Int., Ch. XII, Sec. 2.*

Clause (f). This is the "Reno" clause. A large and increasing number of families have divorces in them. It can happen to anyone, including those who are members of religious faiths which do not recognize divorce or restrict their recognition to divorces for particular causes. Of those who get divorces a substantial number will seek the quick, relatively painless procedure offered by Nevada and such competitors for the divorce trade as Florida, Idaho, and Arkansas. A large number of these quick-and-painless divorces are technically

other upon death; children of the said marriage shall be considered as legitimate, and their status as heirs and next-of-kin shall be the same as if they were legitimate. Provided, however, that where a special power of appointment is created by this will and any " spouse " is an object of the power, no person other than a legal spouse shall be included in this term.

(g) Where a child under the age of 21 has been adopted, such adoption shall have the same effect, for all purposes of this will, as if such child had been legitimately born to the adopting parents.

(h) All references to my trustee hereunder shall be construed to apply to substitute, successor or additional trustee or trustees, where the context permits. All references to my executor herein shall be construed to apply to administrators with this will annexed, where the context permits.

(j) No purchaser from or other person dealing with my executor or trustee shall be responsible for the application of any purchase money or other thing of value paid or delivered to either of them, but the receipt of my executor or trustee shall be a full discharge; and no purchaser from or other person dealing with my executor or trustee and no issuer, or transfer agent or other agent of any issuer, of any securities to which any dealing with my executor or trustee shall relate, shall be under any obligation to ascertain or inquire into the power of my executor or trustee to purchase, sell, exchange, transfer, mortgage, pledge, lease, distribute or otherwise in any manner dispose of or deal with any securities or any other property held by my executor or trustee or comprised in my estate.

(k) For purposes of this will a person shall not be considered to survive another if he shall die within thirty (30) days of the death of such other, provided that this Clause shall not apply in any case where its application would cause any provision of this will, which would otherwise be valid, to be void under any applicable rule against perpetuities, rule limiting suspension of the power of alienation, or other similar rule.

void for lack of domiciliary jurisdiction. This fact involves no practical inconvenience until one of the parties remarries. Then, since this marriage is technically bigamous, the parties are not " husband " and " wife " of each other and their children are illegitimate. Clause (f) undertakes to remedy this situation so far as this will is concerned. The last sentence of Sub-clause (2) is necessary because *I. R. C.* § *811* (*f*), as amended in 1942, does not treat such quasi-spouses as " spouses," even though it treats illegitimate children the same as legitimates.

If a Testator is personally opposed to divorce and therefore questions this Clause, it should be pointed out to him that, if he does not have such a clause applicable to issue, he is penalizing the innocent children of the second marriage, not the parents whose conduct he disapproves.

Clause (*g*). Adoption statutes make the adopted child the heir of his adopting parent, but do not usually make him a " child " or " issue " of the adopting parent as a matter of the construction of wills of third persons. This clause performs that function. *Cf. Mass. Gen. Laws, Ch. 210,* § *8.*

Clause (*j*). Under an extraordinary and indefensible common-law doctrine, one who purchased from a fiduciary was liable if the fiduciary did not properly apply the purchase money to the trust purposes. *3 Scott on Trusts* § *321.* Clause (j) removes this liability and thereby facilitates the sale of trust property. This clause further facilitates transactions of the executor and trustee by not requiring persons dealing with them to examine the will and get an opinion of counsel as to whether the trustee is authorized to engage in the particular transaction.

Clause (*k*). This is the " common disaster " clause. Its purpose is to eliminate the litigable questions which arise when two or more members of a family are killed in the same accident. One type of " common disaster " clause in common use reads: ". . . if A predeceases me or if we die under such circumstances that it is difficult or impossible to determine which survived the other." This is not recommended; it does not prevent a claimant from litigating the question whether he can prove who survived. How can proof be declared " difficult " or " impossible " until it has been attempted? But watch out for a 30-day provision, as in Clause (k), in New York and any other jurisdiction which does not have a stated number of years, e.g. 21, in its period of perpetuities; you must be sure that there are no gifts to persons unborn at Testator's death which are contingent upon the taker living through that 30-day period. For example, the gift in Paragraph VII (f) (2) (ii) to Gertrude's issue who survive Testator's wife would be void in New York, where the perpetuities statute, as construed, requires that all gifts vest and trusts terminate within two lives in being at the Testator's death;

(m) A power of sale given to any beneficiary of this will over the age of 21 may be exercised, and any assent, request or recommendation required of any such beneficiary may be given, by a guardian, conservator, committee or other like official.

(n) The terms " spouse," " husband " and " wife " as used herein shall be construed to include the meanings " widow " and " widower " where the context permits.

(o) In designating clauses in this will the letters " i " and " l " are skipped to avoid confusion with typewritten numerals.

X

My executor shall pay out of the residue of my estate as an expense of administration all estate taxes, inheritance taxes and other death taxes of any nature which may be imposed upon or with respect to the following:

(a) Any devise, legacy or appointment made in this will, including the forgiveness of indebtedness in Paragraph VI;

(b) Any real or personal property which at my death my said wife and I may own in any form of co-ownership;

(c) Any life insurance upon my life which may be payable to my said wife;

(d) Any gifts which I have made or may make during my life to my said wife.

the issue of Gertrude who might survive the Testator's wife might be persons not born when Testator died, and their interests will not vest until 30 days after the wife dies. The protective proviso is therefore vital.

Clause (m). A considerable proportion of people are *non compos* during the last years of their lives, and some are afflicted earlier. It is necessary to make provision for this eventuality by permitting powers of sale to be exercised and assents given by guardians so that desirable flexibility in the estate is not lost. In this particular will the provisions which, apart from Clause (m), might be rendered nugatory by a case of insanity are the power of sale of the New Hampshire property (Par. III), the power to assent to retention of Parsons & Eldridge stock beyond two years (Par. XI), the power of the trustee to lend to the family (Par. XII(d)), and requests and recommendations as to fiduciaries (Par. XV). Note that Clause (m) carefully avoids using the horrid word "insanity" or any synonym therefor.

Paragraph X

Death taxes, federal and state, are so large an item in any substantial estate that the testator should give the most careful consideration to determining what funds are to bear this burden. The " gross estate " for federal tax purposes may include much property which the testator does not own at his death — life insurance, certain trusts he has created during his lifetime, gifts which are found to have been made in contemplation of death, etc. Certain statutes deal with the apportionment of taxes between residuary legatees, other legatees, beneficiaries of inter vivos trusts, beneficiaries of insurance policies, and the like. *I. R. C. § 826; N. Y. D. E. L. § 124; Mass. Gen. Laws, Ch. 65A, § 5.* Some, at least, of these are " challenging studies in ambiguity." See *Paul, Federal Estate and Gift Taxation, § 13.54.* In each case it is desirable to examine the particular testator's problem and work out a practical solution as to how much the residue of his estate should bear. In some estates it will be desirable for each devise and legacy, each insurance beneficiary and each inter vivos donee to pay the tax on the benefit accruing to him at the testator's death. In other estates, it will appear desirable to pay all taxes of all types out of the residue. Paragraph X is an intermediate solution tailored to the circumstances of this particular testator. The important thing is that the problem be considered and solved by the testator rather than left to litigation after his death.

XI

Notwithstanding any power to retain investments given to my executor or trustee, I direct that such shares of Parsons & Eldridge, Inc. (or any successor or other corporation engaged in the same general enterprise now being conducted by Parsons & Eldridge, Inc.) as I shall own at the time of my death shall be sold within two years, unless such of my wife and children who for the time being are living and over the age of 21 shall assent in writing to further delay or delays in selling the same. Such sale may be made either by my executor or by my trustee and no decree authorizing such sale shall be required.

XII

I give to my trustee the following powers, in addition to and not in limitation of its common-law and statutory powers:

(a) Except as provided in Paragraph XI hereof, to retain any property, real or personal, which it may receive as trustee, even though such property (by reason of its character, amount, proportion to the total trust estate, or otherwise) would not be considered appropriate for a fiduciary apart from this provision.

(b) To sell, exchange, give options upon, partition or otherwise dispose of any property which it may hold from time to time, at public or private sale or otherwise, for cash or other consideration or on credit, and upon such terms and for such consideration as it shall think fit, and to transfer and convey the same free of all trust.

(c) To invest and reinvest the trust estate from time to time in any property, real or personal, including (without limiting the generality of the foregoing language) securities of domestic and foreign corporations and investment trusts, bonds, preferred stocks, common stocks, mortgages, mortgage participations, even though such investment (by reason of its character, amount, proportion to the total trust estate, or otherwise) would not be considered appropriate for a fiduciary apart from this provision, and even though such investment causes a greater proportion of the total

Paragraph XI

This direction meets a peculiar danger inherent in Testator's ownership of a large block of stock of a small corporation in which the element of safety during Testator's lifetime is his personal and intimate knowledge of what is going on inside the company.

Note that unanimous consent of the adult family is required for waiver of the direction to sell within two years. The history of the United Nations illustrates the power which a requirement of unanimity gives to a single obstructive member. A Testator should be warned that he should carefully weigh the consequences of such a requirement before imposing it. Still, within a family, one should be able to count upon something more than the Muscovite brand of reasonableness and cooperation.

Paragraph XII

In drafting powers for a trustee it should be realized that these powers perform three functions. First, they give to the trustee additional discretion beyond that permitted to any trustee by law. Second, they facilitate transactions with third persons by making express provision for some types of discretion which the trustee would probably have anyway but which might involve an element of doubt sufficient to impede transactions, at least to the extent of requiring an opinion of counsel. Third, they obviate the necessity of the trustee obtaining court instructions or authorizations for various administrative acts (e.g. compromising claims).

Clauses (a), (b) and (c) greatly expand the field of investment that is open to the trustee and the types of transactions by which he can make or manage investments. Such clauses give flexibility to the investment scheme. Expressed in general terms, such clauses reduce the degree of caution in investments which would otherwise be required of a trustee, without reducing the requirements of care and skill. See *2 Scott on Trusts*, §§ *227.1–227.3* and § *227.14*. Most testators, after discussion, decide that it is wise to pick a trustee they feel they can trust and then give him powers which will let him exercise his own judgment fully. Failure to give broad powers to the trustee tends to drive him, for his own protection, into ultra-conservative investments. Incidentally, ultra-conservative investments are not necessarily safe. First mortgages can suffer heavily from a sustained drop in the real estate market. Government bonds can lose much of their real value through inflation.

trust estate to be invested in investments of one type or of one company than would be considered appropriate for a fiduciary apart from this provision.

(d) To make loans, secured or unsecured, in such amounts, upon such terms, at such rates of interest, and to such persons, firms or corporations as it shall think fit. Specifically, I empower my trustee to make unsecured loans to any of my issue or their spouses at any interest rate or without interest, if such loans and the terms thereof are assented to in writing by such of my wife and issue over the age of 21 as shall be living at the time of any such loan.

(e) To acquire property returning no income or slight income and/or retain any such property so long as it thinks fit without the same being in any way chargeable with income or the proceeds thereof in case of sale being in any part deemed income. However, my trustee may in its discretion pay out of principal to any income beneficiary such amount as in its judgment is reasonable compensation for losses of income due to the acquisition and/or retention of property returning no income or slight income.

(f) To improve any real estate comprised in the trust estate, including power to demolish any buildings in whole or in part and to erect buildings; to lease real estate on such terms as it thinks fit, including power to give leases for periods that may extend beyond the duration of the trust; to foreclose, extend, assign, partially release, and discharge mortgages.

(g) To borrow money, to execute promissory notes therefor, and to secure said obligations by mortgage or pledge of any of the trust estate.

(h) To renew or compromise, upon such terms as it thinks fit, any claims, including taxes, either in favor of or against the trust property or itself as trustee; to pay claims upon such evidence as it thinks sufficient.

(j) To employ such brokers, banks, custodians, investment counsel, attorneys, and other agents, and to delegate to them such of the duties, rights and powers of the trustee (including, among others, rights to vote on shares of stock held by the trustee) for such periods as it thinks fit. If there

Clause (d). Loaning money may be the best way to use it where money is tight and interest rates high. For example, extremely high interest rates were available for " call " money during the stock boom of the 1920's.

The second sentence of this clause is a means of giving to Testator's family a limited access to principal and, at the same time, being sure that any use of principal is charged up against the share of the user.

Clause (e). In the absence of this type of provision the trustee cannot properly retain or acquire unproductive property; and if he should do so the income beneficiary is entitled to a share of any proceeds of sale. *2 Scott on Trusts* §§ *240, 241.1*. It may well happen that, due to the state of the market for the property concerned, a forced sale would be unwise. The purpose of this Clause is to give the trustee desirable freedom of action and make it possible for the trustee to see that the income beneficiaries are not harmed thereby.

Clause (f). It is clear that a trustee, apart from such a clause, could not do many of the things here permitted.

Clause (g). Where a need for cash arises, e.g. to meet a tax payment larger than anticipated, a loan may be wiser than a forced liquidation of assets. The trustee should have power to hypothecate assets of the estate for this and other similar purposes.

Clause (h). Without this clause a trustee might have to apply for leave to compromise where a settlement is being made; and in self-protection he might feel he would have to insist on being sued upon some claims which a person conducting his own business would pay without action. It is not to the interest of the estate to require either of these things to be done.

Clause (j). In the absence of this clause the trustee's employment of agents of various types is subject to attack on the ground that it is an improper delegation. *2 Scott on Trusts* §§ *171–171.4*. Delegation as between co-trustees is a practical necessity. The last sentence is desirable because many corporate and other trustees find it convenient to carry securities in the name of a nominee (usually a brokerage firm). See *2 Scott on Trusts* § *179.5*. A number of statutes specifically authorize the use of such nominees but, even in a state which has such a statute, the clause should be included in the will to take care of various problems of conflict of laws.

shall be more than one trustee at any time, any trustee may delegate any of its powers to any co-trustee for such period as such trustee thinks fit. The trustee may keep any of the trust estate in the name of a nominee without mention of the trust in any instrument of ownership.

(k) To participate in any merger, reorganization or consolidation affecting the trust estate, and in connection therewith to take any action which it could take if it owned in its individual capacity the securities concerned.

(m) To hold, manage, invest and account for the several shares which may be held in trust, either as separate funds or as a single fund, as it thinks fit; if as a single fund, making the division thereof only upon its books of account and allocating to each share its proportionate part of the principal and income of the common fund and charging against each share its proportionate part of the common expenses.

(n) To keep any or all of the trust property at any place or places in Massachusetts or elsewhere in the United States or abroad, or with a depositary or custodian at such place or places.

(o) To determine, as to all sums of money and other things of value received by it, whether and to what extent the same shall be deemed to be principal or to be income, and as to all charges or expenses paid by it, whether and to what extent the same shall be charged against principal or against income, including, without hereby limiting the generality of the foregoing language, power to apportion any receipt or expense between principal and income and to determine what part, if any, of the actual income received upon any wasting investment or upon any security purchased or acquired at a premium shall be retained and added to principal to prevent a diminution of principal upon exhaustion or maturity thereof.

Clause (k). Without this clause the right of a trustee to deposit shares with a protective committee and to make exchanges for purposes of merger and reorganization might be questioned. *2 Scott on Trusts* §§ *193.4, 231.4.*

Clause (m). Where, on the death of the life tenant, there are several small trusts being held for children it is often better for all concerned that the several trusts be treated as shares in a single fund.

Clause (n). In the ordinary transaction of business this may prove to be a convenient provision. It might be very important if bombs started falling on the eastern seaboard. Carol of Rumania was not the first to discover that investment overseas may be sound diversification.

Clause (o). The rules determining which receipts are principal and which income, and which expenses are chargeable against principal and which against income are fruitful in litigable controversies. *2 Scott on Trusts* §§ *233–233.5*. There is a *Uniform Principal and Income Act* (not adopted in Massachusetts) which seeks to straighten out some of these difficulties. But a testamentary provision like Clause (o) is the most workable solution.

The problem as to securities purchased at a premium is illustrated by the following case. In 1947 the trustee purchases for $1,100 (i.e. at a premium of $100) a 5% corporate bond which will be payable at par in 1957. The coupon on this bond is $50 annually. But the true income is less, since the bond, for which $1,100 was paid, will bring in only $1,000 ten years from its date of purchase. Therefore, out of the annual return of $50, there must be withdrawn enough to restore in ten years the principal loss of $100. Thus, in each year, $10 will be allocated to principal and $40 to income. *2 Scott on Trusts* § *239.2*. Clause (o) permits the trustee to amortize these premiums or not, at its discretion.

Mines, oil wells and quarries are other typical wasting investments, and these involve very serious problems of accounting between life tenant and remaindermen. *2 Scott on Trusts* § *239.3*. If it is expected that any substantial property of this type will be found in an estate the testator should give detailed specific consideration to it — as our Testator gave particular attention, on other grounds, to the Parsons & Eldridge stock in his estate. But for property of this type which casually turns up in an estate Clause (o) is satisfactory.

Note that Clause (o) is a power of appointment in a small way — that is, it permits the trustee to cause something to go to the life tenant that would, without the trustee's exercise of this power, go to the remaindermen, or vice versa. The same is true of other trust powers — for example, Clause (e). These "fringe" powers of appointment may prove troublesome. If they last longer than the period of perpetuities they may be void from the outset. Leach, *Perpetuities*

(p) In dividing the trust estate into shares or in distributing the same, to divide or distribute in cash, in kind, or partly in cash and partly in kind, as it thinks fit. For purposes of division or distribution, to value the trust estate and any part thereof, reasonably and in good faith, and such valuation shall be conclusive upon all parties. To whatever extent division or distribution is made in kind my trustee shall, so far as it finds practicable, allocate to the respective beneficiaries approximately proportionate amounts of each kind of security or other property in the trust estate.

As to each trust created herein or hereunder the foregoing powers shall exist for the term of that trust only. After the termination of any trust and until such time as all of the assets of such trust have been distributed my trustee shall have additional powers identical to the foregoing. All of the powers and discretions herein given to my trustee may be exercised by it without application to any court.

XIII

I give to my executor, in addition to and not in limitation of its common-law and statutory powers, all of the powers and discretions given to my trustee in Paragraph XII hereof. All such powers and discretions may be exercised without application to any court.

XIV

No executor or trustee shall be liable for the acts, omissions or defaults of any agent appointed with due care or of any co-executor or co-trustee. No executor or trustee shall be liable for failure to contest the accounts of any executor or trustee, or otherwise to compel any executor or trustee to redress a breach of trust, unless in writing requested so to contest or compel redress by a devisee, legatee, beneficiary, or a guardian or guardian *ad litem* thereof.

in a Nutshell, 51 HARV. L. REV. 638, 652 (1938). If such a power is held by a trustee who has an interest in the estate, this may have the consequence of bringing the whole trust estate into such trustee's "gross estate" for tax purposes under *I. R. C. § 811 (f)*. See *Paul, Federal Estate and Gift Taxation (1946 Supp.) § 9.30 et seq.* So far as these powers permit the trustee to treat as principal what would otherwise be income, they provide for an accumulation — and this may run afoul of statutes on that subject. See *Leach, Cas. Fut. Int., Ch. XX, Sec. 2.*

Clause (p) gets rid of a knot of problems discussed in *3 Scott on Trusts §§ 347 et. seq.* Note that *N. Y. D. E. L. § 125* invalidates any provision that an executor or trustee shall have power to make a "binding and conclusive fixation of the value of any asset. . . ."

The *final provisions* as to the duration of powers look like mumbo-jumbo but are a wise precaution. It is possible that, either because some of the trust powers are like powers of appointment or because of an unwise rule of law, the Rule against Perpetuities will be held to strike down powers which may last beyond the period of perpetuities. Powers may last beyond the period of perpetuities for two reasons: either because the particular trust lasts beyond that period, or because the powers are so given that they last beyond the life of the trust during the cleanup period when the trustee is making final distribution and getting his accounts allowed. The important thing to do is to create various sets of powers — one for each trust and one for each final clean-up period — so that, if one set is held void in whole or in part, this will not affect the validity of the other sets. Note that the trusts directly created in the present will all terminate at the end of lives now in being; but powers of appointment are given which may be exercised in such a way as to create trusts under this will far exceeding the period of perpetuities; and, of course, the clean-up periods may be of considerable duration if litigation develops. On this, see Leach, *Powers of Sale in Trustees and the Rule Against Perpetuities*, 47 HARV. L. REV. 948, 975 (1934).

Paragraph XIII

The basic differences between an executor and a trustee are such that it should not be assumed that powers given to a trustee are also appropriate or sufficient for an executor. However, an examination of the powers given in Paragraph XII indicates that they are also the powers which the executor of this estate needs.

Paragraph XIV

The first sentence eliminates a type of fiduciary liability which seems basically unfair. See *2 Scott on Trusts §§ 224–225.2*.

The second sentence is designed primarily for the benefit of the estate, not of the fiduciaries. In the absence of such a provision a trustee may feel that, for his own self-protection, he must contest the account of an executor or a predecessor trustee, appealing the

XV

(a) I am now providing financial assistance to the widow and daughter of my deceased son, Sheldon, and expect to continue to do so for some time. If, at my death, these persons are still in need of help and I am in a position to give it, it is important that this help should not be interrupted during the administration of my estate; and this Clause of my will is designed to prevent such interruption. I therefore bequeath to said Della Langhorn Thomas, if she is living, or to said Gertrude Thomas, or her guardian, if said Della is not living and said Gertrude is living, One Hundred and Fifty Dollars ($150) per month commencing with the date of my death, subject to the following:

(1) Said monthly amounts shall be increased, decreased, stopped, or resumed, as my wife may from time to time direct in writing addressed to my executor, but in no event shall such amount exceed Two Hundred and Fifty Dollars ($250) for any month.

(2) I request my executor to pay these amounts in the months in which they accrue. If my executor shall fail to make payment in the month when any such amount accrues hereunder, interest at six per cent (6%) shall run upon the amount accruing.

case to the court of last resort; and such litigation is often wasteful. The provision permitting any interested party to request a contest is adequate protection in cases where substantial breaches of fiduciary duty have occurred. See *2 Scott on Trusts* §§ *223–223.3*

Here is the place where, if at all, a clause is to be added relieving the executor and trustee from other liabilities. Many wills contain a provision that "no executor or trustee shall be liable except for actual fraud" or "— willful malfeasance or default." If the fiduciary is a member of testator's family, there is substantial justification for such a clause; testator knows the person he is appointing, is familiar with the degree of care and skill to be expected of him, and perhaps should eliminate those possibilities of family turmoil which might arise from claims of negligence in fiduciary administration. But in the case of a corporate fiduciary this particular justification is certainly lacking. Does the trust company wish to take the position that its officers may be negligent but that, if they are, the loss should fall on the beneficiaries of the trust and not on the trust company? Safety is a principal reason for having a corporate fiduciary, and a broad exculpatory clause seriously reduces this factor. Many corporate fiduciaries discourage exculpatory clauses for reasons of public relations. In some states they are forbidden by law. *N. Y. D. E. L.* § *125.*

Paragraph XV

If Testator's assets were distributed the day after his death this Paragraph would be unnecessary. But the administration of his estate is bound to take a year to two years, and various provisions must be made in the light of that fact.

Clause (a). It is plain that Della and Gertrude cannot exist in a state of suspended animation until the Testator's estate has been administered. They need (or may need) a constant flow of the kind of help Testator is now giving them. On the other hand, the executor cannot be absolutely safe in paying out money to legatees until he is sure there is going to be a net estate after debts and taxes are paid. One way to handle this situation would be to create a revocable *inter vivos* trust to take care of the payments to Della and Gertrude both before and after Testator's death. Such a trust would continue after his death without interruption. But for such a small project an *inter vivos* trust is too cumbersome. Clause (a) attempts to induce the executor to run the risk of making payments. If this fails, it creates a situation in which it should be easy for Della and Gertrude to get loans by assigning their rights against the executor. Of course, the Clause should tie into Paragraph VII(d) so that the latter takes over wher the former leaves off.

(3) Said Della or said Gertrude may, as each amount accrues hereunder, assign the right to receive such amount. (It is my hope that, if my executor is unable or unwilling to preserve the continuity of payments to Della and Gertrude, the members of my family will provide such continuity by purchasing such assignments at their face value.)

(4) No amounts shall accrue after both of the following have happened:

(i) Said Della has married or died;

(ii) Said Gertrude has married, reached the age of 25, or died.

(5) No amounts shall accrue after any one of the following has happened:

(i) My executor has made a distribution to my trustee sufficient to permit my trustee to comply with the provisions of Paragraph VII(d). My executor's determination as to whether sufficient distribution has been made shall be conclusive.

(ii) Any payment has been made under Paragraph VII(f)(2).

(iii) Any payment has been made under Paragraph VIII(b).

(b) Except as herein otherwise provided persons to whom specific devises, legacies or appointments are made shall receive income earned after the date of my death by the property devised, bequeathed or appointed, and persons to whom pecuniary legacies or appointments are made shall receive interest thereon commencing with the date of my death.

(c) Net income earned, during administration, upon my estate or upon property appointed by me (except income earned on property specifically given or appointed) shall become part of the residue of my estate. My trustee shall treat such income as income of the trust.

XVI

(a) I nominate as executor of this will Francis Embree of Belmont, Massachusetts. I request that no sureties on

Clause (b). In Massachusetts pecuniary legacies, with some exceptions, bear interest from one year after testator's death; income accruing at any time after testator's death upon property specifically devised or bequeathed passes to the specific devisee or legatee. *Newhall, Settlement of Estates in Massachusetts (3d ed. 1937)* §§ *203, 301*. Differing rules on these matters will make no sense to the testator or beneficiaries. Therefore, a provision such as Clause (b) promotes uniformity and simplicity.

Clause (c). Where property which is ultimately used to pay debts, taxes, administration expense and pecuniary legacies, earns income during the course of administration, there are conflicting rules as to whether such income constitutes principal or income of the residuary trust when established. See *2 Scott on Trusts* § *234.4*. Clause (c) disposes of this difficulty by a method which is simple but which, in large estates, will cause a very heavy payment of income to the life beneficiary at the outset. Other possible methods are discussed in *Scott*, and still others will readily occur to the practitioner, once the existence of the problem is observed.

Paragraph XVI

In the selection of an executor and a trustee different considerations are relevant. An executor performs a relatively short-term

his bond as executor be required unless my wife or some one of my issue over the age of 21 shall, either at my death or at any later time, request that he give bond with sureties. If said Francis Embree predeceases me, I nominate as executor of this will City Trust Company, of Cambridge, Massachusetts.

(b) I nominate as trustee under this will City Trust Company, of Cambridge, Massachusetts.

(c) If City Trust Company should decline or cease to serve either as executor or as trustee, I request that the court appoint in its place such corporate fiduciary as shall be recommended by such of my wife and issue as shall then be living and over the age of 21.

(d) I request my executor and trustee to consult with my son, Samuel Arthur Thomas, as to all matters of general policy pertaining to my estate and the trusts thereunder.

IN WITNESS WHEREOF I, the said Joseph Albert Thomas, herewith set my hand to this my last will, typewritten on twelve (12) sheets of paper (including the attestation clause and signatures of witnesses) upon the margin of each one of which I have also written my name, this twenty-eighth day of May, nineteen hundred and forty-seven.

JOSEPH ALBERT THOMAS

On the twenty-eighth day of May, nineteen hundred and forty-seven, Joseph Albert Thomas declared to us, the undersigned, that the foregoing instrument, was his last will, and he requested us to act as witnesses to the same and to his signature thereon. He thereupon signed said will in our presence, we being present at the same time. And we now, at his request, in his presence, and in the presence of each other do hereunto subscribe our names as witnesses. And we and each of us declare that we believe this testator to be of sound mind and memory.

FREDERICK T. CURTIS,
15 Lincoln St., Concord, Mass.
ARTHUR F. BENDER,
38 Pine St., Boston, Mass.
EARL A. MURPHY,
87 Naples Rd., Brookline, Mass.

function of liquidation and distribution; an important factor is knowledge of the testator's affairs and family. A trustee performs a relatively long-term function of investment and administration; a controlling factor is skill and experience in the handling of large income-bearing estates.

Embree is a good choice here as executor. He has worked with Testator, and knows about his finances and his family. Professional help — chiefly in probate court proceedings and tax matters — can be provided by lawyers who also start with a knowledge of testator's background. An arrangement in advance can be made by Testator and his family with Embree as to Embree's compensation as executor. Even without such an arrangement some economy will usually result from the employment of an individual executor, familiar with the estate, and selected counsel.

The question of a bond should not be tossed off lightly. A bond with sureties is an inconvenience and some expense; but there have been tragic cases of defalcation. The provision of Clause (a) is a good compromise in this case, particularly when coupled with Clause (d) which gives to the most substantial member of the family constant access to the affairs of the estate. Of course, no bond is required of a corporate fiduciary.

APPENDIX I.

SELECTED STATUTES ON WILLS, INTESTACY AND ADMINISTRATION.

In this Appendix are set forth (A) certain excerpts from the basic English statutes upon which the American law of wills has been constructed, and (B) a number of sections from the New York Decedent Estate Law which indicate the trend of present-day legislation. All students should become generally familiar with the volume of Michigan Legal Studies entitled Simes and Basye, Model Probate Code (1946). This volume contains, not only the Code which may set the pattern for two decades of legislation, but also exhaustive analytical studies of existing state legislation of the greatest practical help to lawyers working in the probate field.

A. ENGLAND.

THE STATUTE OF WILLS, 32 Henry VIII, c. 1 (1540) . . . all and every person and persons, having, or which hereafter shall have, any manors, lands, tenements or hereditaments, . . . shall have full and free liberty, power and authority to give, dispose, will and devise, as well by his last will and testament in writing, or otherwise by any act or acts lawfully executed in his life, all his said manors, lands, tenements or hereditaments, or any of them, at his free will and pleasure; . . .

THE STATUTE OF FRAUDS, 29 Car. II, c. 3 (1677). V. . . . all devises and bequests of any lands or tenements, devisable either by force of the Statute of Wills, or by this Statute, or by force of the custom of Kent, or the custom of any borough, or any other particular custom, shall be in writing, and signed by the party so devising the same, or by some other person in his presence and by his express directions, and shall be attested and subscribed in the presence of the said devisor by three or four credible witnesses, or else they shall be utterly void and of none effect.

VI. And moreover, no devise in writing of lands, tenements or hereditaments, nor any clause thereof, shall . . . be revocable, otherwise than by some other will or codicil in writing, or other writing declaring the same, or by burning, cancelling, tearing or obliterating the same by the testator himself, or in his presence and by his direction and consent; . . .

STAT. 25 Geo. II, c. 6 (1752). . . . if any person shall attest the execution of any will or codicil . . . to whom any beneficial devise, legacy, estate, interest, gift or appointment of or affecting any real or personal estate, other than and except charges on lands, tenements or hereditaments for payment of any debt or debts, shall be thereby given or made, such devise, legacy, estate, interest, gift or appointment, shall, so far only as concerns such person attesting the execution of such will or codicil, or any person claiming under him, be utterly null and void; and such person shall be admitted as a witness to the execution of such will or codicil, within the intent of the said Act; notwithstanding such devise, legacy, estate, interest, gift or appointment mentioned in such will or codicil.

THE WILLS ACT, Stat. 7 W. IV & 1 Vict. c 26 (1837) . . . IX. . . . no will shall be valid unless it shall be in writing and executed in manner hereinafter mentioned; (that is to say), it shall be signed at the foot or end thereof by the testator, or by some other person in his presence and by his direction; and such signature shall be made or acknowledged by the testator in the presence of two or more witnesses present at the same time, and such witnesses shall attest and shall subscribe the will in the presence of the testator, but no form of attestation shall be necessary.

XIV. And be it further enacted, that if any person who shall attest the execution of a will shall at the time of the execution thereof, or at any time afterwards, be incompetent to be admitted a witness to prove the execution thereof, such will shall not on that account be invalid.

XV. And be it further enacted, that if any person shall attest the execution of any will to whom or to whose wife or husband any beneficial devise, legacy, estate, interest, gift, or appointment, of or affecting any real or personal estate (other than and except charges and directions for the payment of any debt or debts), shall be thereby given or made, such devise, legacy, estate, interest, gift, or appointment shall, so far only as concerns such person attesting the execution of such will, or the wife or husband of such person, or any person claiming under such person or wife or husband, be utterly null and void, and such person so attesting shall be admitted as a witness to prove the execution of such will, or to prove the validity or invalidity thereof, notwithstanding such devise, legacy, estate, interest, gift, or appointment mentioned in such will.

XVII. And be it further enacted, that no person shall, on account of his being an executor of a will, be incompetent to be admitted a witness to prove the execution of such will, or a witness to prove the validity or invalidity thereof.

XVIII. And be it further enacted, that every will made by a man or woman shall be revoked by his or her marriage (except a will made in exercise of a power of appointment, when the real or personal estate thereby appointed would not in default of such appointment pass to his or her heir, customary heir, executor, or administrator, or the person entitled as his or her next of kin, under the Statute of Distribution).

XIX. And be it further enacted, that no will shall be revoked by any presumption of an intention on the ground of an alteration in circumstances.

XX. And be it further enacted, that no will or codicil, or any part thereof, shall be revoked otherwise than as aforesaid, or by another will or codicil executed in manner hereinbefore required, or by some writing declaring an intention to revoke the same, and executed in the manner in which a will is hereinbefore required to be executed, or by the burning, tearing, or otherwise destroying the same by the testator, or by some person in his presence and by his direction, with the intention of revoking the same.

XXI. And be it further enacted, that no obliteration, interlineation, or other alteration made in any will after the execution thereof shall be valid or have any effect, except so far as the words or effect of the will before such alteration shall not be apparent, unless such alteration shall be executed in like manner as hereinbefore is required for the execution of the will; but the will, with such alteration as part thereof, shall be deemed to be duly executed if the signature of the testator and the subscription of the witnesses be made in the margin or on some other part of the will opposite or near to such alteration, or at the foot or end of or opposite to a memorandum referring to such alteration, and written at the end or some other part of the will.

XXII. And be it further enacted, that no will or codicil, or any part thereof, which shall be in any manner revoked, shall be revived otherwise than by the re-execution thereof, or by a codicil executed in manner hereinbefore required, and showing an intention to revive the same; and when any will or codicil which shall be partly revoked, and afterwards wholly revoked, shall be revived, such revival shall not extend to so much thereof as shall have been revoked before the revocation of the whole thereof, unless an intention to the contrary shall be shown.

XXIII. And be it further enacted, that no conveyance or other Act made or done subsequently to the execution of a will or of relating to any real or personal estate therein comprised, except an Act by which such will shall be revoked as aforesaid, shall prevent the operation of the will with respect to such estate or interest in such real or personal estate as the testator shall have power to dispose of by will at the time of his death.

XXIV. And be it further enacted, that every will shall be construed, with reference to the real estate and personal estate comprised in it, to speak and take effect as if it had been executed immediately before the death of the testator, unless a contrary intention shall appear by the will.

B. NEW YORK.

DECEDENT ESTATE LAW (as amended through 1946).

§ 17. *Devise or bequest to certain societies, associations, corporations or purposes*

No person having a husband, wife, child, or descendant or parent, shall, by his or her last will and testament, devise or bequeath to any benevolent, charitable, literary, scientific, religious or missionary society, association, corporation or purpose, in trust or otherwise, more than one-half of his or her estate, after the payment of his or her debts, and such devise or bequest shall be valid to the extent of one-half, and no more. The validity of a devise or bequest for more than such one-half may be contested only by a surviving husband, wife, child, descendant or parent. . . .

§ 18. *Election by surviving spouse against or in absence of testamentary provision*

1. Where a testator dies after August thirty-first, nineteen hundred and thirty, and leaves a will thereafter executed and leaves surviving a husband or wife, a personal right of election is given to the surviving spouse to take his or her share of the estate as in intestacy, subject to the limitations, conditions and exceptions contained in this section.

(a) In exercising the right of election herein granted a surviving spouse shall in no event be entitled to take more than one-half of the net estate of the decedent, after the deduction of debts, funeral and administration expenses and any estate tax, and the words " intestate share " wherever used in this section shall in no event be construed to mean more than one-half of such net estate.

(b) Where the intestate share is over twenty-five hundred dollars and where the testator has devised or bequeathed in trust an amount equal to or greater than the intestate share, with income thereof payable to the surviving spouse for life, the surviving spouse shall have the limited right to elect to take the sum of twenty-five hundred dollars absolutely which shall be deducted from the principal of such trust fund and the terms of the will shall otherwise remain effective.

(c) Where the intestate share of the surviving spouse in the estate does not exceed twenty-five hundred dollars, the surviving spouse shall have such right to elect to take his or her intestate share absolutely, which shall be in lieu of any provision for his or her benefit in the will.

(d) Where the will contains an absolute legacy or devise, whether general or specific, to the surviving spouse, of or in excess of the sum of twenty-five hundred dollars and also a provision for a trust for his or her benefit for life of a principal equal to or more than the excess between said legacy or devise and his or her intestate share, no right of election whatever shall exist in the surviving spouse.

(e) Where the will contains an absolute legacy or devise, whether general or specific, to the surviving spouse in an amount less than the sum of twenty-five hundred dollars and also a provision for a trust for his or her benefit for life of a principal equal to or more than the excess between said legacy or devise and his or her intestate share, the surviving spouse shall have the limited right to elect to take not more than the sum of twenty-five hundred dollars inclusive of the amount of such legacy or devise, and the difference between such legacy or devise and the sum of twenty-five hundred dollars shall be deducted from the principal of such trust fund and the terms of the will shall otherwise remain effective.

(f) Where the aggregate of the provisions under the will for the benefit of the surviving spouse including the principal of a trust, or a legacy or devise, or any other form of testamentary provision, is less than the intestate share, the surviving spouse shall have the limited right to elect to take the difference between such aggregate and the amount of the intestate share, and the terms of the will shall otherwise remain effective. In every estate the surviving spouse shall have the limited right to withdraw the sum of twenty-five hundred dollars if the intestate share is equal to or greater than that amount. Such sum shall, however, be inclusive of any absolute legacy or devise, whether general or specific. Where a trust fund is created for his or her benefit for life, such sum of twenty-five hundred dollars or any necessary part thereof to make up that sum shall be payable from the principal of such trust fund.

(g) The provisions of this section with regard to the creation of a trust, with income payable for life to the surviving spouse, shall likewise apply to a legal life estate or to an annuity for life or any other form of income for life created by the will for the benefit of the surviving spouse. In the computation of the value of the provisions under the will the capital value of the fund or other property producing the income shall be taken and not the value of the life estate.

(h) The purported grant of authority in a will to an executor, administrator, c.t.a. or trustee, or the successor of any of them (1) to act without bond or (2) to name his successor to act without bond or (3) to sell assets of the estate upon terms fixed by him or (4) to invest the funds of the estate in other than legal investments or (5) to retain in the assets of the estate investments or property owned by a testator in his lifetime or (6) to make distribution in kind or (7) to make a binding and conclusive fixation of values of assets in the distribution thereof or (8) to allocate assets either outright or in trust for the life of a surviving spouse or (9) to conduct the affairs of the estate with partial or total exoneration from the legal responsibility of a fiduciary, shall not be deemed either singly or in the aggregate to give to a surviving spouse an absolute right of election to take his or her intestate share; but the surrogate's court having jurisdiction of the estate, notwithstanding the terms of the will, shall have power in an appropriate proceeding by the surviving spouse or upon an accounting to direct and enforce for the protection of the surviving spouse an equitable distribution, allocation or valuation of the assets, and to enforce the lawful liability of a fiduciary, and shall have power also to make such other direction consistent with the provisions and purposes of this section as the court may deem necessary for the protection of the surviving spouse.

2. Where any such election shall have been made, the will shall be valid as to the residue remaining after the elective share provided in this section has been deducted and the terms of the will shall as far as possible remain effective.

3. The right of election shall not be available to a spouse against whom or in whose favor a final decree or judgment of divorce recognized as valid by the law of the state has been rendered, or against whom a final decree or judgment of separation recognized as valid by the laws of this state has been rendered. Nor shall such right of election be available to a spouse who has procured without the state of New York a final decree or judgment dissolving the marriage with the testator where such a decree or judgment is not recognized as valid by the law of this state.

4. No husband who has neglected or refused to provide for his wife, or has abandoned her, shall have the right of such an election.

5. No wife who has abandoned her husband shall have the right of such an election.

6. The election as herein provided may be made by the general guardian of an infant, when authorized so to do by the surrogate having jurisdiction of the decedent's estate, or may be made in behalf of an incompetent when authorized by the supreme court.

7. An election made under this section shall be in lieu of any right of dower, and must be made within six months from the date of the issuance of letters testamentary or if letters testamentary have not been issued from the date of the issuance of letters of administration with the will annexed, and shall be made by serving written notice of such election upon the representative of the estate personally or in such other manner as the surrogate may direct and by filing and recording a copy of such notice with proof of service in the surrogate's court where such will was probated. The time to make such election may be enlarged before its expiration by an order of the surrogate's court where such will was probated, for a further period of not exceeding six months upon any one application. If a spouse shall default in filing such election within six months after the date of issuance of such letters, such surrogate's

court may relieve the spouse from such default and authorize the making of such election within a period to be fixed by order, provided no decree settling the account of the fiduciary has been made and provided further that twelve months have not elapsed since the issuance of letters. . . .

9. The husband or wife during the lifetime of the other may waive the right of election to take against a particular last will and testament by an instrument subscribed and duly acknowledged, or may waive such right of election to take against any last will and testament of the other whatsoever in an agreement so executed, made before or after marriage. An agreement so executed made before the taking effect of this section wherein a spouse has waived or released all rights in the estate of the other spouse shall be deemed to release the right of election granted in this section.

§ 21. *Manner of execution of will*

Every last will and testament of real or personal property, or both, shall be executed and attested in the following manner:

1. It shall be subscribed by the testator at the end of the will.
2. Such subscription shall be made by the testator in the presence of each of the attesting witnesses, or shall be acknowledged by him, to have been so made, to each of the attesting witnesses.
3. The testator, at the time of making such subscription, or at the time of acknowledging the same, shall declare the instrument so subscribed, to be his last will and testament.
4. There shall be at least two attesting witnesses, each of whom shall sign his name as a witness, at the end of the will, at the request of the testator.

§ 22. *Witnesses to will to write names and places of residence*

The witnesses to any will, shall write opposite to their names their respective places of residence; and every person who shall sign the testator's name to any will by his direction, shall write his own name as a witness to the will. Whoever shall neglect to comply with either of these provisions, shall forfeit fifty dollars, to be recovered by any person interested in the property devised or bequeathed, who will sue for the same. Such omission shall not affect the validity of any will; nor shall any person liable to the penalty aforesaid, be excused or incapacitated on that account, from testifying respecting the execution of such will.

§ 22-a. *Validity of wills executed without the state*

A will executed without this state in the mode prescribed by the law, either of the place where executed or of the testator's domicile, shall be deemed to be legally executed, and shall be of the same force and effect as if executed in the mode described by the laws of this state, provided, such will is in writing and subscribed by the testator.

§ 23. *What wills may be proved*

A will of real or personal property, executed as prescribed by the laws of the state, or a will of real or personal property executed without the state in the mode prescribed by the law, either of the place where executed or of the testator's domicile, provided such will is in writing and subscribed by the testator, may be admitted to probate in this state.

§ 24. *Effect of change of residence since execution of will*

The right to have a will admitted to probate, the validity of the execution thereof, or the validity or construction of any provision contained therein, is not affected by a change of the testator's residence made since the execution of the will.

§ 26. *Child born after making of will*

Whenever a testator shall have a child born after the making of a last will, either in the lifetime or after the death of such testator, and shall die leaving such child, so after-born, unprovided for by any settlement, and neither provided for, nor in any way mentioned in such will, every such child shall succeed to the same portion of such parent's real and personal estate, as would have descended or been distributed to such child, if such parent had died intestate, and shall be entitled to recover the same portion from the devisees and legatees, in proportion to and out of the parts devised and bequeathed to them by such will.

§ 27. *Devise or bequest to subscribing witness*

If any person shall be a subscribing witness to the execution of any will, wherein any beneficial devise, legacy, interest or appointment of any real or personal estate shall be made to such witness, and such will can not be proved without the testimony of such witness, the said devise, legacy, interest or appointment shall be void, so far only as concerns such witness, or any claiming under him; and such person shall be a competent witness, and compellable to testify respecting the execution of the said will, in like manner as if no such devise or bequest had been made.

But if such witness would have been entitled to any share of the testator's estate, in case the will was not established, then so much of the share that would have descended, or have been distributed to such witness, shall be saved to him, as will not exceed the value of the devise or bequest made to him in the will, and he shall recover the same of the devisees or legatees named in the will, in proportion to, and out of, the parts devised and bequeathed to them.

§ 29. *Devise or bequest to child or descendant, or to a brother or sister of the testator not to lapse*

Whenever any estate, real or personal, shall be devised or bequeathed to a child or other descendant of the testator, or to a brother or sister of the testator, and such legatee or devisee shall die during the lifetime of the testator, leaving a child or other descendant who shall survive such testator, such devise or legacy shall not lapse, but the property so devised or bequeathed shall vest in the surviving child or other descendant of the legatee or devisee, as if such legatee or devisee had survived the testator and had died intestate.

§ 30. *Reception of wills for safe keeping*

The surrogate of any county, upon being paid the fees allowed therefor by law, shall receive and deposit in his office, any last will or testament of a resident of the county in which such will is to be deposited which any person shall deliver to him for that purpose, and shall give a written receipt therefor to the person depositing the same. A subscribing witness to any last will or testament may make and sign an affidavit before any officer authorized to administer oaths setting forth such facts as he would be required to testify to in order to prove such will. Such affidavit may be written upon said will, or on some paper securely attached thereto, and may be filed for safe keeping with the last will or testament to which it relates. There may also be filed with such will, affidavits of certified medical examiners, under the provisions of the insanity law, certifying that the maker of said will was of sound mind at the time of its execution, together with any facts supporting such opinion.

§ 34. *Revocation and cancellation of written wills*

No will in writing, except in the cases hereinafter mentioned, nor any part thereof, shall be revoked, or altered, otherwise than by some other will in writing, or some other writing of the testator, declaring such revocation or alteration, and executed with the same formalities with which the will itself was required by law to be executed; or unless such will be burnt, torn, canceled, obliterated or destroyed, with the intent and for the purpose of revoking the same, by the testator himself, or by another person in his presence, by his direction and consent; and when so done by another person, the direction and consent of the testator, and the fact of such injury or destruction, shall be proved by at least two witnesses.

§ 35. *Revocation by marriage*

If after making any will, such testator marries, and the husband or wife survives the testator, such will shall be deemed revoked as to such survivor, unless provision shall have been made for such survivor by an ante nuptial agreement in writing; and such surviving husband or wife shall be entitled to the same rights in, and to the same share or portion of the estate of said testator as he or she would have been, if such will had not been made. Such husband or wife shall be entitled to such share or portion of the estate from the devisees and legatees in proportion to and out of the parts devised and bequeathed to them by such will. No evidence to rebut such presumption of revocation shall be received, except to show the existence of such ante nuptial agreement. This section as amended shall apply only to wills executed prior to September first, nineteen hundred thirty; and wills executed after such date shall not be affected in any way by the provisions of this section as heretofore contained herein or as amended.

§ 37. *Bond or agreement to convey property devised or bequeathed not a revocation*

A bond, agreement, or covenant, made for a valuable consideration, by a testator, to convey any property devised or bequeathed in any will previously made, shall not be deemed a revocation of such previous devise or bequest, either at law or in equity; but such property shall pass by the devise or bequest, subject to the same remedies on such bond, agreement or covenant, for a specific performance or otherwise, against the devisees or legatees, as might be had by law against the heirs of the testator, or his next of kin, if the same had descended to them.

§ 47. *Validity and effect of testamentary dispositions*

The validity and effect of a testamentary disposition of real property, situated within the state, or of an interest in real property so situated, which would descend to the heir of an intestate, and the manner in which such property or such an interest descends, where it is not disposed of by will, are regulated by the laws of the state, without regard to the residence of the decedent. Except where special provision is otherwise made by law, the validity and effect of a testamentary disposition of any other property situated within the state, and the ownership and disposition of such property, where it is not disposed of by will, are regulated by the laws of the state or county, of which the decedent was a resident, at the time of his death. Whenever a decedent, being a citizen of the United States or a citizen or a subject of a foreign country, wherever resident, shall have declared in his will and testament that he elects that such testamentary dispositions shall be construed and regulated by the laws of this state, the validity and effect of such dispositions shall be determined by such laws.

§ 47-b. *Testamentary directions to purchase annuities*

If a person hereafter dying shall direct in his will the purchase of an annuity, the person or persons to whom the income thereof shall be directed to be paid shall not have the right to elect to take the capital sum directed to be used for such purchase in lieu of such annuity except to the extent the will expressly provides for such right, or except to the extent that the will expressly provides that an assignable annuity be purchased. But nothing herein contained shall affect or lessen the rights of election by a surviving spouse against or in absence of testamentary provision as provided under section eighteen of this chapter.

§ 81. *Descent and distribution to same persons and in same shares*

All existing modes, rules and canons of descent are hereby abolished. The determination of the degrees of consanguinity of distributees of real and personal property shall be uniform, and shall be in accordance with the rules as applied immediately before the taking effect of this section to the determination of the next of kin of an intestate leaving personal property. All distinctions between the persons who take as heirs at law or next of kin are abolished and the descent of real property and the distribution of personal property shall be governed by this article except as otherwise specifically provided by law. Whenever in any statute the words heirs, heirs at law, next of kin, or distributees, are used, such words shall be construed to mean and include the persons entitled to take as provided by this article.

§ 85. *Advancements of real and personal estates*

If a child of an intestate shall have been advanced by him, by settlement or portion, real or personal property, the value thereof must be reckoned for the purposes of descent and distribution as part of the real and personal property of the intestate descendible and to be distributed to his distributees; and if such advancement be equal to or greater than the amount of the share which such child would be entitled to receive of the estate of the deceased, such child and his descendants shall not share in the estate of the intestate; but if it be less than such share, such child and his descendants shall receive so much, only, of the personal property, and inherit so much only, of the real property, of the intestate, as shall be sufficient to make all the shares of all the children in the whole property, including the advancement, equal. The value of any real or personal property so advanced, shall be deemed to be that, if any, which was acknowledged by the child by an instrument in writing; otherwise it must be estimated according to the worth of the property when given. Maintaining or educating a child, or giving him money without a view to a portion or settlement in life is not an advancement. An estate or interest given by a parent to a descendant by virtue of a beneficial power, or of a power in trust with a right of selection, is an advancement.

§ 86. *How advancement adjusted*

When an advancement to be adjusted consisted of real property, the adjustment must be made out of the real property descendible to the distributees. When it consisted of personal property, the adjustment must be made out of the surplus of the personal property to be distributed to the distributees. If either species of property is insufficient to enable the adjustment to be fully made, the deficiency must be adjusted out of the other.

§ 87. *Effect of divorce, abandonment, or refusal to support upon rights of former husband or wife to distributive share*

No distributive share of the estate of a decedent shall be allowed under the provisions of this article, either

(a) to a spouse against whom or in whose favor a final decree or judgment of divorce recognized as valid by the law of this state has been rendered;

(b) or to a spouse who has procured without the state of New York a final decree or judgment dissolving the marriage with the decedent, where such decree or judgment is not recognized as valid by the law of this state;

(c) or to a husband who has neglected or refused to provide for his wife, or has abandoned her;

(d) or to a wife who has abandoned her husband.

§ 124. *Apportionment of federal and state estate taxes; executor or administrator to deduct taxes from distributive shares*

1. Whenever it appears upon any accounting, or in any appropriate action or proceeding, that an executor, administrator, temporary administrator, trustee or other person acting in a fiduciary capacity, has paid a death tax levied or assessed under the provisions of article ten-c of the tax law, or under the provisions of the United States revenue act of nineteen hundred twenty-six, as amended by the United States revenue act of nineteen hundred twenty-eight, or under any death tax law of the United States hereafter enacted, upon or with respect to any property required to be included in the gross estate of a decedent under the provisions of any such law, the amount of the tax so paid, except in a case where a testator otherwise directs in his will, and except in a case where by written instrument executed inter vivos direction is given for apportionment within the fund of taxes assessed upon the specific fund dealt with in such inter vivos instrument, shall be equitably prorated among the persons interested in the estate to whom such property is or may be transferred or to whom any benefit accrues. Such proration shall be made by the surrogate in the proportion, as near as may be, that the value of the property, interest or benefit of each such person bears to the total value of the property, interests and benefits received by all such persons interested in the estate, except that in making such proration allowances shall be made for any exemptions granted by the act imposing the tax and for any deductions allowed by such act for the purpose of arriving at the value of the net estate; and except that in cases where a trust is created, or other provision made whereby any person is given an interest in income, or an estate for years, or for life, or other tem-

porary interest in any property or fund, the tax on both such temporary interest and on the remainder thereafter shall be charged against and be paid out of the corpus of such property or fund without apportionment between remainders and temporary estates. For the purposes of this section the term " persons interested in the estate " shall have the same meaning with respect to both state and federal taxes as is given it by section two hundred forty-nine-m of the tax law.

So far as is practicable and unless otherwise directed by the will of the decedent the tax shall be paid by the executor as such out of the estate before its distribution. In all cases in which any property required to be included in the gross estate does not come into the possession of the executor as such, he shall be entitled, and it shall be his duty, to recover from whomever is in possession, or from the persons interested in the estate, the proportionate amount of such tax payable by the persons interested in the estate with which such persons interested in the estate are chargeable under the provisions of this section, and the surrogate may by order direct the payment of such amount of tax by such persons to the executor.

No executor, administrator or other person acting in a fiduciary capacity shall be required to transfer, pay over or distribute any fund or property with respect to which a federal or state estate tax is imposed until the amount of such tax or taxes due from the devisee, legatee, distributee or other person to whom such property is transferred is paid, or, if the apportionment of tax has not been determined, adequate security is furnished by the transferee for such payment.

2. The surrogate, upon making a determination as provided in subdivision one of this section, shall make a decree or order directing the executor or other fiduciary to charge the prorated amounts against the persons against whom the tax has been so prorated in so far as he is in possession of property or interests of such persons against whom such charge may be made and summarily directing all other persons against whom the tax has been so prorated or who are in possession of property or interests of such persons to make payment of such prorated amounts to such executor or other fiduciary.

3. This section shall not apply to estates of persons dying prior to September first, nineteen hundred thirty.

§ 125. *Limitations on powers and immunities of executors and testamentary trustees*

The attempted grant to an executor or testamentary trustee or the successor of either, of any of the following enumerated powers or immunities shall be deemed contrary to public policy:

1. The exoneration of such fiduciary from liability for failure to exercise reasonable care, diligence and prudence.

2. The power to make a binding and conclusive fixation of the value of any asset for purposes of distribution, allocation or otherwise.

3. The exemption of a successor executor or testamentary trustee from giving a bond where such executor or testamentary trustee is designated by a predecessor executor or testamentary trustee pursuant to a power given in a will, unless such successor executor or testamentary trustee is a corporate fiduciary authorized to act as such under the banking law or the federal reserve act or is acting or is to act jointly with such a corporate fiduciary.

The attempted grant in any will of any power or immunity in contravention of the terms of this section shall be void but shall not be deemed to render such will invalid as a whole, and the remaining terms of the will shall, so far as possible, remain effective.

Any person interested in an estate or trust fund may contest the validity of any purported grant of any power or immunity within the purview of this section without diminishing or affecting adversely his interest in the estate or fund, any provision in any will to the contrary notwithstanding.

The provisions of this section shall apply only to the wills of persons dying after the date this section shall take effect.

§ 204. *Proof of lost will in certain cases*

But the plaintiff is not entitled to a judgment, establishing a lost or destroyed will, as prescribed in this article, unless the will was in existence at the time of the testator's death, or was fraudulently destroyed in his lifetime; and its provisions are clearly and distinctly proved by at least two credible witnesses, a correct copy or draft being equivalent to one witness.

APPENDIX II.
ASPECTS OF THE REVENUE ACT OF 1948.[1]

The power to tax is not only the power to destroy but the power to change the structure of the national life. It can create nouveaux riches by tax exemptions or nouveaux pauvres by high imposts on unearned income, weaken a capitalistic system by draining the incentive which is its life blood, force reliance on cradle-to-grave welfare by making it impossible for a man to meet his family responsibilities, nationalize education by eliminating tax deductions for the charitable gifts upon which private education lives, and do a multitude of other things which are good or bad according to which side of the tracks you live on, which Sunday School you go to, whether you prefer Karl Marx's beard to Roger Babson's, and whose ox is being gored.

The Revenue Act of 1948 was no mere tinkering with the technicalities of the tax laws. In a magazine article analyzing the Act Dean Griswold pointed out that for a quarter century before 1948 the middle class had been taking the brunt of almost every change in the tax laws, but that the 1948 Act reversed this trend. He named his article, "Something for the Middle Class."[2] And by the middle class is meant executives at all levels and in all callings including government, businessmen, professional men — the sales manager of United Shoe Machinery, the owner of the corner drugstore, the doctor, the president of Local 603, the assistant trust officer of the bank, the college professor, the lawyer, the member of Congress. Yes, it is important that the middle class includes most of the Senators and Representatives in Washington, because it may well be that the origin of the two-thirds vote that overrode President Truman's veto of the 1948 Act can be traced to an event which, in 1948, was of recent memory. Congress had undertaken, with solid popular and press support, to raise its own salaries and had discovered that income tax rates were such that a substantial rise in congressional salaries produced very little increase in take-home pay. Congress solved the immediate problem by an expedient potentially dangerous — granting to its own members a sum as "expenses" which, uniquely, was tax exempt whether or not actually spent for business purposes. But there can be no doubt that this vividly per-

---

[1] See generally Casner, "Estate Planning under the Revenue Act of 1948," 62 Harv. L. Rev. 413 (1949).
[2] Fortune, January, 1949, p. 125. See also Lloyd, "The Marital Deduction," Atlantic Monthly, June 1949, p. 58.

sonal indication of the diminished value of additional gross income — and the diminished incentive to productivity — made its impression upon the legislators.

In any event, as Dean Griswold says, the 1948 Act " provides a great and welcome boon to the beleaguered middle class." I repeat, this may be good or bad depending on your views (mine are obvious); but from our common point of view as students we can join in recognizing that in the 1948 Act Congress was utilizing its taxing power to alter the structure of society to a degree that may prove to be important. The means by which this was done and the effect of the Act upon the lawyer's part in estate planning for clients is the subject of the rest of this Appendix.

A. PROVISIONS OF THE ACT: INCOME SPLITTING AND WEALTH SPLITTING.

The husband-and-wife provisions of the Revenue Act of 1948 resulted from the pressure of non-community-property states to get for their married couples the income tax advantages enjoyed for many years by married couples in community-property states — *i.e.*, the privilege of splitting the couple's aggregate income between the husband and wife and thereby, in the usual case, incurring taxes in a much lower surtax bracket than would be incurred if the husband had to return all his income. The community-property states insisted upon wealth-splitting changes in the Estate and Gift Taxes at the same time. However, it is important to recognize that both the income-splitting provisions of the Income Tax amendments and the wealth-splitting provisions of the Estate and Gift Tax amendments are devices for computation of taxes, nothing more; they do not bring it about that the income or wealth of one spouse is actually divided with the other. For example, where a husband earns $20,000 in a year and the wife has no income, their income tax is computed as if the income were earned one-half by the husband and one-half by the wife; but the husband still owns it all, and the wife has not one more penny in her bank account at the end of the year than she had before except as the husband elects to give her some money.

Calling attention to the fact that any simplified statement of tax law is necessarily inaccurate in detail,[1] I here set forth in broad outline the changes worked by the Act:

(1) *Income Tax* (Revenue Act of 1948, sec. 301, amending I.R.C. sec. 12). Husband and wife are permitted to treat their aggregate income as split between them for tax purposes. If H has an income

---

[1] For a full statement, including the text of the Act, see Alexandre & Greenfield, Marital Deductions, Split Income and the Revenue Act of 1948 (ABA Practicing Law Institute, 1948); Shattuck, An Estate Planner's Handbook, 485 et seq. (1948).

of $23,000 and W an income of $2000, before 1948 they paid one tax on $23,000 and one on $2000; under the 1948 Act they file a joint return and pay two taxes on $12,500.[2] Thus for the first time in history in common-law states it really becomes true that "two can live as cheaply as one." Indeed, if one spouse has a large income and the other has little or none, it well may be that marriage is a very profitable enterprise. A new type of marriage of convenience may be in the offing.

(2) *Estate Tax* (Revenue Act of 1948, sec. 361, amending I.R.C. sec. 812). In computing the net estate upon which the Estate Tax is levied a "marital deduction" is allowed for assets comprised in the gross estate which are received by the wife up to 50% of the "adjusted gross estate." In other words, the gross estate of H is considered (for tax purposes) as belonging half to W, and to whatever extent she gets this it is tax free. The "gross estate" — an artificial conception of the tax laws — includes property owned by the decedent when he died, life insurance, gifts made in contemplation of death, property subject to certain powers of appointment, revocable gifts, gifts intended to take effect in enjoyment on death, and certain other items. The "adjusted gross estate," of which 50% can be received by the surviving spouse tax free, is the gross estate less debts and administration expense. Where H dies the marital deduction is allowable as to property W receives by devise or bequest, by inheritance, as life insurance, by inter vivos outright gifts which are included in the gross estate, or under a testamentary trust which gives the whole income to W for life and a general power of appointment at her death — these being the principal items that can be included in the marital deduction.[3]

---

[2] The statutory language which accomplishes this result is ingeniously simple: "In the case of a joint return of husband and wife . . . the combined normal tax and surtax . . . shall be twice the combined normal tax and surtax that would be determined if the net income and the applicable credits against net income . . . were reduced by one-half."

[3] The statutory sections are very complex with numerous exceptions and limitations. The following quotations may prove useful. The marital deduction is specified as follows: "An amount equal to the value of any interest in property which passes or has passed from the decedent to his surviving spouse, but only to the extent that such interest is included in determining the value of the gross estate. . . . The aggregate amount of the deductions allowed . . . shall not exceed 50 per centum of the value of the adjusted gross estate. . . ." Trusts qualify for the marital deduction " if under the terms of the trust his surviving spouse is entitled for life to all the income from the corpus of the trust, payable annually or at more frequent intervals, with power in the surviving spouse to appoint the entire corpus free of the trust (exercisable in favor of such surviving spouse, or of the estate of such surviving spouse, or in favor of either, whether or not in each case the power is exercisable in favor of others), and with no power in any other person to appoint any part of the corpus to any person other than the surviving spouse . . . [and] if . . . such power in the surviving spouse to appoint the corpus, whether exercisable by will or during life, is exercisable by such spouse alone and in all events."

(3) *Gift Tax* (Revenue Act of 1948, secs. 372–374, amending I.R.C. secs. 1000, 1004). There are two changes, the first as to gifts from one spouse to the other, the second as to gifts from a married person to an outsider. It simplifies exposition if we assume that the husband, H, is making the gifts. (a) Where H makes a gift to W he is entitled to a marital deduction of 50% if the gift is one of the specified types; and these include outright gifts, the creation of co-ownership interests with W, and the creation of a trust of which W has all the income for life followed by a general power of appointment over the corpus. Since the Gift Tax permits an " annual exclusion " of $3000 for each donee in each year, this means that H can give W $6000 per year without exceeding the exclusion. Since, in addition to the exclusion, the Gift Tax gives a life-time " specific exemption " of $30,000 for each donor, the marital deduction permits $60,000 of tax free gifts from H to W above the annual exclusions, provided that H has not made any gifts to others in excess of the annual exclusions. (b) Where H makes a gift to some third person, X, and W gives her assent, this gift is treated as being made one-half by H and one-half by W. Thus, if H gives $6000 to X with W's assent, the whole gift will fall within the combined annual exclusions of H and W. Similarly, gifts by H can take advantage of the combined specific exemptions, totalling $60,000, to which the two spouses are entitled.

Community property is dealt with in detail in the 1948 Act. This matter is too complex to be treated in this brief statement.[4]

B. ESTATE TAX CHANGES RELATING TO POWERS OF APPOINTMENT.

Within the 1940's three different phases of the Estate Tax have been in effect with reference to powers of appointment. These substantially affect estate planning. To avoid potential confusion these three phases are now stated.

Phase One — Before the Revenue Act of 1942. Section 811(f) of the Internal Revenue Code included in the estate of a decedent property subject to a *general* power of appointment which the decedent *exercised*. As a matter of estate planning this form of the statute gave great popularity to a trust under which a wife or child was given the income, a power to consume principal, and a fairly broad special power or a general power to appoint upon death. Where a general power of appointment was given, nice questions arose as to the taxability of " appointments " to persons who would have taken anyway in default of appointment.

Phase Two — Revenue Act of 1942. It was felt by the Treasury

---

[4] The Practicing Law Institute pamphlet, supra n. 1, covers this question.

and by Congress that the above state of the law made it possible for the donee of a power to have substantially complete control over the property without incurring a tax in his estate and that this was a violation of the basic principles of the estate tax.[5] Therefore, amendments were passed which had the following effect as to including in a decedent's gross estate property over which he held a power of appointment:

(a) Taxability was made to depend upon the *type* of power alone, not upon whether it was exercised. (Compare the pre-1942 law under which no tax was incurred unless the decedent *exercised* his general power.) An exception to this was that an exempt type of power became non-exempt so far as it was exercised by creating a new power.

(b) A power in a life tenant incurred a tax in his estate to whatever extent he could (1) exercise a power to consume principal during his lifetime or (2) appoint to any person other than spouses of the donor or donee, issue of the donor or donee, spouses of such issue, or charities.

(c) Special powers given to a person who had no other interest in the trust estate invoked no tax. This meant that powers given to trustees to permit a life tenant to consume principal or to appoint among a group which did not include the trustee or his estate did not incur a tax.

The Act produced these results by declaring that all property over which the donee held a " power of appointment " was includible in the donee's gross estate, and then defining " power of appointment " to exclude (a) powers to appoint only to spouses, issue, and spouses-of-issue of the donor or donee, or to charities and (b) fiduciary powers.[6] To permit estate planners to adjust to the new state of the law

---

[5] I once pointed out an extreme example of potential abuse in Delaware, due to a Delaware statute which caused the period of perpetuities to be computed from the date of exercise of all powers. 24 ABA Journal 807 (October 1938). There is no indication that anyone ever executed or contemplated executing a will containing the rather fantastic dispositions which were theoretically possible; but the proponents of the 1942 Act repeatedly referred to this school-teacher's concoction as a loophole that demanded plugging. To that extent I am an unwitting and unwilling parent of the 1942 Act. See also Griswold and Leach, Powers of Appointment and the Federal Estate Tax, 52 Harv. L. Rev. 929 (1939).

[6] The amendment to I.R.C. sec. 811(f) describing property subject to powers which is includible in the gross estate is as follows:

(f) *Powers of Appointment.*—

(1) *In General.*— To the extent of any property (A) with respect to which the decedent has at the time of his death a power of appointment, or (B) with respect to which he has at any time exercised or released a power of appointment in contemplation of death, or (C) with respect to which he has at any time exercised or released a power of appointment by a disposition intended to take effect in possession or enjoyment at or after his death, or by a dis-

liberal provisions were made for releasing nonexempt powers or cutting them down to exempt powers by partial release without incurring either estate or gift taxes.[7]

The 1942 Act required substantial changes in estate plans and in certain clauses of wills and trusts. It became practically compulsory to create powers of appointment so that they fell within one of the two accepted types. It made it dangerous to include among the trustees a person who was also a beneficiary of the trust, for it might happen that certain broad trustee powers, basically administrative in nature, would prove to give to the trustee-beneficiary a " power of appointment."[8]

Is the foregoing discussion of the 1942 Act rendered obsolete by the provisions of the 1948 Act? Only to a limited extent. The 1948 Act makes it desirable to create general powers of appointment only

---

position under which he has retained for his life or any period not ascertainable without reference to his death or for any period which does not in fact end before his death (i) the possession or enjoyment of, or the right to the income from, the property, or (ii) the right, either alone or in conjunction with any person, to designate the persons who shall possess or enjoy the property or the income therefrom; except in case of a bona fide sale for an adequate and full consideration in money or money's worth.

(2) *Definition of Power of Appointment.* — For the purposes of this subsection the term " power of appointment " means any power to appoint exercisable by the decedent either alone or in conjunction with any person, except

(A) a power to appoint within a class which does not include any others than the spouse of the decedent, spouse of the creator of the power, descendants of the decedent or his spouse, descendants (other than the decedent) of the creator of the power or his spouse, spouses of such descendants, donees described in section 812 (d), and donees described in section 861 (a) (3). As used in this subparagraph, the term " descendant " includes adopted and illegitimate descendants, and the term " spouse " includes former spouse; and

(B) a power to appoint within a restricted class if the decedent did not receive any beneficial interest, vested or contingent, in the property from the creator of the power or thereafter acquire any such interest, and if the power is not exercisable to any extent for the benefit of the decedent, his estate, his creditors, or the creditors of his estate.

If a power to appoint is exercised by creating another power to appoint, such first power shall not be considered excepted under subparagraph (A) or (B) from the definition of power of appointment to the extent of the value of the property subject to such second power to appoint. For the purposes of the preceding sentence the value of the property subject to such second power to appoint shall be its value unreduced by any precedent or subsequent interest not subject to such power to appoint.

[7] See Paul, Federal Estate and Gift Taxation (1946 Supp.) sec. 9.41. The time limit for release of powers has annually been extended beyond the date of July 1, 1946 mentioned by Paul. These provisions as to release of powers, together with provisions which eliminate the tax in certain cases where a person dies without exercising the power, appear in the 1942 Act at section 403 (d) and section 2 of P.L. 635, 80th Congress (House Joint Resolution 395).

[8] See discussion, supra, at the bottom of p. 279 and the top of p. 281. A form of exempt power of appointment appears at p. 260. A form of power to consume principal designed to achieve maximum flexibility with minimum taxability appears at p. 258.

where (a) the donee of the power is a surviving spouse, (b) the property qualifies as a marital deduction, and (c) the estates of the two spouses are of such relative sizes that it is more economical to include the property in the future gross estate of the surviving spouse than in that of the decedent spouse.

Phase Three — Revenue Act of 1948. This Act (more fully discussed in the first pages of this Appendix) allows a marital deduction as to property which is given in trust to pay all the income to the surviving spouse for life with a general power of appointment in the spouse as to the corpus. This once more brings into popularity the general power of appointment; but it does so only in certain situations and for reasons quite different from those which were operative before 1942. Under the pre-1942 version of I.R.C. sec. 811(f) estate planners gave the surviving wife a life estate in the trust plus a power to consume principal and a general power of appointment, with a gift in default of appointment to the children, in the expectation that she would exercise the power to consume only so far as she needed principal for family purposes and that she would probably not exercise the power but would allow the property to pass in default of appointment; if this happened, the trust property would not be included in her gross estate although of course it would be included in her husband's. Under the 1948 Act planners give a general power to the surviving wife so that the property will not be included in her husband's estate; but the provisions of the 1942 Act, above set forth, will cause it to be included in her estate when she dies, whether or not she exercises the general power. Of course, if she exercises her power to consume principal, the property consumed will not be included in either estate.

C. ESTATE PLAN OF J. ALBERT THOMAS: CHANGES REQUIRED BY THE REVENUE ACT OF 1948.

In Chapter XI of this book is considered an estate plan for a hypothetical testator, J. Albert Thomas. This was worked out, and a will drawn, in early 1947. It is obvious that, after the passage of the Revenue Act of 1948, this Testator should be informed by his counsel that revision is required. At the time of the original estate plan counsel took the precaution of getting from the Testator authority to conduct periodic review of his estate plan and will;[9] this authority should now be exercised.

Let us consider the situation as we, Mr. Thomas's counsel, should put it up to him.

You will recall that Mr. Thomas has a probable gross estate at death as follows:

[9] Page 245, supra.

Stocks and bonds	$420,000
Residence held in tenancy by the entirety for which he paid purchase price	28,000
Furnishings of residence	18,000
Summer home	25,000
Furnishings of summer home	2,000
Joint bank account with wife	2,000
Personal bank account	10,000
Life insurance payable to wife	40,000
Auto	2,000
Total	$547,000

His wife has a probable separate estate of $50,000 which comes from her family. The Thomases have a family comprising two married children, the widow of a deceased son, and several grandchildren.

Thomas's 1946 estate plan and will were along the following lines:

(a) The residence, joint bank account and life insurance go to his wife automatically.

(b) He bequeaths the furnishings of both houses and the auto to his wife outright.

(c) He devises the summer home to his wife for life with special power of appointment for the benefit of issue and their spouses.

(d) After a few pecuniary legacies he bequeaths the residue in trust to pay to his wife the income for life plus distributions of principal to take care of taxes and medical expense, with a special testamentary power of appointment in the wife for the benefit of issue and their spouses.

Tax-wise it was a major objective of this plan to assure that most of the property left by Thomas would not pay a second tax in his wife's estate when she should die. It is for this reason that she was given life estates with special powers in the summer home and the residuary trust. The probable Estate Tax liability of Thomas' Estate at his death under the 1942 Act was as follows:

Gross estate	$547,000
Less estimated 10% for debts, administration expense, etc.	55,000 [10]
Balance ("adjusted gross estate")	$492,000
Less exemption	60,000
Net estate	$432,000
Tax	$123,940
Top rate of tax	32%

It is plain that the 1948 Act requires substantial change in this estate plan if maximum tax savings are to be realized. This Act

[10] The figures on p. 240, supra, do not take into account the deductibility of debts and administration expense. This was an error of over-simplification.

permits Thomas to obtain for his Estate a marital deduction of $246,000, being 50% of his adjusted gross estate of $492,000. If he takes advantage of this possibility his tax figures will be:

Gross estate		$547,000
Less:		
Debts, etc.	55,000	
Exemption	60,000	
Marital deduction	246,000	
		361,000
Net estate		$186,000
Tax		$46,500
Top rate of tax		30%

How can we procure this marital deduction for the Estate of J. Arthur Thomas? The following assets already qualify without altering the will as drawn in 1946:

Survivorship interest in the residence	$28,000
Furnishings of residence	18,000
Furnishings of summer home	2,000
Joint bank account	2,000
Life insurance	40,000
Auto	2,000
Total	$92,000

Thus, Thomas should be informed that, as his Estate is now constituted, he can obtain a further deduction of about $155,000 if he makes further gifts in that amount either to his wife outright or in trust for her for life with a general power of appointment.

The first obvious step is to amend the will [11] so that the summer home is given to his wife outright. This adds another $25,000 to the assets which qualify for the deduction.

Should he take steps to bring a portion of the residuary trust — say $130,000 — within the marital deduction? He can do this either by bequeathing $130,000 to his wife outright or by setting this amount up in the trust in such a way that she has the right to the full income plus a general power of appointment over the principal. But he should not be too hasty in arriving at the conclusion that this is wise. In the first place he should not let tax considerations dominate his testamentary scheme; tax savings may prove a pyrrhic victory if they are produced by dispositions which are unwise from the family point of view. (Is his wife competent to handle this amount of money? Has she business experience? Can she resist importunities from her children to do unwise things?) In the second place, Testator should realize that when he gives his wife

---

[11] Paragraph III at p. 250, supra.

$130,000 outright or by an appropriate type of trust, this amount is added to her estate and, if the property is not dissipated, will increase the estate taxes payable on her death. So let us examine her probable gross estate if Thomas should take advantage of the maximum marital deduction. On the rather fanciful assumption that she would retain until her death all property which she had at her husband's death or received from his Estate the figures would be as follows:

Gross estate			
	Her family inheritance	$ 50,000	
	Residence and furnishings	46,000	
	Summer home and furnishings	27,000	
	Bank account	2,000	
	Life insurance	40,000	
	Bequest or trust	130,000	
			$295,000
Less:			
	10% for debts, etc.	30,000	
	Exemption	60,000	
			90,000
Net estate			$205,000

Mrs. Thomas will probably cut down this amount to some degree by expenditures and inter vivos gifts. It therefore appears that in this particular case there is no *tax* reason why J. Arthur Thomas should not take the full marital deduction. But in other cases, where the wife has substantial property of her own, it may be false economy for the husband to take the full marital deduction. On the basis of tax issues only, the aim should be to have the net estates of husband and wife as nearly equal as possible.

Thomas' counsel should call his attention to various incidental matters arising out of the Revenue Act of 1948:

(a) Gifts up to $6,000, rather than $3,000, in each year to any number of persons fall within the Gift Tax " annual exclusion " if Mrs. Thomas assents.[12]

(b) The Gift Tax " specific exemption " of $30,000 can be extended to $60,000 if Mrs. Thomas assents to the additional gifts, although they should both be warned that this uses up her " specific exemption." [13]

(c) Thomas can make gifts of $6,000 annually to his wife within the " annual exclusion," since there is a 50% marital deduction for the Gift Tax.

(d) Before the Act of 1948 it was often wise for a father to make

---

[12] See p. 240, supra.
[13] See p. 241, supra.

a testamentary gift to his son's wife rather than to his son. This would bring it about that the income on this gift would be returnable by the wife at low rates of income tax rather than by her husband at high rates.[14] Under the 1948 Act there is no longer any income-tax purpose in making a gift in this way since the son and his wife can split their income for tax purposes anyway. However, if the family situation is such that the property given will amost certainly get to the son's wife eventually there is an obvious Estate Tax saving in having the property pass through only one estate (the father's) rather than two (the father's and the son's).

(e) Since the " marital deduction " of the 1948 Act does not apply to the inheritance taxes levied by many states, these taxes may in some instances take on a new significance in estate planning.

There are certain types of testamentary clauses, common before the 1948 Act, which should not be used in creating any trust which seeks to qualify for the marital deduction. One requirement of such a trust is that the " surviving spouse is entitled for life to *all* the income." Therefore any powers in trustees which may be exercised in such a way that the life tenant's income is cut down should be avoided. Examples of such powers are:

(a) a power to make loans without interest,

(b) a power to acquire or retain property returning no income without compensating the life tenant,

(c) a power to determine conclusively what is income and what principal and what expenses are chargeable to income and what to principal.[15]

Furthermore any gift to the wife which is designed to be included in the marital deduction should go to her net, *i.e.*, free of taxes. Otherwise the deduction is allowed only as to the amount she actually receives. Thus, all taxes payable with reference to gifts to the wife should be paid out of that portion of the residue which does not qualify for the marital deduction.[16]

Comment by Professor A. James Casner: " The Estate of J. Arthur Thomas, which is the basis of the foregoing discussion, is a very simple one so far as the problem of adjusting an estate plan to the Revenue Act of 1948 is concerned. Thomas has made no significant inter vivos transfers; his Estate seems relatively immune to serious fluctuation before death; his wife's family estate, present or prospective, is unimportant tax-wise. Change any of these factors and you get a much different and more complex situation both in the matter of planning and in the drafting of testamentary clauses to effectuate the plan. Your estate involves no consequence of the changes in the law as to the deductibility from the gross estate of property previously subjected to a gift tax, and this can cause a lot

[14] See par. 5 on p. 241, supra, and clause f at the bottom of p. 260.
[15] See clauses d, e, and o at pp. 276 and 278, supra.
[16] See Paragraph X at p. 272, supra.

of trouble.[17] You suggest an amendment of the residuary trust so that $130,000 of it is given to the wife for life with general power; but the state of Testator's affairs at his death may be such that $130,000 is too much to qualify for the marital deduction or too little to take advantage of the whole deduction. The drafting of a clause which will cause the corpus of this trust to be just the right amount takes some skill and ingenuity."

I concur with all that Professor Casner says but point out, in confession and avoidance, that students who take this course have not usually had a full treatment of federal taxation, particularly the Estate Tax and Gift Tax. Therefore my purpose is only to lay before the student enough understanding of the tax problem so that his thinking on estate planning and property law is reasonably realistic. When he takes his full-treatment course in federal taxation he must synthesize what he gets there with what he got here.

PROBLEM

On the basis of the foregoing discussion, draft a codicil to the will of J. Albert Thomas.

[17] See Revenue Act of 1948, sec. 362, amending I.R.C. sec. 812(c).